STO

ACPL ITEM
DISCARDED

ALLEN COUNTY PUBLIC LIBRARY
3 1833 03865 8271

D0573233

DOT COMS TO START

101

Best

101 Best

DOT COMS TO START

Best

THE ESSENTIAL SOURCEBOOK OF START-UP WISDOM, FINANCIAL TIPS, AND INSIDE SECRETS FOR BUILDING A BUSINESS ON THE INTERNET

The Philip Lief Group
Lynie Arden and Tom Nash, Ph.D.

BROADWAY BOOKS

NEW YORK

BROADWAY

101 BEST DOT COMS TO START. Copyright © 2000 by The Philip Lief Group.
All rights reserved. Printed in the United States of America. No part of this
book may be reproduced or transmitted in any form or by any means,
electronic or mechanical, including photocopying, recording, or by
any information storage and retrieval system, without written permission
from the publisher. For information, address Broadway Books, a division of
Random House, Inc., 1540 Broadway, New York, NY 10036.

Broadway Books titles may be purchased for business or promotional use or
for special sales. For information please write to: Special Markets Department,
Random House, Inc., 1540 Broadway, New York, NY 10036.

BROADWAY BOOKS and its logo, a letter B bisected on the diagonal, are trade-
marks of Broadway Books, a division of Random House, Inc.

Visit our website at www.broadwaybooks.com

Library of Congress Cataloging-in-Publication Data
101 best dot coms to start: the essential sourcebook of startup wisdom,
financial tips, and inside secrets for building a business on the Internet /
Philip Lief Group and Lynie Arden and Tom Nash—1st ed.
            p.   cm.
    1. Electronic commerce.   2. Electronic commerce—Management.
    3. New business enterprises—Computer networks.   4. Internet.
I. Title: One hundred one best dot coms to start.   II. Title: One hundred
    and one best dot coms to start.   III. Title: Best dot coms to start.
    IV. Philip Lief Group   V. Arden, Lynie, 1949–   VI. Nash, Tom, 1945–

                HF5548.32 A17 2000
        658.8′4—dc21   00-039774

                FIRST EDITION

            Designed by Chris Welch

            ISBN 0-7679-0604-7

    00   01   02   03   04   10   9   8   7   6   5   4   3   2   1

Contents

Introduction xiii

Glossary xxxi

ARTS & ENTERTAINMENT

Art Posters 3

Digital Publishing 11

Digital Recordings 16

Magic Shop 22

Online Games 28

Photo Gallery 34

Sports Art 40

Contents

BUSINESS TO BUSINESS

Accounting Services 49

Auction House 55

Customer Service 59

Employee Training 64

Management Consulting 69

Meeting Planner 75

Professional and Business Coach 79

Public Speaking Seminars 84

CAREERS

Job Boards 93

Inventor Representative 99

Professional Placement Services 106

CHILDREN

Asian Educational Materials 115

Children's Videotapes 119

Hand-Painted Children's Furniture 126

Mail Club for Kids 132

Party Planning 138

Unique Toys 144

CLOTHING & ACCESSORIES

Antique Jewelry   153

Clothing Discount Outlet   158

Dance Shoes   163

Diamond Jewelry   169

Girls' Custom Clothing   177

Men's Ties   183

Specialty Jewelry   188

COMPUTERS/HIGH TECH

Software Developer   195

Technical Support   200

Web Content Provider   204

Web Site Designer   208

Web Site Program Reseller   214

Web Site Promotion   219

FOOD & DRINK

Chocolate   227

Coffee and Tea   234

Hot Foods   238

Organic Groceries   243

Personal Chef   248

Restaurant Ordering Service   253

Contents

Specialty Wine 259

Wine Shop 264

GARDENING

Exotic Plants 271

Landscaping 277

Seed Supplier 282

GIFTS

Cakes for College Students 289

Creative Gift Baskets 295

Flowers 300

Guy Stuff 305

Refrigerator Magnets 310

Regional Products 316

Sports-Related Gifts 320

Theme Gift Baskets 326

HEALTH & FITNESS

Bodybuilding 335

High-Tech Cosmetics 342

Medical Advice 348

Nutritional Supplements 353

Weight Loss 359

Contents

HOBBIES & COLLECTIBLES

Antiques   367

Antique Quilts   372

Collectible Horses   378

Collectible Sports Cards   385

Dollhouses and Miniatures   389

Science Fiction Collectibles   394

Stencils for Home Decorating   399

Turkish Plates   403

PERSONAL SERVICES & LIFESTYLES

Childcare and Eldercare   411

Delivery of Web Purchases   416

Matchmaking Service   421

Personal Shopper   430

Religious Specialties   436

PETS

Animal Gifts   445

Aromatherapy for Pets   449

Dog Daycare   455

Exotic Pets   461

Pet Locator Service   466

Unique Pet Supplies   472

Contents

REAL ESTATE & HOME IMPROVEMENT

Antique Reproduction Furniture   479

Asian Home Furnishings   484

Hardware Store   489

Home Contractor Referral Service   496

Home Improvement Information   501

SPORTS & RECREATION

Cycle Retailer   511

Destination Travel—Dude Ranch   516

Golf Pro Shop   521

Kites and Wind-Powered Equipment   525

Mountaineering Gear   530

Racquet Sports Supplies   534

Sports League Scheduling   540

Water Sports Outfitters   545

TRAVEL

Bed and Breakfast Reservations Service   553

Business Travel Accessories   558

Specialty Tours   563

Travel Auctions   571

Travel Information   577

Contents

WEDDING

Custom Wedding Accessories   585

Honeymoon Travel Agency   591

Wedding Registry   597

Introduction

WHAT IT TAKES TO SUCCEED IN CYBERSPACE

In a race the likes of which have not been seen since the days of the California Gold Rush, entrepreneurs are sprinting to stake their claims in the wilds of cyberspace. Is it any wonder? Research groups agree that the global e-commerce marketplace will generate more than $1 trillion over the next two years. That's a lot of virtual cash!

The Internet has become a global marketplace where businesses can sell their wares and services to customers they'll never meet—without the high overhead of a physical location. This multibillion-dollar market is irresistible, so what are you waiting for? There'll never be another time like this, another opportunity so golden. So decide what you're going to offer, hang out your cybershingle, and ask your bank for more deposit slips.

Introduction

Not all e-businesses are alike, and there is no cut-and-sew pattern that will assure success to anyone who follows it. But if you understand some basics, you can be one step ahead. Here are some of the best tips to start you on the way to a successful e-business:

- Find a niche market within a big and growing market.
- Do it for the love of it.
- Know your customers.
- Choose a good domain name, one that people can remember and that ties into your offering.
- Design a site that is well organized and easy to navigate.
- Hire "experts" only after getting referrals and seeing samples of actual work.
- Do your homework. There are free tutorials all over the Web to teach you everything from HTML to the finer points of Internet marketing. The Glossary in the next chapter defines a lot of the e-lingo you'll need to know.
- Choose an ISP with 24/7 technical support.
- Offer secure shopping.
- Make it easy to order.
- Fill orders promptly and have a tracking system in place.
- Ask your first customers for feedback, and post testimonials on your site as soon as possible.
- Post as many ways to contact you as possible.
- Respond to e-mails quickly.
- Know what your competition is doing.
- Be prepared for bumps in the road.
- Stop talking about it and start doing it.

WHAT'S THE BIG IDEA?

The first—and most important—step in starting an e-business is to come up with the "big idea." Remember, it doesn't have to be a product—it can be a service. And you don't have to market just to consumers either. As a matter of fact, it is estimated that over 70 percent of e-commerce is being (quietly) conducted within the business-to-business sector.

As you read through this book and surf the Web, you'll come up with loads of ideas. That's the hallmark of a true entrepreneur. You may find that your challenge is not in coming up with a great idea but in deciding which one to pursue. Two essential pieces of advice:

- **Make sure you love what you're going to do.** When the going gets rough—and it will—your passion for your pursuit will see you through.
- **Find your own niche.** There may be a finite number of industries, but, by putting a new spin on any one of them, you can corner your little part of cyberspace.

Sure, in every industry there's already a 500-pound gorilla like Amazon.com or MonsterBoard.com. But Amazon.com doesn't control the market for Asterisk comic books, and MonsterBoard.com isn't the industry leader in announcing jobs for the educational market.

The gift market, for example, is huge (both online and off-line). It's overrun with gorilla sites like Gifts.com and click-and-mortars (see Glossary) like Fingerhut. But that traffic jam didn't deter Chris Gwynn from starting fridgedoor.com, a site that provides a fabulous array of refrigerator magnets for all those little gift-giving occasions. Why refrigerator magnets? Says Gwynn, "I had first looked around for a target product, and books and CDs were the perfect ones, but they were taken. So, looking at a lot of things, I looked at my fridge one day and realized it was covered with magnets. I started with 20 items in May of 1997 to see if people would buy them, and they did, from day one. Now we have 1,500 magnets—far more than any competitor. It's also something that's not available in mass merchants (big stores). Actually, with magnets, to find good ones it takes a lot of work. They're usually sold through funky specialty shops. My idea was to create one place on the Web where that was all that was available."

Once you've found your niche, stay focused. Oliver Mittermaier of CareGuide.com says that staying focused is the biggest challenge. "It's hard to fathom how big this [caregiving] market is. We have the ability to take it in all kinds of directions, but we make sure we don't stay from the core need of our customers. Our focus is caregiving." Mittermaier argues that his potential customers are part of a huge demographic, so the challenge is always to not "get sucked into the appeal of starting to do things for the easy money—like straight advertising or meaningless sponsorships. Such activities dilute the value of what we do."

CHOOSE A BUSINESS MODEL

In the real world, there is really only one business model. You sell a product or service to a buyer, charging enough over and above your costs of doing business to make a profit. End of story.

In cyberspace, the story doesn't end there. There are different ways of doing things, different ways of looking at things, different ways of turning a profit. If everyone agrees, and it works, do it. To keep things simple, though, the two main ways to make a profit from e-commerce are charging for ad space and selling products and services.

The Digital Billboard: Charging for Ad Space

The beauty and uniqueness of the Internet has always been that it's a great resource for the most valuable commodity of all—information. Since the Net's inception, people all over the world have logged on, clicked in, and retrieved information on any subject imaginable—all for free. The question for entrepreneurs is: how do you make money by giving away anything for free? The answer is simple: by selling ad space. Since the hardest part of being successful on the Web is getting noticed, any site with traffic is considered a great place to hang a digital billboard.

The business model works like this: the more extensive and valuable the content on your site, the more traffic you're likely to have; the more traffic you have, the more attractive your site is to potential advertisers trying to lure those same visitors to *their* sites. Compare it with television. Local cable TV ads are cheap because there are relatively small numbers of viewers, but the same ads run on network TV cost thousands, sometimes millions, of dollars. And you don't even have to own a network TV station to cash in.

After working as a professional home builder and remodeler for over 20 years, Tim Carter decided to launch Ask The Builder.com, an ad-supported content site. He made a few calls—four, to be exact—to manufacturers of home-building products just to test the waters and see if there was any interest in advertising on his site. On the fourth call he sold his first banner ad for $12,000, getting paid up front, and his site hadn't even launched yet. That was in December 1995, the dark ages of e-commerce, when it took real vision to launch an active site. Carter took $5,000 of that $12,000 to launch his site, and today he grosses in the neighborhood of $1 million a year from advertising fees. All because the content, which is free to visitors, is excellent and draws tons of viewers.

Step Up to the Checkout Line: Selling Products and Services

The face of the Internet is quickly changing, and it is questionable how long the advertising model will continue to be viable for budding entrepreneurs. Most new e-businesses are opting for the more direct approach: selling products and services right to consumers for a profit. All you need is something to sell, a secure ordering system, and fulfillment (handling, packing, and delivering) capabilities.

Ideally, you will have chosen a product that is unique and not easily found in the local WalMart. The Web can be a great resource for finding suppliers. But remember to compare prices carefully and check their reliability with existing customers. To keep start-up costs low, look for suppliers who are willing to drop-ship the products (send them directly to your customers from their warehouse), so you don't have to invest in inventory. Except to pay a little more for this service.

You must have a secure ordering system. The easiest way to do this is to start with an Internet service provider (ISP) like Bigstep or Yahoo! Part of their site-building packages (which are free) includes access to their secure shopping cart systems.

Be prepared to fill orders immediately. Check with as many shippers as you can before you start to compare costs and delivery times. Make sure you work with one that offers a good tracking system. A great way to make your customers feel secure is to e-mail a tracking number upon shipment so they can see for themselves where their order is.

JUST DO IT

Numerous e-business operators told us the same thing: "Just do it, and do it *now*." Like the land claims of the 1880s, those who hesitated were left with nothing but dust in their faces. Don't worry about how much things are going to change over the next few years. That would be like refusing to buy a computer because there will be a fancier, less expensive one out next week. The phenomenon of obsolescence will always create a shadow, but if you keep waiting, you'll never get into business at all. As long as you have a good offering and a good idea of what you want to accomplish, now is the time to get online. It doesn't have to be completely refined. Things will change anyway as you learn the ropes of e-commerce, a realm that is different from the real world. When you're doing things that haven't been done before, you're going to make mistakes. It's how you react to those mistakes that makes all the difference.

If you think you have a good idea for a Web site, you need to have something up within ten weeks. At least that's the consensus among our business owners. You should assume that if you have an idea, someone else has it, too. If you wait for the perfect time or stall while creating the perfect site, you'll never make it. Karen DeMars, cofounder of eCrush.com, says, "In e-business, there is no time to come up with a better solution. There is always going to be something better and a better way to do things, but if it takes two months to come up with it, it'll be too late."

When Karen and her partner Clark Benson dreamed up

eCrush.com, a service that pairs people up with those they have a crush on, it was late December. Without a marketing budget, they knew their best chance for success was a media tie-in for Valentine's Day. Sure, they knew how to make a business plan and follow it to the letter. But they decided to go with their instincts and forego the traditional market research. "We got the site up in four weeks flat," says Karen. "I was absolutely determined to get that [Valentine] PR angle for launch. We killed ourselves to get it done in time, flying by the seat of our pants, but we did it!" So stop talking about it and start doing it!

START SMALL

As competition gets stiffer in cyberspace, organizations are spending more and more to get their ventures under way. Some of our e-business owners feel that, to start today, you need to seek heavy funding from venture capitalists. But the majority still believe that entry into the marketplace can be achieved with little, or even no, capital whatsoever. It just takes a little more creativity.

Several of our entrepreneurs got their digital toes wet in e-commerce by first testing the waters on eBay.com. Ragan Hughs, founder of PipperSnaps.com, actually sold things she found around the house, not unlike having a virtual yard sale. She was able to make a little extra cash while getting a feel for what it was like to do business on the Web. When the closets were empty, she chose a product of her own, hand-painted children's furniture, and tested that on eBay.com, too. Not until it was apparent that hers was a product in demand did she go forward with plans for a Web site of her own.

TECHNICALLY SPEAKING

As you consider technology in the start-up scheme, several possibilities present themselves. Sometimes a Web-based service provides a good entry point into business. If you merely want to see how the Net works as a sales channel, contact the Yahoo! Store or a similar server. For a few dollars, you can launch a limited operation. If you are committed to the Web as part of your total business operation, contact an ISP that will allow you to start small and move forward at a controlled pace. Finally, if you are sure that the Net will become the center of your business, think about hiring a professional designer and getting your own server.

The most common mistake among new e-entrepreneurs is getting hung up on the design of the site. Sure, a visually appealing design is nice, but what shoppers really desire is to be able to find what they want easily and quickly. And that doesn't require a high-priced Web designer. You can set up a neatly organized store, complete with shopping cart, order tracking, and automatic confirmation e-mails for free. It won't have streaming video or cute Java aplets, but it will be a true working store.

A number of companies offer quick and easy e-commerce building, but three of the best are Bigstep.com, Yahoo!Store, and IBM Small Business Solutions.

Bigstep.com

Bigstep.com's big deal is that you can build a site for free. With their software templates, store building is easy, and you can sell as many products as you like. They charge a little extra to add a merchant account (so you can accept credit cards). Right now, that's $14.95 a month plus 20¢ per transaction, but that fee is pretty standard. The biggest advantage of Bigstep is speed. It's quick and easy. For example, it took Stuart Brotman only two days to go online with his store, Travel Dynamics. And he had absolutely no technical experience. Today, the store runs itself.

Yahoo!Store

Yahoo!Store currently has 15 store templates that make it a snap to build in a hurry. The software is free; the hosting charge is $100 per month for up to 50 items in your catalog. Both Bigstep and Yahoo!Store are a bit limited in their design capabilities, but with Yahoo!Store you can add your own HTML pages to the site. Not so with Bigstep. The biggest advantage of going with Yahoo!Store is having your store automatically placed in the Yahoo mall. Sure, it's a bit crowded in there, but if you're unique, you can rely on Yahoo! to send you traffic practically from day one.

IBM Small Business Solutions

IBM offers several plans depending on your individual e-commerce requirements. The Web site-building software, *Home Page Creator*, is free and requires absolutely no technical knowledge or skills.

Rosemary Zraly, aka ChampagneLady.com, had just a book cover and a domain name when she discovered IBM. "They were fabulous," she says. "They helped me put in the extra visual touches like the rising champagne bubbles and the millennium countdown. And they didn't charge for the help." As part of its service, IBM includes most of the "back office services," such as online transactions and credit card verification. They also have a top-notch PR firm ready to help you launch your marketing plan. Zraly's advice: "Go with IBM. You really need the clout and the credibility of someone who takes care of that technical stuff. For $60 a month, I couldn't ask for more."

Building Your Site on Your Own

If you're ambitious and know exactly what you want to accomplish—particularly if you already own a business and are looking to expand through a Web presence—you might want to set up your own site. The downside is it can cost a lot to build your own pages. Even if you're technically adept, there will be many challenges and issues to face on your own, like security. On the other hand, you'll have unlimited design possibilities, a must for big sites. Be prepared to pay the price, though. For the necessary components such as site development, hardware, bandwidth, secure server, and maintenance, you'll be investing thousands of dollars before you open your doors. Believe it or not, some design firms charge up to $250,000. Dull that blow by bartering as much as you can for services.

E-Commerce Hosting

Somewhere between using an e-commerce building company and creating a site on your own is the option of going to an ISP that offers e-commerce hosting. Using an ISP is appealing because you receive valuable support and services from them at every step. Further, the ISP approach allows for growth and change at meaningful stages. Recently ISPs have been offering licensed versions of e-commerce software that will allow you to build your own store. Even though the tools won't be as helpful as those from a site like Bigstep.com, you can plan to add special pages and creative features without serious problems. Instead of having to begin from point zero, you can use the ISP materials to augment your own customer databases and product descriptions. Generally speaking, the ISP package requires HTML programming. If you can't work with HTML, you'll have to pay for a technician. However, in the end, you'll probably be happy with the results.

Whichever way you decide to go, the most important factor in choosing your host is making sure you get 24/7 technical support, meaning 24 hours a day, seven days a week. If your ISP's server goes down, you lose business as surely as if your store door was suddenly locked. Since e-commerce has no set business hours, it is crucial that someone is keeping a watchful eye and keeping things running all the time, not just Monday through Friday between the hours of nine and five.

ATTRACTING CUSTOMERS

In retail businesses in the brick-and-mortar world, the universal slogan is location, location, location. But in cyberspace, there is no location, at least in the traditional sense. For e-tailers, marketing, marketing, marketing is the golden phrase. Bringing customers to your site is critical. Even the most glorious and appealing interactive site can't turn a profit if nobody clicks on to your logo. Luckily, some of the best marketing methods in cyberspace are also the cheapest.

Search Engines

Most visitors—as many as 80 percent—come to a site as a result of search engines. Think about it. When you want to find something on the Web, what's your first move? You go to a favorite search engine, whether it's Excite, GoTo, or Yahoo!, and type in the description of what you're looking for. What you get back is a list of possible sites that match your description. It's widely accepted that for a search engine to be of any value to a business, that business must be listed within the top 20. Why? Because most people will search through 20 listings before getting tired.

A search engine is a site that indexes Web site information, based on content. Different search engines operate differently, but most utilize meta tags (key words and descriptors), a page title, some information on the content of each page, and, in some cases, clues about the number and types of external links to the site. A search vehicle, sometimes called a spider or a bot, gathers information after you've provided the appropriate URL in the registration phase.

For search engines to know about and index your site, you must register it with them. Every search engine has a registration page on its site. Just follow the instructions. But first you'll need to be prepared with meta tags on your own pages. Search engines release their spiders to make an index for your pages, using meta tags as keys. These meta tags are descriptors and key words that lie in the preliminary (or "head") section of your site. When you launch a search through an engine, the description you view onscreen is the meta tag information. For the best possible search ranking, you should dwell on productive key words, those that you know searchers will type into place when they want to find your type of service or product.

Some search engines ignore meta tags and instead go directly to the first characters in your document that appear after the head section. Just make sure you put clear, succinct descriptions there.

Registering with search engines is a time-consuming job, especially if you're vigilant about staying in the top 20. Many engine registering services will continually register for you, usually on a monthly basis. Most cost under $100 for six months of service.

Naturally, you'll want to register with the most popular search engines first. Excite, GoTo, Yahoo!, AltaVista, and Google are among those. But don't stop there. There are about 1,500 search engines available, so find as many as you can and register whenever you have the time.

Affiliate Programs

Selling your products through affiliate programs is like hiring a huge salesforce and putting them to work without spending a dime on salaries. It's a simple concept: another Web site establishes a link with yours and directs its visitors to click through to you. If the visitor then buys something from you, you pay a commission—10 percent is the norm—to the originating site owner. It's a great advantage because you don't actually pay for any advertising up front. You pay only after money is jangling in your pockets.

You can build your own network of affiliates by surfing the Net, finding sites that are compatible but not competitive with yours, and sending an e-mail offering the opportunity. To build a big network fast, you can go through an affiliate program like LinkShare.com or BeFree.com, companies that will establish those links for you. Not only will they find affiliates to boost your sales, but they'll take care of the messy paperwork, too.

One of the sites profiled in this book, 800trekker.com, gets most of its customers for the sci-fi collectibles it sells from its pool of over 4,500 affiliate sites. Says owner David Blaise, "We got a lot of them by signing up with affiliate programs and the rest by sending out a targeted e-mail to other sci-fi sites, letting them know they could earn money from their sites. It works particularly well for us because we have individual 'stores' set up within 800trekker, such as the Star Wars Store and the Buffy the Vampire Slayer Store. It's set up through banners that, when you click on them, take visitors not to the home page of 800trekker but directly to that particular store page. So, if an affiliate is a Buffy fan club, click-throughs will go directly to the Buffy Store. This allows us to keep the traffic as tightly targeted as possible. That's why the affiliate program has worked so well. And, of course, visitors do have access to the other pages ('stores') if they want."

Making link exchanges is a favorite way to use networking on the Web to build business. It's like having affiliates, except you don't necessarily pay commissions to the participating site. For example, you can seek the services of LinkExchange.com. Simply sign with the BannerNetwork, and you can start to post banner ads on other Web addresses without charge in exchange for agreeing to sponsor banner ads on your site. Of course, there are other methods of making links. It's just as profitable to arrange your own link exchanges. Just find a compatible site that isn't a direct competitor—one that could obviously benefit from the exposure. Use e-mail to make a connection, and express some notions about why you think the links would be mutually helpful. It's as simple as that.

Promotion

One great thing about starting a niche business is that you probably have a story to tell. If it's new and interesting, you can get publicity. And that's a good thing. If the media talks about you, they're making an implied endorsement. So send a press release, outlining your story, to as many media contacts as you can.

In terms of paid promotion, the most popular form on the

Web is banner ads. Unfortunately, these can be expensive, and it's often questionable whether they do the job. The problem is, it takes a lot of hits to get a customer, not unlike in the world of print ads and mail order. The average site gets less than a thousand hits a week even properly tagged, and only 1–2 percent of these hits will respond, so you have to be realistic about your expectations before investing in banner advertising.

Finally, don't forget the real world. Put your Web address on everything:

- Brochures
- Business cards
- Yellow Pages ad
- Letterhead
- Print ads
- Newsletters
- Promotional items like pens and magnets

Don't ignore offline advertising. For businesses with a local customer base, advertising in the local newspaper and shoppers makes a lot of sense. If you're thinking of starting a business with a target market, look for industry or trade magazines and newsletters that focus on the same topic. For instance, a wine shop would do well to consider advertising in *Wine Spectator* or *Gourmet*. Also consider radio and TV. The owner of Champagnelady.com got most of her customers from radio spots in New York.

KEEPING CUSTOMERS HAPPY

It takes a lot of time and money to get customers to your site, so it's imperative that you do everything you can to keep your visitors happy.

Customer service should be your top priority. Although customers are shopping in the virtual world of cyberspace, they want to deal with real people. At the very least, you should constantly monitor your e-mail and answer it as quickly as possible. You wouldn't ignore a ringing phone in your store, would you? Send e-mails to customers letting them know their order is on the way, and *thank them*. If there's a delay, let them know immediately. Use autoresponders to address common questions, try to hold regular online chats, and make sure customers can reach you in a variety of ways.

Some smart e-tailers like NorthlandMarine.com think it's so important to talk to customers that they don't have a shopping cart on their site. Customers are forced to call the 800 number. Laura Boers of Northland says, "The Internet shoppers know what they want. You're just finalizing what's in their minds. The biggest thing is making sure you give them what they need, not just what they *think* they want. Normally, return rates for e-commerce sites can be 35 percent on the Internet. That's the last thing we want [returns]. Our returns are only 5 to 7 percent."

To keep customers coming back, don't let your site go stagnant. Update your content frequently, add new inventory, and provide interactive opportunities.

THE LANGUAGE OF CYBERSPACE

The Net has spurred a whole new lexicon; to stay ahead of the pack, you first have to learn the jargon. Before you launch into the body of this book, we recommend that you spend some time reading the Glossary, which appears directly after this introduction. These terms appear in the discussions of the individual e-businesses we profile. So sharpen your pencils and open your minds. Trust us, it'll be fun!

Glossary

affiliates: Sites that send visitors to another commercial site, usually in a related business or subject area, in exchange for a commission, typically 5 percent, if a sale or purchase is made from a visitor that came from the affiliate's site.

auditing: Process of verifying the number of visitors to a Web site or page. Auditing also includes "hits" or page and file "requests."

autoresponder: An automatic response sent to an incoming e-mail. Generally, it is used to confirm orders, confirm that a message was received, and notify customers.

back room, back office, back end: These are the mechanics behind e-commerce (in the real world, these transactions often occur in a back office), including online transactions, credit card verification, CGI script support (see definition below), and so on.

banner ad: A graphic image, much like the shape of a banner, that advertises a site on another site. Viewers can click on the banner and be "hot linked," or instantly linked, to the sponsoring site.

brick and mortar: A business operating in the real world, such as from an office building or storefront.

buzz: Excitement over a site that can result in strong word-of-mouth sales.

CGI (common gateway interface): A common programming language used for online Internet applications. These programs are stored on the host servers that are used by visitors to Web pages.

click and mortar: A brick-and-mortar business that also operates online.

click rate: Also called "ad click-rate" or "click-through-rate." The number of times an ad is clicked on versus the number of times it is simply seen but not clicked on. When an ad is viewed (seen only), this is an "impression." Simple math: If an ad has 100 impressions (i.e., is seen by 100 people), and 10 of them actually click on it, then you would say that it has a click rate of 10 percent.

click-throughs: Also called "ad clicks" or "requests." A click-through occurs when a visitor clicks on a hot-linked banner ad and is transported to the site of the banner's advertiser.

.com: Indicates a commercial site (however, a commercial site can also end with .net or .org).

cookies: Coded information about you (the browser) that is gathered by Web sites you visit.

CPM: A term used in the traditional advertising world. It refers to the total cost of designing an ad seen by 1,000 people. On the Web, it is thought of as the cost for 1,000 impressions, ad views, or exposures.

drop-ship: This term refers to when a Web site receives an order for a piece of merchandise and immediately sends the order to the manufacturer or distributor to be filled and the manufacturer or distributor sends the product directly to the customer.

e-: A prefix meaning "electronic" (e.g., e-business, e-entrepreneur, e-mail).

FAQs: Frequently asked questions.

Frontpage: Microsoft's software for building Web sites.

FTP (file transfer protocol): The standard method used to transfer files over the Internet. It enables the sending (uploading) and receiving (downloading) of files, programs, and so on.

hit: A single request from a Web browser for a single item from a Web server.

HTML (hypertext markup language): The computer code used to create a web page.

hypertext: Text that contains links to other documents.

impressions: Also known as "ad views" or "exposures." Each time a Web site visitor sees a banner ad displayed on a Web site, whether or not he actually clicks on it, it is called an impression.

intranet: A network inside an organization that is similar to the Internet but is used only internally.

ISP (Internet service provider): The company that hosts a Web site.

Java: A programming language designed for writing programs that are downloaded from the Internet to your computer. Small Java programs, called Aplets, are used to create animations, calculators, and other nontext functions.

JPEG (joint photographic experts group): The most common format for image files, particularly preferred for photographic images.

key words: Words that describe your Web site page, product, or offering. They are used by search engines to identify and categorize your page(s).

link: A connection from one Web page to another, usually by clicking on a highlighted word, phrase, or icon.

meta tags: Special HTML labels that provide information about a Web page, such as key words, the owner of the Web site, description of the page's content, when it was last updated, and so on.

nondomain name: A URL, such as http://www.hoflink.com/~your-name, that points to somebody else's Web server. Generally used only because it is free or the desired domain name is taken.

opt-in mailing: The digital version of direct mail. When people register on the search engines to receive free information about a special interest or to enter a contest or complete a short survey, they choose to "opt in." Companies that run the surveys or contests then sell the consumer information to Web site clients. Those Web sites then send targeted information, such as a promotional letter, to the names on their list.

page views: Also known as "page requests" or "page transfers." This occurs when a Web page is presented to a Web site visitor. Generally, home pages get many more page views than subpages.

platform: The underlying hardware or software for a computer system. It is often interchangeable with the term "operating system."

portals: Sites that act as a port of entry and have a catalog of Web sites, proprietary guides, a search engine, and other services, such as e-mail. Examples of portals include Yahoo! and Excite.

search engine: An automatic indexing system whereby a user types in a word or phrase and finds a list of URLs related to that request; a site that indexes information, in this case Web sites, on a content-oriented basis. They are currently the only tool for users to find sites of interest.

shopping cart: A credit card ordering system for making purchases from Web sites.

spam: Unwanted, or "junk," e-mail.

spider: A search vehicle, sometimes called a bot, for gathering information from Web sites to be used for search engine indexing.

spiral: Word of mouth at its best. For example, one person tells two people about a Web site, and each of those two people in turn tell two or three people, and so on.

SSL (secure socket layer) secure server: This protects data being transferred for viewing by outside parties. It's the system used for credit card transfers.

stickiness: A site's ability to keep visitors on the site for long periods of time, usually because of top-notch content that holds their attention.

submitting a URL: To index your site on the Internet, and allow people to find your site, you must submit it to several Web site search engine indexes.

24/7: 24 hours a day, seven days a week.

unique host impressions: Exposures to new visitors as opposed to repeat visits.

URL (universal resource locator): A Web page address, usually beginning with *www*.

USENET: A worldwide system of decentralized discussion groups. Discussion areas, called newsgroups, cover thousands of different topics of interest.

VC (venture capital): An infusion of cash from a third-party source to start or grow a business.

viral marketing: A buzzword that describes extremely rapid growth of an e-business, akin to the spread of a virus. The "virus" is spread by encouraging customers, who effectively serve as your salesforce, to pass on the word.

virtual domain name: A URL (e.g., www.your_name.com) that points to a Web server and makes it appear as your own. Usually it is the Web hosting company that owns the server, but many companies own their own servers and have direct connections to the Web. They have true domains.

Web page: A mixture of text, graphics, sound, and animation in the HTML format, to make information accessible in an easy-to-understand format using the Internet.

Web site: A collection of Web pages connected (linked) by hypertext clickable links.

WWW (World Wide Web): One part of the Internet; the connection of every Web site and Web server networks all over the world.

Arts & Entertainment

Art Posters

Start-up expenses: $100,000
Special requirements: *Extensive database and a paid employee who can manage it continually*
Best advice: *"Have realistic expectations. This business is hard work. The Net is growing and changing so quickly. You have to stay flexible and stay 100 percent involved at all times."*

B are walls are dull. Naturally, then, people plaster their living spaces with artwork of all kinds, including posters. For many of us, posters help us articulate our wishes and desires, our secret lives and alter egos, our tastes and our prejudices. Walls can bear the likenesses of Pearl Bailey or Pearl Harbor, Lisbon Antigua or Liz Taylor, the Rocky Mountains or Rocky Balboa. The subjects are endless, and the styles range from high camp to high art—Andy Warhol in the foyer, Velvet Elvis in the den, Michelangelo's *David* in the library, and Nine-Inch Nails in the Teen Ghetto. Millions of posters are sold every year in the West, and not all of them come from brick-and-mortar shops. Needless to say, the poster business is well suited to the world of e-commerce. It is therefore no surprise to find plenty of poster addresses in that giant mailbox called cyberspace.

One of the specialty niches in this field is art posters. Ann Reiter and Jane Henley are partners in TimelessTraveler.com, an e-shop whose name sounds like that of a travel bureau but really deals in art posters and prints. "We specialize in the *hottest*," says Reiter. "That's to differentiate us from others who try to carry every print in the world. A million prints? Who has the time to look at them?" Reiter and Henley list only the newest and most trendy art posters and prints, leaving the problems of massive inventories to other businesses. As a result, they have carved a special niche, one that began as a traditional catalog-sales business.

Originally the partners sold wholesale art prints. Then they ventured into retail sales, marketing through their own print catalogs. Reiter and Henley had always advertised in art magazines, but they soon discovered the limitations of operating in the world of bulk mailings and print-shop deadlines. "We finally decided to forego the paper catalog," says Reiter, "because the mailing costs, printing costs, and fulfillment costs became very expensive." When the partners started their Web site in November 1998, they thought it would just supplement their catalog business. But it didn't take long to realize the Net was "a better economic decision." As Reiter says, "This industry changes a lot, and every time something new comes out, you have to change the inventory and the catalog and the mailing base. That's really expensive and difficult normally. But on the Net, it's a lot easier."

A Tale of Two Cities

Ann was a sales manager for 15 years, working in Chicago, while Jane specialized in graphic design projects in Minneapolis. With the advent of the Net, geographic distance became a small, almost infinitesimal, disadvantage to the art poster partnership. Today, Henly provides Web design service for not only TimelessTraveler.com. but other companies as well. Reiter also does business outside the partnership, serving as art director for a large Chicago corporation. Despite their busy work schedules, the partners have learned a number of skills appropriate to the Web. Both are technically proficient. Henley does the company's Web site design and maintenance, and Reiter also knows her way around a computer keyboard.

Working from separate cities has not been a problem thus far, perhaps because both partners have kept current in technology. But the process was not easy for art specialist Reiter. "When the business started, I knew only what the average user knows," she says. "There's a big learning curve with HTML coding. It isn't as easy as people think." Reiter discovered, along with other small e-business owners, that Web site maintenance was going to be a huge expense. So the partners had to assume that job themselves. "If you paid an outsider to do your Web site maintenance," she says, "I don't think you could stay in business. It's too time-consuming and too expensive. You have to have a strong business in place before you can afford to hire out Web maintenance." She adds that many e-commerce neophytes think they'll become Amazon.com overnight. Not so. In reality, says Reiter, most fledgling businesses are at least a year away from even making a profit.

Keep It Simple, Keep It Friendly, Make It Secure

The TimelessTraveler.com. site is easy to use and doesn't require much time to load. The partners continuously upgrade and modify their site, offering new products and prices on a regular basis—something that was impossible with the paper catalog albatross. "We went out of our way to structure our site for ease of use," says Reiter, "and we get a lot of good feedback on that. If you click on an image you want, it goes into the shopping cart. Then, when you're ready, it's waiting for you at the checkout." It's simple, easy, and—as the partners emphasize—secure.

Security is always an issue in virtual businesses. As Reiter reminds us, the Internet has diverged from its originally intended path. Originally it was designed for academic discourse, not for commerce. Now people are shopping online for birthday gifts and anniversary mementos and paying by credit card. Two years ago, says Reiter, people would say, "I'm not going to put my credit card number out there in space." Indeed, TimelessTraveler.com still receives plenty of phone orders from the cyberphobics, but the ratios are dwindling. More people are feeling comfy about Web purchases with credit cards.

"We had to advertise on the home page that we're secure," says Reiter, "so that people would conquer their fears, so they'd feel comfortable." TimelessTraveler.com also has a policy of sending a confirmation, with a "Thanks" and an estimated arrival time for the print or poster. Reiter says that there's an additional follow-up only if shipping has been delayed beyond the normal two- to three-day interval. The partners don't use buyer names in any other communications and refuse to sell their mailing lists. Says Reiter, "I don't think people appreciate getting e-mail boxes full of monthly specials from other businesses. That builds resentment. We respect their privacy."

LOCATION, LOCATION, LOCATION

As in retail brick-and-mortar sales, success on the Web often depends on three things: location, location, location. Search engines are troublesome and time-consuming for the business partners but terribly important. A strong placement on the search engines is the rough equivalent of a brick storefront at the corner of Rockefeller Avenue and Vanderbilt Street. As Reiter explains, the key to sales through search engines is *placement, placement, placement.* How far up the search ladder you're listed depends on how a buyer types in a search category. "Sometimes we're seventh," she says, "and sometimes number 407." It all hangs on the key-word choice. Furthermore, Yahoo!, one of the largest engines, "is *so* difficult," according to Reiter. "They change their search criteria continually." Taking a lead from other small Web businesses, TimelessTraveler.com does no banner advertising. The returns simply do not justify the expense.

Web site marketing has proven a different game than traditional sales for Reiter. The newness of Web business can present puzzles. "There's no textbook for this," she says, referring to e-commerce. "When we started, there was no expert to go to. Everyone was just finding her way, like we were." Small problems can become big ones quickly in cyberspace. For example, there are many elements in a Web page. Changing one can have a cascading effect. "Sometimes you're not sure what makes a Web page click," says Reiter. "If you change it, the page may not click at all. Then you have to go back to the drawing board."

The partners keep track of traffic volume to their site, but they stress that it's not the volume that's important. Rather, they try to figure out what's bringing people to the Web page and what brings them back again. In virtual sales, change is one of the few constants. "What works today may not work six months from now," says Reiter.

Posters and art prints are not impulse buys. A typical customer goes to the site, sends e-mail questions, then waits a week or so before ordering from TimelessTraveler.com. On a regular basis, the business partners have to ask, "What's going on? The buyers are making decisions on some basis, but what? Redecorating a home? Outfitting a new office?" Whatever the reason, Reiter and Henley must continue to upgrade their site to guarantee that the selections are "hot" and the prices low.

ODDS OF SUCCESS: 50 PERCENT

Low prices and trendy selections provide TimelessTraveler.com with its special edge in this niche market. Other considerations also help. The company offers custom framing as well, a subcontracted service. Despite the need to expand services, the partners are not enthusiastic about framing. Reiter explains, "If a customer receives a poster that's not the right size or color, they can return it. No problem. But once we have made the frame, it could be a problem. In this case, a brick-and-mortar business would work better. They could discount the framed print to get rid of it. We can't." As a result, TimelessTraveler.com emphasizes poster sales, and the partners are clearly concerned about seeing a big advance in orders for custom frames.

Another edge comes from competitive pricing. The partners recognize that they're competing not just for art dollars but for consumer dollars in general. When the Christmas season rolls around, for example, buyers will spend some of their holiday budgets on posters but will also consider electronics, books, toys, and household appliances. Finding the right advertising for the limited purchasing power of consumers is difficult—and expensive. Therefore, TimelessTraveler.com keeps prices low, operating on a narrow profit margin. "That means there's a lot of work for a small dividend," says Reiter. Such narrow margins spell trouble for underfunded businesses and those without competitive pricing. Many of TimelessTraveler's online competitors will be out of business within the year. Say the partners: "It's a very competitive marketplace."

Even with the fierce competition, the odds of long-term success in e-business are approximately 50 percent. That's much better than the one-in-five odds for survival in traditional business. Reiter and Henley, however, warn against underfunding. They invested about $100,000 initially and suggest that those who start with less are almost surely "throwing it away." Another must is good suppliers, ones who are reliable. Finally, the poster business demands an extensive database. Poster images are formatted in JPEG files and must be handled by experienced managers, preferably working full-time.

BE FLEXIBLE, BE CREATIVE, BE DILIGENT

Expect your e-business venture to cost twice as much as you anticipated, say the owners of TimelessTraveler.com. Further, you can expect to work twice as hard as you anticipated. Entrepreneurs make a huge mistake when they set up a Web site and walk away. "This is not an absentee business," says Reiter convincingly. E-commerce ventures like the poster business are growing and changing daily. Those who survive must stay atop of trends and anticipate movements in the poster market. People always assume that Amazon.com is the model for their own enterprises. Not so. Amazon went online when there were no competitors, establishing name recognition before like businesses had even considered the Internet play. Today, unless you have a special niche in mind, the competition is already out there selling products online. And the name recognition is theirs.

"Be flexible, be creative, be diligent. Focus on good marketing techniques and artful presentation. Continuously evaluate the products—and the pricing. And rely on the instantaneous tools of the Net," say the owners. "If you want to make a marketing change or a pricing switch, do it today. Do it now. And when you look back to see the path of your journey, stop for a moment to savor the scene. It's a satisfying part of the exciting and changeable world of e-commerce."

Web address:

www.TimelessTraveler.com

3 1833 03865 8271

Digital Publishing

Start-up expenses: $3,500
Special requirements: *Digital music components*
Best advice: *"It has to come from the heart. Too many people are Stanford grads who only work for the money. Many are successful, many are not. But if you work at something you love, it gets you past the rough stuff. Don't get sucked into trying to be the next Bill Gates. Do the right thing, and the right thing will come to you."*

The Internet is rapidly changing the music world. Distributors are establishing Web sites that do everything musical but tune your guitar. At TrueFire.com, Loop DeVille offers artists' works for sale through a site directly linked to the consumer. That's right. No more CDs, tapes, or vinyl. You can download your favorites and even view artists in performance at TrueFire.com.

Here's what you get. TrueFire promotes education, music,

and other arts through these categories on its Web site: visual arts, literature and education, original music, music instruction, and reference and how-to. Packaged in cross-platform digital formats such as Mp3, PDF, and others, the programs offered by TrueFire.com arrive at your computer for a small fee. The artists' works are original, without censorship or alteration.

TrueFire.com offers artistic experiences that sometimes go beyond virtual. Poets don't just contribute to a text file—they read their works aloud as the text runs. In a music lesson, you see the sheet music and hear the tunes in Real Audio or Mp3, with the artists commenting as you proceed. Content comes directly from musicians and teachers. DeVille and his staff make no attempt to remake the works or editorialize.

For artists, the concept is ideal. Small bands, individual players and performers, and even unknown novelists can display their intellectual properties online, sharing the profits with TrueFire.com. As DeVille says, this arrangement means "no rejection letters, no editing, no quibbling with editors, no production fees, and no publisher headaches." Sounds great. The artists retain all copyrights and can pull the plug on their project at any time. They receive 50 percent of the royalties, a huge portion by comparison with normal publishing agreements.

In a certain sense, TrueFire.com serves as an Internet music and arts store. Buyers can purchase the music or entertainment they want. Or they can use the True Fire Alert feature to reach friends, publishers, or the media—even to dispense a press release. TrueFire.com also presents the opportunity for artists to send mass-market promotions into cyberspace. Frankly, for musicians, writers, and fans, it sounds like the "Stairway to Heaven."

A New Paradigm?

Loop DeVille comes from a background in music. With friends in the business who couldn't get their work to the public, DeVille recognized a niche. "There are too many barriers," he says. His Web site was designed to give artists an advantage. After 20 months of research, DeVille and fellow founders felt confident that they could deliver a site that broke down barriers. When the shopping cart and sign-up procedures finally worked perfectly, the company went online. Now an artist can upload intellectual properties in about a half-hour, complete with images, descriptions, pricing codes, and tools for producing statements. The artists can also begin checking immediately for hits and revenue.

DeVille expects viral marketing to carry his site. He employs no advertising, no banners, no opt-in e-mail. In eschewing ads, DeVille thinks he may be establishing a new paradigm on the Net. Part of the word-of-mouth concept depends on 100 board members representing the five disciplines supported by the site. With 100 supporters and organizers nationwide, TrueFire.com depends on friends telling friends about the company.

DeVille admits to having issued a single press release once upon a time, but he prefers to think of TrueFire.com as a grassroots effort. He says, "We really thought we would have to work a lot harder spreading the news." But the Web visitors seem to arrive well educated about the site, having been clearly informed by friends and fans.

The one promotional ploy is True Fire Cash. When a customer signs on, the buyer receives $10 credit. "That may not sound like much," says DeVille, "but look at the prices." Indeed, you can get a guitar lesson from Steve Ross-Elliot for six bucks, along with your 15-cent rebate in the form of True Fire Cash. The site even offers a free preview of the lesson before you pay.

The lesson uses several platforms—PDF, Mp3, and Tablature. It's the kind of lesson that, assuming you could even get the attention of a professional, would cost at least $50 in real life. On the site, you download the clip for use again and again, whenever you want to crank up the old Fender or dust off those drums. DeVille asks rhetorically, "Can you imagine getting a lesson from Zep's axe-man Jimmy Page?" If so, hurry. It's free for a short time as a promotion.

A DREAM COME TRUE

DeVille is clearly following the best e-advice available. He's working at something he loves. "I have never had more fun in my life," he says. "I love these folks I do business with. I love the enthusiasm, the artists. It's a dream come true." Perhaps DeVille's labors with garage bands and university lessons were necessary dues for this opportunity. At any rate, he says the new digital consciousness makes the business viable, and the results have been astonishing. In DeVille's own words, "We have found The Beach."

Part of the lure of The Beach is being able to relax. At TrueFire.com, DeVille makes sure that people aren't hassled when they venture online. He says, "It's clear that people don't like others trying to make a buck off them every time they click through a new page." He compares a typical Net visit to walking through Times Square and being harassed by sidewalk vendors and overwhelmed by billboards. "Our site is clean," he proposes. "It's like the Dewey decimal system for art." DeVille rejects on-line banners, spamming, and selling customers' names.

The closest thing to "noise" at TrueFire is the Cool Link section, where other related sites—ones that DeVille judges are compatible with his site—are listed. DeVille must be careful even with these links. After only two months online, TrueFire.com was receiving 500,000 page views a month, without promotion. Clearly, everyone in the business wants to jump on this train.

With businesses like TrueFire meeting immediate and overwhelming success, it becomes clear that a new paradigm is forming in cyberspace. At least for some entrepreneurs, the site sells itself. A viral campaign that draws half a million responses immediately must be tapping into an enormous well of interest. Such stories may prove the norm in future years. At least we think others will play a similar tune.

Web address:
www.TrueFire.com

Digital Recordings

Start-up expenses: $3,400
Special requirements: *Access to musicians and artists*
Best advice: *"You have to be able to complete and create value. You have to know what you're doing and have talented people around you, preferably ones involved in the music industry. This is not something your average computer scientist can understand without having known the music business."*

S *chooby-dooby-do....* Still playing those old Sinatra records on your creaky turntable? Boy, are you overdue for an update. How about digital music, the kind that emerges from your computer? The Mp3 variety is the most common at the moment (although the entire music industry is changing rapidly). With a few clicks of the mouse, you can buy Mp3 music and download it at home, keeping the tunes in a convenient file. You can even get Sinatra.

Jim Milton is the owner of Digital Music Corporation, an online distributor representing more than 1,000 artists from 60 different countries. At the tender age of 20, Milton has developed two separate sites, one offering free selections and the other promoting sales. The sites work together. In addition to listing established groups, the free-of-charge Audiosurge.com address introduces the music of emerging artists. After you download your favorite old and new tunes, the site directs you back to BuyMP3.com, a pay-per-selection site. If you really like the selections you've heard from a South African ska band or a South Philly hip-hop group, you can order a CD-length sampler. Get out your credit card.

FIRST, THE DOMAIN NAME

While still in his teens, Jim Milton purchased the domain name BuyMP3.com. At that time, he had no organization, backing, or experience. But Milton paid attention to the lawsuit between the recording industry and Diamond Multimedia, the makers of the portable Mp3 player called the Reel. "At that time," he says, "they had made no offers to the industry for any level of security, so Diamond Multimedia was shipping players that the industry felt would cause more piracy and make it portable for people downloading." Milton decided this controversy was promoting a business opportunity. He jumped on it.

The audience for Mp3 was clearly made up of college students, a computer-savvy clientele who craved music—with lots of variety and selections—and had a reputation for pirating artists' work and trading it among themselves. Milton decided he could tap this market and make it advantageous for college types to buy music instead of "borrow" it. "Whether it's Mp3 or a more secure format," he says, "I thought maybe consumers would embrace my idea and that I could provide a more organized place for them to acquire their music."

The idea was simple and direct. Milton offered a retail location for anyone who wanted to sell digital music, both independent artists and commercial labels. He figured that the Net might offer a level playing field, lending the same advantage to Warner and No-Name Records. "What should matter," says Milton, "is the quality of the music." In his business plan, Milton provided a clean, clear, compact place for people to give their music exposure and a virtual storefront for marketing their compositions and collections.

A MYSTERIOUS PHONE CALL

Early on, while still sitting on the domain name and contemplating an online business, Milton took a phone call in his dormitory room. The man who called wanted to buy the business name and address. It was all very shady. Says Milton, "I didn't know he represented buy.com because the man gave his name but not his position or company name. I had to go to a reverse directory on another Web site to find his e-mail address. Then I discovered that this person had a lofty title at buy.com. He had lied about wanting the business name for personal use."

According to Milton, the business executives at buy.com wanted his domain name badly. "Apparently, they contacted me that particular morning because, an hour before the call, the music industry held a press conference announcing the beginning of SDMI, the Secure Digital Music Initiative." The initiative lumps the five major recording labels with some technical companies "to create security specs for selling digital music on the Net." Says Milton, "It meant Mp3 could potentially be a container that could be protected." As a result, the concept was becoming suddenly more relevant.

"Things were starting to get interesting," says the young entrepreneur, who was clearly wading in shark-filled waters. "I decided to do something. I got together with four other college students—engineers, programmers, and computer science majors. We set out to create a company that could distribute music." The result was two sites, Audiosurge.com and BuyMP3.com.

TWO INTERLACING SITES

To sell something, first give something away. This prevailing online strategy attracted the partners, and Milton's troops established Audiosurge.com so that people could download new music without charge—catching the breeze of new artists and labels. Then they launched BuyMP3.com, a pay-per-download site. In the meantime, Milton established a cross-promotional strategy to lure the listeners from the free site to the fee-based one.

Over the course of several months, Milton's team conducted lots of research, gauging how to take advantage of market opportunities. They looked at how the business they'd conceived was relevant and how much leverage they had in the industry as a whole. "Along the way," says Milton, "we made great strategic alliances with companies like Internet Cash and Cybergold." Internet Cash offers prepaid cards for people without standard credit cards, a perfect match for their demographic, heavily loaded with teenagers and younger college students. They also liked iPIN.com, another site at which you can buy Mp3 selections. The iPIN.com plan allows buyers to charge their purchases to a monthly bill rather than pay immediately for each selection.

Despite early successes for BuyMP3.com, the winds could always change. The music business is in rapid transition—constant technological development alters the industry. But Milton and his associates are ready. Says Milton, "We believe from a retail standpoint, BuyMP3.com will have to morph into something like buydigitalmusic.com, where we are a format-agnostic retailer, meaning we are not really putting emphasis on Mp3 format because it will soon be outdated." With planned obsolescence in mind, Digital Music Corporation sees itself eventually as an e-commerce portal and one-stop destination for purchasing digital selections. The advantage? Says Milton, "Consumers won't have to run around to ten different sites to get what they want."

Easier to Buy Tunes Than Steal Them

Unfortunately, cyberpiracy is an accepted way of life on the Net. The ease of information sharing reduces people's inhibitions about acquiring intellectual properties without paying fees or royalties. Amazingly, Milton and his company have a business plan that makes it advantageous to pay for online digital music rather than to pilfer it. Accessibility and one-stop shopping are the keys. "It is crucial," says Milton, "to make it easier to buy music than to steal it."

Apparently, the strategy is working. With more than 1,000 independent artists registered at Digital Music Corporation, Jim Milton has an incredible catalog of free and for-sale music. Word-of-mouth advertising helps the cause, bringing lots of new inquiries from aspiring artists and new packagers. Says Milton, "They come to us looking for a way out of the traditional business paths of the music industry. That means you are picked up and given a contract by a label. Because major companies sign more people than they promote, some are left stagnant. It's not so great for them." Artists who choose to deal with Milton, on the other hand, are allowed to sell their own downloadable CDs directly.

The music industry—from the days of wax and vinyl to the current digital approach—has always been controversial and changeable. With downloadable Mp3 programs, Jim Milton's company has established a secure promontory in a stormy landscape. For the meantime, the tunes are great, and lots are free. Say, Jim, do you have any downloadable versions of "Strangers in the Night"?

Web addresses:
www.Audiosurge.com
www.buymp3.com

Magic Shop

Start-up expenses: *None*
Special requirements: *Background in magic*
Best advice: *"It just takes work, pure and simple. Most business owners wouldn't put the same amount of labor into this job. It takes me full-time, seven hours a day to promote the site."*

Now here's something to get for that hard-to-buy-for relative who likes Penn and Teller, David Copperfield, and the Amazing Kreskin. It's the David Blaine Magic Kit. If you've never seen David Blaine, you're missing a real hoot. Recently on a televised special, the magician was shown traveling around the world, amazing onlookers from Wall Street to the Great Wall. Everywhere he goes these days, Blaine, an improbable street magician who dresses in a T-shirt and jeans, astonishes audiences with simple props like a deck of cards and a shiny new quarter.

So, now that your interest is piqued, where do you buy a

David Blaine Magic Kit? Why not try MagicTricks.com, the joint online venture of Peter and Jackie Monticup. Peter is the magician, and Jackie is the marketing head. Together they sponsor a Web site that makes any frown disappear into thin air.

Fun All Around

The Monticups are having fun. "This is like my child," says Jackie Monticup. "My husband is extremely enthused about magic. It is all he has done all his life. I have a passion for the marketing and Web site part. Between the two of us, we absolutely love what we are doing." Now that's a nice arrangement.

Even with the day-to-day glitches, ghosts, and goblins that haunt any Web site, Jackie Monticup manages to see her business as an extended party. "It's a great adventure," she offers. The adventure, of course, includes a good bottom line. "The last time I looked at statistics," she says, "we had more than 63 percent repeat customers. That is exceptional." Indeed. But the Magic Tricks.com site is also hard work. And Monticup is the first to say that a site like hers depends on sweat equity. People who aren't enthused, thrilled, and captivated by their e-businesses are simply not going to put in the requisite number of hours. In this anecdote is a valuable lesson for start-up owners: you've gotta love it.

The Headless Chicken Trick

MagicTricks.com is just what the name suggests: a magic shop. From that address, Jackie Monticup markets "all kinds of cool magic tricks" and the associated accessories—more than 1,200 tricks! There's also a Pandora's box full of great stuff, such as a directory of magicians and magic clubs, a series of magicians' biographies, a section on the history of magic tricks, and loads more. The shop exists as a brick-and-mortar retail outlet in Charlottesville, Virginia, as well as a Web site. In the retail shop, relying on his long-standing expertise in the magic arts, Peter Monticup sets the stage. Having studied magic since age seven, when he served as apprentice to Professor Henry Bessette, part of the Miracle Team, Monticup drags most anything from behind your ear.

One of the things to try at MagicTricks.com is a video. Consider the one on David Blaine where he levitates three inches above the sidewalk in downtown Manhattan or the one where he removes the head of a chicken, then reattaches it. Or perhaps you'd like to see the magician push a cigarette through the middle of a quarter.

MORE THAN JUST MAGIC

In addition to finding magic on the Web, you can also come to the Monticups' real-world store for a demonstration. Says Monticup, "We feel that, if we can get you interested in magic, you will become a lifelong customer, not just a one-time buyer." As a result, when an inexperienced customer walks into the brick-and-mortar shop, asking to see a specific trick, Peter Monticup leads the customer toward gags that are the least frustrating. Says Jackie, "That means he may steer him away from a $100 trick toward one that is [easily] successful, even if it's only a $3 trick."

On the Net, the Monticups are very careful about their offerings, since it's not as easy to move online shoppers toward the approachable tricks. "We don't just sell anything," says Jackie. "There are a lot of tricks that would disappoint people, some that are a bad value." In response to the need for quality, the Monticups actually put together some of their own magic kits, thinking that the commercial varieties tend to be either chintzy or too difficult for beginners.

A BACKGROUND IN MARKETING IS A PLUS

Jackie Monticup comes from a background in English literature, later acquiring an M.B.A. in marketing. Prior to starting a business, she was a college professor of marketing. In 1983, she formed her own advertising agency and booked her husband for several corporate magic shows—ones like Marketing Magic, where Peter helped the company salesmen perform magic tricks at banquets and trade shows. "We got tired of traveling," she says, explaining how they found themselves in a storefront magic shop.

By 1996, Jackie saw the promise of the Internet. She bought a computer and spent a year teaching herself HTML code, as well as everything else about establishing a Web site. As she recalls, "I would sit up literally all night long, from midnight to nine in the morning, visiting Web sites with tutorials on how to learn the Net, how to market, how to write code, and how to build a Web site. I just immersed myself."

FRONTPAGE IS LIKE MAGIC

Monticup claims that one of the designers of *Frontpage* software is a magician. Metaphor or not, her observation is high praise.

Using *Frontpage*, her favorite tool, Monticup built one of the largest sites ever posted through that service. But the task took some preparation. As she says, "You have to remember that I already knew HTML, so I used *Frontpage* as a shortcut for basic coding to get it slapped up. Then I tweaked everything." Monticup believes *Frontpage* is an excellent organizational tool, one that allowed her to get past some serious barriers while constructing an eighty page-site.

INVENTORY AND A CUSTOMER BASE

Beyond the Web problem, Monticup recognizes that virtual business mirrors real-world business in many ways. For example, she knows the importance of a mailing list and excellent customer service. She relies on thanking customers for their orders. In all her daily plans, she reaffirms the idea that keeping a customer is easier than finding a new one. That lesson has been lost on some e-tailers, she suggests. "I am appalled at the low level of service on the Web," she says. "It's as if the anonymity of the Web has made companies and people rude and difficult to deal with." Such poor customer relations, says Monticup, are a primary problem with the Net.

Customer service has become Monticup's first priority. Using her own experiences with Web commerce, she anticipates problems and prepares solutions. Also, the simple expedient of asking customers how the company can solve problems has paid benefits.

KEEPING TRACK OF ORDERS

With increasing sales volume, Monticup relies on a high-quality tracking system in her site. Within 72 hours of ordering, customers can track their own orders. Says Jackie, "People are leery of the Web. If they haven't talked to a real person, they are worried that the order didn't get through. Previously, the only way to check was to call our toll-free number. That was expensive for us." To cut costs and provide better service, Monticup contacted a programmer, who wrote a special software key to supply the company its own tracking system.

For tracking information, the customer types in a phone number. The program explains what day the package was shipped and where the order is located at that time. With a direct feed to the U.S. Postal Service, the software automatically tracks the order on its journey. "The buyers don't even have to know their tracking numbers," says Monticup. "It makes people feel their orders are on the way, and it helps us from getting blamed for delays caused by the delivery system." In Monticup's memory, the company has suffered no customer complaints over shipping and delivery. "It's well worth the efforts," she says.

So if you want a little magic in your life, click onto MagicTricks.com. It's a rich and engaging site, full of surprises and wonders.

Web address:
www.MagicTricks.com

Online Games

Start-up expenses: *Variable*
Special requirements: *Games technology*
Best advice: *"You have to be madly in love with your idea because nine out of ten people are going to tell you it stinks. If you aren't in love with it, you should work for somebody else. You have to communicate that passion."*

Remember Super Mario, Donkey Kong, and Tetris? The prehistoric era of computerized games, which began with ones like Pong, captured the imaginations of teenagers and adults alike, back when computer games were available almost exclusively on floppy disks. Today, of course, the floppies are passé. The Internet is awash with games, and the varieties are endless. Not only are preadolescent boys wasting their time on game screens, but so are little sister Sally and Grandma. There's some serious market potential out there. If

Grandma can shoot down alien ships or play backgammon in cyberspace, anyone can do it.

Games have been the number one use of computers since day one. Since the first bouncing Pong ball, computer geeks—mostly young boys and men—haven't been able to get enough games like Pac Man and Alien Invasion. Today the obsessed can turn to the Internet, where entrepreneurs are finding ways to turn gaming passions into big bucks. One example is the online firm Gamesville.com, a database marketing company that masquerades as a games company.

Steve Kane, the CEO of Gamesville, takes a whimsical attitude toward his business, best displayed in the company slogan: "Wasting Your Time Since 1976." While online gaming may be a waste of time to many, it's a million-dollars-a-year hobby for Kane, whose firm turns the simple act of online registration into a fail-safe marketing strategy.

IF THE GAMES ARE FREE, HOW DO YOU MAKE MONEY?

Gamesville.com is the world's largest online game site. As such, the company gets tremendous exposure and viral publicity. Despite appearances, however, Gamesville.com is actually a database marketing company that employs games and prizes as an inducement for consumers to contribute their time and data. This is how it works: all but the most casual visitors to Gamesville fill out a membership form during the registration process. Subsequently, Kane's firm uses the data to create highly specific target marketing for each registrant. In the meantime, Gamesville telecasts ads during and between the games. The total package is enhanced by a rich series of prizes for skilled game players. In a typical month, Gamesville gives out 3,500 checks to game winners, who are not gambling, because the games are free. The Web site puts the scope of this financial package into perspective: "Our bank statements are so massive they have to be delivered by UPS." The statements, of course, are jammed with the records of the lucky 3,500 winners.

At Gamesville, each product ad is literally one-to-one targeted so that one player sees something completely different from someone else. If you're twentysomething in Peoria, you get an entirely different message than a twentysomething in Santa Fe. If you move from Peoria to Tacoma, the online message also changes. This skillful manipulation of demographic information can happen only on the Net, where there is no limit to the power of the algorithm. Says Kane with considerable accuracy, "You can't do this targeting in any other medium." He's right. Even with direct mail, you can only hope for loose targeting at best. On the Net, every individual can be specifically targeted. That's the premise on which Gamesville.com operates.

HOW DOES IT WORK?

At Gamesville.com, Kane's employees take the geographic model used by direct marketers (mailing to all residents in an affluent ZIP code, for example) to a new level, building detailed and complex profiles of people based on the registration information. That data is worth money. Despite the obvious temptations, Gamesville.com *never* sells its information to other marketers, according to Kane, who has a better business plan. He says, "You can't come to me and buy my names." However, you can go to Kane with an ad budget and say, "I want access to people in the Gamesville database who might use my products." For example, Virgin Airlines advertises in only a few markets in the United States. But because Gamesville.com targets geographically, Virgin has an opportunity to reach players who would never normally see a Virgin ad (i.e., they don't live within fifty miles of an airport Virgin services). "We offer Virgin an extremely efficient use of their money," says Kane.

Gamesville has other important strategies. When the company examines the results of ad campaigns using closed-loop marketing, Gamesville uses feedback from the first campaign to design new ones. For instance, perhaps a number of women students were targeted by ads for athletic shoes. Kane's staff analyzes the feedback on young women who clicked onto the ads but didn't buy the shoes. As a result, Kane might change prices, lifestyle slant, or some other factor to see what might start to generate sales. Says Kane, "The great thing is, on the Net, this all happens at incredible speed. The whole thing is predicated on consumers willingly and happily spending a lot of time with us and giving us their data." And while they're entertained by the online games, the players are contributing information that adds up to trends.

RETRO IS BACK

In the past, computer games were thought of as "Toys for Boys." They always involved warriors, combat, aliens, and big, fast action. In truth, says Kane, everybody who uses a computer likes games. The most popular computer game ever is Microsoft's Solitaire. Everybody plays.

Gamesville's secret weapon is accessibility. "We offer instant gratification," says Kane, uttering the mantra of cyberspace. "We are actually closer to a game show like 'Wheel of

Fortune.' " Kane suggests that the average player can pick up the rules and conventions of a game in less than 15 seconds—without guidebooks. Now that's instant gratification.

"We have a principle here called *yesterday's technology today*," says Kane. Gamesville will not release anything that hasn't been tested with a dinosaur-like AOL 1.0 on a 486 PC with a 14-baud modem and a tiny, outdated monitor. Not only can you play the games with any ancient platform or technology, but you can *win* the games. "There is absolutely no advantage to having a new computer," says Kane, "so you can kick butt on a super geek at Harvard with a T1 line connected to the best laptop money can buy." As Kane suggests, no one else in the games industry has adopted *retro* as its code word.

Computer games, Kane admits, are still aimed at the tech lover, but demographics are changing. Today the typical games player looks like the average reader of *People* magazine. A surprising 63 percent are females. The average online player is thirty-four or thirty-five years old. Says Kane, "The same people who watch prime-time TV love us." The image of the computer geek with the pocket protector is no longer valid as a portrait of the online gamester.

So How Do I Get There?

Don't expect to find Gamesville.com in banner ads or media blurbs. Its advertising budget is low—very low. "We have spent zero on marketing since day one," says Kane, "and we've been profitable for years." Gamesville survives primarily by viral advertising, the word-of-mouth publicity that money can't buy. People like the site—it works, they understand it, they tell their friends. And they return, again and again. In the meantime, the players' digital fingerprints provide data that pays for those winners' checks and profit statements. It sounds like fun.

Kane has some words of advice for others who are thinking about similar online businesses. "It's all entertainment," he says, "first and foremost." Gamesville succeeds because the venture plays to the American obsession with entertainment and distraction. Gamesville's brand of interactive play puts thousands of people into competition with each other for real prizes and serious money. It's exciting and interesting. The winners—even the losers—tell their friends and invite them to join the action. It's positively viral!

As a final consideration, CEO Kane says that, to succeed, you must love your business. Even if everyone else thinks you're crazy, you many have a great idea. Meanwhile, keep people around you who believe in it as much as you do. Why? You're convincing people that, even though there's no business here today, tomorrow will be different. That line calls for an act of faith and some coconspirators who trust your judgment.

To summarize his first days in business, Kane quotes a great military leader. When asked about his most important job during World War II, General Dwight D. Eisenhower said simply, "It was to smile." Kane sees himself in the same role in the early days at Gamesville—a leader ready to encourage the troops and boost morale. Now that the main battle has been waged, Kane no longer has to force a smile.

Web address:
  www.Gamesville.com

Photo Gallery

Start-up expenses: *$500 plus inventory*
Special requirements: *Digital camera*
Best advice: *"Have your business plan well thought out. Have a targeted approach, not a broad base, and focus on quality. First, you must have a good idea, a targeted idea—something unique. Then decide whether you're going to emphasize value or volume. You should be able to support yourself for a year or two because, if you start to feel pinched on the money end, it will hamper your decision making and create unnecessary stress."*

Sometimes the origins of an e-business are decades old, lying dormant, waiting for the rush of Internet technology. In Seattle, just such an opportunity occurred when Jill Bennett approached famed Northwest photographer Josef Scaylea, a man who has spent 35 years snapping pictures of the Evergreen State. When Bennett built a Web site featuring Scaylea's award-winning photos, many of them originally featured in the pages of the *Seattle Times*, she held a digital mirror to Seattle and the Northwest.

Today fans of Scaylea (and others who just appreciate the striking photographic images) can click onto SeattleGallery.com for a view of the Space Needle, Snoqualmie Falls, the Narrows Bridge, or Alki Beach. Bennett's company distributes prints of the photos to buyers that include corporations, small businesses, and individuals. Despite the name SeattleGallery.com, there is no gallery, at least in the traditional sense. The business is entirely an online venture, one that provides Bennett with a great deal of satisfaction and a growing income.

THE PERSUASION GAME

Despite a long and successful career, Scaylea was not a prime mover in the SeattleGallery business. In fact, he stalled. But because Scaylea is the father of Bennett's best friend and college pal, he at least listened. After years of resistance, the photographer agreed to Bennett's plan to buy 1,000 autographed black-and-white images for distribution on the Net. Scaylea's work is now widely available for the first time, despite the artist's long and celebrated career.

Scaylea, who is in his late eighties and retired, had captured on film a lifetime's collection of Northwest scenes and characters. Some of the most popular images are of horses, followed by a famous photo of the Blue Angels flight team performing at Seattle's Seafare celebration. Another popular addition is "Perfection," a scene that features a crew team on Lake Washington. The photo, with its perfect pooling of oars, is a favorite with Seattle-area businesses. For many, the immaculate coordination of the oars represents the ideal corporate image of collaborative precision.

A MIX OF THE OLD AND THE NEW

When Bennett finally secured the artist's permission to sell his photos, she put up her Web site with assistance from a neighbor in her apartment building. First, she contacted a venture capitalist, someone with ties to BigStep.com, the Web hosting company. Together they established the site and put up pictures in about two weeks. By the end of the third week, they had secured a credit card system, and SeattleGallery.com went online in 1999.

Unlike many businesses that make the transition from brick-and-mortar to online services, SeattleGallery.com was launched exclusively as an e-commerce venture, although much of its advertising takes a traditional form. Bennett and her colleagues place pictures around the Seattle area in restaurants, bars, and small businesses, hoping to spur interest. Each of the photos includes the Web address.

"Our market is highly targeted," says Bennett. "We concentrate on the Northwest and its people. We have pictures of sailing, pictures of animals, pictures of local scenes." Bennett also places small black-and-white ads with sample pictures in publications such as the magazine for the Washington Athletic Club. "It paid for itself in a nanosecond," says Bennett. Recently the *Seattle Times* published an article about Scaylea's prints, one that featured the SeattleGallery address, and the company immediately received 2,600 new hits.

Web links have not been fruitful, admits Bennett, who has returned to traditional advertising modes such as placing ads in newspapers and putting up fliers on bulletin boards. People are still finding their way around the Net, she argues, and SeattleGallery.com is hard to find. "There are *so many* businesses out there," she laments. "People have to be experienced with the Web to find what they want. Web users are just beginning to develop their own search expertise. Most of them need help through standard offline advertising."

NOT GOING BACK, IT'S TOO MUCH FUN

Bennett found her way to e-commerce through a natural channel. She worked most of her career in the computer industry—in sales and marketing of digital equipment. Most recently she worked for WRQ, a small software company that provides networking infrastructures, serving as sales and marketing regional director. After taking a leave of absence in July 1999 to launch the Web site, Bennett has not returned. "Honestly," she says, "it looks like I'm not going back. This is too much fun."

One of the first important steps for SeattleGallery.com was Bennett's cyberstroll through domain names. For this information, she went to Network Solutions, the registry point for domain titles. "I wanted to have a company name that was the same as my Web site, so I started working on a Web name first," she explains. "But I had a hard time finding one that spoke to a higher level, an umbrella name that wouldn't pigeonhole me or force me into a corner." She was looking for something broad and descriptive, like Clickapic.com, which, of course, was taken. After finding that her next 25 or 30 choices were also taken, Bennett gave up and decided to focus on a Northwest audience, settling on SeattleGallery.com as the URL address and the business name.

The decision to regionalize was a wise move. Bennett admits she doesn't have a nationwide view for her business. "What I do have," she says, "is the vision of pulling in Northwest artists and art media." In addition to photography, Bennett loves pottery and glass (the world-famous glassblower Dale Chihuly is a

Tacoma resident.) SeattleGallery expects to someday include the glasswork and pottery creations of Northwest artists.

In imagining her business, Bennett decided her primary goal was complete customer satisfaction. "We want zero returns," says Bennett. For that reason, she has chosen a carefully managed approach to growth, wishing to move slowly at the cost of volume. Ironically, one of her first business decisions was to buy an enormous inventory of a thousand pictures. "I needed to have some security," she admits, "so I bought a huge inventory from Scaylea and paid a royalty for each." After having each photo printed and signed by the author, she found that her initial costs were well above expectations. However, Scaylea's advancing years convinced her to move decisively.

Happily, the artist is still working. At age eighty-seven, he says he still hasn't taken his best picture. On day trips through the region with Bennett, Scaylea still shows an intimate knowledge of the Northwest and is still snapping photos of the people and places that fascinate him.

PEOPLE STILL WANT TO TALK TO SOMEONE

E-businesses cater to customers who have different comfort levels with the Net, and Bennett finds that SeattleGallery.com buyers mostly want to buy over the phone. Many people simply won't order online, primarily for security reasons. A few have been burned by giving out credit card numbers in the past, and others are not yet Net-smart. Bennett has taken steps to ensure credit card security, but she still realizes that telephone orders will dominate her business. She understands, saying, "These pictures are not inexpensive. Many people just want to talk to someone before committing that amount of money."

Besides concerns about credit cards, potential buyers often ask to see the pictures in a real visit rather than through digital image. For them, a field trip is in order. On her site, Bennett lists some of the locations where several Scaylea prints hang, such as a well-known café near the University of Washington. After viewing the prints in natural light—and perhaps touching the frames or glass—customers usually find their way back to SeattleGallery.com.

Other problems involve advertising. Bennett initially thought, "If I build it [the site], they will come." Nope. She admits her Pollyannaish predictions were wrong, leading to a big disappointment. "We thought we just had to put up our pictures, and our job would be done," she says. "But we were just starting. The Web site is a great way to take orders, offering tremendous business efficiency. But the site in no way replaces standard basic marketing tasks."

On the other hand, once people reach the SeattleGallery.com site, they are captivated. The high-quality pictures don't need selling. "That's our advantage," says Bennett. "We have good stuff." Scaylea's work is so well known and appreciated in the Seattle area that his 35-year reputation serves as a natural publicity foundation for the e-business. In addition, even though there are only eight photos displayed at a time on the Web site, people will call, remembering a past photo, and Bennett sends Scaylea looking for the negative.

As a bit of advice for the prospective e-business venture, Bennett suggests a careful study of your audience. She is convinced that a targeted approach is superior to a broad one. With a bright idea and a good sense of audience, all that remains is high-quality execution. Putting a great product, like Josef Scaylea photos, before the eyes of a carefully screened audience has a strong prospect of success. It certainly paints a rosy picture!

Web address:
www.SeattleGallery.com

Sports Art

Start-up expenses: $50,000
Special requirements: *Knowledge of the art world*
Best advice: *"Hurry up. You can never get started too soon. Just plunge right in. But understand that e-business can be the ultimate black hole. It is a huge commitment. First, ask yourself, 'Why am I doing this? Why am I going online rather than building a brick-and-mortar business?'"*

If someone were to say "golf art," you might be tempted to think of kitsch like "Dogs Playing Poker" or a velvet Elvis. But art expert Taba Dale has another view. With sales approaching a million dollars a year, her collection of golf-themed art is not the stuff of garage sales and flea markets. Instead, her buyers are often the corporate executives of companies such as Merrill Lynch, MCI WorldCom, and IBM. These are just some of the people (and companies) who might want an oil painting of the eighteenth fairway at Pebble Beach or a pen-and-ink likeness of the late Payne Stewart.

Golf is an important pastime in America. Not only do millions of people play, but the sport has a certain cachet in board rooms and executive suites around the country. Fairway condos are popular among the jet-setters, and more than one "big deal" has taken place over an eighteen-foot putt for par. Naturally, then, interest is growing in paintings and sculpture with a golf theme. The well-known images of Tiger Woods, Arnold Palmer, and Betsy King have long adorned posters, key chains, T-shirts, and coffee mugs. Now Dale is collecting more serious iconography and distributing golf art both online and offline through her company, the Scottsdale Collection.

HIGH-END CONTEMPORARY ART

Dale founded TABA, Inc., in 1979, forming the parent company as a fine art outlet. She worked then (and still does) with private collectors and as an art consultant for corporations seeking high-end contemporary art pieces. In 1988, Dale built a house in the golf community of Avenal, Maryland, the host city for the Kemper Open, a regular U.S. Golf Association event. "It's a beautiful golf course community," says Dale. "I found myself living on a golf course and loving it." Even though Dale did not golf at the time, she appreciated the "magical experience" of golf—the beautiful scenery, the beautiful people, the beautiful moments.

Although golf art was not in her plans, Dale began to receive special requests from corporate clients. "If a client asks for something, you say *yes*," she says emphatically. "Then you go find it." Dale entered the marketplace looking for golf art and found very little.

Today, Dale's golf division, the Scottsdale Collection,

promotes top golf artists and contains some exclusive artistic presentations. Dale's company also functions as an art agency, representing painters and sculptors in the business world. Says Dale, "This business is a wonderful way for me to blend my love of golf and art. The artists I deal with are world-class." With the golf art experience in hand, Dale now is looking into theme art for other sports such as baseball, basketball, and running.

DOING BUSINESS ON THE FOURTEENTH FAIRWAY

At first, Dale was simply pleased to find art for her immediate clients. But she soon discovered that golf art, like the sport itself, was in a growth spurt. More and more artists were contributing pieces based on the game and its famous players. When Dale began collecting and distributing golf art, there were twenty-four million golfers and twelve thousand courses. Now there are in excess of twenty-six million golfers in the United States alone and more than fourteen thousand courses, with another three hundred added each year, according to the National Golf Association. In a short time, interest in golf has exploded. Dale felt that the wave of interest in the sport signaled an opportunity for her.

In fact, after doing extensive research on golf art, Dale became one of America's foremost experts. Building a Web site devoted to that specialty was the next logical step. The Net approach was so successful that she closed her brick-and-mortar showroom, saying, "It made no sense to carry the overhead when I could do as much from my home. Besides, it's great doing business on the fourteenth fairway. I just love working at home and being close to the course." She says that the Net allows anyone to create a million-dollar or multimillion-dollar company that can compete with the brick-and-mortar stores on a high level and in a professional way.

She launched the Web site in 1997. At that time, Dale was already learning about the Net through her affiliations with Golf.com and Golfweb. Back in the Gold Rush days of the Net, when everyone was pioneering, Dale approached those companies and asked about setting up an art gallery within their sites. It took a few years, but the Web site soon became "a huge revenue stream." In the early stages, says Dale, "I had a big learning curve to get past." But Dale now has a partnership with new high-tech people who have an intimate understanding of how cyberspace works. "I have to rely on the techies to guide me," Dale admits. Interestingly, early in 1999 the site was reviewed by the USGA in a magazine called *Golf Journal*. The USGA agreed that scottsdalecollection.com remains the best online source for golf art.

On the technical side, life has become more complicated with each passing month. To compete, Dale has assembled legal, marketing, and technical teams. She sees her business (and e-commerce in general) entering a more sophisticated era. To be ready, her technical experts have composed a new Web site, one that she calls "definitive."

A SITE FOR FUN AND PROFIT

Because she carved a niche in the industry at an early stage, today Dale does virtually no marketing. She explains, "I get calls and e-mails all the time from people who say they searched for golf art or prints on search engines, and that's it." People suggest that they simply found scottsdalecollection.com and "had a blast" looking through the site. Dale says that people know what they want even before they click onto her site, so business transactions almost write themselves.

Dale believes that she can find most anything that a customer wants in golf art. Her resources, she suggests, are vast, meaning that she has access to a huge number of works by artists and associated galleries. She cites a recent example of her successes. Someone wanted a sculpture for about $500. Dale e-mailed the woman and asked for more information about the recipient. She ended up very happy with a spectacular piece valued at $1,300. "It was a sculpture that wasn't even on my site," says Dale. "But the woman wouldn't have known about the work if she hadn't come to my site to investigate."

From her experiences at building a successful e-business, Dale has some sage advice. For one thing, she has a professional Web master. "I am the visionary, the art dealer, the content leader," she says. "I don't do the other stuff."

Dale believes that the Gold Rush era is about to close for new Net businesses. "Hurry up!" she says. Now is the time to get wired for e-commerce. Who knows how much longer the golden opportunities will last. But, even in haste, be sure to have a plan and a commitment. "Make the fundamental choice to be successful, or else you will be rocked like a toothpick in a stormy sea," she says. "People who think they just have to have a Web site—because that's what business trends dictate now—well, it's just not a good reason." Without a solid business plan, warns Dale, even a great Web site won't be of much value.

Finally, says Dale, if you're going to build a company and take it to the highest level, be aware of the importance of seemingly small things. She suggests a catchy name and Web address, a well-designed logo, and some research into brand management (to assure high-quality products). Needless to say, the Net is a tremendous resource for each of these concerns.

Today, Taba Dale is successfully marketing golf art online. Her house on the fourteenth fairway is also her office. And yes, golf is no longer just a theme for her business. Every now and then she throws her clubs in the golf cart and pulls out onto the greens for a round.

Web address:
www.scottsdalecollection.com

Business to
Business

Accounting Services

Start-up expenses: $4,400
Special requirements: *Accounting experience and CPA certification*
Best advice: *"Be patient. Nothing ever happens as quickly as you expect it to."*

Ken Downing is the founder and owner of Netcontroller.com, a Princeton, New Jersey–based firm that keeps financial records, supports accounting services, and generates fiscal reports. Downing says, "We are like the accounting department down the hall—but we're not." The online service is not an accounting firm either, so Netcontroller.com is not appropriate for audits and complicated tax questions. Rather, Downing's firm offers online support for accounting practices.

Hard to follow? Here's how it works. If you're running a business, you need financial statements for investors and tax

49

purposes or just to see if you're making money. Downing's company assists small businesses that are not in a position to receive high-level accounting services from large firms. As Downing explains, "We provide that service by posting records right on the Internet."

Usually a small business owner tries to keep records in his office or hire a local bookkeeper. In these cases, the company's needs are not complex. The books don't need full-time attention, but they do require expertise. Day-to-day operations call for someone to write checks or to handle collections. "That is the easy stuff," says Downing, "not at all complicated." But a few steps further along, accounting problems become more troublesome. When firms try to raise capital or have to deal with the IRS, they can't expect Bill's Bookkeeping Service to keep in stride.

MOVING THROUGH THE RANKS

Even though Downing is a CPA (as are others on his staff), the company doesn't actively provide complete accounting services. Instead, it works to give support from the CPA level on down. That strategy means the firm provides plenty of expertise in areas such as reporting information, organizing accounts, and generating documents. As Downing explains, his employees bring hard-copy documents into the main office. Then the staff breaks the information down and puts it onto the computer. Next is an upper-management review with a CPA level of expertise. Finally the company generates formal reports using general accounting principles that satisfy the requirements for bank loans, IRS audits, and other investment concerns. Whew! It sounds like hard work. Other companies are providing similar services, but not with the same approach.

SETTING YOUR OWN SCHEDULE

A number of small business owners don't have the time to review reports during normal hours. They usually want to look at records during the evening—maybe as late as 11 P.M.—an inconvenient time for Bill's Bookkeeping Service. Downing says, "The owners settle down after dinner, go back to work, then eventually want to look at reports online." When the owners are relaxed and prepared, they want to see who owes what amounts, how much cash they have on hand, and where their own funds are headed.

Downing's Net-controller.com system places the fiscal reports and numbers online so business professionals can review their status anytime, day or night. "The hardest part," he says, "is that not everybody is up to speed with technology. Not everyone has high-speed Internet access, even though that's the way the world is going."

FLEXIBLE SPENDING

As for pricing, Downing strives to be flexible. "Not everybody wants everything," he explains. Those who want only a portion of the available services can expect to pay less. Downing asks potential clients whether they want help with accounts receivable or payroll. Then he questions them about the number of employees, the usual range of customers, and other procedural matters. Prices for service can then range from $500 a month for a one-person Internet shop to $3,500 a month for complex transactions.

CAN BILL'S BOOKKEEPING
SERVE TOKYO?

Does Bill's Bookkeeping Service reach Tokyo? No. But Downing's Net-controller.com can. The company has clients all over the world, one huge advantage of the Net. "We have an electronic equipment manufacturer from Japan setting up operations in the United States," says Downing, "and we have other clients in New York, California, Oregon, and throughout the globe." The services provided don't need any local control, nor is any face-to-face contact required. Unlike most CPA practices, centrally located for ease of operations, the Net-controller.com site is an office without doors. Downing says the Net helps eliminate the obstacles of getting information from point A to point B.

Before the launch in October 1999, Ken Downing worked in the Wall Street arena, where the best way to reach new clients was through referrals. He finds that referrals are still the best method for attracting new business. Response to his site has been good. "We have ads in newspapers, and we've done mass mailings," he says, "but the best methods are the search engines and referrals."

GETTING AHEAD

The biggest challenge so far has been optimizing the search engine placement. With thousands of companies in competition, getting to the top is hard work. Downing admits that "getting our positioning has taken longer than I expected. It's more complicated than I thought." Although Downing paid an expert to design his Web site, he takes some credit for the pages, having first written out the plan. "I am no graphic designer," he says without shame. Downing wrote out ten pages of what he wanted to sell and took it to a designer, saying, "Here's what I want. Make it look good and work well." The designer, an information technician from an ISP, remains the site maintenance expert.

PEOPLE ARE COMFORTABLE SENDING DOCUMENTS

At first Downing worried that customers would be afraid to send financial documents to an outside service. That concern has been unwarranted. And, as Downing says, "There are lots more sensitive documents flying around in FedEx folders. Invoices and canceled checks aren't much of a risk."

None of the exchanges on the site have generated much anxiety for clients. Few people, he says, seem uncomfortable with the Net's security. "Once a week, the client collects all the documents, approves them, overnight expresses them (that's pretty cheap), and then we receive them," says Downing. After accepting the packages, Downing's employees break down the information, enter it into the system, generate reports, put the reports on the Internet, and send them on their way. Some files go first into *Excel* and then are e-mailed to their destinations. Perhaps with added bravura, Downing says, "We can do everything from soup to nuts."

COMMUNICATION IS KEY

Communication is an important part of the business plan at Net-controller.com. Downing explains, "We have someone on our side who acts as liaison with clients, so that we have some idea what's going on." He adds, "We try to communicate on a scheduled basis and keep in touch so nothing breaks down in the process." According to the owner, customers like the company's policy because it reduces turnover problems. "If issues come up," says Downing, "you have someone to call." Reassuringly, he adds, "And we don't say, 'You owe us $150 for answering your phone call.' "

There isn't much you can't find on the Internet. If it's support services for matters of accounting, consider Ken Downing at Net-controller.com. He can probably even balance your checkbook.

Web address:
www.Net-controller.com

Auction House

Start-up expenses: *$500,000 + (high costs associated with expensive programming and large inventory)*
Special requirements: *None*
Best advice: *"You have to have a good idea. It should be something that is unique, not like what others are doing."*

MakeUsAnOffer.com is the online brainchild of Michael and Kathy Morell. This site is definitely one of a kind. At MakeUsAnOffer.com, you negotiate with a cartoon character for the best price on a watch, a sofa, or a sweater. Chester is the artificially intelligent salesman, and he likes to haggle.

At first glance, it looks like the pair of twenty somethings set out to go head-to-head with the 500-pound gorillas in the online auction market, eBay and Priceline. But actually, the concept is the exact opposite. Instead of asking customers to come and offer the highest price for an item, they're prompted to bid lower.

Opening a store without price tags was Michael's idea. But he probably didn't learn about haggling at Harvard, where he earned a B.S. in economics. Haggling is as old as Baghdad. But MakeUsAnOffer.com is no ancient bazaar, and the underlying technology that uses artificial intelligence to haggle with bargain-hungry shoppers is cutting edge, even experimental. The Morells are positioning themselves as haggling technology experts.

CHESTER DOES ALL THE WORK

At the "haggle" site, the digital puppet, Chester, sells more than 1,300 brand-new products across six major departments: electronics, fashion and beauty, housewares, travel and leisure, holiday gifts, and the ultimate bargain basement "under $20" area. The prices are open to negotiation, and you must bid through the Web page. The virtual shopkeeper likes to banter and joke, so you can expect to hear comments like, "Come on, Lou, why don't you make me an offer on this luggage?" or "All right, Mary, I'll sell this fine piece of luggage for only $20 because I like you."

A customer starts by browsing the neatly organized store. Then, once a product captures interest, Chester shows a large picture of the product, offers a thorough description, and reveals the retail price. From there the interaction resembles one at your local flea market.

Chester informs a buyer of the normal retail price for an item, then invites him to make a lower offer. Unlike traditional stores, where sales are periodic events, the products at MakeUsAnOffer.com are always on sale—at least to those who can outduel Chester. How is this possible? Chester's programming allows him to analyze on the fly the inventory levels and customer demand, letting him compute the minimum acceptable price.

In fact, this immediacy is one major feature that separates MakeUsAnOffer.com from the slew of existing online auction sites. Here, customers complete a sale and walk away with the prices they asked for within minutes. There's no waiting, and no competition from other customers. It's the immediacy of the whole process that makes it work. In 1996, Kathy tried a mail order version of the haggling concept and it failed. Bidding by mail simply took so long, people lost interest.

It was Mike's programming skills that made the e-commerce version of haggling a reality. "The best part of the system," says Kathy, "is that the software he created makes the bidding process instantaneous, rather than slow and cumbersome, such as online auction sites, where transactions take days to complete." The haggling takes just a few minutes. Then the product goes to the shipping ramp, and the deal is complete.

LIQUIDATION STOCKS FILL THE SHELVES

Chester's willingness to haggle stems from the fact that the inventory at MakeUsAnOffer.com. is all liquidation merchandise. That's why the prices are so low. For example, the company recently carried a music box listed for $14.95. Chester unloaded a crate of them for as low as $9.45 each. One customer picked up a lady's gold watch and bracelet, normally priced at $695, for only $225. The prices and discounts range considerably, depending on customer demand and the inventory levels. In the winter, a designer cowl-neck dress listed at

$92 sold for almost half price at $47. Chester must have been napping.

With a background in retail and marketing, Kathy Morell takes responsibility for hunting down the liquidation items for sale on the site. The company has borrowed one popular aspect from online auctions: they make room for guest hagglers. After receiving many requests from visitors to have Chester haggle off products for them, the Morells added the "guest haggler" feature to the site. It allows an outside, independent party to place a product on the site for haggling. While the feature doesn't provide an instant response to the customer and the seller yet, it's the first step toward an interactive classified service for haggling.

Web address:
www.MakeUsAnOffer.com

Customer Service

Start-up expenses: *Variable*
Special requirements: *None*
Best advice: *"Remember the importance of customer service. If you focus on being the best customer service company, issues like pricing go out the door. The companies that provide the best service will be the winners."*

In e-commerce, customer service is critical. But online businesses have been slow to get the point. A couple of years ago on the Net, customer service was the last consideration when owners and corporations put up a Web site. "Contact Us" pages were an afterthought, hastily prepared and poorly conceived. Naturally, there were predictable results. The worst thing that could happen became, in fact, a regular event: throughout the e-commerce world, dissatisfied customers spread the word that they couldn't return a product or contact the seller.

Today, people are deservedly cautious. Nobody wants to take any unnecessary risks, and they won't buy from firms that ignore customers' questions and concerns. In such a business climate, firms that specialize in customer relations have a niche. One such venture is LivePerson.com, the leading provider of interactive customer service and sales solutions for Web sites. Using real-time technology, the people at LivePerson.com use chat rooms to allow customers to communicate with sellers and service representatives.

HOW DOES IT WORK?

There is no software installation or special hardware involved with the services at LivePerson. As the name suggests, customers of a given Web site with questions contact a live—yes, live—person. Clicking on a LivePerson.com link initiates an online chat that is designed to solve problems ranging from how to program the VCR to how to get biscuits to rise.

Here's how the process works. A customer clicks onto a company's Web site with a question and is directed to the LivePerson icon. The next click raises the LivePerson window. After customers log in, they choose an operator and begin clacking out their questions. The "conversation" happens in real time while the customer toggles between the window and the business owner's Web site, which keeps the customer's eyes at least partially focused on product information even while receiving technical assistance.

The operators, who work for the client companies, respond to both a visual cue and ringing bell when a question comes in. They can respond to visitors' queries with either preformatted responses or a customized text response. Each LivePerson.com operator maintains as many as four conversations at a time and can toggle between queries.

The system is geared for smooth running. There are no special plug-ins at the LivePerson.com site, and it does not use the gee-whiz special effects of Java. Virtually anyone can use the LivePerson service, even those on funky, out-of-date computers. LivePerson.com works with standard browsers using Netscape 3.0 to 4.6 and with Internet Explorer versions 3.0 to 5.0. With AOL, LivePerson.com reacts to Explorer versions 3 and 4. Because of the low-tech applications, the LivePerson.com service is fast, efficient, and trouble free. And, no surprise, LivePerson.com is open 24 hours.

THE HUMAN TOUCH INCREASES SALES

Robert Locascio is the CEO of LivePerson.com. He says that valued customer service is not only courteous and helpful—it dramatically increases the bottom line. According to Locascio, about 1–2 percent of hits on the Net eventually turn into sales. That's the international average. With live interaction, however, the number jumps to 35 percent. "It's actually an old idea," he says, "a one-on-one chat." In a previous era of commerce, the neighborhood butcher sold more hamburger when he asked, "How's your arthritis, Mrs. Schwarz?" Today an online chat can also be a powerful inducement to sales.

When asked why the service is needed, Locascio says that people desire the immediacy that the Net has promised. When buying or researching products, people want feedback, answers, and personal attention—and they want it now. In the brick-and-mortar world, offers Locascio, when you walk into a store, you do one of two things. Either you find a product, touch it, check the price tag, and see how it's made, getting enough information to put it back on the shelf or take it to the counter. Or you decide that you need some assistance, so you ask a salesperson your questions.

On the Net, you can't touch the products, and there are no salespeople to hail. The Net is largely self-service. "So far," says Locascio, "e-mail has been utilized [for customer service], but it's a poor solution." The CEO compares sending an e-mail question with dropping a note in the suggestion box at a department store and waiting for a letter in response. Good luck. And while 800 numbers are useful, you can't use them if you have only one phone line, which is tied up while you're online. Live interaction, he insists, is the best answer.

WHO PAYS THE BILLS?

The client companies at LivePerson.com each pay a one-time fee of $500, with an added monthly charge of $250 per operator. LivePerson.com does not supply the operators, only the technology. Obviously, there is another niche opening here. A company that could supply the operators to LivePerson.com and their clients would have a ready-made business opportunity. (Just a hint for enterprising readers!)

So far, LivePerson.com has been able to attract some important clients. Technology juggernaut Intuit is among the customers, as are e-commerce companies like Tickets.com and Flowers&Gifts.com. The e-tailers have been able to dramatically decrease the number of abandoned shopping carts since adding the LivePerson.com icon to their Web pages. In addition, some Net-based finance companies like NextCard have experienced higher conversion rates, thanks to Live-Person.com's immediate access capabilities.

The clientele attracted to LivePerson has thus far fallen into three categories, with others, of course, that defy cataloging. First is the high-touch business operation—services such as insurance companies and mortgage companies, where scores of forms clutter the application processes. Forms are difficult for online customers, and a question-and-answer button keeps people from giving up in frustration at line 24.

Second are e-commerce companies that sell products and have customers with questions that need instant answers. "It's a great way to up-sell and cross-sell, too," offers Locascio.

Third are companies that want to offer their customers sales support or even tech support. Intuit customers, for instance, might have problems with the installation of *Quicken* software. Instead of poring over the manuals and wildly punching buttons, the customers can ask a LivePerson operator for step-by-step assistance.

It all sounds perfect. But we have a question. "Operator, what do we do with the three mystery bolts left over from assembling Junior's big red bubble-tire Schwinn bicycle with the ooooga horn?"

Web address:
www.LivePerson.com

Employee Training

Start-up expenses: $2,500–$4,000
Special requirements: *None*
Best advice: *"Start small. Don't try to do too much at once. We stalled in the first 18 months because we kept looking at the whole pie instead of taking one bite at a time. You can't go from where you are to where you need to be in one giant step without sinking an awful lot of money into it."*

In many businesses today, the clients are driving the trend, forcing companies into early upgrades of technology, especially in their demands for better and faster Web access. Throughout the commercial world, it's increasingly true that people won't even accept hard copies of business proposals. They want the instant access of Web sites and e-mail attachments. Everything has to be in real time, and clients want to deal primarily with corporations—even shops—that are technologically advanced. The Systema Corporation is one such enterprise that has been caught in the tide of the technology surge—and pulled along in the wake.

Systema is a corporation that provides sales training for corporate clients. Employee training is a $2 trillion industry, according to *Training Magazine*, a periodical that does annual assessments. Even so, the industry continues to get bigger and bigger, due primarily to new technology and new products. In partnership with sales management representatives, Systema offers a variety of tools to enhance sales methods and performance. In business for thirty years, Systema has been ensuring its success by staying ahead of business trends and adjusting to the new realities of the commercial marketplace. Today the challenges involve technology. Back in 1997, clients began to clamor for Web access. "Do you have a Web site yet?" was a persistent question. In response, Systema developed an online presence, one that helped secure its position as a player among midsize employee training firms.

After nearly twenty-five years of standard operating procedures, the Systema Corporation launched its e-business component, recognizing that even the smallest firms were beginning to plug their Web sites. They needed an edge. In employee relations, a lot of the work is procedural training teamed with technical training. That combination outlines the area of greatest growth potential. Systema felt in the late '90s that an online presence was necessary to maintain its position in the industry.

SOFT SKILLS, HARD SALES

Judy Oliver is manager of operations at Systema. She differentiates between two kinds of employee services. Hard skills come into play when a manager instructs a bank teller how to do a job—how to take a deposit, how to cash out a drawer. Soft skills, on the other hand, describe how to greet customers, sell products, work with upper management. "We deal more with soft skills here at Systema," says Oliver. As a result, the company's programs concentrate on cooperation, efficiency, and measurable sales performance.

Oliver notes that employee training is a very competitive industry, but it is very fragmented, meaning that there are a few big players but a large number of smaller ones. There are thousands of small firms with only one or two employees. Systema is a midsize company, one of about fifteen or twenty comparable firms in the United States. As Oliver explains, "There is quite a lot of room for the small firms. They tend to be industry experts, like insurance specialists or independent consultants. For the most part, they're industry specific." And they've found a niche.

Most employee training firms are strictly service firms, meaning that they offer only consulting or training. Typically, the small players don't have products. The bigger ones do. Oliver's company markets its own products, such as a packaged sales training program. "It's interactive," says Oliver. "It's a three-day program you can buy from the shelf. We'll also run a workshop for you, or you can take home a kit to teach yourself and your own people." Systema also sells a variety of self-study materials that support its competency-assessment program.

Systema promotes the idea of increased effectiveness in sales. It provides a wide range of products and services that include training materials, sales strategies, hiring guidelines, and other benefits to sales staffs. Through the site, the company explains that it can help clients increase sales performances, remotivate experienced salespeople, develop stronger ties between clients and customers, and enhance job satisfaction, among other things.

STATIC OR INTERACTIVE SITES?

Oliver agrees that the Web site provides an important presence. Sometimes clients go to the site first, sometimes not. Systema is listed on the major search engines. With so many people looking for vendors on the Internet, Systema makes significant contacts online. But the start was rocky, Oliver admits: "It took a good 18 months just to decide what we were going to do. The hardest thing was getting our foot in the door. We went through two Web site designers before we found one we liked. It was a saving grace to finally find someone who understood our business."

Still, despite Systema's Web presence, its customers are not predominantly "wired." New clients make contact mostly by phone. Some use e-mail. Usually a customer locates Systema's phone number on the Web site. "We have to talk to them first," says Oliver. "After we find out what they need, we send them more information. We also direct people to the Web site to see what services we provide." The Systema Web address appears on the company's printed materials and in professional directories. Other than that, the site is not advertised or promoted.

Systema executives understand that their Web site needs upgrading. Says Oliver, "We really just got the static Web site up, knowing eventually we have to expand it and make it interactive." Systema also is engaged in more aggressive marketing, searching for ways to pull people toward the Web site. Like so many companies, Systema recognizes that people enjoy the interaction of the Web, the two-way exchange of information. "In the past," admits Oliver, "we just needed a Web presence. Now it needs to be a dynamic presence." The clients keep raising the bar, making companies acquire more technology.

Many competing companies in employee training also support only static Web sites, but Systema has an added concern about going interactive. It sells and licenses intellectual capital. "We are afraid that people will go to the site and download material—maybe making multiple copies. If we lose control over our material, in the world of intellectual property it can be considered public domain." Oliver stresses that her company must be vigilant so that competitors don't steal Systema materials. Sadly, she offers, theft is fairly rampant in this industry.

"If we exposed too much intellectual property, we'd soon have ten little shops competing with us and using our own materials," says Oliver, "so we don't even list our courses on the Web site—certainly no outlines. We only share that information after we talk to clients and qualify them." Admittedly, Systema could use more information technology specialists. One IT person on the staff of a midsize business isn't able to set up the "fire walls" necessary to keep out pirates and, at the same time, keep the company on the cutting edge of new technologies.

Web address:

www.systema.com

Resource:

www.TrainingSuperSite.com/publications

Management Consulting

Start-up expenses: *Variable*

Special requirements: *Consulting expertise*

Best advice: *"A lot of firms really shoot themselves in the foot with poorly thought-out Web sites. Ours is always under review and construction. Your site should contain the most updated information on what you are doing, whom you are working with, and what you are discovering. Even [only] an annual review is a mistake. The site has to be a dynamic document to get the results you want."*

Increasingly, the Net is a sanctuary for executives and technicians who walk away from the high-rise corporate world. After the stressful hours and travel tortures, the fresh air of cyberspace is invigorating. E-commerce ventures seem to attract people who enjoy their business specialties but don't want to work full-time or can no longer take the corporation grind.

And the coffee tastes better if you brew it in your own cappuc-
cino maker.

Consultants constitute one such group of intrepid adventurers.
In many cases, consultants were originally management-level employees with special expertise. A large number of these people find
their way to Expert Marketplace, a subsidiary of PENgroup.com, a
clearinghouse for consultants. Expert Marketplace maintains a
database network of over 1,000 prequalified independent consulting affiliates, representing more than 8,500 consultants with expertise in management, information technology, marketing, sales, and
human resources. Corporations—or anyone seeking consultants—can go to Expert Marketplace and post their needs. Then
the affiliates respond. Finally, the corporation chooses the best
consultant for the planned project. It's great exposure for all parties
concerned—and an excellent use of the Web.

The alliance with Expert Marketplace worked especially well
for Transformations Consulting. The clearinghouse reviewed
the company's credentials, checked into its work history, and
spoke with typical clients. After getting positive answers to
questions, Expert Marketplace determined that the company
met Marketplace standards. Transformations Consulting became an affiliate, earning an opportunity to view postings from
a broad range of companies that seek consulting services.

SENIOR-LEVEL FORTUNE 50 MANAGERS OPT FOR E-BUSINESS

Transformations Consulting is typical of businesses registered
with Expert Marketplace. The company, which began business
in March 1993, specializes in coordinating joint ventures and
collaborative opportunities. It was created by three senior-level

financial managers from Fortune 50 corporations. They knew each other and joined forces "to get out of the corporate rat race and to do something a little different in the consulting field."

Patty Dogen, managing partner for Transformationsgroup. com, says that the partners decided, based on their experiences, to use their marketable consulting skills in a series of private ventures. They contacted people they respected and said, "We're thinking of going into business for ourselves." They described their methods and tools, asking colleagues if their companies would be interested. They were.

Within 60 days, Transformations Consulting had sold its first contract. It was huge and lasted two and a half years. The general feeling was "Hey, this is easy." But even while they worked to finish their first assignment, Dogen and her partners began to redefine their business. From their first venture, they learned what consulting skills and techniques they could use to best advantage in further commercial ventures.

The practice changed from its original concept—general management consulting—to its present approach, helping companies join forces to gain a competitive edge. "It's a matter of doing things differently from most other companies," says Dogen. "We seek major competitors and explore ways in which joint ventures can help both businesses." Obviously the collaborative business style has been popular. Dogen's client list includes diverse groups such as Compaq, the Internal Revenue Service, Youngstown State University, Digital Equipment, the American Health Care Management Company, the Corporation for Public Broadcasting, the Bureau of Land Management, Honeywell, the Public Broadcasting System (PBS), and Kent State University.

A Marriage of Public and Private

The very name Transformations suggests a new approach. In fact, the company has been innovative, changing business practices among its clients while increasing sales and effectiveness. "We have capitalized on the ability to make changes, especially in the media and broadcast industries," says Dogen. Their work with PBS is the company's best example of creative thinking. At PBS, Dogen's firm commingled the concerns and methods of public and private sectors, creating a broadcasting approach that is both popular and educational.

Transformations Consulting works with government, public, and private entities to coordinate efforts, and today those efforts focus largely on the Net. Dogen admits that the company was late finding the benefits of e-commerce, primarily because the bulk of their business had come from networking and referrals. But the Internet applications of recent months have had a significant impact on business.

"It was through the Web presence that we were able to develop our second business, a sponsorship marketing agency," says Dogen. That approach was suggested by a referral in early 1999 from Expert Marketplace. Dogen's partners had talked about the second business strand and were planning to conduct research throughout the year. But once they made connections through Expert Marketplace, "it was *boom, boom, boom!*" Dogen and her colleagues immediately found themselves with three new clients, all interested in corporate sponsorship deals.

DESIGN YOUR SITE CAREFULLY

As Dogen says, the Web is a great place to expand business opportunities, but in consulting, the rules are different. Consultants must understand that they are selling credibility and confidence. A client must first believe that the company has both the reputation and the tools to get the job done. While a Web presence can open those doors, the Net's primary advantage lies in its networking aspect. Simply using the Web is not enough to build a successful consulting practice unless you are the creator and property-rights owner for some concept or model. If you write a book or establish a new management trend, for instance, the Web site gains importance.

But most consulting firms are not the holders of creative properties. They sell services. Therefore, the Web site is a place to meet and educate new clients, a method of establishing links and building a business reputation. Dogen emphasizes, however, the necessity of building a top-notch Web site. She urges hiring a professional Web design team. "There are a lot of do-it-yourself kits," she says. "Most consulting people who use that approach end up with a Web site that looks unprofessional. For most businesspeople, unless you have specialized technical skills or unless it's a budget issue, you should not build the site yourself." Use someone with Web expertise, says Dogen. It's worth the investment.

An experienced Web design team will consider the special needs of a consulting firm. As Dogen says, "Take your strategic business plan and your marketing plan and set goals with trigger points. That way, you will invest a little more money in Web presence as you progress." Building the Web site haphazardly is not a good idea. At Transformations Consulting, Dogen's partners constantly upgrade the Web presence, always seeking the most current approaches and information. And the review process must be continual, she urges. Once a year is not enough. Business trends move too quickly.

A PERSONAL APPROACH

Even with the Web advantage, consulting businesses like Dogen's must maintain personal ties with their clients. Dogen likes to spend 10 to 15 minutes on the phone with people who've approached the firm on the Web. It's necessary to explain in detail the company's methods, its strengths, and its limitations. "We are selling our experience and expertise," says Dogen. "The Web site has given us the opportunity to have such an interaction with our clients. It is critical from that standpoint." But the Net is also a portal for Dogen's group. Much of the heavy lifting still takes place in phone or personal conversations with clients.

An impressive site is an important introduction to clients and a chance for Transformations Consulting to explain how its business practices may be different. Dogen's company has 15 consultants, but only eight or ten work at any given time. Some are semiretired and work when they have the time. Others wait for a project that fits their expertise. "It has been a great way to expand," says Dogen, who prefers the loose alliance of consultants to the tight restrictions of payroll and corporate rules.

In American business, flexibility has always been an advantage. Today, the Internet offers an economic pliability that is unprecedented in business history. Firms such as Transformationsgroup.com, working with a major clearinghouse like Expert Marketplace, are rewriting the book on consulting. In the end, everybody profits.

Web address:
www.Transformationsgroup.com

Meeting Planner

Start-up expenses: $3,500

Special requirements: *Background in advertising, travel, marketing, or communications*

Best advice: *"The most important thing is a good technology manager. You can't wing it. We are investing in technology more than anything else. The right information technology system is the number one priority. And information technology experts are getting harder and harder to find because everybody wants them."*

Have you ever attended a big conference where nothing went right, from errors in the program to mismanaged hotel reservations? Hosting a conference is a big responsibility, one that requires intensive planning, meticulous coordination, innovative implementation, and follow-through. Experienced companies exist that specialize in event planning, and many are found online. It's all part of a huge $100 billion industry.

Event planners handle services including marketing and publicizing the conference, promoting attendance, searching for hotels, managing and staging exhibits, organizing registration, implementing on-site logistics, making the travel arrangements, and paying bills. That's a lot of work. Volunteers can rarely handle all the details, and even paid employees without experience usually founder under the burdens.

MeetingsPlus.com is a company specializing in high-tech business conferences, such as user conferences that attract large numbers of customers, in the Bay Area. Technology businesses and computer companies like Hewlett Packard and Sun Microsystems know that a user conference is often the single most important marketing opportunity of the year. Under those circumstances, it pays to hire professional planners rather than to ask Jack in public relations to pretend he's Andy Hardy and "put on a show." With a little guidance, MeetingsPlus.com cofounder Carolyn West can organize a conference package that is worthy of Baghdad by the Bay.

LOOKING FOR ROOM

A large portion of the work performed by MeetingsPlus.com centers on hotel searches. "Site search is when a client asks us to look for a hotel—it's the foundation of what we do," says West. "It is amazing how technology can affect something like this. It used to be a tedious thing, such as finding a place for a special off-site dinner in the south of France. It's a snap now. It is so easy to communicate with our international partners. It's made the whole thing faster."

In the old days, the process started with a call to Hyatt or Westin. The data was passed to the company's national reps, and it took days to find out if there were enough rooms available for a conference in Cincinnati. But now the hotels are online, too, so it takes just a couple of hours to find out everything the planners need to know.

A High-Contact Business

West founded MeetingsPlus.com as the union of two industries. She joined the creative promotional services of a public relations approach with the traditional expertise of professional meeting planners. Today, her firm markets to technology-driven companies such as software makers, networking specialists, computer builders, and medical suppliers. Employing 61 full-time professionals, MeetingsPlus.com operates more than 50 conferences and programs annually. MeetingsPlus.com even includes a full-service corporate travel department. The company, which has grown at an average rate of 45 percent over the past five years, has one of the highest customer retention rates in the industry.

With all these services, West's firm has greatly benefited from Web presence and its technology. The company went online not to promote the business but to manage the programs. "We don't even market ourselves online," says West. "People find us through the search engines, but we still sell person-to-person and over the phone. This is a very high-contact business." West's company manages everything online—from registration for conference members to paying the providers' bills after the event. Registration hassles have been greatly reduced by online technology. For example, instead of fielding thousands of faxes and phone calls, MeetingsPlus employees collect conference registration forms from the Net. Online registration is as convenient for attendees as it is for the meeting planner.

This setup has special advantages for services like handling registration for international meetings. As West quips, "Have you ever tried to read handwriting from someone in Thailand?"

Online access eradicates time-zone problems. Says West, "We don't have to worry about that anymore." The Net makes time differences irrelevant. Clients in Italy can log onto MeetingsPlus.com and pull up all the details about an upcoming meeting, including a list of registrants, speakers, accommodations options, and so on. "They have instant, up-to-the-minute access," says West. "The customers don't have to wait until the doors are open so they can call us."

Customers can also check the layouts online. "We do a lot of trade shows, and we manage the exhibits through our Web site." West explains, "Typically we have, for a large conference, maybe one hundred exhibitor booths. Clients can go to our site and find out how big the booth is, the colors, the floor layout, everything. We do every aspect of that online."

Planning a conference, a meeting, or a program is complicated. It's hard to imagine how such events ever became reality in the pre-Net world. There's a lot of negotiating, purchasing, facilitating, and organizing. So the next time you receive a conference flyer in the mail, look closely at the fine print. Perhaps the entire extravaganza is being organized by an events coordinator such as MeetingsPlus.

Web address:
www.MeetingsPlus.com

Professional and Business Coach

Start-up expenses: $2,300
Special requirements: *Public speaking experience*
Best advice: *"Set up the business right the first time. The biggest challenge perhaps comes when you don't think through the various aspects of launching a business. How do you really establish the business? Build on a good foundation. If your company grows beyond what you can handle, then go back and rework it."*

Football, basketball, soccer, track and field, volleyball, lacrosse—these are sports for which you'd expect to find a coach. Off the field, you'd add coaching opportunities such as speech, drama, or modeling. But have you heard of a business coach? In the corporate world, businesspeople need every advantage to succeed. And sometimes the best way to gain an edge is to consult someone who knows the ropes. A business coach synthesizes psychology, philosophy, spirituality, and finance—not to mention the various aspects of commerce.

Coaching is a growth industry, according to Jackie Nagel, who launched her online approach in December 1997. Jackienagel.com is part of a new wave of business coaches, and a professional organization, the International Coach Federation, is currently establishing certification criteria for coaches.

Coaching fosters the highest potential in sales and executive professionals. It's low key and philosophical, such as in Stan Adler's popular book *The Zen of Selling*. For others, coaching is more hands-on. Nagel says there are about 10,000 such business coaches out there, many of them with business cards printed in cyberink.

BURNT OUT BUT STILL INTERESTED IN PEOPLE

Nagel brought to her online business a background in sales and training. After 20 years in the front lines, she was ready for a change. Since she wanted to continue helping people, she started a quest to establish a career that would lend fulfillment and add an income. She says, "At the time, I didn't know that business coaching existed—at least in an organized fashion— until a friend told me about it." In 1997 the friend recommended seeing a business coach for advice.

The coaching idea continued to incubate. Nagel took training at two schools, Coach University and Corporate Coach University, two virtual colleges with long-distance learning packages and phone exchanges. With senior coaches in the professors' chairs, these virtual schools take about 20 students per class. The student body appears from all over the world, following an intense and comprehensive curriculum.

With her training complete, Nagel began the coaching business from her home in Bremerton, Washington—not exactly a metropolis—but her services are in demand across the country and across the oceans. Today she does all her coaching by e-mail or phone. After she launched her Web site, Nagel began to draw an international audience. She believes the Net offers a one-of-a-kind marketing advantage for her venture, allowing her to avoid the pitfalls of geography and regional competition.

A WEALTH OF E-SERVICES

When Nagel decided to take the virtual approach, she knew nothing about Web sites. She didn't even have a list of reasonable questions to ask site designers. Perhaps that's why she has gone through three technicians. "I found out there are three kinds of designers," she exclaims, rather ruefully. Nagel's first designer was an HTML person who knew the coding but was not familiar with matters of content or presentation—especially color and design. The second hire was a better choice, someone familiar with HTML who also knew rudiments of color, design, and Web content. The third choice had it all—a designer with expertise in HTML and great competence in content and design who also specialized in marketing.

It was an expensive and frustrating journey for Nagel, who passes on sage advice. You need to initially ask important questions of the Web designer, such as: What services do you provide? What can you offer in terms of designing, creating, and marketing a site? What is your experience in marketing Web sites?

Today, Nagel is happy with her site. In it, she has a private client area that customers can visit for additional resources. The private section supports clients through difficult decisions and dilemmas. People who are stuck at midnight, when they don't have access to a coach, can find some ideas, perhaps solutions, to perplexing business problems. "When you own a service like mine," says Nagel, "you can't always be available." The online responder puts a virtual coach on the sidelines whenever there's a game.

How to Find a Business Coach

People look for coaches on the search engines and reach Jackienagel.com through links with associated addresses. Wherever there is a publicized class online—like a virtual workshop—Nagel registers her site. This exposure brings customers back to her site. Nagel also offers a weekly e-zine, which she also submits to other sites. "It's free, of course," she says. "My articles give me exposure elsewhere, and they always have links to my site. Naturally, I make sure that my Web address appears on my collateral pieces, like brochures, business cards, and press releases."

Customer Profile

Primarily, clients are small-business owners and people in transition, whether it's someone looking for a career change or people in a corporation looking to develop new leadership ideas. Nagel offers a good example of the average customer. A carpet cleaning company—an exceptional firm in many ways—was having a hard time financially. It was working hard but not realizing a payoff. "So we worked together for three months on one commercial aspect that they wanted to develop, which has been a successful part of the business." After the coaching stint, revenue at the company jumped 220 percent. "That was really exciting," says Nagel. "They were really happy."

The carpet company managers had always been enthusiastic about their prospects, and to finally see some results was rewarding. Nagel charged them $750. In the meantime, the carpet company's revenues leaped from $600 a week to more than $2,000. And that was just in the single area that they were focusing on. "A pretty good return on investment," says Nagel. "They hired me for my basic small-business service," says Nagel, "which includes 30 to 40 minutes of weekly phone conversations for three months. In addition, the owner and I touch base for 5 or 10 minutes during the week, depending on what we're attempting, at no extra charge." The carpet company executive would regularly fax the project details to Nagel, and the two would then chat about the next steps. "I really like helping people," says Nagel, who added no extra fees for unscheduled phone conferences to her $250 monthly assessment. "That is a very fair price for the value and their return."

Web address:
    www.jackienagel.com

Public Speaking
Seminars

Start-up expenses: $2,500
Special requirements: *Expertise in public speaking*
Best advice: *"Never hire somebody to do marketing for you. If you don't know how to market yourself, you will get a line about what it should cost. My theory is I don't care how many hits you have. What matters is how much money people are putting in your pocket. You don't need a million hits. How much business did you actually book? If you get ten visitors a month and ten do business with you, that is all you need. Focus on getting the right kinds of clients."*

L enny Laskowski is a professional speaker, consultant, seminar leader, and keynote speaker. With expertise in presentation and communication skills, he is in huge demand across the country. He charges $4,000 for half-day seminars and a minimum hourly rate of $175 for consulting. Although Laskowski has been doing business successfully for

25 years, his site offered an entirely new opportunity. Without doubt, the Net has made Laskowski a wealthy man.

But ljlSeminars.com has also helped people in need of instruction, advice, or entertainment. The Web site allows interested consumers to browse through freely posted articles, arrange speaking dates, or e-mail queries about communication skills. Laskowski's Web pages also display his résumé, along with enthusiastic referral letters from satisfied clients.

AN EARLY ONLINE PRESENCE

In 1996, Laskowski entered cyberspace. With an engineering background, he found the Net a compatible friend. Now he makes 90 percent of his booking arrangements online. Although he still receives phone calls, most business arrives through his computer. In 1999 alone, Laskowski received 2,047 requests. He had time to book 109 programs. That's a lot of frequent flyer miles. As of mid-February 2000, Laskowski had already booked 79 shows from the Net for the year. At that rate, he can expect to own a part of United Airlines in the near future.

Laskowski maintains a huge database. His free newsletter, *Simply Speaking*, goes out to 19,000 people. On the Web, he sells books and videos in more than 78 countries. "Some countries I had to look up in the atlas," he says. "I didn't know they existed. But that's OK. MasterCard and Visa work on the other side of the world, too."

Part of Laskowski's success on the Net probably depends on his willingness to offer something of value without charge. On his site, he displays 106 free articles, available for anyone to download. As a result of that presence, he is well received by important industry magazines like *Presentation*—a "biggie" in the communications industry. The periodicals regularly ask permission to reprint his essays and articles. "It's great exposure," says

Laskowski, "because my article sits in a magazine next to an ad costing $4,000. The free articles generate awareness of my services." More than 3,000 of Laskowski's essays were downloaded and printed in 1999 alone.

ONLINE EXPERTISE

"People are looking for experts," says Laskowski. "The Net— that's how I was invited to author a book for Warner Books, *10 Days to More Confident Public Speaking*." Plus, many magazines have published articles that were found on the site. With all his exposure, Laskowski can afford to be confident. "I walk away from $20,000 a week in business because there is only so much time," he says. "That's a nice position to be in." We agree.

When prospective clients call, Laskowski knows they've been to his site and seen his information sheets. "They don't call asking questions," he says. "They call looking for bookings. The sale is already done." With the Net, the red tape and repeat explanations are gone. It's all on the site, says Laskowski. "I am ecstatic about what the site has done for me," says Laskowski. "It has been so successful that in October 1999 I was invited to be the keynote speaker at Columbia Business School, to talk about Internet marketing." Laskowski receives about 60,000 to 90,000 visitors a month (that's *visitors*, not hits or page views) to his site. That's a lot of traffic! "The key," says Laskowski, "is to have the site properly designed. It has to be content rich and search engine friendly."

Search engines index only about 25 percent of Web sites, and only 20 percent are properly designed, says the author-speaker. Most people don't provide external marketing, but "you have to do that," says Laskowski. The advantage of the Net comes from the level playing ground it provides. "If you design your site correctly, you should be in the top ten," says Laskowski, momentarily forgetting that, according to the laws of mathematics, not everyone in a group of 100 registrants can be in the top ten.

WEB SITES REQUIRE CAREFUL PLANNING

To maximize the effectiveness of his site, Laskowski links heavily with other sites, choosing carefully those that enhance or complement his own. "Your site needs good content," he says. "Good statements that are key-word-rich. You also need META tags, and if the key words match the content of your page properly, you will score well on the search engines. You can't fool the search engines. That's an important issue." Laskowski believes in multiple pages for multiple doors, so that once browsers enter a site, they'll find it easily navigable. "You achieve that goal through text links, not graphic links," he says. "Search engines can't do graphic links."

Despite Laskowski's fine-tuning of the site, he admits that the communications business is commonly a word-of-mouth proposition. Laskowski is primarily a public speaker who provides keynote addresses, seminars, workshops, and consulting. The bulk—about 65 percent—of his business comes from the public addresses, with another 25 percent coming from seminars and workshops. A few more dollars derive from coaching clinics and individual consulting. Laskowski is listed with the speakers' bureaus, but nine out of ten appearances come from his own efforts.

Even in a word-of-mouth industry, Laskowski knows his Net presence really made viral advertising efficient. Typically, people locate him through the search engines after typing in "public speaking skills" or "presentation skills." Anyone who takes these steps will find ljlSeminars.com, he says. "In fact, in some cases, I am the *entire* top 20 in a search engine category." By the time customers reach Laskowski on the phones, he offers, they have passed six or seven qualification levels. Laskowski uses the e-mail autoresponder to present testimonials, prices, and other information. So when a customer finally reaches the speaker himself, "I don't have to waste time on sales calls."

Laskowski loves the benefits of his Web presence. Luckily, when the publisher of *10 Days to More Confident Speaking* sent the book's proposed table of contents, the topics on the outline fit almost exactly his articles on the Web site. "It was a no-brainer," he said.

A TIME SAVER

All things considered, Laskowski could do his job without the Net. But the Web pages make everything so much quicker and easier. The Net is a huge time saver for corporations, as well as individual businesspeople, he insists. Corporations call about 100 times a month. Neither he nor the corporate executive on the other end of the line has the leisure to chat about workshops and addresses. With e-mail contacts and guest book information, Laskowski can keep on top of his requests. His 2,000 e-mails a month and constant phone calls make it important for him to use time wisely. He says, "If people call you trying to do business, you should be ready to respond." The Net helps make it possible. As Laskowski says in his succinct manner, "The idea of the Net is to build relationships with people." He seems to be setting records in that department.

With colleges and universities clamoring for Laskowski's services, with corporations and industries phoning for booking dates, with individuals and groups searching out his books and tapes, Laskowski is on top of the public speaking industry.

Without the Net, it would no doubt take a phalanx of office people to head him out the door each day in the direction of his appointments.

Web address:
www.ljlSeminars.com

Careers

Job Boards

Start-up expenses: *As low as $2,000*
Special requirements: *Searchable database*
Best advice: *"The trick to establishing a successful job board is to find the right niche. If you can think of a particular type of job that is highly sought after and then identify and target that market of workers, you are looking at the beginnings of a successful business."*

Web-savvy job seekers know they have the leg up when it comes to finding the perfect job fast. They know that people no longer have to dirty their hands thumbing through newspaper classifieds looking for a job or print out résumés, lick stamps, and hope that snail mail will arrive before job openings are filled. And they aren't confined to their own locales either. Most newspapers post their classified ads on the Internet for free, so you can browse the help wanted ads from any area in the country. Plus, more and more jobs are actually being performed in cyberspace rather than high-rises. You won't find those jobs in your local paper—you'll find them only on the Internet.

There are literally hundreds of job boards on the Internet, and more are springing up every day. General boards can be huge, like MonsterBoard, which boasts over 250,000 job listings on any given day. But the real gold for independent entrepreneurs won't come from listing every possible kind of job, from accountant to zookeeper. The trend is toward specialty job boards like Ink Spot, a hot job spot for writers, and NetTemp, a great site for technical personnel who are always on the lookout for the next contract. When starting a job board e-business, the more specific you can get, the better.

AT HOME IN CYBERSPACE

By 1993, the work-at-home phenomenon had come into its own, and the percentage of Americans who worked at home, at least part-time, topped 40 percent. The work-at-home job trend was led by millions of baby boomers looking for the same kind of freedom and control in their work that they had come to expect in other parts of their lives. Technology made it possible to perform a lot of jobs at home, and working at home soon became the most enviable work style.

In 1993 Stephen St. Louis took a peek at the future on his computer and liked what he saw. He was just starting to "play around" in cyberspace and knew he wanted to start an e-business, but the Internet was still under construction and there wasn't much available. But then he heard through the grapevine about a small association called the International Homeworkers Association, a traditional business that was looking for a buyer.

"The operation was basically stagnant, not really going anywhere," St. Louis recalls. "They lacked vision." But St. Louis saw potential for a technological makeover and snapped it up for $17,000. All he really got for his money was a roster of roughly 1,500 members and a bunch of printed directories with work-at-home jobs and business opportunities. The directories were hard copies, of course, that were printed and sent through the post to members. The problem for members was the delay in getting the information. Often, many of the opportunities were already gone by the time anyone heard about them. "When I first took over," says St. Louis, "I was just on CompuServe and only improved the service by using e-mail instead of snail mail. But soon I put up our first Web site and things changed in a hurry."

The new Independent Homeworkers Alliance (St. Louis kept the initials but changed the name) now has over 30,000 members worldwide. Its Web site is www.homeworkers.org, posting hundreds of new job openings every day, all jobs that can be done at home. St. Louis says, "I have made contacts with a number of outsource companies that need all kinds of telecommuters, from medical transcribers to computer programmers. A good 30 percent to 50 percent of our postings are from these contacts; the rest are dug up by our researchers from newspapers and other specialty job sites."

IHA inputs the job information into a database called Jobvertise. It's a free database program available to any business that wants to use it. Members can then search the database by job discipline, state, country, or date.

FIND A NICHE

Anyone can start a job board. There are lots of big general job sites where owners make their money from advertising revenue. It's possible to compete with them, but it would take a lot of capital and marketing savvy. However, there's plenty of opportunity for specialty boards.

The trick is to find the right niche. If you can think of a particular type of job that is highly sought after and then identify and target that market of workers, you're looking at the beginnings of a successful business. IHA, for example, lists over 60,000 jobs in its database. There are many sites, though, with just a few dozen listings that do just fine because the jobs are highly specialized, such as physicians.

Most job boards list job openings for free and make their profit by charging employers for the postings. It's the same as a newspaper charging for running help wanted ads in the classified section. But in cases like IHA, where the jobs are highly sought after, it makes more sense to charge the job seeker for the privilege of checking the postings. Fees to access specialty job boards range from a low of $24.95 for three months to a high of $1,500 per year. IHA members pay as little as $19.95 per month for unlimited access to the job board.

ADD SERVICES, ADD PROFITS

A stand-alone job board can be profitable, but why settle for just one profit center when you have the attention of a targeted market? It costs nothing more to offer additional services to your customers, and you can multiply your profits with each new service. IHA offers dozens of products and services to members; some are free, some are not. Among the free services are forums, each of which is led by an expert in the area. Some of the forums cover topics like résumé writing, work and family issues, language translation, employment counseling, and medical-related jobs. There are also resource libraries where members can go to find information that will help them succeed in their jobs or businesses.

Some of the value-added services include medical and disability insurance at group rates and distance-learning programs. There are 44 job courses offered through distance-learning programs, where members can learn new job skills such as Web mastering, legal transcription, and medical billing. It's a favorite service among members even though the price tag can run as high as $700.

One particularly hot area for home workers is medical transcription. Not only does IHA offer a training program, but it has made arrangements with 20 employers who have agreed to provide internships to graduates of the IHA course. Pay rates for interns are set just slightly below those for experienced workers, which is great because most medical transcription jobs require at least two years of experience. These kinds of value-added services keep members enrolled and paying dues month after month, year after year.

PRESCREENING RÉSUMÉS TO PROTECT YOU AND YOUR MEMBERS

Until recently, the IHA job board included contact information for members to use at their own discretion. This was not such a hot idea. Cyberspace is often like the Old West, where bandits snatch and grab whatever they want and have no qualms about reselling it themselves, ignoring copyrights and other laws that work better in the real world than in cyberspace. Now contact information is kept under lock and key, although all the other job information is still available for viewing. If a member wants to apply for a job, the applicant must submit a résumé directly to the association, where it is screened. If it meets the employer's requirements, IHA submits it directly to the employer.

There was resistance to this procedure at first, but it turned out to be a very good move for everyone. Stephen St. Louis explains, "In the past, employers often got overloaded with worthless résumés from job seekers who sent out résumés to anyone and everyone, regardless of qualifications, that were clearly stated in job postings. The result was that only 5 percent of employers came back to post more jobs. Now that résumés are being prescreened, almost 50 percent of IHA employer contacts are retained, and employers who left before are back on board. "That means more job postings for members and less cost getting new postings from employers."

GETTING THE WORD OUT

Attracting new customers to your job board doesn't have to cost much. For example, you can place cheap classified ads on AOL to get started, but to really boost exposure, you'll need to go where job seekers hang out. You can place ads, paid or for free, on various general job sites to lure people to your site and create awareness. Once they're there, make your pitch. IHA attracts new members by posting free job listings on big job boards like Select Jobs and Career Shop. After seeing those free listings, new visitors log on to the IHA site and find that 10–20 percent of the day's job listings are posted for free there as well. Banner exchanges also work, but nothing beats being able to give away free samples.

Today, Stephen St. Louis is enjoying a booming e-business. "When I first took over IHA there were only two staffers handling the orders," he says. "Now, business is so good we've got 23 in-house employees plus 14 telecommuters, and it's all we can do to keep up!"

Resource:
　www.homeworkers.org

Inventor Representative

Start-up expenses: $8,000
Special requirements: *Contacts in the industry*
Best advice: *"We opened our doors with the reputation as experts in what we do. Our business was already 21 years old. So, for us, it was different than for someone starting from scratch. Our biggest chore came down to getting the right Web site, one that explains who we are and how we do things."*

New Funtiers, despite the curious name, is a clearinghouse for inventors. What do you want to patent? A corkscrew for left-handers? A wrinkle cream for pets? A golf ball that doesn't slice? Believe it or not, people are probably working on these projects right now in the basements of America. To be sure, somebody has to help the inventors get those ideas for glow-in-the-dark flea collars to the manufacturers. That company is Paul Lapidus's New Funtiers.

Lapidus, founder of the company, works to create products

for manufacturing clients and to license them on a royalty basis. Lapidus says, "We do design and development work for those clients for a fee." Many of these clients, as well as others in associated industries, pass the name New Funtiers to independent inventors. The inventors, who usually have few contacts with manufacturers, solicit Lapidus's firm to review their Bigfoot insignia watches and bean-bag rocket launchers. The New Funtiers team helps determine which products are strong enough to be represented.

"We are an innovative design and development company," says Lapidus, the former design director for PlaySkool Co. In 1978, Lapidus started the Together Group, adding his new company, New Funtiers, in 1989. "New Funtiers works with independent inventors," he explains. "It is not a big company— only three people—but New Funtiers keeps what we do separate from the larger company so that we can keep control over the billions of pieces of paperwork."

NOTICE! WEB PRESENCE REQUIRED

In 1999, Lapidus and his colleagues decided that they needed a Web site. "We'd been talking about it," he says, "but we finally made a commitment in January and went online the first day of June. We thought we had to." Because New Funtiers is well known in the industry, Lapidus does not advertise. Nevertheless, he realized the necessity of a Web presence, if only to explain the company's role to new inventors and manufacturers.

But working with the inventors proved different from working with manufacturing clients. For the most part, the inventors have already contacted manufacturers or called on industry associations. Says Lapidus, "So we have all these people coming to us by referral. We needed a better way to describe what we do and how to do it. The Web site gave us a forum, a much better exposure than the photocopied package we had been mailing." Lapidus, like so many people these days, built his site on Yahoo! He feels the Yahoo! tech representatives were a terrific help in the Web site construction.

Happily, the New Funtiers site has simplified business, especially the interaction with inventors. Say Lapidus, "They start with a great deal more knowledge up front. The site has increased our business dramatically. Now we must adjust how we do business on the Net so we don't get overwhelmed."

MAKING THE GRADE

For a first effort, the New Funtiers site is getting good marks. Lapidus says, "People give us good feedback, just as we hoped. The site is easy to read, and it makes us more available to people overseas." Lapidus argues that overseas customers seek his firm online because the American toy industry—their specialty—is the biggest in the world. With an online presence, toy manufacturers and toy inventors, especially those from distant corners of the globe, have immediate access to the company and a good online sketch of their services. The site allows Lapidus to provide photos in a way that brings to life particular inventions. Previously, New Funtiers simply handed out black-and-white photocopies of potential products, a method everyone agrees was ineffective.

"WE DON'T SEARCH FOR CUSTOMERS"

Unlike most e-businesses, Lapidus's firm has no concern about maintaining customer traffic. He says, "Keep in mind that we don't seek out the people who come to us. At least 75 percent arrive after being referred by another site, by a manufacturing client, or by an organization like Toy Manufacturers of America." Those recommendations help in gaining automatic credibility. Even with reputation and credibility assured, however, Lapidus always warns everyone visiting the site, whether they sign on or not, to work with trustworthy companies and representatives—a group that has the backing of a credible source. Hundreds, probably thousands, of people have dealt with invention-marketing companies only to be "ripped off," according to Lapidus, who laments the number of charlatans in the industry.

INDUSTRY WATCHDOG

Lapidus has even accepted the role of industry watchdog in many cases. He says, "We were responsible in one significant case for getting back $8,000 for a lady who spent $11,000 on one of these companies now under indictment. After she contacted us, I told her to contact the attorney general and the Federal Trade Commission." The woman followed through on Lapidus's advice and won a judgment. "Basically, this company, like many others," says Lapidus, "tells you they can show your product to the industry people. They can't. They are perpetuating fraud." Now with the defrauded woman's blessing, Lapidus advises others about invention-industry scams, using her story as an example of how to get money back from the crooks. There's more. Says Lapidus, "We also keep track of sites with class action suits pending against them. I play an active role in keeping track of suspicious people."

Lapidus says he is watching the industry scofflaws as a favor to manufacturing clients and also to maintain a moral distance from some of the shadier members of the business. The fact that New Funtiers is recommended to people is an advantage. Says Lapidus, "The Net is a form of advertising, so some people arrive without recommendations. In those cases, I have them contact manufacturers or the inventors' protection sites, like National Invention Fraud Center and Patent Café, which list all the companies who have been served with complaints." Lapidus adds, "We feel very comfortable getting information from other professionals, so they can decide whom to work with."

TRUTH IN ADVERTISING

At New Funtiers, Paul Lapidus and his coworkers do not tell inventors they have "the greatest idea in the world," because they don't relish having to sit face-to-face with exasperated manufacturers who feel their time is being wasted with impractical inventions. An honest assessment of possibilities is better for everyone involved. Lapidus admits that the odds against success for first-time inventors are huge. He estimates that about 98 percent of all products reviewed show no promise in the commercial world.

Part of the problem for inventors is overlap in the marketplace. Even though there may be public demand for a refinement of an idea or a new version of the widget, patents and licenses often prohibit manufacturers from acting. Sometimes both manufacturers and consumers like an invention, but that point is irrelevant if the product overlaps items already in the marketplace. Price is another concern. As Lapidus says, there is a whole range of licensing requisites to be met before a new product can be considered.

"The valuable new products that we see are interesting because they provide a twist on something that the industry would never imagine." For instance, in the toy industry, it's easy to say, "Every toy has been invented. Everything has been tried." But independent inventors, those who aren't colored by industry perceptions and attitudes, sometimes propose "nice twists on things." Adds Lapidus, "The important thing for our inventor clients is we will only show our [manufacturing] clients great products."

Concern for patents and licenses is a major thrust of the Web site at New Funtiers. According to Lapidus, "We have found generally that inventors just want to do a different version of what has been out in the marketplace, and most of the time it is so close to another product, we can't use it." On two separate Web pages, Lapidus explains that, even though an inventor has great products and ideas, the company may not be able to license them. Even so, sometimes it takes up to six years to get an OK. Other times, manufacturers say no initially but yes much later, adding to the confusion. To enter into a licensing agreement, manufacturers might pay hundreds of thousands of dollars for development. Needless to say, they need to be sure. As Lapidus explains, success in the inventions business truly depends on being in the right place at the right time. And it is very speculative.

CONSTANT CHANGES

Things are changing rapidly in Lapidus's industry. He is coping with those changes in part with the Web presence. "The site has been a terrific way to get across a great deal of information," he says. "It's very much a piece of us. It represents our company more than letterhead with information. That has been terrific. People now have a sense of who we are as a business entity." Before the online emergence, the only way to publicize was through a slick package—not the image the company wanted to portray. Now the New Funtiers pages are well done but certainly not slick.

Without doubt, the Web addition has been healthy and vital. Lapidus also sees Web communications as part of the new wave. He says, "Our e-mail is up dramatically, just within the last year. Our lines of information between manufacturers and inventors—all aspects of communication—are coming together in a much more straightforward way and with much more fluidity. We are trying to make sure that we adjust to take advantage of ways of doing things better." The Net is a perfect medium for growth, according to the owner of New Funtiers. It is easy, convenient, and natural. Besides, says Lapidus, "It is fascinating, a lot of fun, and the best part is that we get to play with toys."

Web address:
    www.stores.yahoo.com/lapidus/profbac.html

Professional
Placement Services

Start-up expenses: *Variable*
Special requirements: *18 months' cash reserves; multiple phone lines*
Best advice: *"Don't go into this business undercapitalized. Do not believe that you will make a fortune quickly."*

If you need a job or want a change, you can easily go to the classifieds section of the newspaper. Good luck. Or if you're in Miami and want to move to Seattle, you can always call a headhunter with ties to the Evergreen State. But these days, there's a cyberselection process making job placements accurately and efficiently, with fewer problems for both the corporation and the prospective employee. Yes, the Internet has become the favored recruiting tool of American business on many levels.

Today online placement services facilitate the high-level recruiting of executives and technical specialists in several fields.

Journalists, writers, teachers, scientists, and, of course, computer nerds can use the Net in the computerized version of what used to be called "pounding the pavement." Fewer people are burning up shoe leather in the e-society of the twenty-first century. More are burning a hole in cyberspace with online queries, résumés, and applications.

Experts estimate that young Americans can expect to change jobs more than half a dozen times in their careers. Some futurists suggest that even these surprising statistics are hopelessly conservative. In truth, the trend has already begun. People with solid training and special skills are becoming highly mobile, climbing not one corporate ladder but several in succession. Even *Doonesbury*'s high-flying e-couple, Mike and Kim, are having trouble hanging on to their technology *wunderkinder*.

In the midst of this clamor for new and better jobs are large and small recruitment services. Clearly the leader is Management Recruiters International (MRI), the largest search and recruitment company on Earth. The 4,500 professionals at MRI place approximately 34,000 employees each year, using (among other things) tools like the MRI job site, BrilliantPeople.com. This site, according to MRI marketing director Karen Bloomfield, is "state-of-the-art technology" linking all 900 MRI offices into a consortium of information and recruitment.

UNLIMITED UPSIDE POTENTIAL

"It's amazing how much money there is to be made in this business," says MRI's Bloomfield, who adds that the incredible growth in the recruitment industry "is not going to slow down soon." But it's not just the high-rolling services such as Management Recruiters International that are having success. Large numbers of niche businesses also benefit from the change of winds in corporate America. One such niche belongs to Phyllis Moffitt, owner of Career Placement Systems. Moffitt specializes in the recruitment and placement of physicians.

Physicians? Surely you mean lab technicians, phlebotomists, or bedpan washers? No. Things have changed over the past ten years in the medical arena. Believe it or not, the country has too many doctors. The current glut of general practitioners (and even some specialists) has lowered salaries in many fields of medicine. Among general practitioners, says Moffitt, the salary declines in recent years have averaged about 40 percent. Under such conditions, doctors—like everyone else in America who feels financial pressure—are looking for new and better opportunities. That's where Career Placement Services enters the picture.

Moffitt began operations in 1989 and went online in 1996, recognizing that the business was truly national, with doctors and potential positions coming from virtually every state. "It was logical to use the Net," she says. Moffitt's father-in-law is a physician, and at the time she started the business there was a shortage of doctors in America. Finding physicians for clinics and hospitals around the country therefore seemed a natural opportunity. Now that the ratios have changed, it is the doctors who are often looking for new jobs. Regardless of this reversal of fortunes, Moffitt continues to find physician recruiting a flourishing enterprise.

IT'S WISE TO SPECIALIZE

Career Placement Services is a niche business that is competing in a burgeoning industry. Moffitt's system is to contact hospitals, find out what specialties they seek, then put such descriptions on her Net site. If a clinic needs an internist or a vascular surgeon, the online ad will solicit physicians with the right skill. When physicians apply, Moffitt's employees request a résumé, or CV (curriculum vitae), as it is called in the medical and academic world. Then they check for malpractice claims and legal problems. Once the background check is complete, Career Placement Services then refers the doctors to hospitals and clinics that match the physician's credentials. The hospitals often request visits and frequently make an offer.

Seldom, however, do doctors accept first offers. Ninety percent of the time, serious negotiations ensue, especially when specialties in demand are involved. Doctors with special skills still command top salaries, despite the general trends.

Hospitals, on the other hand, have their own priorities. Clinics and hospitals often want American-trained doctors, if only to avoid the complicated licensing processes visited upon foreign-trained physicians. Sometimes a rural community may need an orthodontist or a thoracic surgeon. That's where specialty placement services such as Moffitt's may fill an important demand.

Today there's a big demand for Spanish-speaking doctors in America. Career Placement Services can help employers locate such physicians because Bruce Moffitt, Phyllis's husband, is fluent in Spanish. Many applicants, he finds, claim to speak Spanish but, when interviewed in the native language, cannot communicate. By winnowing out those with a year of high school Spanish, Moffitt can protect hospitals from wasting their time on pointless recruitments.

Although Moffitt warns that quick profits are not automatic in referral services, it's clear that recruitment fees are substantial. Says Moffitt, "You might be able to get $25,000 for an orthopedic surgeon and generally around $18,000 to $20,000 for an internist." But fees are negotiable and highly dependent on circumstances. Often Career Placement Services shares fees

with another placement service, especially in the case of a difficult placement, such as a brain surgeon for a tiny hamlet in
Colorado. Sometimes a placement that is usually worth
$20,000 will command a fee of only $12,000. In another instance, it's worth far more than the average placement fee.
Whatever the case, says Moffitt, the money is significant.
Recruiting in general pays a percentage from the client of 20 to
25 percent of one year's salary. Considering doctors' wages,
even in a depressed market, that's serious money.

BEGIN WITH ADEQUATE CAPITAL

Specialty recruitment requires a good nest egg. Moffitt says it's
dangerous to enter such a business without adequate capitaliza-
tion. Career Placement Services offers a Web site, consisting of
30 to 40 pages, with each page registered separately. The big
site, supported by proper meta tagging and site positioning, is
an important advantage when people log on to search engines.
"With 40 pages," says Moffitt, "you have a real advantage."

Moffitt suggests that a reliable recruitment service needs 18
months of cash reserves, in addition to the usual hardware such
as a fax machine, computer, and phone lines. But the real investment, according to Moffitt, is in the cash reserve. "Recruiting is
a business where the response (people coming to your site) is
instant, but the procedure isn't," says Moffitt. In short, the delay
time between recruitment and payment can be long. Moffitt
also suggests, "There is a lot of phone work involved with both
parties." Recruitment is labor intensive, requiring long and
complicated negotiations. Finally, she says, "Don't waste your
time with candidates who are not qualified. Such searches will
only anger the employers. They will not want to work with you
in the future."

A Brave New E-World

The idea of e-recruitment is here to stay. At least in specialty fields such as medicine, science, and technology, there is significant demand for intelligent and well-trained workers. As Karen Bloomfield of Management Recruiters International says, "It's a matter of population demographics. There are simply more jobs than people entering the workforce." Predictably, both workers and employers want the same thing: a recruitment service that respects confidentiality, rewards integrity, and protects privacy. For firms such as MCI and Career Placement Services, it is both a challenge and an opportunity.

Web address:

www.premiersystems.com/recruit/index.html

Children

Asian Educational Materials

Start-up expenses: $900
Special requirements: *None*
Best advice: *"Know your target audience and be clear on what you are trying to achieve. It's easy to get wrapped up in the technology end and forget who the customers are. That's what it comes down to—the customers—and how you are going to serve them. We have had our site for a long time, and we learned that success doesn't happen automatically."*

Many educational materials today still represent inaccurately or negatively cultures and languages of the world. Selina Yoon's products are not among these. Yoon is the president of Master Communications, a company focusing on helping children, especially Asian American children, learn languages, even when their parents are not fluent. Believing that second language skills are essential for children, Yoon's enterprise markets more than 1,000 products, all displayed in a 64-page color catalog. Everything is also available online at Asiaforkids.com.

Yoon came to America in 1976 as an ice skater. When her career was cut short by an injury, she enrolled at Smith College, earning degrees in math and art. Later she took an advanced degree in business from the University of Chicago. From there she worked in marketing and brand management at Procter and Gamble, handling international marketing and global publicity efforts. Her experience with a large, globally oriented corporation gave Yoon initial experience and the confidence to start her own broad-based venture.

GETTING STARTED

In 1994 Yoon began Master Communications, a mail order catalog operation. A year later, she distributed her Asia for Kids catalog, featuring language books, trade books, videos, software, CD-ROMs, dolls, games, posters, crafts, audiocassettes, T-shirts, and source materials for parents and teachers available for many countries, including Vietnam, China, Japan, Korea, the Philippines, Laos, Cambodia, Taiwan, Thailand, India, Bangladesh, Pakistan, Bali, Indonesia, Nepal, Burma/Myanmar, Tibet, and several Middle Eastern countries.

Asia for Kids even offers bilingual posters with messages in Spanish, Chinese, Japanese, Korean, Vietnamese, and Hmong, as well as English. The company's *Sing n' Learn* CDs and tapes are available for parents interested in helping their children with Chinese, Korean, Vietnamese, or Japanese. Yoon's company ships nationwide and to more than 30 foreign countries. She says that all the Asia for Kids offerings have been tested with children, parents, and educators, adding, "We look for educational value, quality of illustrations, and accuracy and authenticity in everything we carry." Asiaforkids.com guarantees authentic cultural content and illustrations and precise language models.

The site clearly meets educational needs, including hard-to-find resources for personal libraries, classrooms, and community libraries. Yoon's effort to make the rich Asian heritage available to others has been a remarkable success. Asia for Kids is the winner of the Parents' Choice Seal of Approval every year since 1996, and the program garnered the 1998 Seal of Approval from the Multicultural Education Council.

INTERNATIONAL BUSINESSES FLOURISH

Yoon launched her Web site in 1996. She reasoned that more exposure was necessary and that the catalog itself had limitations. "The biggest difference about going on the Net was the immediacy," says Yoon. "With mail order customers, they first call to request a catalog. Then we mail it. After they see our products, they mail or call in an order. That takes weeks." The Net, of course, is instantaneous—or nearly so. Yoon notes that her customers locate her site through the search engines or through links. As a result, the time frame is greatly reduced. And she adds, "So is the speed with which people are becoming aware of our business!" Yoon really likes the online approach to sales, particularly because it reduces expenses dramatically. In the old business plan, Asia for Kids spent $4 each on catalogs. Now the products can be displayed or listed online for a fraction of the cost.

About 67 percent of Asians in developed countries are wired for the Net, says Yoon, a huge proportion by any standard. That statistic makes Asiaforkids.com a venture with a large potential audience. But Yoon's customers are not restricted to Western countries or industrial nations. The company enlists buyers from all over the world, an advantage they did not have with the mail order program alone. Yoon says there have been few problems at AsiaforKids.com, and shipping, even to far-away places, has been smooth and trouble free.

Actually, the international business climate has prospered from the convenience of the Net. Says Yoon, "Since it's electronic, you can even converse overseas. It doesn't cost anything and works great." Customers worldwide usually don't need to return products (even though everything can be returned without fee for 30 days) because the site has provided ample opportunity to investigate the materials in depth.

Today, despite the search mechanisms and the links to associated sites, Asiaforkids.com draws most of its customers by word of mouth. The press has also contributed some helpful articles and timely publicity, including a feature article in *Business Week*.

UNTAPPED MARKET

Yoon has one problem that other online businesses would like to have. AsiaforKids.com has virtually no competition. Strangely enough, Yoon believes that a few more Web sites with a similar focus would be a good thing. "They would help develop critical mass for awareness," she says. "Awareness of an industry is something you really need in cyberspace."

Yoon has targeted a business that seems likely to flourish. There are an estimated ten million Asians living in the United States, and the numbers are growing. With such a potential buying population and no visible competition on the horizon, the view looks sunny indeed.

Web address:
www.Asiaforkids.com

Children's Videotapes

Start-up expenses: $20 *plus inventory*
Special requirements: *Inventory of children's tapes*
Best advice: *"Run a lot of experiments and try a lot of ideas. Make sure you know what's going on. There are no real experts. You have to investigate the market yourself. Don't shell out a lot of money to some big expensive Web hosting company. Start small. Don't let somebody talk you into spending money unless you have big bucks and a big vision. Just do a specialty niche and start off cheaply. Then work your way up. A lot of people spend big money for ShockWave and Streaming Video when they should have used that money for marketing."*

People with bumper stickers that read "Kill Your Television" may have seen one too many slasher movies on the tube. Children, of course, are the primary victims of commercial television's demise into violence, violence, and more violence. And the selection in the video stores is no better either. "Do you think little Sally would like me to bring home *Terminator, Alien,* or *Friday the 13th*?" Ask any parents who think carefully about what their children watch, and chances are they will tell you that most children's television programs and videos are violent, scary, condescending, devoid of content, silly, inane, or even depressing.

So, if you want something educational, enlightening, and entertaining for your children's viewing, where do you turn? Try a children's video site, one that can send you the adventures of *Curious George, Madeline,* or *The Velveteen Rabbit.* One such site is GreatTapes.com, a venture started by Margaret Levine, a computer whiz who retreated with her family to Vermont and wanted to start an online business. Levine, one of the original authors of *Internet for Dummies,* was particularly qualified for Web design and e-commerce. She also has young children. It was clear to her that good children's videos were hard to find.

A BUSINESS YOU CAN RUN FROM HOME

Levine established her site in 1996, running it from her home. After building the site, she added a database. If you sell a product, you need a database to catalog new orders, back orders, and purchase orders; generate mailing labels; and so on. It's not unlike running a brick-and-mortar store in that regard and requires some of the same business skills. With a cornucopia of computer experience, Levine had no difficulty managing the Web site and database. From there, she found some local Vermont videos that weren't available elsewhere. These videos gave her the idea to sell children's films through a Web address.

"These films were not ones you can get in the supermarket," she says. "They're not violent. They're not commercial. They're not so sickeningly sweet that you can't stand to sit through a third showing." Levine began to find movies that kids and adults could enjoy—not just once, but many times over. "We make it easy for parents to pick out titles," she says, "because we post a lot of information." GreatTapes.com offers a full description of each movie and includes the appropriate age level. Adding a personal touch, she even lets customers know what her own children think about the selection.

RABBITS, HATS, AND BIG MACHINES

At GreatTapes.com, Levine stocks a variety of movies, including lots of *Rabbit Ears* videos, a popular line that circulated for about ten years before closing its doors. The *Ears* producers hired Hollywood actors to narrate their stories and to take character roles, so the voices were familiar to children and adults. Now the series is rarely available in stores, but Levine's company is able to find and distribute used copies. "One of the best things about Web sales," says Levine, "is that you can put items on and take them off when they're no longer available." Unlike a catalog, the Web is flexible that way.

GreatTapes.com also sells the *Arthur* series, *Blue's Clues Too*, the *Madeline* collection, and selections from *There Goes . . . (Big Machines in Action)*. A Vermont favorite is a local production, *Let's Go to the Farm: A Vermont Dairy Farm*, a film narrated by a local storyteller who plays the farmhand. Levine says *Let's Go to the Farm* is popular with adults as well as children. "It's very gentle and lovely," she says.

In her film business, Levine offers more information about tapes than you'd find on reel.com or Amazon.com. Because Levine hand selects the movies, she knows them well. Her customers are assured, says the owner: "If it's on our site, it is appropriate for little kids and not violent." The viewing range is generally from ages one through eight, but Levine admits that that's liable to change as her own children grow up. "We test our kids and our neighbors," she says, "to get a sense of what kids enjoy. Sometimes we think a film is going to be great, but the kids just wander off. For reasons we don't understand, it's not compelling." When the little Siskels and Eberts leave the room, it's the same as a double thumbs-down.

To find suppliers, Levine took the simple route. She asked the local video store owner. Now she buys from three sources. One specializes in children's tapes, but it doesn't have commercial blockbusters like *The Wizard of Oz*. The Disney films and major Hollywood productions come from regular distributors. A third source is the individual producers—their videos are often available only through direct purchase. "I like that approach," says Levine. "When we get some films that big distributors don't sell, we often find little gems."

MARKETING FOR DUMMIES

Traditionally, book and tape sellers experience half of their yearly sales during December, so GreatTapes.com had to prepare for the Christmas rush. In December 1998, Levine was driving daily to the FedEx box, starting with twice-a-day trips. Then the business slowed to one FedEx drop a day. And on December 23 it was over.

Despite the seasonal nature of the business, Levine enjoys it, especially the direct contact with customers. "When someone has a three-year-old who loves trucks, a video with lots of hauling and actual big truck noise is going to make the child happy," says Levine. "It's a simple thing, but I appreciate being in that role."

Despite having a serious edge in computer and Web knowledge, Levine had one significant business problem: She didn't know anything about marketing. "The Net is a very big place," she laments. "How could people find the site?" Subsequently, she made contact with the search engines, and that exposure helped, although Levine admits that she doesn't do the suggestive maintenance, such as constantly tweaking the meta tags to improve her rankings.

Advertising, Levine reasoned, would not be profitable. In a small niche business like children's tapes, advertising doesn't really pay. Link exchanges with appropriate sites, however, is a good idea, and Levine got some publicity from sponsoring the local public television station. Most of her customers today come from the search engines, however. Generally, browsers type the name of a character, like "Lassie," or fill in the full title, like *The Grinch Who Stole Christmas*. Bingo, the GreatTapes.com site comes up. Fortunately, that kind of single-character or title prompt doesn't bring up reel.com or Amazon.com because you can search for movies only after logging on to their site.

START-UP COSTS ARE NEGLIGIBLE

Like many niche businesses, Great Tapes was launched without much investment. Levine started with a computer and a Web site that was hosted without charge. She estimates that an appropriate Web presence should never cost more than $20 a month for similar services. At first, Levine started small—very small. In fact, during the first three months of operation, she was testing the notion of working as an Amazon.com affiliate. As a result, customers at GreatTapes.com actually had their orders filled by Amazon. In this test period, Levine learned some valuable lessons, without an investment.

Building an inventory was also inexpensive. After severing the Amazon ties, Levine simply contacted distributors and made small orders. The inventory was much more modest than one for a brick-and-mortar video stop. Levine immediately recognized that e-business was cheaper and simpler than what her storefront competitors were experiencing. "It's more like a catalog business," says Levine, "except that you don't need the four-color glossy catalog or the huge postage bills."

Despite the ease of entry into the film sales business, Levine warns that the Net is not a sure-fire cash cow. Someone entering the e-world of film sales needs to understand that, while the job is fun and sales can be strong, the product has a small margin. The children's films cost about $8, and Levine sells them for $13. "It takes a lot of orders to make money," she says. For those who really want to make serious money, a product with a higher margin seems the ticket.

It's easy to believe that e-commerce is invincible. In Levine's case, she launched her operation after only two weeks of planning. The start-up costs were almost nil. To casual observers, success might seem as simple as a sweep of Mickey's wand in *The Sorcerer's Apprentice*. But appearances are deceiving. "Yes," says Levine, "the doors are open. I'm in business. So where are the customers?" Well, they're out there, but they won't be visiting your site until you do some marketing experiments, track their results, and begin the hard work of making sales.

DON'T BE AFRAID TO EXPERIMENT

Small business on the Net is uncharted territory. People are making the rules as they go. In such an atmosphere, experimentation makes sense. Because there are no real experts in many fields, especially niche businesses like children's videos, entrepreneurs have to try new ideas. As Levine suggests, don't put your cash into high-powered Web sites and glitzy online displays. Start small and find out what works in your niche.

With the advantage of the Net, small e-business owners can keep costs down while building a clientele. In the case of GreatTapes.com, Levine found she had unlimited space for displaying her products. "You are only limited by how much you want to put into inventory," she says. Unlike catalog sales, where glossy photos of film jackets are prohibitively expensive, e-commerce allows you to list your inventory at a fraction of the cost. And unlike brick-and-mortar outlets, where storage and inventory are limiting factors, the e-commerce site requires a fraction of the inventory and space.

So, if you want to share some childhood memories with your own children, click onto GreatTapes.com and order something special. Do you remember Madeline's big round hat that was always catching in the wind? Well, in a few days it could be flying across your television screen to the delight of your own little ones.

Web address:
    www.GreatTapes.com

Hand-Painted Children's Furniture

Start-up expenses: $4,800
Special requirements: *None*
Best advice: *"Pick something you love. Otherwise, you'll hate
e-business. I picked a business in a field I truly enjoy. I love children, and painting furniture for the little ones is fun for me."*

S omewhere, there's a Norman Rockwell painting of Dad or
Grandpa (or both) working with loving hands on a rocking horse or a toy chest. It's apple pie, it's *The Saturday
Evening Post*, it's "Mayberry RFD." Building furniture, especially
on a scale for children, is difficult (as Dad could tell you as soon
as he's finished cutting this chair leg for the fourth time). Give
Dad a chance, and he'll unplug the saw and see what's available
online.

Well, a whole range of kids' furniture is for sale in cyberspace.
It's a thriving business and a productive niche in the larger world
of children's goods. Go bandage that thumb, Dad, and let's see if

you can find the perfect chair at PipperSnaps.com. This online venture is an enterprise started by Ragan Hughs, who orders pre-made products and then provides the paint, finally packaging the furniture for sale all over the world.

A LITTLE IMAGINATION

Using her creative touch and imagination, Hughs paints or stains high-quality desks, chairs, tables, bookcases, and other furniture for the little ones. Her furniture is painted with non-toxic, lead-free finishes, guaranteed safe. For potential buyers, the Web site catalogs both furniture pieces and design plans. If you want a step stool in antique teal, just find the right descriptors and click. Hughs cracks open a shipping crate and puts the finishing touches on your order.

Hughs also offers custom designs. With a phone call, Dad can discuss specific features. Even though the general array of design choices is made for tables and chairs, Hughs is flexible. She adapts designs for any of her products, including bookcases, bedroom sets, and hobbyhorses.

AVOID WORK, HAVE FUN, MAKE MONEY

Yes, this is another of those "I'm doing what I love" stories. They're pandemic in e-commerce. When Hughs had a baby, she wanted to stay home for an extended period. With finances tight, however, she knew she would have to return to work after only twelve months. She was motivated to find something else. "I didn't want to leave this precious little bundle," she says. "Looking around, I found eBay.com and started selling things—

things I had around the house, sort of like a yard sale." Of course, she finally ran out of things to sell.

For a while, she bought and sold children's clothes, but it was neither a high-profit venture nor consistent. "Right away," she says, "I knew I wanted a Web site of my own." Hughs didn't want to be dependent on others and even began to worry that eBay would falter. So she looked into her own e-business. Because she already knew the Net and loved its accessibility, Hughs knew "it would be perfect." Besides not having to find start-up expenses for a storefront, Hughs recognized that she could devote lots of time to her child without the distractions of having to deal physically with customers. It was a perfect fit.

Next came the dilemma—which business to try. When Hughs worked as a nanny some years before, she had painted a rocking horse as a Christmas present, and the little boy loved it. So her husband said, "Why don't you paint a rocking horse again?" Even though she couldn't find rocking horses immediately, Hughs did locate some appealing table and chair sets. First, she offered her creations on eBay to see if anyone was out there waiting for hand-painted furniture. Yes.

The next stop was Yahoo!Store. For $100 a month, Hughs loaded her catalog with 50 items. She sampled the free software before signing up and found it easy to use. As she says, "You can build a test store and fool around with it. Yahoo! has tons of templates for designs. I know just enough HTML to tweak the site, which I learned from a book." After several hours of fine-tuning, the site was ready. She tries to keep "the flashing things" on her site to a minimum, reasoning that a clean, easy-to-access site looks more professional.

Hughs swears that anyone can do what she accomplished with Yahoo!Store. She uses *Microsoft Publisher* to design her lo-gos and graphics. But the serious *PhotoShop* and HTML tasks she leaves to Yahoo!Store. With no reservations, Hughs recommends the Yahoo! services, even the credit card program, relishing the preprogrammed features of the host.

A RETURN POLICY THAT NO ONE USES

Here's a tribute to great merchandise. Hughs has a 100 percent guaranteed return policy. She's pretty sure it's effective, but she'll have to wait for a return to be sure. So far, no takers. "I constantly get e-mails from people who love what they get," says Hughs. Her guarantee is a comfort to prospective buyers. "People have faith in me," she says, "because I have faith in them."

In addition to her product guarantees, Hughs cites a good customer service policy. "I bend over backwards to make my customers happy," she suggests, "and it works because I get many, many repeat sales and referrals." Despite her best intentions, however, all has not been smooth on the fulfillment side. During the hectic Christmas rush of 1999, UPS could not deliver some orders on time. To placate customers, Hughs offered a rebate, refunding the shipping costs and adding a polite "I'm sorry." Even though she lost some money on the shipping fiasco, the customers returned, bought more, and dragged their relatives along. "It worked beautifully," she beams.

WORK CLOSELY WITH THE SHIPPING COMPANIES

Painting the furniture and the occasional assembly project are easy parts for Hughs. Shipping and handling are the chores. At first, she had problems because her boxes were so large. Fortunately, most of the pieces come assembled, so Hughs can reuse the packing crates: "I just take the chair out, paint it, and repackage the box." Using bubble wrap on the corners prevents damage to the furniture, and Hughs employs foam sheets to protect the tops and sides where fresh paint has been added.

Every so often, Hughs also uses drop-shipping to advantage. When the customer wants a piece with a natural finish, she can send the information directly to the manufacturer, saving time and money.

"You really have to work with the shipping companies," says Hughs. "If you have large items or if you are shipping in quantity, call everybody to find out who has the best rates and what they'll do if you have oversized packages." In her own research, Hughs asked about pickup and delivery. Would the shipper come to her business address, or would she have to schlep everything to the relay point herself?

Hughs says that, when facing the shipping dilemma, new business owners should "sit down with them [shippers] and put together a concise shipping table." Once she passed that essential step, says Hughs, everything was easy. Besides, Yahoo!Store lets e-tailers plug in their shipping tables. From there, everything is automatic. The billing orders are based on weight, cost, or order, and Yahoo! will tell the customer the shipping costs as the order is being placed.

TONS OF TRAFFIC AND TWO THUMBS UP!

For many reasons—plenty of them economic—Hughs loves Yahoo! services. She gets her customers primarily from the search engines, and Yahoo!Store tracks their paths to PipperSnaps.com. As a result, she knows what campaigns are effective and which aren't. Through the Yahoo!Store, Hughs automatically registers with Yahoo!Shopping as well. As an added benefit, she found herself rush-listed into the search engine in a mere two weeks, much less than the normal six-month waiting period. "I think it helped to add a note that I was a Yahoo! customer," says Hughs. Indeed.

Despite her appreciation for Yahoo! services, Hughs also dabbles in other engines. She likes GoTo.com, even though there are fees. "After Christmas, I invested a lot of money in GoTo," says Hughs, "but it paid off." With GoTo.com, you pay for each click-through, regardless of sales, so Hughs warns that "you have to watch it." Clearly, however, the ploy has been productive for PipperSnaps.com. "I get tons of traffic from there," says the owner.

In many ways, Hughs is living the Horatio Alger story. She has a little apartment in downtown Washington, D.C. If she stands in the middle of the street outside her front door, she sees the pillars of the White House. Nevertheless, she runs a booming business from her own home. In words full of thanks and gratitude, Hughs says, "This is just a super thumbs-up to capitalism!"

In closing, Hughs says, "If I can do this, anyone can!" Surely she exaggerates, but the message is clear enough: if you find an e-business that really inspires you, and if you work diligently and with purpose, your chances for success are as lofty as the Washington Monument.

Web address:
   www.PipperSnaps.com

Mail Club for Kids

Start-up expenses: $12,000

Special requirements: *None*

Best advice: *"It is really important to have a decent product. You can put together a decent Web site, but if you don't have a quality product, you are going to find yourself in trouble. I spent a lot of time developing a good product and finding good suppliers, then making sure I could do what I promised. Don't spend all your time promoting your site and not developing a quality product."*

D ear Kelsey,
I am writing this letter to tell you how much I loved your Mother's Day gift. The Pokemon Magic Set is wonderful. Thank you. You are a sweet little girl. Daddy and I both love you.

P.S. Please clean your room.

You've got mail! The real thing, with a stamp and an envelope and with neat stuff inside—if you're a child, that is, because MailJust4Me.com delivers only to kids.

Karen Tinley is the owner and founder of this online mail club for youngsters, a business that swept into the virtual realm in February 1999. "I wanted to do something creative and something I could do at home," says Tinley. MailJust4Me.com served that impulse. With an M.B.A. in marketing and experience in her field, Tinley knew she could manage the business part of an e-commerce site. She just wasn't sure what to venture into.

Finally Tinley got an idea from her four-year-old son, who was so excited when he received pieces of mail. At first she tried researching the idea on the Net and in the library but couldn't find any resources. Apparently, no one else had ever dabbled in mail for kids.

JOINING CYBERSPACE

Tinley knew she had hit an untapped market. Launching the site was a series of steps. First, Tinley decided on a theme-based approach. She decided to focus on holidays like Halloween and Valentine's Day, occasions that inspire ideas for envelope stuffing. Then Tinley started looking for suppliers, people who provide the materials for the overflowing envelopes. Finally, she had to build the site. Tinley knew how to surf the Net but had no expertise in HTML or search engine maneuvering. Big problem.

"I basically knew nothing, so I started from scratch," says Tinley. "I hired a graphic designer who was really responsible for building my site." Ironically, Tinley located the designer while surfing the Net, discovering a graphics style that seemed perfect for Tinley's own project. "She helped me," says the site owner, "and showed me how to do things for myself so I didn't have to ask her constantly (and pay her) for changes and site maintenance."

After a period of training and collaborating with the Web designer, Tinley has now taken over the Web duties. "I do things myself now," she says, explaining that her designer didn't use an editor, so Tinley had to learn HTML anyway. With experience in code writing, Tinley felt confident to take over all Web duties except graphics, which she still farms out.

A VALENTINE FOR JOHNNY?

Tinley's business approach is fundamental. Customers can order one themed mailing or a membership for three-, six-, and twelve-month increments. The longer the membership, the lower the cost per mailing. The site has a shopping cart, so all ordering and processing is done online. Each mailing includes a two-page newsletter touting activities related to the theme of the day. Children might receive crafts pieces or art materials, and Tinley usually adds a book list for parents, often old favorites that focus on Christmas, Hanukkah, Easter, Chinese New Year, or the current holiday theme.

"My target is three- to eight-year-olds," says Tinley. "I include everything they need to make a simple craft, so for instance on Valentine's Day, they get a little bag with pom-poms and glitter, as well as instructions on how to make valentines." Also they receive some stickers and—the pièce de résistance— a personalized letter on themed stationery that is signed according to instructions from the purchaser.

PRODUCT LINE

Tinley believes her products speak for themselves. She encourages word-of-mouth advertising, partly by providing a testimonial page on the Web. As she explains, "Ten to one, people will tell you when something is wrong, but positive response is something you have to solicit. When I get good feedback, I ask permission to post it on the testimonial page." Good idea.

Having a one-of-a-kind line helps Tinley's bottom line. "I have something so unique people aren't looking for it," she says, half in complaint. "They don't even know MailJust4Me exists, so I have to come up with a way for people to stumble upon my site." To that end, Tinley does a regular traffic report. She finds that most visitors type in her URL directly, meaning they've found the address through publicity or word or mouth.

People simply don't go looking for personalized mail sites for kids, argues Tinley. There must be another route. Many people find her site by typing in a holiday name on a search engine. Links to other sites also bring in business. She has even received publicity from parenting magazines and—the best draw—articles in the local paper. "But now," she says, "most people are coming from word-of-mouth advertising." Eventually, viral publicity takes over when a site is hot. Says Tinley, "A lot of people's kids see their friends receiving mail and want to get in on it."

SOME DIFFICULT LESSONS

"I have learned some things the hard way," says Tinley. In addition to losing money on banner ads, with their high click-through rates, she laments the time spent learning to successfully promote her Web site. It is extremely time-consuming to do promotional tasks, she argues, adding, "If you are not willing to put in the time, you are going to have some problems." The constant tedium of upgrading the site is a drain on physical and mental resources. And it took a long time to learn the right strategies.

Just adding a page and registering it takes time, she suggests. "You could literally sit at the computer twelve hours a day and not do everything necessary to promote the site." During the first six months of search engine scrambling, says Tinley, "I pulled out my hair to get into the top 20." But now she ranks high on all the engines, because they eventually list sites according to popularity, as measured by click-throughs. You have to put in the meta tags, too, she agrees, but spending a lot of time on meta tags didn't seem to help her climb the charts. "For other sites," she admits, "meta tags are probably more important."

Banner ads have been expensive and nonproductive, says Tinley. "You really have to target ads," she continues. "Eventually the price will come down so that ads will be reasonable. Then maybe it will make sense." In the meantime, she says, "I wouldn't recommend banner ads to anybody." Tinley prefers trading newletter ads. She won't sell ads ("it's too commercial"), but trades with creative sites and well-targeted newsletters have produced results. Her own newsletter, with a circulation of 1,200, is popular with other site owners for children's products, many of whom like the idea of creative links.

Search engines do bring customers, but the traffic surges during holiday seasons when people type in "Christmas" or a similar key word. MailJust4Me surfaces on these occasions because Tinley emphasizes holiday themes. "For instance," she says, "people typing in a search for Valentine's Day will usually bring up my site. Even just the key word 'Valentine' works, because there aren't a lot of sites out there that have anything to do with that holiday." Because Tinley features a Valentine's Day page, people follow the link from her index and arrive directly at the targeted page.

EMPHASIS ON GRAPHICS

Unlike many sites, where the designers minimize graphics to promote easier navigation, Tinley loves graphics, arguing that they promote a professional-looking site. Some of her graphics icons are free, courtesy of donor sites. Regardless of the source, Tinley believes that solid graphics encourage people to use their credit cards. "I see a lot of sites that I don't trust enough to put my number out," she says. In most cases, people are shopping the Net for convenience, she notes. But there's still a lurking suspicion about online buying. To alleviate those fears, she uses graphics as part of a trust-this-site image.

ANSWERING SERVICE VS. VOICEMAIL

Originally Tinley used a service to answer her phones, but that idea came to a halt when she realized the operators were stretching most calls into long conversations. "The service charged by the minute," she says, "and you'd be amazed at the amount of time they spent on the phone with each caller." A query that took Tinley twenty seconds to answer would take the service operator six minutes or more. Tinley fired the phone service company, opting instead for a voice-mail box, one that gives the callers the option to press one number to order. Then the call rings through to Tinley on a dedicated line.

The holidays are coming, and your little tyke might just like a note from Grandma or a card from Uncle Chuck. Keep MailJust4Me in mind. Tinley is glad to make sure your message is filled with fun and signed with love and kisses—just the way you'd choose for little Jim.

Web address:
   www.MailJust4Me.com

Party Planning

Start-up expenses: $8,600

Special requirements: *A background in party planning*

Best advice: *"Here's the key: have something that sets you apart from the rest, some kind of unique product or content—or something you really know about and can develop on the Internet's special resources. There should be a nice synergy between what you are doing and the potential of the Net."*

It's a long way from Sesame Street to Wall Street. But that's the path for Party Makers, an enterprise dedicated to planning parties large and small—from children's birthdays to elaborate corporate hooplas, sometimes for as many as 10,000 people. That's a lot of noisemakers and party favors!

Linda Kaye has been a professional party planner for 24 years. Until 1998, when the firm went online, Kaye's company designed parties for children and organized special events, such as safari-theme birthday celebrations for children at the Central

Park Wildlife Center in New York—something they still do. But gradually the firm moved toward education. These days, Partymakers.com sells information. If you want to throw a big birthday bash and make sure it's a success, put on your party hat and click on to Partymakers.com. The site takes you step-by-step through the party planning process—from themes to cakes to activities, even safety issues and clean-up tips.

FOR STARTERS, A WEB DESIGN CLASS

In 1997 when Kaye decided that the Net was a natural medium for her business, she signed up for a three-day Internet class—at a time when Internet commerce was still on the runway. Kaye believed that children's party planning was a perfect fit because, in 20-plus years of her work, she had discovered incredible amounts of valuable information about planning festivities for kids. She says, "So many people have two-career families, so the ability to find out what works—and to get some ideas from other parents—made sense. Working parents just don't have the leisure time to learn these things."

BRINGING CONTENT TO THE VIRTUAL WORLD

With filing cabinets filled with content and tips, Kaye knew she had the resources to describe the perfect party. And the Internet was the place to do it. Today Partymakers.com takes a parent through the entire planning process. "We actually give them professional tips," says Kaye. "For instance, when parents are interviewing an entertainer, they download a form with the right questions to ask." With these procedures and other expert advice given on the site, parents can be assured that the entertainers they hire are reliable, responsible, and appropriate for children. Kaye adds, "From years of expertise, we have developed a package that allows parents to plan their own events in a professional manner. In this way, they will have fewer chances for mishaps."

One of the stops on Partymakers.com is the entertainer locator. Parents can search these pages by theme, after considering their child's interests and personality. For example, a parent can type in "dance" as a topic. The screen then shows a description of a dance party and where the party can be held. By typing in the local area code, a list of locales, such as ballet studios, appears on the screen. Visitors to the site can construct a fail-safe party package, according to Kaye.

A FAMILY AFFAIR

Kaye's daughter, a veteran of the technology industry, helped Kaye navigate the technical aspects of the Net. Along with her husband, she created the site for Mom. The daughter's experience included writing stints with iVillage and ParentSoup, so her online background in creative expression helped her package the content. Kaye's daughter also worked for America Online in its beginning stages, so she was at the cutting edge "when things started to pop."

The elder Kaye admits, "I *absolutely* did not do the Net work." Even though she had been computer literate for many years (her business is fully computerized), Kaye left those details to the relatives. However, she says in general that her work with computers was instructive. "You must have a logical, sequential mind for party planning," she says, "because there are so many details. I was able to take that logical mind-set and use it to help parents work through the process for creating a perfect party."

"We try to direct the process so that parents don't get overwhelmed," says Kaye, who believes that experience is the key. "We have done so many of these parties," she says, "that we are in a position to offer a lot of value, along with the convenience of having just the right products available online." Some of the products offered are balloons, cakes, and paper goods. In addition to finding useful suggestions for the gala affairs, Kaye wants visitors at her site to say, "These are great paper plates. Why not buy them now while we're online?" Kaye's ongoing vision is to create new lines of party products to sell on her site.

OTHER SERVICES ADD TO THE BOTTOM LINE

In addition to party products and information, Partymakers. com supports a message board, where parents ask questions and other parents are invited to comment. This hub allows parents a place to share and exchange ideas. For example, they may say, "I have a seven-year-old, and I'm giving a party with lots of adults in attendance. Should I serve food to the parents? If so, what?" Kaye notes that parents have lots of reservations about proper protocol at birthday parties, asking, "What's the best theme for a child who likes art?" "How can I plan a party around the *Stuart Little* movie?" The message board encourages such interchanges. If the question needs a personal response, parents directly e-mail Kaye's employees, and the message board personnel respond.

One important item available for purchase at Partymakers.com is birthday cakes. In most cases, Kaye's colleagues work with local bakers, just as FTD works with local florists.

"We are pretty resourceful even when we don't have a baker in mind," says Kaye, who says she can tell from a phone interview if the baker can produce cakes of the desired designs and quality. "We make follow-up calls to check on them," the owner says. "What we offer is a simple cake. We don't do theme cakes. It's too complicated. Traditional decorations are the best."

A BUSINESS PLAN THAT'S ICING ON THE CAKE

At this point, the profit center on Partymakers.com is the party products, but other avenues are opening through affiliate links. Kaye operates a cobranding enterprise with toy maker FAO Schwartz—an attempt to link her content with the well-known toy store's exclusive products. Eventually, Partymakers.com plans to develop, through its affiliate links, a boutique site that includes special additions, like party costumes.

Kaye believes that her business is best defined as "reaching out to people from all over the world." When she receives orders from every corner of the globe, she marvels at the way the Net brings people in contact with one another. She says, "Although the customer might have a post office box in Texas, he might live overseas. It's wonderful to get orders from foreign countries." Perhaps it's obvious to some that children's parties are universal and predictable. "I like to see people responding the same way to kids," says Kaye, "no matter where they live." For the founder of Party Makers, the same elements go into party planning, whether it's a fete in Spain, California, or Hong Kong.

Partymakers.com has certainly broadened its customer base. In the old days, each month Kaye's troops planned scores of parties for clients, but now their efforts focus on education, information, and planning. In the future, says Kaye, her focus will be on the site and its opportunities: "That's where growth in this business will be."

Since Partymakers.com consistently ranks in the top ten with search engines—at least when you type in "children's birthday parties"—Kaye is confident that her Web presence is working. She admits that she hasn't even changed the original meta tags. She says, "I think that, as I look at the other sites, we still have something most people don't. Our business existed before there was a Net." Those added years of experience in the real world were the proving grounds for the virtual business. "Now," says Kaye, "we can expand any way we choose."

Web address:

www.Partymakers.com

Unique Toys

Start-up expenses: *None*

Special requirements: *A child's imagination*

Best advice: *"Not any one of us alone [a mother and two children] could have built this business. If you don't have the combination of organizational skills, retail background, and technical skills, costs could be prohibitive. You would have to hire people to do all that. We don't even live in the same town or state and didn't while the site was under development."*

Mom and Pop businesses have always thrived in America. Andersons' Swedish bakery, Zingo's magazine stand, Marcelli's Shoe Store—these were places where that particularly American combination of hard work and eternal optimism flourished, where couples young and old found a niche or a comfortable address, where small businesses grew or faltered or stayed about the same—but, above all, painted a Norman Rockwell picture of the country and its people.

With the advent of the Net, things have changed, and Norman Rockwell is no longer the artist capturing it all on canvas. But the picture of small business in America still has appeal. Consider the family business called BananaJunction.com, a Web site for one-of-a-kind toys. First, it's not a Mom and Pop store but a Mom and Kids business, organized by Barbara Mozingo. Second, BananaJunction.com is not a well-lit store with a picture window gleaming under a big green awning on Main Street. It's a Web address. Third, the owners of BananaJunction.com actually live in three widely separated locations—Tennessee, Georgia, and Minnesota—creating a panoramic portrait of the family cyberbusiness.

A Brick-and-Mortar Beginning

Barbara Mozingo founded BananaJunction.com after a first attempt at a brick-and-mortar store in Minnesota. "The store would have done well in a different location," she says, "but Minnesota is too conservative." Mozingo's storefront was called Anna Banana, a moniker borrowed from Mozingo's mother, Anna, whose older brother long ago used the name to tease his little sister. Located in a mall, Anna Banana was a "fun store" for children, with unusual toys and creative learning packages available from many providers.

In the retail outlet, Mozingo was selling San Rio (Hello Kitty) products and girls' dress-up clothes, as well as boys' policeman caps, kites, puppets, and a long list of items for under a dollar, toys appropriate for kids wandering the mall with only small change rattling in a pocket. Plastic snakes were popular. Says Mozingo, "People insisted it was the most fun store they'd ever been in, but we needed to sell $500 a day to make the expenses of being in a mall. We never made it."

Despite its financial wobbles, Anna Banana was a popular idea. After the Web site appeared, one of the largest malls in Montreal called Mozingo to inquire about opening a storefront there, thinking that Anna Banana was a brick-and-mortar operation. But Mozingo declined, citing the high overhead costs of mall enterprises. Instead, Mozingo and her children decided to stress the online operation, partly as an advertising presence for the storefront property. In the virtual world, Mozingo advertised a full complement of products from the Anna Banana store but altered slightly the unusual business name.

"It was my son's idea to go online," says Mozingo. "We were hoping we could grow really fast and thought it would save the store. But it didn't work out that way." The store closed, and BananaJunction.com took its place. Mozingo's son, an IBM employee, became the Webmaster. Mozingo's daughter, with more than 20 years of experience in retail sales, knew where to find "neat stuff" like juggling equipment and "other things you can't find at Kmart." Asks Mozingo, "Where do you get juggling supplies if you live in Iowa or Montana?" Apparently, nowhere. That's how BananaJunction.com found its niche.

WE'RE NOT IN MINNESOTA ANYMORE, TOTO!

While Duluth may be conservative, Paris is not. Neither is Sydney, Rome, or San Francisco. After establishing the online address, Mozingo's business started to field orders for unusual, even exotic, toys and hobbies from South America, France, Israel—all over the world. In international sales, BananaJunction.com finds boomerangs a huge seller (unfinished, so that the buyers can customize them). Other hot products include glow-in-the-dark juggling balls, puppet theater showcases, and kites. As the Web site says, BananaJunction.com carries items that are hard to find else-where, things that support all levels of involvement—from be-ginners to pros.

Other favorites are Dragalongs, huge high-quality stuffed toys like dragons, unicorns, and spaceships. "Kids can use them as giant pillows," says Mozingo, "and daydream about them or just nap inside. We really love those products. The dragons are especially popular." At BananaJunction.com, the business part-ners stress quality of manufacturing and uniqueness. They like to sell items with educational value, excellent craftsmanship, and clever designs. The company has lots of great ideas for the parent or relative who wants to promote learning and creative thinking. But BananaJunction.com also caters to hobbyists with unusual projects, ones that go beyond the normal resources of storefront suppliers.

ORDERS DOUBLE EVERY MONTH

To attract customers, Mozingo regularly visits the search en-gines, registering and updating meta tags and key words. There is no advertising campaign beyond the Net resources. "We don't even do reciprocal advertising," says Mozingo, "especially exchange programs and affiliate programs. That's because you don't have control over those you're in business with." Mozingo stresses that reputation and image are important, especially when dealing with children's products. There are some useful links, however. "We pick and choose those," says Mozingo. "We like to have high-quality links to high-quality sites."

The plan is working. As the founder explains, orders double every month. The site has always paid for itself. In fact, the own-ers did not invest any cash in the online project, beginning the endeavor with a credit card. In the meantime, the owners have maintained their other jobs. Barbara Mozingo is a tax preparer. Her daughter is a buyer, and son Paul remains with IBM. Despite the part-time approach, Mozingo sees the incredible potential for online sales. As Barbara Mozingo explains, "We can offer things to people that they can't find anywhere else."

Making Headway

The first technology contact for Mozingo was Yahoo! Store, but the Web demands soon took the partners to EarthLink software, primarily because the new programs perform more complicated functions. "We're especially excited to offer CyberCash as a payment option," says Mozingo. "It's like a phonecard. You can buy it at common stores like Wal-Mart in increments of $50 or $25 a card." In this way, buyers without credit cards pick up a card at a store and use it at participating merchants. "It's also great to give as a gift (particularly to a kid)," says Mozingo, "because they use them at stores just like credit cards." BananaJunction.com is one of the charter members of the CyberCash program. The owners like the association because they foresee strong post-Christmas sales from kids whose parents put CyberCash cards in their stockings.

No Problemo

Although the business is growing rapidly, BananaJunction.com has not had significant problems. Yes, there were some shipping glitches at Christmas—always a challenge. But Mozingo uses priority mail for merchandise, taking advantage of the tracking numbers to determine whether items had been delivered. "We like the security of knowing when a package has been delivered," she offers. Sometimes, at Christmas, it's not shipping that causes the most concerns. During the 1999 Christmas season, the company ran out of finger puppets and the puppet theater kits, and the supplier had no more in stock. Nonetheless, complaints have been few, and Mozingo says, "We rarely get returns."

Fulfillment is more complicated for overseas orders, of course. Says Mozingo, the company doesn't predict shipping costs or possible delays. "We e-mail the costs and let them respond if they want to. In some countries we are limited in the size or weight we can ship—or the cost is prohibitive. But we try all avenues and let the customer know the choices before deciding to buy." By allowing the customer access to the nuts-and-bolts of shipping, Mozingo tries to keep frustrations to a minimum for overseas orders. However, she says, "Once an order is filled, we make sure to e-mail the customer that the package has been shipped and when to expect it." Adds the owner, "That's my job!"

NOT ALONE IN THIS MARKET

In addition to fulfillment responsibilities, Mozingo is in charge of inventory control. At first, when the virtual doors opened, BananaJunction.com had little inventory. "We started with the idea of selling something first and then contacting the supplier," says Mozingo. But if the item is hot, you can't do that." Indeed, the partners finally decided to establish a good-size inventory, keeping most everything in stock. "Now," says the owner, "we don't put anything on the site unless we have it in inventory. And on the Web site, we say 'temporarily out' in those circumstances."

Toys and hobbies are big plays on the Net. BananaJunction.com has many competitors, some of which are mega companies. But

Mozingo is confident that her niche business offers items unavailable on most other sites. For the most part, the big players sell items in high demand like GI-Joe and Monopoly. "They are only offering the public more choices from among the mass-produced items," observes Mozingo. "The kinds of products we buy are from the toy and gift markets where mass marketers don't go."

Mozingo's product lines are more gift oriented than those of most toy stores and online marketers. She says, "We like to feature new products that have never been seen before." One popular example is Starlight and Stardust, little space particles that come in vials and sit on a desk or display case. Although pricing is important at BananaJunction.com—and Mozingo really tries to keep costs reasonable throughout the product lists—there are a few high-end items, like a castle that a child can sit in, selling for $200. The moat, we assume, is extra.

As for advice, Barbara Mozingo stresses the idea that a good cyberbusiness like hers requires a combination of skills—technical expertise, organizational prowess, and retail experience. If one person can't muster all these qualities, that entrepreneur must form a partnership or pay others. For her, the Mom and Kids partnership filled the bill perfectly.

Web address:
www.BananaJunction.com

Clothing & Accessories

Antique Jewelry

Start-up expenses: $7,900
Special requirements: None
Best advice: *"Persistence. The Web presents a whole different way to market. I offer everything in pristine condition. You have to be honest. You can't just throw up the site and wait for the money to roll in. It takes as much time to market an e-business as it would to do a [trade] show or sit in a shop. But this approach is the way to go. I am able to cut back on shows, and that process works for me. You really need a niche and to offer good-quality products. And offer service. Everyone wants a prompt e-mail reply!"*

Many people believe that children and families are the greatest benefactors of Internet commerce, because many e-business owners wanted to spend more time with their families. Do you agree? Ann Mills, owner of annscollection.com, an online antique jewelry company, entered the e-commerce world because she "had young kids and decided to be with them." Hers is an increasingly common story.

"I was in the business world," Mills says, "when I started to think about ways to spend time with my children." Because Mills always loved antiques and instinctively knew she should always follow her passions, she sought advice about an antique jewelry shop. Unfortunately, she believed that required too much effort, and why bother? It would leave her no time for her kids. But she thought at least she should give the concept a try and began attending antique shows near her home in northern Michigan.

One day by chance Mills surfed the Net and found the Web site of her mentor antique dealer Gloria Quincy. Mills thought she'd follow Quincy's lead. That was 1997. Soon after, Mills launched a Web site, and the online presence has given her the freedom and support to be a success in vintage jewelry products.

HATS, GLOVES, PURSES, AND CAMEOS

Today, Mills displays a wide selection of accessories and primary pieces such as cameo and portrait jewelry, vintage handbags, solid perfumes, hats and gloves, men's accessories and cuff links, and designer jewelry (both signed and unsigned). She skips most of the antique shows now. There's too much happening on the Net.

"The true collectors are my customers," says Mills. "I sell mostly upper-end accessories and jewelry and especially vintage handbags." With many clients in New York, California, and Japan, Mills realizes that she would never have achieved such market breadth from upstate Michigan, where the roads north, east, and west lead only to water or tundra. Japan is one of her best markets. "People in Japan love everything American," she says. Also collectors in Hong Kong and Taiwan frequently visit, with Atlanta, New York, Los Angeles, and Chicago serving as the most productive American markets. Here is another business that simply would not have been possible without the Internet.

GREAT TREASURES

Mills sells antiques that are "pristine" and at a reasonable price. Occasionally, buyers ask why her prices are so low. For example, a Manhattan customer recently e-mailed a query about a bakelite butterfly pin listed for $45. Eventually the two settled on a price of $30. After considering her bargain buy and the excellent condition of the pin, the woman, who wanted the bauble for her mother, asked, "Why so cheap?" Mills finally explained that the cost was low because "I'm in Michigan, not New York."

A week later the same customer wrote back and said she was thrilled with her purchase. Mills likes this personal interaction. She admits that people don't want to buy antique jewelry on eBay or other auction sites. "It's too impersonal," the antique dealer complains. With high-end items especially, people want feedback, personal attention—for security and assurance. "I enjoy one-on-one interaction a lot," says Mills. Apparently, her customers agree.

MEMBERSHIPS INCREASE AWARENESS

Despite her antipathy for eBay, Mills does maintain a site there. She finds eBay buyers a different sort. They click from eBay directly to annscollection.com, but not many buyers, by comparison, make the leap. Mills has other connections that work better. She has a membership in the Internet Antique Shop, www.tias. com. She started with that group in 1997, when thirty two dealers held memberships. At that time, the Antique Shop worked one-on-one setting up online shops. Now, with more than 200 members, the association offers other services, including a template-style make-a-shop program. Although Mills still belongs to the organization, she considers herself an independent, using the Antique Shop now as a server and a backup system for her site.

The Internet Antique Shop is like a virtual antique mall. "It's good," says Mills, "because people are more comfortable coming there than to an individual site they don't recognize. The link helps your reputation." Mills likes the online service and appreciates their assistance. "I also like discussing collectibles versus antiques," she says, "and crafts versus antiques—how they don't mix." She has tried to advise the Internet Antique Shop to screen applicants carefully, separating the genuine antique dealers from the arts and crafts types. She says, "If you dilute the membership, then the antique market isn't pure."

The Internet Antique Shop was among the first online. Mills still has to do her own "shop" promoting, but the service has fast uploads and a secure line for credit card ordering. "They are like my guts," says Mills, stretching for an analogy.

PROMOTING THE SITE

Another helpful organization is JewelCollect, a news group with a bulletin board system to post buys and sells. Some people only buy through such a service. Qtiques Mall is another affiliate that brings customers. Mills also dabbles in mirroring, a technique of taking the home page of her site and placing it on another server or site. When people check into QtiquesMall, they see Mills's home page and can click on it if they choose. The rest of the site data is not farmed out, only the home page. But once a visitor clicks on the home page, they are transported to the real Web site. As Mills says, "It's like putting up a mirror. I keep my name active in Jewel Collect."

For added exposure, Mills places a link in *Echoes* magazine, a '50s periodical. The privilege costs $40 a quarter, but the link is worth it, she suggests. Search engines are a necessary evil for Mills, but she prefers the business advantages of rich links. "It only costs me $15 for the capability to put links into other people's sites and to accept them," she says. "You must get your name out there." For additional visibility, Mills puts her domain name on her checks, business cards, and media releases. She even gives refrigerator magnets to her customers. "You can't just stay with the computer world," she argues.

Communication is central to a business such as annscollection.com. Mills is lucky, she says, to have reliable contacts for buying inventory. She receives a number of excellent lines, and the Web keeps her in communication with buyers and other dealers. Her e-mail lines smoke regularly. The suppliers e-mail to say things like, "We've got Regency Butterfly pins." Then they send JPEG images from a digital camera and add, "Would you like to accept some on approval?" The e-commerce flexibility and speed makes it possible for Mills to find virtually anything for a customer. She says, "If a woman wants a bakelite horse pin, it's out there somewhere. In the old-fashioned commercial world, the customer would probably never find it."

There are downsides to e-commerce. Mills says people spend $500 or $800, and she never sees or hears from them again. The personal nature of e-business is also cold and detached. On the other hand, she's seeing a lot more customers than might drop by on a typical snowy day in Northern Michigan.

Web address:

www.annscollection.com

Clothing Discount Outlet

Start-up expenses: *Cost of inventory*

Special requirements: *A thorough understanding of the retail industry*

Best advice: *"Make sure you really understand what your target customer wants and that you are serving all those needs. People spend too much time analyzing business models and revenue streams. Businesses end up with a potential customer base that needs more functions filled—or they're paying for services they have no interest in."*

Somebody needs to write a book about domain names, explaining why and how people choose their monikers. For instance, consider BlueFly.com No one would guess that the Web site sells clothing at a discount. Here's the story.

THE NAME TELLS IT ALL

The company owners wanted something "hip," but nothing with the words "off-price," "outlet," or "discount," fearing negative connotations. How they came to BlueFly.com is a puzzle, however. Ken Seiff, the chief operating officer, says, "We looked for something memorable, and when we thought of our warehouse in five years, we imagined an enormous building with products flying off the shelves. We liked the idea of a fly as an icon because it is fast and quick, able to change directions on a dime and ever so unpredictable. The idea of adding blue was to make the name fun and friendly."

Names aside, the company has a plan. BlueFly.com is like an online store in a factory outlet mall, but one with a tremendous number of brands rather than just one. They tout great prices and a large selection. And maybe they're right about the name. It certainly looks as though products are starting to fly from the virtual shelves.

THE ORIGINAL PLAN
DEVELOPED A SLICE

BlueFly.com began online operations in the spring of 1998, four months after the company's reinvention. Its predecessor was selling golf clothes to department stores. The market was competitive for two reasons. First, the retailers felt the need to make profits at the expense of small wholesale brands. Second, the well-known clothing companies felt pressure to expand offerings in high-growth categories, where there was less competition. As a result, the original company took a good squeeze from the retailers seeking higher margins and from the wholesalers looking to capture a larger share of the market.

"We had successfully introduced golf lifestyle sportswear to department stores," says Seiff. "That was our innovation." But change was needed. In the presence of growing threats from both sides of the industry—and because the company had raised $7.5 million the previous year from an IPO—the management team decided to research new types of investments. They felt diversity was the best avenue, removing the company from the department store squeeze play. "Our first instinct," says Seiff, "was to lever our brand name, Pivot Rules Brand, and take the brand directly to consumers through our own retail stores, catalogs, and a Web site."

As Seiff's staff explored the Web strategy, they discovered two surprising facts. On the one hand, there were no sophisticated Web retailers selling golf clothing. On the other, no Net-based firm was making serious online efforts to sell apparel in general. Opportunity was knocking with a boulder! "We quickly shifted our business development toward exploring the online apparel sector," says Seiff. The partners studied the early moves of Amazon.com and cdnow.com, e-commerce firms that succeeded on a value proposition that combined both great prices and broad selection.

SEWING PRICE AND SELECTION TOGETHER

Among its many commercial advantages, the primary key to success at BlueFly.com is excellent prices. How does the company manage to keep costs so low? Seiff says he goes to the brand name distributors, the retailers, and the consolidators at the end of each season. BlueFly.com buyers scan the inventories and look for lines that remain in style. In one season, the hot items are aqua; in another, crimson. "We are always in sync with fashion trends," says Seiff. He says that a supplier might have 20,000 shirts, but BlueFly.com will order only 1,000 units— only the ones in vogue.

Tying price and selection was harder for an online apparel firm, says Seiff: "If you sell a broad selection, the vendors don't want to see their products sold at discount rates. Therefore, if you sell at discount rates, you can't expect to offer a broad selection." Seiff further says it's possible to buy items from the close-out market to sell at discount prices. But even though that ploy assures a broad selection, the inventory is plagued by a lack of sizes (too many smalls and not enough larges).

There was a solution. In traditional off-price retail stores like T J Maxx and Ross, customers who receive great prices must dig through racks and search bins for bargains. BlueFly.com set out to bridge the gap between the miserable experience of rooting and the unhappy alternative of high prices. In short, they developed a feature called My Catalog, which allows customers to select favorite brands, apparel categories (socks and shirts), and appropriate sizes.

To order at BlueFly.com, customers initially fill out the "My Catalog" questionnaire, creating a personalized catalog that reveals only those products matching their requirements for size, category, and brand. "In many ways," says Seiff, "this method let us reinvent the way consumers shop for off-price clothing and accessories."

Besides offering T J Maxx prices and the convenience of the Net, BlueFly.com also stresses customer service, emulating Nordstrom's or Bloomingdale's. "Our plan," says Seiff, "was to offer the best of the full-price world with the best of the catalog world and the best of the price world." Whew! Only the Net could facilitate such an assertive business plan.

How It Works

Don't try to order by phone or fax. It won't work. BlueFly.com operates entirely from its Web site. Seiff says security is one of the reasons for Web-only operations: "We are trying to protect the confidentiality of our customers' information. We just decided it is much better protected when the customer enters it herself online." Seiff also wants to maintain a compelling selection and price schedule. Such goals are best met without overhead, and the Net is the ultimate enemy of overhead costs. Says Seiff, "The cost savings come from customers entering their own data online. It is one less function we need to pay for, and it gives customers a better discount. When we launched, we offered phone ordering, but nobody took advantage." Gratefully, BlueFly.com pulled out the phone jacks.

Most people find the BlueFly.com site in one of four ways. First they see BlueFly.com ads in consumer magazines. Second, buyers have clicked through a banner or link from a major portal like AOL, Lycos, Excite, or Yahoo! Third, customers pick up on word-of-mouth recommendations—a huge draw. Finally, visitors arrive having read about BlueFly.com in newspapers and magazine articles.

The main competitors to BlueFly.com are major players like the Gap. "We are fighting for the same share of the wallet," says Seiff. But there is no direct competitor with the same business model. "We think we are in the best position in our section," says Seiff, citing a wealth of market research. "When you are designing a business from the ground up, you have the advantage of going to the customer and asking about designs or customer needs." Apparently the feedback has merit.

Web address:
   www.BlueFly.com

Dance Shoes

Start-up expenses: $3,350
Special requirements: *High-speed computer lines*
Best advice: *"Technology. Depending on the business, you need
    certain kinds of tech developments. To sell products on the Web,
    you should have a good tie-in from your shipping to your inven-
    tory control, customer service, and accounting systems. You need
    someone who is good at managing and maintaining the system.
    Upgrading is absolutely critical, as is securing your supply lines.
    Without either, you can't handle quick and efficient fulfillment. It
    won't work."*

If you've been out of touch and out of style since the Glenn
Miller era, you're in luck. The Swing Era is back. Expect
clarinets, trombones, zoot suits, and midair collisions on
the dance floor. Welcome to the past. If you want to get back
into the swing, you'll need shoes. No, you can't wear those
clunky saddle shoes or those slippery oxfords drawing dust

mites in the back of your closet. You'll need the official shoe of the Retro Swing Dance Craze, a lightweight special order made in Germany called Bleyers. And in this country, you can buy Bleyers dance shoes only on the Net.

SWING IS BACK

DanceStore.com, a business owned by partners Buck Smolow and Gay Shepardson, is an exclusive distributor of these shoes. The shoes are great! But even if you can't dance, you can join the Blast from the Past in other ways when you shop at this site. DanceStore.com also sells Swing Era clothing, instructional videos, and special collection CDs for dancers. If you click onto the site, you'll probably see the owners and their friends' dancing Swing steps, including some pretty wild aerials.

OK, while you crank up the latest tunes from Big Bad Voodoo Daddy or Royal Crown Revue, you can tap your toe and get the rhythm.

DANCING ON TO THE NET

How did the new swing revival spawn an online business like DanceStore.com? In January 1998, Smolow and Shepardson learned that the best swing dancers in the world preferred the special German-made shoe. When they investigated, they found that no more than 50 pairs existed in the United States. The word *niche* came to mind. On April Fool's Day of that year, the partners—themselves avid swing dancers—went online. They found themselves catering to a craze already full in progress, and one that grew even greater with the advent of a Gap TV ad featuring swing.

Smolow says, "At that time, there were plenty of black-and-white shoes out there, but we wanted a shoe that would allow you to dance well and protect both feet and knees." That description fit only the Bleyers footwear, shoes that weigh one-third as much as Bass saddle shoes and one-sixth as much as other popular brands. "We wanted to wear our dance shoes," says Smolow, "not have the shoes wearing us."

When Smolow, Shepardson, and their partners danced their specialty, the Lindy Hop—a high-flying spectacle with lots of aerial throws—they needed the freedom to kick and fly, but they also needed support and a lightweight shoe that wouldn't cause a concussion in an accident. Smolow says, "You can easily get knocked out by a pair of real shoes with hard leather and wooden heels topped by a leather or rubber bottom." While such sturdiness is admirable in a walking shoe, it doesn't facilitate good dance moves. Smolow says he's been kicked in the head by a Bleyers-wearing partner and lived to tell the tale. "It doesn't really hurt that bad," he adds.

WHAT'S HAPPENING HERE?

Smolow and his partner noticed early on that the swing fad encouraged a particular clothing style. Some dancers embrace a Rockabilly style and want bowling shirts or Hawaiian prints. Others love the Hollywood lounge-singer style with cufflinks and tie bars. Still others opt for the '20s and '30s zoot suit fashions, the ones associated with Cab Calloway. They want oversize coats with huge lapels and high pants with suspenders. So Smolow looked for suspenders, tie bars, knee-length coats, and other such fashion statements. Eventually he and Shepardson started their own private label of clothing to meet these needs. But the business really revolves around the dance shoes.

Smolow says, "We started the business with just a small shipment of Bleyers shoes, selling them from the back of our car to
dancers."

THE PLAN

Realizing that no one else was meeting this need, Smolow proposed a business arrangement. He also argued that, if you spend
time and money on a commercial venture, he needed exclusive
rights to the shoes. He caught a plane to Germany and signed
an agreement at the Bleyers Company.

Now DanceStore.com owns exclusive Western Hemisphere
rights to sell the Bleyers products. Such a licensing arrangement, of course, meant that Smolow and his partner needed
some way to advertise and distribute the products. Shepardson,
a graphic designer and Web creator, argued for the Net. It was,
she said, the most cost-effective way of distributing. "Once we
had the rights," says Smolow, "we had a niche that was really
worth our money and time. The rest of the business could stand
on that foundation." With the relatively quick and inexpensive
entry demands of the Net, Smolow and Shepardson went online almost effortlessly.

WHERE TO KEEP THE INVENTORY

There was an initial problem, however. Without a storefront,
the partners lost their houses to office space and inventory storage. Both live in residential areas. Trucks began to roll in from
the airport to Shepardson's house, the warehousing area.
Smolow was forced to install high-speed computer lines and
equipment to download photos in his home, which became the

office. For a year, the partners struggled with these arrangements, finally giving in to the need for a real warehouse-office space. Now they open the warehouse to the public twice a month for on-site sales.

GRASSROOTS MARKETING IS THE KEY

Even though the partners faced an immense problem with marketing, they decided to play on their strengths. They didn't spend money on advertising but distributed flyers at dance halls and classes. Smolow traveled the world, everywhere asking dancers to spread the word. In a stroke of brilliance, the two encouraged the world's best swing dancers to endorse the shoes. Their spokespeople, who demanded high-quality products for themselves, seemed eager to represent the company. They loved the shoes. Says Smolow, "We had a good product, and we had a good attitude." The combination worked.

With a commitment from a worldwide dance community, DanceStore.com hit its stride. The partners involved key dance people in decision making, so that the dancers felt they had ownership in the company's future. Such an implied association has made DanceStore.com popular with the retro players.

MEETING A NEED

The only serious problems (outside the year of losing control of their homes) came for the partners when they faced fulfillment demands. Shipping and delivery, always a concern for new Web businesses, didn't always go smoothly. Being out of stock at inopportune times also hurt the business picture. But Smolow and

Shepardson persevered, working out these glitches and keeping customer response foremost. "We don't sell things people don't want or need," says Smolow. "And we take cues from the dance community about what to sell." So far, business is hopping.

Web address:
    www.Dancestore.com

Diamond Jewelry

Start-up expenses: $20,000

Special requirements: *Knowledge about jewelry and jewelry design*

Best advice: *"I watched a lot of companies like Ebay and amazon.com, and I recognized a pattern: if you base your business on what you love, you can actually afford to make quality of life the most important thing."*

Would you like a copy of the 1989 Super Bowl ring worn by Joe Montana? Do you want a pendant made from that uncut diamond in your safe deposit box, the one that Uncle Joe brought back from South Africa in 1921? Have you always wanted a duplicate of the elvish rings in the Tolkien novels? Well, you can take your wishes to the local jewelry store and hope for the best. Or you can type in "Tradeshop.com" and connect with Ray Elsey, the widely respected dean of American diamond cutters. His Web site is a two-fold operation—diamond trade and custom jewelry design.

Trade Shop was the first diamond search engine on the Net, beginning in August 1997. At that time, Elsey sold his interest in Associate Jewelers, a union jewelry shop that he had owned in partnership for 24 years. During those early years, Elsey had built a successful brick-and-mortar business, processing more than 50,000 orders a year from jewelry stores and chain outlets around the country. But when Elsey retired and began his online enterprise, his company immediately soared above the competition, largely by paying close attention to people's needs. "There are no rules at my shop," says Elsey, "except that the customer comes first." While others might make such a homespun claim shamelessly, Elsey seems to live by the credo. As Jaclyn Easton says in *Internet Business*, "Solving customer needs is Tradeshop's hallmark." Trade Shop is not about profit—although Elsey is clearing a cool $1.1 million a year—but about serving customers' needs.

THE CROWN JEWEL OF THE INTERNET

By his own admission, Elsey's Web site is messy. Even though *Internet Business* Magazine called TradeShop.com "the crown jewel of the Internet," Elsey also received an award for having "the most chaotic site next to Texas and Southwest Airlines." Amenities like spelling and grammar are not high priorities on Elsey's site. He explains, "I wrote all 1,400 pages of content," says Elsey. "Now there are over 2,000 megs." Haste is partly to blame, says Elsey: "I'm not a great speller, but I can type fast." In the beginning, Elsey wrote content as answers to people's online questions. He wrote what he knew, often without much regard for style. Oddly, it seems to work. As Easton says, the spelling "is so bad and so pervasive that, after noticing the 15th error, it ceases being annoying and actually becomes entertaining."

The Trade Shop owner makes no apologies for his site. He remembers the early days of posting on Prodigy, when every one of his messages would draw 20 e-mails saying, "How smart can you be if you don't even know it's *i* before *e*?" When he went on to the Net in 1994, he was again bombarded with criticisms. But the grammarians have apparently decided to cut Elsey some slack of late, probably because he maintains a tone and style that people believe is genuine, including occasional stage directions such as "[Grin]" or even "[Grinning very widely now]" when he drops a line like, "This will crack you up, folks!" Besides, Elsey's unspell-checked site has won the Net Guide 5-Star Award for content and was featured in StrikingitRich.com as one of America's "23 incredibly successful sites."

"THIS SITE IS FOR THE PEOPLE"

Elsey's foray into Web design began modestly. He bought an Apple computer "when the first one came out" and continued to upgrade each time a new model rolled out of Silicon Valley, adding new varieties of software as they became available. "I learned my computer skills as a hobby," he says. In 1994 Elsey created a Web site in his family room, then ran it from his jewelry shop. "It took off like crazy," he says with some amazement, "so I sold my interest in the wholesale business and started a pure Internet business."

By Elsey's own admission, "The growth has been legendary." He has had offers, but he chooses not to take Trade Shop public. Wall Street representatives have been waving offers at

Elsey, but he has no interest in becoming an IPO. "If they take over," he says, "there will be no follow through. This site is for the people." Elsey is proud that his workers are all jewelry master craftsmen, people who can talk knowledgeably about gems and settings and do so with complete authority. As he says, "We have no salespeople." Every representative is also a bench jeweler, a creative artist with credentials at grading, cutting, and evaluating precious gems. So when a customer e-mails a question or an order, any of the Trade Shop employees can offer a confident and final answer.

Elsey is particularly critical of telemarketing sites and warehousers who have a separate sales staff. "It's stupid to have the typical salespeople who don't know anything about diamonds and don't really care. They say the corporations don't provide training, but that's a cop-out. If you are doing something you believe in, you should have product knowledge." At Trade Shop, the artisans can make special arrangements for people that would be well beyond the capabilities of a typical sales representative. As Elsey says, using one of the newest cyber verbs, We interface with the customer and, using our product knowledge and experience, we can engineer a project to produce the customer's dream."

EVERY DAY IS CASUAL FRIDAY

Some executives probably model themselves after Michael Eisner or Bill Gates or even The Donald, but Elsey's alter ego is madcap surgeon Hawkeye Pierce. Like Pierce, Elsey doesn't take himself too seriously, as a trip to his Web site can confirm. "But," he says, "we take our customers and services very seriously." The secret to this paradox lies in Trade Shop's general atmosphere. "I'm in this for the long haul," says Elsey, "not the money." In fact, the unstructured business style—a definite no-no at Harvard Business School—serves the diamond cutters well. Employees enjoy the business atmosphere at Trade Shop, and Elsey sees that quality of life comes first: "If someone has a sick child, that employee can go home. It is a culturally centered business." Everyone has a Power Book and is wired for the twenty-first century, so people who need to be away from the main office can do their work online.

Elsey pictures himself with golf shoes and a Hawaiian shirt, directing traffic and fielding inquires in the headquarters of TradeShop.com. In the spirit of Hawkeye, he worries not about the masses on the Internet but the one person online at that moment who wants a chain or a pendant or an engagement ring. "That is the real secret of our business," says Elsey. "We bring the customer into the process. When I design a ring, a particular young man is building his own ring. He doesn't walk up to a counter and point to the one he wants." In that manner, business can be personal, even while being lucrative. Elsey normally charges 20 to 25 percent over cost for diamonds and custom-made jewelry, a tremendous bargain considering the traditional 300 percent markup.

The Trade Shop office looks like FAO Schwartz (it's literally full of toys)—and apparently a bit cluttered. Elsey says, "I work 15 hours a day at least six days a week, so the first piece of equipment I got is a sleep sofa." Perhaps that schedule is necessary because TradeShop.com is actually two businesses. One is the diamond trade. Elsey's diamonds come with lab reports on color and clarity and with statistically accurate measurements. "There is no better product to sell on the Internet," he says, "because the diamonds are so accurately described." Diamonds are the most carefully documented objects for sale on the Net, argues Elsey. Besides, TradeShop.com provides intricate photos of the diamonds, and the result, according to *Internet Business's* Easton, is "a 100 percent satisfaction rate."

The second business is custom jewelry design. That half of the trade brings the chaos, according to its owner. Even though diamonds are the safest possible purchase on the Net in Elsey's opinion, "There is nothing more dangerous than custom jewelry." You have to be part craftsman, part psychologist. It's never easy trying to understand what a customer really wants in a ring or bracelet. But Trade Shop's distinct advantage here is the photo gallery on the Web site. Customers can see photos of their work in progress and communicate with the artists at every step of design and construction. Needless to say, customer satisfaction is much enhanced through this interchange.

Trade Shop uses a standard Nikon CoolPick 950 camera, one that cost less than $1,000—just a consumer model. Elsey gets a kick out of companies that boast about $13,000 cameras wired through computers. Elsey has his own photo shop on site, and one of his jewelers also works at Apple in Tech Support. That up-to-date knowledge translates to a digital camera that goes straight into the computer with no scanning. The entire process is done on the computer—hand operated, without automation. Says Elsey, "In a full digital production like this, you are truly in control." The jeweler doesn't miss the old days of running down the street to have a photo processed, running back to put in on the scanner, cutting it up, and then working it down from 600 DPI to 72 DPI. The Nikon produces a 72 DPI photo simply and easily.

Elsey says, "Having this photo capacity is part of what makes our service work. I am getting ready to upload so this guy will see his ring just a few hours after it's done. On Friday I always have a big project that comes up for a guy with a great sense of humor. So I take a photo at the end of the day and let him claw at his monitor all weekend. Then I ship it on Monday." Trade Shop uses Federal Express Overnight A.M. delivery—a highly dependable service. And all shipments are insured, although long ago Elsey had to order a second-party carrier policy custom-designed for his needs because traditional insurers could not keep pace with his volume. "I do business all over the world," Elsey offers, "so I have to be covered for international business as well." In addition to insurance, Elsey guarantees every product for a full year, citing his experience as a technician for this added layer of caution and care.

JUST SEND CHOCOLATE, PLEASE

When asked about the competition online, Elsey admits there isn't much, perhaps for two reasons. First, TradeShop.com was first on the Net, and being first is terrifically important in e-businesses. As Elsey says, "I feel we have an unfair advantage." But staying on top is equally important, and Trade Shop manages its success by remembering to treat customers as individuals who want a special product at a good price. "I am not interested in how big we can get," says Elsey, "but how effective we can get. That's very different."

In fact, Trade Shop's business plan is stupendously effective. In addition to strong and growing revenues, the jewelry company has inspired uncommon levels of customer loyalty. For example, Elsey mentioned in his online biography that he liked chocolate. Within six months he had received 500 boxes of chocolate in the mail from happy customers. When he mentioned that he liked Godiva chocolates, Elsey began to receive boxes of specialty chocolates from Paris, Rome, and other locations around the world, with the senders claiming, "No, try these. They're made in this little shop." Once he opened the mail pouch and found 60 pounds of Texas ribs sent in a hot box. Regularly a customer from England sends packages of caramel candy powder, a confection that Elsey had never seen before.

"It is a wonderful expression of personal thanks," says Elsey of the gifts from customers, "and one that the telemarketers will never enjoy." Elsey claims that the large chains of jewelry outfitters might get written up in redherring.com for their sales volume, but Trade Shop is the kind of business that makes headlines in *Consumer Reports*. "We go after the hearts and minds of the people," he says, "and we will let everyone else slap up banner ads."

A final success story comes from Louisiana, where a young man bought a one-quarter carat diamond for his girlfriend. He had only $350 to spend, and every store he went to told him he could get only garbage for that little money. Says Elsey, "I sold him a really nice diamond for $350, and I must have gotten $300 worth of food over the next six months from him." On almost the same day Elsey took an order for a customer in New York City, who made a $95,000 purchase. "But I worked harder for the guy from Louisiana," he says. "I like that. It tells me we still have integrity. That is real important. I run this place from the heart, and it wouldn't be possible if I went public. Customers yammer that I should go public, but I never will."

Web address:
   www.TradeShop.com

Girls' Custom Clothing

Start-up expenses: *Under $500*
Special requirements: *Sewing machine and sewing skills*
Best advice: *"Do the research. Otherwise, you could put a lot of effort into doing something that isn't going to succeed. Work with a good Web design group that will provide you with food for thought."*

If you want to buy from the rack, climb in the car and head for Macy's, Nordstrom's, the Gap, or JC Penney. If you want to catalog shop, make a call to L. L. Bean, Eddie Bauer, or Bernie's Big and Tall. But if you want something breathtaking in a trendy new fabric or something traditional in an unusual weave—maybe even a garment that you've only dared to imagine—it might be time to shop the Internet. In fact, just click on the appropriate fabric, size, and design—perhaps add a special flourish or two of your own—then wait for the UPS truck to arrive.

Custom-made clothes are usually the result of fittings, consultations, and fabric choices. But specialty clothing is an industry that seems perfect for the Net. Sewers in Des Moines create gowns, prayer shawls, and knee socks for customers in Montpelier, Dallas, and Cheyenne. Designers in San Rafael show mock-ups of special orders to buyers in Seattle, Athens, and Duluth. As an added advantage, if you want to lie about your waist size on the Net, no one will ask you to hold up your arms while saying, "Let's check that measurement."

A READY-MADE SITE—WITH CUSTOMERS!

Ladon Brumfield sells custom clothing (mostly dresses) for babies and little girls, with matching dresses for their dolls. The dolls are not just Chatty Cathys or Bronc-Ridin' Barbies but also brands like Itty Bitty and American Girl Dolls. These varieties are collectibles, especially the American Girl Doll line, which remain hugely popular with little girls and their mothers.

Brumfield started a business selling matching doll and girl dresses on eBay. These designs were similar to the dresses being sold online at the SewnPerfect site. "I wasn't sure there was a market for matching dresses, so I did some research," says Brumfield. "One of the women I contacted during my research was the owner of the SewnPerfect site." Brumfield was impressed with the SewnPerfect.com site, and the business owner said that, despite being overwhelmed with work, she really enjoyed it. After that conversation, Brumfield went ahead with selling on eBay, and the business grew faster than anticipated.

Between December and January in her first year, Brumfield received 35 orders—a huge workload since she was the only one doing the sewing at that time. Between January and Easter,

Brumfield accepted another 45 to 50 orders. "I had no idea that it would grow so quickly," she says. "I had to hire contract sewers to help me fill the orders." In the meantime, Brumfield, who had a small, static site on AOL, began talking with SewnPerfect's Web designer about putting together a professionally crafted page. Just at that moment, a lucky event occurred.

"About that time, the previous owner of SewnPerfect wanted to sell," says Brumfield, who got the news from the Web designer. "She just couldn't handle the volume of orders." At that time, Brumfield was working with the designer on the logistics of a new site and was contacting other Web site designers to get new ideas. "I figured why not get an established site that was already up and running," says Brumfield. Not only was the site running, but it had an overflow of customers waiting for customized dresses.

1,000 Hits a Day—with No Promotion!

At her previous AOL site, Brumfield had begun to make Web page progress. She had established links with eBay so that customers could view dress styles that weren't displayed on the auction boards. But she had no idea what kind of volume an interactive Web page might bring. Almost immediately the site began to average more than 1,000 hits a day, with some days the counters spinning past 1,500, all without advertising or offline promotions. Today, a mother and daughter can visit the interactive SewnPerfect.com site together, viewing dresses in different fabrics, styles, and colors. And the little girl's dolly can shop, too.

Today, SewnPerfect.com continues to provide excellent

feedback so that Brumfield can plan ahead. She gets an automated statistical report every night from her *Web Trends* software. The program tracks how many hits are received at the
home page, how many each page of the site receives, and what
page people are using to access the site. For instance, *Web Trends*
tells whether browsers are bookmarking Brumfield's Party Page.
"If we have a lot of hits on the Party Page," she explains, "we update it a lot. The software tells me what search engines are productive, how many hits come from each user, how many spiders
visit each page, how often they visit, and which pages are least
visited."

Keeping track of customers' habits and styles is important.
Brumfield has discovered that search engines account for approximately 50 percent of new business, with word of mouth
adding another 25 percent. Personal-touch publicity has been
particularly interesting. Says Brumfield, "I have a lot of clients
who love my dresses and have e-mailed me about their mothers, sisters-in-law, neighbors—even people at work—who have
shared the site with their friends." The remaining 25 percent of
customers arrive through online links. Brumfield guesses that
about five people a month contact her about establishing a link.
"There's no reason to say no," she offers candidly.

CHOOSE AN INNOVATIVE WEB DESIGNER

Brumfield has wise advice for those who would follow her steps
to success. She particularly endorses solid preplanning and research, arguing that people can put considerable efforts into
projects that simply aren't likely to prosper. It's easier to drop an
idea in the formative stages than it is after investing thousands
of dollars.

Also, argues the business owner, opt for a great Web design group, one that will provide you with clever ideas for your site, not just technical expertise. "What I love about working with my designers is they always have suggestions," says Brumfield. "And then the ideas are not so technical that I don't know what they're talking about." Brumfield appreciates that her design team helps expand her own ideas. "Too many designers ask what you want, and that's it," she laments. "So you are not benefiting from their expertise." Finally, Brumfield advises new e-business owners to start small and grow at a measured pace. There are plenty of "Out of Business" signs in cyberspace, just as there are downtown.

SewnPerfect seems to attract a number of repeat customers, partly because the company tries to keep prices low, but not too low. Says Brumfield, "Our quality is excellent, so why give it away?" A moderate pricing policy is best. One of the problems that plagues new owners is price tags that are too high or two low. "Don't undersell your work!" says an emphatic Brumfield, recounting that the previous SewnPerfect owner had done just that: "I found from eBay auctioning that the SewnPerfect dresses were going too inexpensively." One of the new owner's first tasks was to bring prices back in line with the quality work her sewers were performing.

MODEST BEGINNINGS

The story of Ladon Brumfield is instructive. She started sewing because she had a young daughter. After making lots of dresses and little-girl clothes, Brumfield found that other parents were interested and wanted to buy. She observed that fashion designers were matching doll clothing to girls' dresses. It seemed like a cute idea. A few hundred thousand stitches later,

Brumfield had a special collection and decided to display it on eBay. After initial successes, she chanced upon a Web designer with talent and foresight who just happened also to know of a unique opportunity to go online where customers were clamoring for matching dresses. By her own description, Brumfield became a successful Internet player simply because she wanted to sew nice clothes for her little girl. Again and again, e-commerce success stories begin with people doing what they love and wanting to share it with others.

SewnPerfect is another good example of a business that seems specially adaptable to the Internet. Time and distance are serious barriers to people who want customized clothing. With the instantaneous responses of the Net and the irrelevancy of geography, buyers should be able to browse for specialty items of every shape, style, and hue. It's a brave new world of fashion out there in the virtual world.

Web address:
   www.SewnPerfect.com

Men's Ties

Start-up expenses: $2,400
Special requirements: *Ties!*
Best advice: *"We had to think globally, instead of asking what people in Connecticut want. Now we get orders from Japan, Germany; we're very big in England, Canada, and Australia. So we have to think, what would those people be interested in? It has made a difference in our selection of merchandise. The different TV shows we export, such as "Dilbert," a big hit in England, have a big impact on the buying habits of people in other countries."*

Here's a gift problem: What to buy crazy Uncle Bill? The one with the joy buzzer and whoopee cushion? He's always hard to shop for. But, of course, there's a solution. Simply click onto absoluteties.com. Maybe Uncle Bill would like a tie with $E = mc^2$ or the face of Peter Lorre. Perhaps the Marx Brothers? How about a tie with the Christmas greeting

"Humbug"? Squirrels? Pirates? Cats playing bridge? Log on to absoluteties.com and see what's available.

From the Window to the Computer Screen

Marilyn Lombardo and her husband own a tie store in Manchester, Connecticut. It's their base of operations, a venture that her husband has backed for three decades. With novelty ties, however, they felt a bigger audience was waiting in cyberspace. They were right. Even people overseas have been checking the site to see what strangeness is newly available in men's neckwear. Instead of looking for a blue tie or a black tie—as might have been expected in the old days—the customers at absoluteties.com are more adventurous. They might want a Betty Boop tie or an Austin Powers tie. The partners also sell lots of neckwear for special occupations and hobbies. As Marilyn Lombardo says, "We try to get something for everybody."

Experience Makes a Difference

Lombardo's husband, with 30 years in the tie business, brought the necessary experience into their partnership when Marilyn proposed that they go online. Marilyn, a great fan of the computer, regularly checked Web sites but couldn't find many with novelty ties. The sites she did uncover were hard to navigate. So she decided to offer the special ties online. It all worked out well. As she says, "We're very excited with the results!"

Having an edge in the field made a difference at least one time, when a competitor downloaded the Lombardos' photo in-

ventory of ties and started showing the digital pictures on his
own site. After stealing the copy, the scofflaw boldly objected
to inquiries, challenging Marilyn Lombardo to "prove the stuff
is copyrighted." A conference with the support people at
Yahoo! and a few well-turned arguments convinced the miscre-
ant to abandon his e-theft. It's probably a good thing. The competitor had lots of pictures and content, but no merchandise.

A START WITH YAHOO!STORE

Marilyn Lombardo took her inspiration for the site one day
when she was browsing through Yahoo! in search of an unrelated product. She saw the ad for Yahoo!Store and logged on.
"You can take it for a test drive," she says, "to see if you can
make it work. It was very do-able." Lombardo started with the
Small Store but has since increased the size. Netscape chose ab-
soluteties.com as its Site of the Week, after only one month in
business. That day, Lombardo welcomed 10,000 visitors.

"There weren't many immediate sales," she says, "but you
don't know how long it will be until they come back to buy."
Such is the advantage of the Net. When the urge to buy re-
emerges, the computer is there waiting. It's not like you have to
drive an hour to a tie shop in Bridgeport.

Most people now find absoluteties.com through Yahoo!
Lombardo says the Christmas seasons have been the most productive, of course. During their first holiday rush, the
Lombardos were unprepared for the heavy volume and spent
several nights working until 3 A.M. to fill orders. As a warning,
they suggest being prepared at all times. Customers expect immediate service, even during peak shopping times.

A NEW PERSPECTIVE ON SALES TERRITORY

At the brick-and-mortar tie shop in Manchester, customer habits are more predictable. In cyberspace, Lombardo has learned to expect the unusual. For instance, a woman called asking for an alligator tie, complaining that a wedding proposal depended on her success. Lombardo sent a digital image of the tie. "It turned out to be an online scavenger hunt," says the owner.

The partners have several steady customers, people who place orders every few weeks, sometimes ordering six or eight ties at once. Schoolteachers are often repeat clients. One man, says Lombardo, orders oddball ties with great frequency. His kids rush to class to see the Tie of the Day. During lectures on *A Tale of Two Cities* and the French Revolution, he wanted one with a guillotine. We'd like to see what he orders when the students read Mary Shelley's *Frankenstein*.

EVERYBODY NEEDS TIES

There are plenty of gift buyers who visit the site, mostly women. Lombardo tries to include gift messages with such orders. She says it works well to make the ties part of a personalized package. The price range is low by comparison, typically between $9.99 and $29.99. Other sites tout more expensive ties, but the novelty niche would not support high-end selections.

Lombardo does enjoy the curious orders from restaurants in particular. Recently, Treasure Island in Las Vegas requested neckwear festooned with red-and-blue guitars. Lombardo at first thought the order was a hoax but later discovered that the ties matched the theme of an ongoing show at the casino-hotel. Restaurant owners often want their waiters to dress in outfits that reflect the special cuisine or the dining ambience. For instance, she sells ties with fish motifs to the owners of a new seafood restaurant and ones with buffaloes for a restaurateur who's trying to unload bison steaks.

The online tie business is fun for Lombardo. She likes the personal interactions with customers, the e-mail messages, and ongoing cyberrelationships. It's more casual than traditional business communications, she notes, but entertaining and engaging. Lombardo has one customer who has made 15 orders, each for six to ten ties.

Even though Lombardo rarely meets her customers face-to-face, she feels there is a close online tie (no pun intended) with several. For instance, when she delayed sending her regular mailing list for a fairly long time last year, one of her regular customers wrote, "What's the matter, Marilyn? I haven't heard from you in awhile. Are you OK?" Now that's a sign of good customer relations.

Web address:
www.absoluteties.com

Specialty Jewelry

Start-up expenses: $2,500
Special requirements: *Digital camera*
Best advice: *"Really put a focus on marketing, not only on registering with search engines but also opt-in mailing and different
partnerships, like Blind Gift, a company that so far is responsible
for 20 percent of our sales."*

During every Olympics, one of the popular traditions is
trading pins. Athletes from Nairobi, Czechoslovakia, and
South Korea sell, barter, and trade pins at a dizzying rate.
Collectors flock to the frenzy, proving that theme and commem-
orative pins have market value. Perhaps that inspiration helped
guide Sherrie Pellisier to become the Pin Lady, or maybe it was
just a simple love of the baubles themselves. At any rate, you can
find what you want at ThePinConnection.com, an online out-
post established in November 1999.

Novel Pins

"Somebody looking specifically for pins would love our site," says Gerry Pelissier, husband of the Pin Lady. "When you come to our home page, you can click on a category. Say you are buying for someone who likes tennis. You can click on "tennis," and the site brings up just those pertinent items—tennis earrings, bracelets, or pins." With a convenient cataloging method and a huge selection, ThePinConnection.com is also apt for holiday shopping. Click on "Valentine's Day" or "St. Patrick's Day," and you find a ready assortment in reds or greens. Your choices are displayed via digital camera photos.

Gerry Pelissier first thought women would be the customers at ThePinConnection.com site. But the ratio is 50:50, primarily because so many men choose the site as a shopping stop for gifts. The most popular category is animals—no surprise perhaps, considering the vast interest in pets on the Net—especially dogs, where 75 separate pins are available. Pelissier notes that other popular categories include sports, hobbies, religion, and special occasions. Besides pins, the site markets earrings, necklaces, and magnets.

Second Incomes for Both Partners

It all started in school. Sherrie Pellissier is a teacher with a penchant for pins. After all, she says, how can you teach kids without a Bambi pin or an Apollo 13 pin or a "School Drives Me Crazy" pin? The kids love commenting on the pins' themes. Her husband wanted to get involved with Sherrie in a business venture, and her flair for the novelty costume items seemed a good start. "We started the business together," he says, noting that it also let him play to his own interest, the Internet, which Gerry saw as the coming attraction of the new millennium.

Gerry had owned a business in the past, a drive-through coffee operation that he started franchising in 1990 before selling out to Chock full o' Nuts. Since the sale, Gerry had been working for the buy-out firm, but he knew he wanted to get back into an online business of his own. The pins fed into Sherrie's interests and provided great conversation pieces as well. The Pin Lady knew from experience that good pins were hard to find. Every time she went into a jewelry store, she looked for new displays but often left disappointed. Sherrie asked, "What if we had a Web site where people could choose from hundreds of pins organized by a theme?"

The first step was finding some resources. The couple went to trade shows and met with manufacturers, finding good outlets and beginning to build an inventory. Today, the Web site displays more than 600 items. Both partners work day jobs, but at night they organize the site and mount the displays for the digital camera. "Business goes on 24 hours a day, seven days a week," says Gerry. "We can keep our day jobs, but our long-term goal is to quit and manage ThePinConnection.com full-time."

YAHOO!STORE TO THE RESCUE

Sherrie's brother built ThePinConnection.com through the services of Yahoo!Store. And the Pelissiers are thrilled with the help they received. "Yahoo! has done a great job of putting together the software," says Gerry, "so you can build it easily. We purchased a digital camera early on and photograph every pin. Then we use PhotoShop to display the pins on our site."

Attracting customers is an ongoing chore for the partners. It requires a substantial commitment to marketing. Getting on the search engines was the first item on their agenda, followed shortly by a venture with opt-in mailing. How does it work? People register with various search engines to receive free information regarding their own interests. Maybe they entered a contest and answered a short survey. At any rate, they somehow chose to "opt in."

CHECKS AND BALANCES

Companies that run the online surveys and contests then sell the consumer information to firms like ThePinConnection.com. Gerry Pelissier says, "I get a list of people who want to know more about jewelry, and I send a promotional letter. If they have a real interest in what you are selling, you get a higher rate of response." In some ways, opt-in mailing is the digital version of direct mail.

Another attractive alliance is Blind Gift, an affiliate that allows people to send gifts to people when gift-givers know only the e-mail address of the intended. It's a nifty idea. Gerry says with a modest grin, "There's a lot of romance on the Net." Somebody who has an e-mail address wants to send a "little something" without invading privacy. The solution? Plug in the e-mail address, and Blind Gift plays Cupid. Blind Gift says, "Someone wants to send you a gift. Where should we ship it?" The giver doesn't receive the shipping address, but with the transaction begun, the gift is on its way. For the Pelissiers, the perfect gift is a pin from their selection lists.

The couple also registers with EpublicEye, a service that tracks customer comments. When people have good or bad experiences with e-commerce firms, they can click onto the company's logo and give some feedback. If they prefer, customers can click onto the site and see what others have said about ThePinConnection.com or another affiliated company. Is the firm rated good or bad? Efficient or sloppy? Safe or risky? Friendly or supercilious? It's all there on EpublicEye. "It's good for anyone who might be skeptical about doing business with an unfamiliar name," says Gerry. "Buyers can click on the site and read how others have done with the firm. That feedback offers a great level of comfort, letting people know that everything went smoothly and properly, that the transactions were on the up-and-up!"

For the Pin Lady, the biggest issue so far has been visibility—always a concern with start-up e-businesses. "Like everyone else, we are trying to get noticed," says Gerry. "There are so many sites out there. You are constantly competing for exposure. Ideally, the Pelissiers would have a full-time marketing manager, but that luxury is not possible yet. On the other hand, with a few zillion more pins on display—and the next Olympics on TV to spur general interest—maybe the couple will find themselves filling that position on a daily basis.

Thinking about the perfect gift—something small and noncommittal, but interesting, and maybe even a conversation piece? Click on to ThePinConnection.com and browse the selections. We promise you'll find something for cousin Sal, that cute guy in the next cubicle, or Grandma Alice.

Web address:
www. ThePinConnection.com

Computers/
High Tech

Software Developer

Start-up expenses: *None, or $1,799 for a Rapid Application Development Tool*

Special requirements: *Pocket protector*

Best advice: *"With rapid application development tools [RADs], making software is a lot easier than you think."*

There are not many businesses that people can start with no capital and virtually no experience. Software development is one. Furthermore, successful developers can expect a big payday—between $50,000 and $1,000,000 a year for those who find the right niche. Needless to say, the field is growing, especially with the advent of prepackaged programs, sometimes called rapid application development tools.

With the latest generation of RADs, you no longer have to be a programmer to develop commercial-grade software of most any type. If you can use software as complicated as a database (like *MS Access*), then you can create your own software. And, because *MS Access* is no more sophisticated than Windows, that means most computer users can also find a role in software production.

Rapid application development tools are daunting at first glance but ultimately user-friendly. Even if you have no programming experience, the RAD smooths out the bumps and gullies in your cyberpath. Clarion (from Top Speed) is a typical RAD. It costs about $1,799 and takes about three months to master. If you're thrifty—and truly want to begin an e-business with only a computer and a chair—the same type of information is available without cost on the Net. But it still takes time to learn software skills and to put a test program into place.

RIDING THE JET STREAM TO PROFITS

Look up. See that vapor trail? It might be Mark Muller, airline pilot. After he lands his jumbo jet, he slips into a phone booth and comes out as Mark Muller, software developer. In his hotel room with his laptop propped up on the bed, Mark writes programs for worldwide distribution. "There is an incredible opportunity right now for people who want to develop software," says Muller. "The Internet gives everyone a printing press and an international market." Muller, who lives in Western Pennsylvania, has sold programs all over the world—in fact, in every English-speaking country on the globe.

Muller began his online business in 1993 during a period when the airlines were furloughing pilots. He felt the need to establish a second income, one that would suit his lifestyle. "I can do most of my work while I travel," he says, "instead of wandering the city aimlessly, looking for something to do during a 22-hour layover." Typically, Muller goes to dinner, drops by a gym for a workout, then retires to his room for a few hours of computer work. "When I am home, that's time for my family," says Muller. "I only fill orders at home," he adds, "and that takes just a few minutes a day."

ADVERTISING BUDGET: ZERO

Muller marvels at the laptop and its ease of application. When he graduated from the U.S. Air Force Academy in aeronautical engineering, a computer could fill an entire room. In 1993, when he felt his job security was threatened, he knew he was out of touch with computer technology. So Muller read some books, talked to computer experts, and began a course of study. "It's nothing anyone can't do with the proper motivation and a few hundred dollars for books and software," he suggests. Muller had never completed any software projects previously—only bits and pieces of code. He essentially began from scratch.

After learning his skills primarily on the Net, Muller began to write source code using *Visual Basic* by Microsoft. He says, "*Visual Basic* takes a lot of the nuts and bolts out of programming, but you still have to go line-by-line and make entries manually. Still, the program simplifies debugging and does speed the development process." Muller markets his products as shareware, available on the Net at software retail locations such as Vdnet, Download.com, softseek.com, and 32bit.com.

Muller's primary software product is *Recipe Calc*, a simple program that analyzes recipes. For instance, if you have a lasagna recipe and want to find out if it's a healthy one, you put the ingredients into the computer and *Recipe Calc* prints a food label, one that looks like the printout on the back of a Chef Boyardee can. The label lists fats, sugar, carbohydrates, sodium, fiber, protein, and other equivalents. The program is popular with Weight Watchers participants and diabetics and has a following among those who work as personal trainers. Muller's software has gained an audience primarily through word of mouth. For example, enthusiasts talk about *Recipe Calc* in Weight Watchers meetings or at the gym. Such publicity has been good for Muller, who says, "I don't spend thousands of dollars on advertising. Actually, I don't spend *any*."

CAN YOU FIND A NICHE?

There are lots of opportunities for software developers, says Muller. In fact, he considers the industry "the most obvious way to make money these days," especially for those who can tap into the Internet market. The most important first step is to pick a niche. Start by looking and listening for problems, as Muller did when he tapped into the weight-loss market, an interest group with enormous potential. Then solve those problems with a programming package such as *Recipe Calc*. Pick projects that you can complete in less than one month, advises Muller. Otherwise, you've lost too much time if the software doesn't sell.

Download.com is a great entry point, according to Muller. They don't get "a piece of the action"—rather, the company relies on advertising for profits. So the larger their library of software, the better for Download.com. Entry is not difficult either. "If you have a good piece of software," says Muller, "it's easy. I just have to establish a link to where my program is stored on the Net, and Download.com sends the customers there." With this ease of operation, there are few problems, and most people who have software programs can handle the link-up requirements for Download.com.

Without advertising, owners of *Recipe Calc* and other programs need strategies for establishing a customer base. Muller advises a four-point marketing plan. First, if possible, get to the top of the search engines. Second, provide press releases to newspapers, e-magazines, and the electronic media. Third, write articles or publicity blurbs for Web forums, discussion groups, and newsletters. Finally, look for ways to promote word-of-mouth advertising, even if it means offering some free services or product samples.

Recipe Calc is just one of many successful programs written by independent software developers, people who have found their electronic niche in the great Business World Without Borders. For those interested in writing software for a specific audience, one that is well defined, there are unlimited opportunities. Lack of experience and money are not even significant boundaries in today's e-commerce climate, because if you spend the time to learn the shortcuts, you can avoid the heavy investments. And, because the demand for new software systems is growing at an ever-faster pace, competition is minimal, at least in the niche markets. So log on to that new rapid application development program and start writing software. Isn't this a great time to be in business?

Resources:

    http://members.aol.com/webhealth/recipe.htm
    http://topspeed.com/

Technical Support

Start-up expenses: $1,000
Special requirements: *Technical expertise*
Best advice: *"Do it from your heart."*

Computers are marvelous tools, but the interface of hardware, software, and hacker leads to troubles sooner or later. Mostly sooner. Sometimes the gremlins are formidable and entrenched, calling for life-saving technical intervention. At other times, a simple click here and there brings a pulse back to the program. But one thing is constant: where there are computers, there are technical problems. Just ask a technical support person.

PUSH ANY KEY, THEN CURSE

A wide-open field for online entrepreneurs is technical support. It takes a lot of expertise and training to enter this business en-

deavor, but the opportunities are endless. There's a lot of reading involved, and keeping up with software changes requires
constant diligence. As soon as the newest Windows hits the
street, Bill Gates's cyber nerds join the race to develop the next
software generation. And other companies, like Red Hat, are
joining the marathon at various points along the route. In short,
a techie must remain current in several user programs, both
popular and emerging.

Victor Rivera recently emerged from the corporate world and
began GroovyMinds.com, an online tech support service. Rivera
worked with customer support as a team leader for .com at
America Online. In his position at AOL, he noticed the overwhelming need for support services. "We got lots of calls—from
simple problems to highly technical crises that we couldn't help."
Sadly, many of the people who called eventually got advice from
the Big Boys, as Rivera calls them, and the counseling was usually
the same: strip the system and start over. The same thing happens
at brick-and-mortar technical support facilities where the solution
to most serious problems is new components or new software.

"I basically wanted to help people," says Rivera. First he began to pack his tools and go to people's houses, helping them to
fix their computers on-site. "Immediately I began to make more
money than at my day job," says Rivera, "and it was a lot more
satisfying." Within a short time, Rivera conceived a Web-based
tech service, one that was simple and competitively priced,
where frustrated computer users could help themselves. But
Rivera's service is not just a Web site. "If they need to, they can
call," he says, "and the price is *very* reasonable. It's a flat fee for
increments of 10 minutes. And most problems can be fixed in
less than 15 minutes." When Rivera has no immediate solution,
he refers customers to people he knows and trusts who are specialists in Web programming or other aspects of computer
technology.

A WEB SITE WITH A HEART

Rivera's business plan was part service, part philanthropy. "I want to be speaking for all the frustrated computer users," he says. "I want to help. If you ask a software company for help, they say it's everyone's fault but theirs." Rivera feels concerned for the elderly and the infirm, people who can't understand or afford high-tech conversations with the Big Boys. Consequently, his Web service is accessible and direct, and for those who get lost, he's available on the phone as well.

Rivera doesn't try to do everything. "If I come across a problem I can't fix, I contract out to people I know can do it. For instance, HTML is not my strong point. But I know a lot of people who do know HTML well. I'll find someone to handle whatever problem comes up." Rivera says that few, if any, are providing the same services.

At GroovyMinds.com, Rivera makes money in two ways. First, his profits come from customers who call and request service. Second, he sells advertising on his site. Increasingly, Rivera is moving toward his goal: "My five-year plan is to make the company name the one people think of when it comes to customer support." In the meantime, Rivera is also making marketing agreements with software companies that need customer support services seasonally—tax preparers, for instance. But, whatever the computer problem, Rivera wants to reduce the anxiety of computer use for the average clacker. "So many people have simple problems," he says, "but ones that are really important to solve. For instance, I heard from a grandfather who was trying to open a digital picture of his grandchild. That was typical."

Rivera built his own Web site for GroovyMinds.com. It is essentially a database. Users can type in the error message they're getting, like "Modem not responding," and the search brings up appropriate help files. Next, the files tell the customer how to check and isolate the problem and how to fix it. Rivera complains that many support systems offer only one solution, then hang up. "They don't give you the opportunity to test the solution," he says.

For impatient or overly ambitious people, tech support is not the right career choice. Dealing with people's computer problems is not unlike counseling. "You have to do it from the heart," says Rivera. "This is customer service. You're going to be dealing with people who are upset. They're having a bad day. If you're not there to help them, this is not your field. You won't be happy in this business." Rivera, on the other hand, takes great satisfaction from his online tech support program. He has helped all kinds of people, with all kinds of skills and expertise. "It feels good," he says, "that I also have something special to offer to people—something that takes skill and makes a difference." Tech support seems like a job for the head and the hands, but Rivera would disagree. It's work from the heart.

Web address:
   www.GroovyMinds.com

Web Content Provider

Start-up expenses: $50,000

Special requirements: *Extensive database and extensive training of personnel and employee screening*

Best advice: *"Stay on top of trends and look at how Web content is different from print content. If you're going to do anything on the Internet, you need to be thoroughly familiar with the new technologies, how they are read and viewed."*

Ask people who've been around the Web a while, and they'll tell you content is king. But valuable content is harder to provide than it first appears. Often e-commerce sites try to cut corners by producing their own content, with dismal results. For writers and editors who have a keen understanding of how the written word can be used to draw visitors to a site and keep them there, opportunities abound.

WriteEdge.com is a full-service Web content provider. Its recent successes include the high-profile Petopia.com site, for which WriteEdge.com produced 1.5 million words of original content in just six weeks. The company has built a reputation for being able to research, write, and proofread original content on any subject and in any style, on a moment's notice.

WriteEdge.com employs an international cadre of 1,700 programmers, graphic artists, editors, proofreaders, and writers. This eclectic gathering of experts is a necessary "edge" in competing for global e-business, according to director Martina Boone, because time and geography are not trade barriers as in the nine-to-five business world. "For example, I have contractors who work from Sweden to New Zealand. When a client asks me for something at five P.M. and needs it first thing in the morning, I have people somewhere in the world who are just getting started on the workday. So we get fifteen hours of work before the client comes back to the office."

20 YEARS OF PREPARATION

Martina's husband, Doug Boone, came to the partnership with both technical and business expertise—including computer and HTML knowledge, an M.B.A. in business, and experience as a project manager. Collectively, Martina and Doug Boone spent two decades working in television, radio, magazine publication, and associated fields before launching the WriteEdge.com enterprise. They worked as writers, editors, public relations reps, and small-business owners, gaining the necessary experience and expertise. When they saw the need for content-based Web sites—to provide information that's useful to the consumer— the Boones also saw that most sites were not very effective. "We thought we could do it better," says Martina.

The first customers to WriteEdge.com came from contacts made while working in the print medium and from people the

Boones had met in their community. Gradually their work became known, and they received lots of referrals. Now, says Martina, "We don't even advertise."

As the contracts increased, the Boones found it necessary to build a large base of contractors—the writers, editors, and designers who do the work. They developed an online application and screening process, complete with competency testing that assures a capable workforce. And the added efforts at recruiting have been good for both the Boones and their contractors: "We now have so many good people we are in an excellent growth position. We obviously want to be able to keep them. We want to give them so much work they don't have time to work for somebody else."

How to Remain Competitive

Web site design is a cutting-edge business. The Boones found it necessary to be realistic about size and strengths. Do what you do best, they say. If you want to remain local and deal with the same people you've known for years in your community, then it may not be necessary to invest heavily in Web page design and content. On the other hand, if you want a national or international market, you must be willing to invest. (They suggest $100,000 as a reasonable bankroll in today's market.) Also it's paramount to stay ahead of technological innovations and trends. Keeping one eye on the competition is mandatory, as is knowing what innovations are cost-effective for your own e-business.

OTHER SERVICES

WriteEdge.com advertises customized site designs that evolve automatically without input from the business owners, establishing a design that "looks different every time the customer loads the page." WriteEdge.com also offers writing services in virtually any genre, as well as consulting services for business owners who want an assessment of whether they should swim with the sharks on the Internet.

Web address:
   www.WriteEdge.com

Web Site Designer

Start-up expenses: $5,000
Special requirements: *At least 256 MB of RAM*
Best advice: *"Know what you're doing and learn the technologies you are going to work with—really, really well. Go into this venture with the understanding that you will get out of it only as much as you put in."*

So how's your Web site doing—the one you patched together after reading *Web Site Building for Dummies*? Then it may be time to consider hiring a professional Web site designer.

It's not surprising that more than 40,000 Web design businesses are operating today, with more virtual doors opening daily. Both nationally and globally, Web page design and site development is big business. Every day, more than 20,000 domains are registered, and most owners will need help in developing their sites. That is *one huge market!*

But the quality and effectiveness of Web sites cannot be measured in dollars. Yes, some design firms—the trendy ones—command $250,000 for one site and yet accomplish little. Conversely, there are huge numbers of Web sites being assembled at Earl Scheib prices ($149.95). Unfortunately, many of the low-cost developers use cookie-cutter templates and give little consideration to the real goals of the business owners.

Since the first blips of the Internet, Web site design has flourished. Only five years ago, programmers were the only people who could figure out how to construct a site. It was a great mystery to everyone else. When Web design software such as *Frontpage* hit the stores, the pendulum swung the other way. Suddenly people who could not program their VCRs were dabbling in Web design. Today the industry is in flux, as market forces require more quality and usability. According to industry experts, the next few years will weed out the overconfident folks who think that *Frontpage* is the magic wand of Web design. As business owners and consumers become more familiar with the Internet, they will demand designers who can *really* pull the virtual rabbit out of the hat.

THREE CATS AND A DOG

Until late 1997, Jennifer Youree was honing her skills as a Web designer for an Internet service provider. At that point, she felt ready to step out on her own. The name of her company, Three Cats and a Dog, is not a competitor with Petsmart. Rather, Youree's business concentrates on Web development and hosting for e-commerce sites. Her sites are custom designed; she uses no packages or prepriced products. And the quality of her work clearly sets her apart from any unsophisticated competitors.

Youree says that most people really don't know what they want in a Web site or how to get it. But they *do* want to be able to compete aggressively in the cybermarketplace. "I start by sitting down with the client," she explains, "to discuss what they want to accomplish for their business, as well as how much they are willing to invest. Then I develop the site to match their needs. If they are on a tight budget, I tell them what they can and cannot do. I won't cut corners on quality. It's just a matter of scaling down the size of the site temporarily. For instance, if it's an e-store, they might want to introduce ten products instead of a hundred. We can always wait a few months to add more."

Reining in clients with unrealistic expectations is an important part of Youree's business plan. Many people have trouble seeing clearly in the nonlinear world of the Internet. It's the designer's job to work out the organizational flow of the site so that visitors can find everything easily and not be overwhelmed. Often Youree has to explain why having a dozen animations on the home page is a bad idea: "It's obnoxious, for one thing, and takes too long to load." As she carefully explains, "The goal of good Web design is to lead the human eye where you want it to go. If there is too much stuff moving around, the eye doesn't know where to go. All you see is movement." Another common mistake Youree encounters occurs when people try to put text the length of *Crime and Punishment* on the first page; two or three paragraphs is about right.

A Service Business with Little Investment

It takes at least one computer with lots of memory to get into the Web design business. Other necessities are a scanner, a printer, a fax machine, and the latest versions of design software, including PhotoShop, Illustrator, and Image Ready. It's also a good idea to have both a Macintosh and a PC with the two most popular browsers—Netscape and Explorer—on each. Why? Because each computer and browser produces an entirely different page design. For instance, on a Mac the difference in the gamma shows a Web site either lighter or brighter in color. And print that looks just fine on a Mac looks like text for the visually impaired on a PC. By testing designs on both machines, users find a middle ground, a design that looks good on both a PC and a Macintosh.

In addition to learning to use the design software, Web designers also need a complete working knowledge of HTML. A fair understanding of Java Script is also important. Designers can get away without knowing a lot about CGI scripts because there are so many prewritten codes available. Web artists, however, need to understand the platform, whether it is UNIX or NT. Ignorance of the platform conventions usually mean the difference between making a CGI script work in five minutes and pulling an all-nighter at the monitor.

Web designers can work at home at first, keeping overhead low while meeting deadlines in their bathrobes. But those who intend to work with local customers must struggle out the door each morning with a briefcase. Ambitious clients want face-to-face meetings. An important early decision to make, says Youree, is whether having people come to your home makes you feel uncomfortable. If not, at least spring for a new robe.

PROTECT YOURSELF
WITH A CONTRACT

Youree is surprised by how many designers work without a contract. "I *never* work without a contract," she declares. "It is important for both parties for several reasons. I often get clients who come to me after working with someone else who didn't offer a contract. The clients were unhappy with the work but had no recourse. There was no 'out clause' to fall back on."

From Youree's point of view, a contract is important because it outlines who owns what, a significant issue in creative industries such as design: "I think over 90 percent of people don't understand that what I create for them is my property. What they are getting is a licensing agreement to use it on their Web sites. They can't take anything from that Web site and use it in print. And likewise, they can't bring me someone else's printed material or artwork from a Web site and expect me to use it. That material belongs to someone else."

A valid contract also spells out costs to the clients. Youree uses an hourly rate as her guide, but she always sets a flat rate for each project. Setting a flat rate discourages people who want to come in several times a week to add this or that. "I don't want to be someone's employee. I do not charge à *la carte* for anything." The normal range for professional designers is $50 to $90 an hour. When calculating a total fee up front, a Web designer needs to take into account the number of meetings with a client, the number of graphics and scans involved, and the number of hours necessary to complete phone calls, attend meetings, and travel for research. Designers who know the business well should be able to produce a small site of five pages (or less) for about $1,000.

BUILD A REPUTATION
TO BUILD A BUSINESS

Like many modern entrepreneurs, Web site designers can work completely on the Internet, serving clients who are unknown beyond the realm of cyberspace. However, Youree warns, because it is so easy for people to perpetuate scams on the Net, today's Web designer must scrupulously carve out a reputation that draws clients. "If you are going to start out just doing business on the Internet, you're going to have to invest a lot in design just to get that legitimacy across," says Youree. "You certainly won't get anywhere if your own site looks like a 14-year-old's. Nothing can be broken. All your links have to be working all the time."

Youree chose to work locally, and it turned out to be a wise decision. She is active in the local Chamber of Commerce and the Rotary Club. She says traditional advertising doesn't seem to work in her business, but word of mouth definitely attracts customers. "The best thing I could have done was to get involved with the community," she concludes. "I have more business than I can keep up with at this point, and it has all come from referrals. Build your reputation, and they will come."

Web address:

   www.3cats1dog.com

Web Site Program Reseller

Start-up expenses: $2,000
Special requirements: *None*
Best advice: *"Anything you sell should be a product you use yourself."*

Web commerce is the most explosive industry on the planet and will remain that way until almost every business has an electronic storefront. Web site program reselling (selling automated software to help small and medium-size businesses build their own Web site) is one business where entrepreneurs can begin with no special talent, backing, or inventory. Formerly, small business faced a huge cost barrier at the portal to the Internet. Web site designers charged from a few thousand to a quarter of a million dollars—just for the main site development—with added charges for maintenance. Needless to say, in the mid to late 90's, many young e-businesses buckled under the financial strain.

SOFTWARE IS THE KEY

New software systems, like the *KronTek Commerce Engine*, make it possible for any small business to have an automated professional Web site for only $995. The *KronTek Commerce Engine* is a turnkey Internet business system that includes a complete package of tools and services that eliminates the costs of Web site construction and maintenance. It allows anyone with minimal computer knowledge to create and automate an Internet operation without significant technical knowledge. The *KronTek* software should not be confused with a shopping cart or Web page generation system. There are plenty of those businesses out there, usually ones associated with hosting services.

So how does this work as a business opportunity? As a *KronTek* reseller, you first get your own *KronTek Commerce Engine* Multi-User License. With that license, you can then resell the *KronTek* software system to clients. The company charges you $1,995 for the license, and founder Tom Bererton says that the only other requirements for the reseller are high-speed Internet access (about $50 a month) and quality Web hosting ($25 a month) for your new business site. It takes prospective resellers only about a day online to learn the engine mechanics and another day to prepare marketing materials. From there, the operation is ready for launching.

To begin your new business, you establish your own Internet domain and resell the software from that site. Each time you sell a "store," your new client simply goes to your Web site and fills out a form. The *KronTek* software automatically does the rest. Then your client—the new store owner—gets a password and downloads the package with little or no assistance. Most of your time is spent on selling, not tech support. The package your client buys includes support materials, primarily video tutorials based on frequently asked questions (FAQs). As a licensee, your spend your time getting customers to your site.

BUILDING A CUSTOMER BASE

Some of the best ways to get customers for this business are offline. Bererton suggests ads in local newspapers and magazines, flyers and pamphlets, contacts with the Chamber of Commerce, and informational seminars. As with most Web business, you're likely to be most successful with word-of-mouth publicity. Happy, satisfied clients who have successfully developed their own sites using *KronTek* software provide your best publicity for free.

Bererton has several useful suggestions for new licensees who want to market online. He has attracted some of his own customers by gaining top positions in the search engines. But he also spends time on press releases, seminars, Web forums, discussion groups, newsletters, and e-zines.

FILLING THE NEEDS OF A CONVENTIONAL E-BUSINESS

Ready to start taking orders? Here's what you're offering to customers. They can have a real-time credit card processing system with a stand-alone order form or they can opt for a real-time credit card shopping cart. Or they can have both. Either system includes an order-tracking database "back end," so that every order comes through the system. This database therefore follows orders whether they are automatically processed in real time or through a secondary means, such as phone or fax. The system can even track live orders from a retail store. Under all circumstances, the software system keeps records, tracks trends, and writes reports.

An order-systems package is also versatile. It produces sales reports for each product, day of the month, or type of customer. If you want data on widgets, your system can track how many green ones are being purchased over the phone by women in Peoria using American Express cards. Another feature allows customers to e-mail questions or comments. Even better, there's a template e-mail that notifies customers when orders are received. Or, if a customer has bought a green widget, the template writes to say, "Have you seen our new lines of widget holders and widget covers?"

There's more. The automated system manages customer support and, if tech support is necessary, the system can organize that service. *KronTek* software also handles site promotion. It has an autopromotion system, which automatically creates a site map page that graphically lays out the entire site and promotes better performance with the search engines. Without additional programming, the software submits to top search engines and promotion sites.

Different pages on the client's site are also automatically linked, and there is an optional forum system so that customers can enter a discussion group, if desired. *KronTek* lets clients designate as many forums as they want, including private ones that require passwords. That advantage is particularly resourceful for company employees who want to exchange proprietary information through the site.

The software covers the common features of function and design that are found on successful, professionally designed business Web sites. As Bererton says, "[The software] is a combination of what we needed for our business plus what other people have found useful on their sites. Furthermore, every feature on such a program can be turned on or off. You don't have to pay a programmer $75 an hour to do it for you."

FOCUS ON THE ESSENTIALS

Time is a thief in most e-businesses. It's important to use your time wisely, says Bererton. A business owner needs to focus on building a customer base and developing products and can't be forced to spend a lot of time on maintaining a Web site. Each moment spent on mundane repetitive tasks is a drain on the efficiency of the venture. To remain competitive in the hyperactive world of e-commerce, owners need to be fast, flexible, responsive, dynamic, and efficient. Anything that is automated *must* be automated. As Bererton discovered when founding his business, "More and more of my time was being absorbed by maintenance tasks. It left almost no time for growth. So, whenever I came across a task that could be computerized, I wrote software for it." Eventually Bererton decided that others could benefit from the software concepts he had taken to free his own hands.

For example, the *KronTek* system works especially well for people who sell electronic products with downloadable materials like e-books or software, also called intellectual properties. Normally, when you sell such a product, you take the order, issue a password, then send the customer downloading instructions. With automated software, the entire process is integrated into the back end, and the store owner performs none of the steps. Everything is designed to maximize the business owner's time.

The competitors for *KronTek* are out there. Many, however, are too expensive or have a high learning curve. Other programs come with poor customer service or are not flexible enough to meet general business needs. However, with the *KronTek* software, resellers take advantage of the software's benefits to build a successful cyberspace business.

Web address:
http://krontek.com/krontek

Web Site Promotion

Start-up expenses: *$1,200, plus $75 month*
Special requirements: *Key word density analysis software and Web page security software*
Best advice: *"In terms of Web site promotions, search engine placement is the best source of promotion for the majority of e-commerce products. Stick with it until you can consistently achieve top positions. As soon as you can consistently achieve top positions, you will have more work than you can handle."*

Remember the movie *Six Degrees of Separation?* The premise is that each of us connects to any other soul in the world through a chain of only six people. Recently, a Notre Dame physicist played on that theme to suggest that we are only 19 clicks away from any address on the Net. Finding the correct 19 clicks, of course, is the problem.

The current solution to finding your way in cyberspace is search engines. If you want a recipe for squash marmalade or a steerage ticket on a tramp steamer, you must usually log onto an engine (like Yahoo! or GoTo) and click your way toward your goal. That process pays big dividends for e-commerce mavens who reside at the top of the search engines. Those residing on page twelve cannot expect banner sales years, no matter how much they pay for banner ads.

If you own an e-business and want to "move up," it may be time to consult a specialist in search engine optimization (SEO). The typical SEO company sells a variety of services. Online, the SEO specialist produces e-zines and newsletters, promotes link exchanges, writes electronic press releases, or boosts traffic to client sites. Helping clients climb the search ladder is probably the primary job of most SEOs.

Lots of Room for SEOs

Thomas Bererton began Position-It.com in March 1997 in the frozen north of Ponoka, Alberta. Bererton, who worked at promoting new and established businesses, opened his e-doors of necessity. He says, "In my efforts to promote other products, I was forced to become a search engine promoter. I turned what I had learned into a business of my own." Like so many of his e-colleagues, Bererton started with no experience. He had some vague skills in product development but nothing to prepare him for the high-tech world of search engine maneuvering.

Nonetheless, despite his lack of experience, Bererton began his niche business with some advanced technical skills. He had a university degree in engineering physics and had been playing with computers since he was 13. Immediately, Bererton found Internet searches a challenge. "They are highly dynamic," he says, "and you have to update your skills continually to stay competitive." In his business, Bererton sells both the software for search engine manipulation (*SEA-Bot*) and other tools for those who want to enter the business.

It should be clear, considering that Bererton is selling his knowledge as well as his services, that he has little fear of the competition. "It's a rapidly growing industry," he says. "As long as there are search engines, there will be a demand for SEO specialists." Bererton explains that there are many people cluttering the search engine scene, but few of them are really competing for the business dollars. Only those with good success rates are making money, and they seem to be overwhelmed with work.

Typically, a good SEO provider can expect to draw fees between $50,000 and $100,000 a year. This particular niche of Web promotion requires more skill because the technician needs a detailed understanding of search engines and their eccentricities. Those who can master those quirks and trends monopolize much of the business traffic. Says Bererton, "There are lots of people calling themselves SEO specialists, but they don't get results. Those of us who can produce are *very* busy." Word-of-mouth referrals help the best specialists find more work, and, as Bererton says, there is room for more players.

DIVERSIFY, DIVERSIFY, DIVERSIFY

Tilting at search engine windmills is frustrating. The engines change so frequently that specialists must constantly review the online data and requirements. The tasks also require some special tools. For one thing, Bererton depends on key word density analysis software, such as *Key Word Net Analyzer* by Planet Ocean. Bererton also suggests excellent Web page security software, with a main function of protecting key words from competitors. The software identifies who is requesting the key word page. If the search comes from an authorized search engine, the code successfully launches the search. If not, the security software switches to a regular page for visitors or a "nonauthorized" code message. The package also allows programmers to separate code pages from visitor pages.

The fledgling SEO expert also may need a packaged course in search engine promotion, which costs $200, and such services as high-speed Internet access and quality Web hosting. It usually takes about three months of training and practice at page design to start maneuvering into top search positions on the Net.

In addition to selling basic services, Bererton also packages his own software tools. He offers his own key word density analyzer, called *Search Engine Analyzer Robot*, aka *SEA-Bot* and a Web page security program titled *Cloak Bot*. Unlike others who want to protect their intellectual properties, Bererton puts all his software on the "For Sale" table.

TOO MUCH BUSINESS?

Strangely enough, there is such a thing as being too successful as an SEO specialist. After struggling to the top of the engine hierarchy with several of his own pages, Bererton actually had to remove them from the lists. Why? Because he was attracting far more business than he could handle. As he explains, "People ask why none of my training pages is at the top of the search engines. I say it's because I couldn't keep up with the business when we were on top. It actually hurts your business to be so successful that you must turn people away."

One reason that Net businesses can be so profitable is the low overhead. As Bererton discovered, "Overhead is so low that even minor successes can amount to significant income." However, those expecting such bountiful incomes must also cope with the changing nature of the search engine business. Today there are several kinds of search engines. For instance, there are pay-for engines like GoTo. These services tend to worry some small players, but Bererton says there is more than enough business space for fee-based services. He says, "People will learn that paid search engines will work for one type of Web site, while free services will be appropriate for others." Also, people today are using meta engines (e.g., META Crawler or Dogpile) more often if they are experienced e-business players.

Everyone must be accommodated, says Bererton. "As a specialist, your job includes getting top positions for all types of search engine users." Flexibility and depth of knowledge are paramount. In the end, of course, it's the bottom line that counts. Bererton says there are a number of ways to get paid in the complicated SEO business. One is by click-throughs, and another is by flat rate, so that the SEO expert gets an established fee for reaching the top ten, with a sliding scale for the top twenty or top thirty. Bererton charges not only for lofty placement on the engines but also for maintaining position. The flat fees can vary from $100 to $500 per placement and also with the competitiveness of the search engine or the time required for placement.

THE 19 CLICKS

The world's greatest directory is at your fingertips. Within seconds you can reach virtually any corner of the world. It's no more than nineteen clicks away. But for those of us who have clicked and clicked until our fingerprints became smooth, it's easy to understand the value of being able to ride the search engines to a goal. The search engine optimization specialist is someone who knows the way. For e-commerce entrepreneurs and Web site preparers, SEO experts provide a map to profits and success.

Resource:

www.position-it.com

Food & Drink

Chocolate

Start-up expenses: $10,000–$50,000
Special requirements: *Sweet tooth*
Best advice: *"Anybody who gets into e-commerce, whether it's with chocolate or anything else, needs to be realistic about the costs and complications. You see so many ads that say* Make tons of money. Invest only $10 and make $4,000 a month. *They are just scams. The cost of entry is fairly substantial. You can put up a site and gain a couple of customers, but if you want to grow, you have to invest in the technology. And you have to understand the technology, or you will be held captive to your provider."*

Oooooh, chocolate. Now here's an online product we can really appreciate. Cheeses are nice; jams and jellies have some appeal; and the Pennsylvania Dutch Sausage Collection can be interesting. But chocolate is more than food. It's a vacation, a celebration, a liaison, a daring adventure. If bratwurst is Pittsburgh on a dreary Monday, then chocolate is the *Rive Gauche* of Paris at dusk. To many, chocolate is the ulti-mate reward for enduring life's frustrations. You never can re-ceive too much chocolate. (I'd like a package of the hazelnut truffles, please. Yes, that's right, the one-pound box.)

Chocolates are available all over the Net, with large and small companies tapping into America's sweet tooth. There are manu-facturer-specific sites such as Godiva's chocolates, and larger oper-ations like GreatFoods.com, companies with a dessert or choco-late page scattered among many food pages and links. The owners at Chocoholic.com have chosen to specialize, assuming that even chocoholics appreciate a wide variety of delicacies and snacks. While Chocoholic.com owners Pete Smith and Corinne Moore predict lots of competitors on the horizon, they have positioned themselves well in the market and are counting on both products and services to keep profits sweet.

As a strategy for getting and keeping customers, Smith and Moore have focused on public relations efforts to garner major me-dia coverage and so far have appeared in *The Wall Street Journal* and *Style* magazine and on the "Early Today Show" with Bryant Gumbel. "That kind of publicity helps a lot," says Smith. But the major affiliate programs work the best. The affiliate matrices have a constituency of customers for whom chocolate is appealing. With a large membership, an affiliate organization can channel a consid-erable body of business to a company like Chocoholic.com.

CHOCOLATE OF THE MONTH CLUB

The fortuitously named Chocoholic.com site was originally founded by several individuals who were chocoholics themselves. In 1996, the group conceived the company, pooled their money, and got the site on to the Web a year later. But the group didn't have the technical background to enhance the Chocoholic site. "It was a good idea," says Pete Smith, "but ahead of its time." The partners couldn't afford to continue paying outsiders for the technical changes necessary to expand the Web site. Smith, however, came from a technical background, and Moore had a marketing background. Today, the combination of Web expertise and marketing know-how contributes to the dynamics of a high-volume site.

Chocoholic.com will send you chocolate delicacies from all over the world, such as Amsterdam, or from a specific manufacturer, such as Harry and David. On the site, chocolates are listed first by geographic region and then by manufacturers, sometimes called chocolatiers. As Smith explains, "The cataloging serves to remind buyers they're not just purchasing an unknown variety of candy from someplace in cyberspace, but rather they're dealing with a real chocolatier in a part of the world they may know or identify with."

At Smith and Moore's Web site, customers can join the Chocolate of the Month Club and receive top-notch selections from featured chocolatiers. The club sends shipments of one-of-a-kind chocolate selections to any office or doorstep. For $25 a month, charged to a credit card, the shopper receives Easter treats in March, Mother's Day delights in May, Christmas cookies in December, and surprises in the months between. Sign-up plans extend for periods of three, six, nine, and 12 months.

Chocoholic.com also offers a reminder service so that Dad won't forget his anniversary, Mom's birthday, Sally Ann's graduation, or Cousin Mark's bar mitzvah. Without charge, the company solicits its customers for important dates of events and then e-mails a reminder two weeks ahead. In addition, Chocoholic sponsors monthly puzzle contests with (what else?) chocolates as the prizes. Every month, the Web page lists free chocolate recipes, often for unusual—even exotic—treats.

Customers like the eclectic approach at Chocoholic.com. Instead of offering only Godiva chocolates or only Brown and Haley candies, the company sells a huge variety. For example, you can get European or West Coast chocolates, specialty brands, and unusual new taste treats.

DARK CHOCOLATES, LIGHT TRUCKS

In foods, there's always lots of competition online. But Chocoholics. com has a remarkable advantage, the Chocoholic name. Today, when a domain name is tied to the industry, it becomes a significant asset. "It's also been instrumental," says Smith, "in attracting top affiliate programs like QuickStar and BigPlanet." Otherwise, people have chosen Chocoholic.com after hearing good things from other customers. A combination of name familiarity and word of mouth (no pun intended) has benefited Chocoholic.com, along with a great record of customer service.

Maintaining customer service has sometimes required creative approaches. The company tracks orders to make sure they arrive on time and in good condition. Sometimes the tracking records reveal inherent problems in sending perishable items such as bon-bons or tarts. In the summertime, for example, people may receive chocolate that is melted or soft, especially if delivery comes at the end of a long UPS delivery route. Smith solved this particular problem by changing from UPS to Federal Express for some of his Deep South summer routes. Why? Well, UPS trucks are dark brown; FedEx trucks are white. It's cooler in the Federal Express vehicles.

One summer, Smith's firm had a customer in Texas. There was a period of more than three weeks when the temperature didn't fall below 100 degrees. During that time, Chocoholic.com agreed to wait until there was a break in the weather before resuming deliveries, to protect the chocolates from softening or melting during transportation. Says Smith, "Going the extra step, talking to customers, making sure the problem is resolved, taking care of any unfortunate circumstances—that is what sets us apart." Smith has had to resend shipments when problems occur. Nobody wants a gooey truffle shaped like a lump of coal.

JUST SAY NO TO BANNER ADS

"We used to look at search engine rating," says Smith, "and we still consider that nowadays, but the bulk of our shoppers come through word of mouth and our affiliate programs." People often ask Smith about his advertising campaigns. In the past, he says, the model for e-business was to pay for banner ads. But they proved to be ineffective and a nuisance. "The only possible exception," he admits, "occurred if you were using a search engine to look for flowers and suddenly a 1-800-FLOWERS banner popped up. That might work, but it's rare."

At least for Smith's business—and probably for a great many more—banner ads don't work. The better model is affiliate relationships. If somebody at another affiliated site sends a customer to Chocoholic.com, a commission goes to the originating vendor. So rather than spending large amounts of money on questionably effective banner ads, e-commerce owners like Smith pay only for actual purchasers. The system is much more effective and—across many segments of the Net—a new standard model for marketing. "It works especially well for those looking for a big return on their investment," says Smith. And frankly, it's hard to imagine many Web sellers who don't want to see a healthy ROI.

YOU'RE NOT OPEN AT 3 A.M.?

Smith and Moore, like many new Web venturers, find that customers are driving the markets with demands for accessibility. From the consumer's point of view, shopping on the Web means both instant and constant accessibility. It is not unusual for the Chocoholic.com help desk to get calls at 3 A.M. In today's business climate, customers simply assume the Web site is always available. The Internet is clearly beginning to break down the notion of regular business hours. Says Smith, "If you publish an 800 number, you'd better have it staffed 24/7 or you'll lose customers." The same can be said for a Web site where people expect immediate e-mail responses.

Another discarded business rule is the need for a strong supply of inventory. "We don't keep much inventory at all," admits Smith. "We have stocked some chocolates—just certain products that we get a good discount on." But because chocolates have a high dairy content and short shelf life, top-notch truffles last only two weeks. So generally Smith's company sees that the boxes and tins come directly from the chocolatiers.

PLAN TO MAKE AN INVESTMENT

Unlike many e-businesses, chocolate distribution may require an initial investment between $10,000 and $50,000—perhaps more—because, among other things, you need a reputable and reliable Web hosting service. Smith warns about ads for free or cheap Web hosting but says that these plans come with caveats. For example, some may work only with Microsoft packages; some won't allow certain kinds of scripting; some place a strict limit on the amount of storage space. Yahoo! and other portals let you set up a storefront, but once the volume starts to increase, it gets complex and you need more "back office" services. There are also accounting complexities. "That's where the investment will be greatest," says Smith, "on the back end stuff." It's critical, he insists, that you have a sophisticated back end that keeps the bookkeeping organized and lets you reconcile accounts with customers, suppliers, and shippers.

Web address:

www.Chocoholic.com

Coffee and Tea

Start-up expenses: $10,000

Special requirements: *Two memory-intensive computers, scanner, digital camera*

Best advice: *"There is a lot of competition in the coffee area. We are concentrating on tea, tea accessories, and china because there isn't as much competition in that area."*

Unless you live in Bog Hollow, Louisiana, or Far Out, Colorado, you've probably noticed that Starbucks is taking over the streets, becoming the upscale, high-octane version of McDonald's. Americans love coffee. And tea. Starbucks is just the most prominent of many young businesses geared toward America's obsession with caffeine. Actually, it's probably not the caffeine that matters (there's plenty of "unleaded" in those paper cups wrapped in java jackets) but the experience. As Patricia Mertes and James Roberts, owners of the Coffee, Tea and Thee Café Web site, say, these potables are not just drinks—coffee and tea are symbols of "passions that may have been lost in this hectic lifestyle that we all seem bound to pursue."

Well, OK. Coffee is not just a pick-me-up drink. And tea is not just Earl Grey, Red Zinger, Sleepy Time, or Ginseng Flower. Each is a time-out in the mad dash through the vanguard years of the twenty-first century. However you define it, the coffee and tea business is big. And like so many other enterprises, it's going online.

LAUNCHING INTO CYBERSPACE

In October 1998, Mertes launched Coffee, Tea and Thee with an initial investment of $10,000 and a natural interest in coffee and tea products such as tea accessories and china to serve the tea in. "We just liked them," says Mertes, who with cofounder Roberts decided to market products that they not only enjoy but that represent a romantic layover in the hectic modern marathon. Mertes and Roberts had no background in coffee and tea distribution, but they were experienced in the business world. Together they had credentials in craft manufacturing and in producing a newsletter (about dolls). Neither business had online support, but when Mertes and Roberts envisioned the Coffee, Tea and Thee site they recognized that exposure on the Net was crucial.

The partners invested $10,000 to get their e-business off the ground. To save dollars (and to get it right), Mertes designed the Web site herself. The remaining costs involved inventory. "We don't have to stock a lot," says Mertes. "We order from suppliers as orders come in over the Internet." It was important to choose suppliers wisely, seeking out those who offer a reasonable delivery time and don't require huge minimum orders. Most of the coffee and tea supplies were located over the Net, although there was an early period of trial and error in finding dependable distributors.

Despite America's unabating passion for coffee and tea,

Mertes and Roberts found it taxing to get their business under way. Mertes was challenged to learn Web design, and both partners found it difficult to identify which advertising methods would be effective. Though she was inexperienced, Mertes completed her Web page successfully—partly because she had spent a couple of years doing print-based layout and design for a photographer. Mertes also credits her personality for some success. "I like to have control," she says. "I learned [Web design] just by researching and looking at what other people had done. I looked to the Internet for training, and I read *a lot* of books."

LINK UP TO A *LATTÈ* SITES

The partners at Coffee, Tea, and Thee discovered that the best marketing plan was to link with other sites, including shopping malls. The partners do some banner advertising as well with one placed on a coffee site. These ventures are not always successful, they warn. "We have one in the Gourmet Mall, and it is very expensive, but it doesn't produce much," says Mertes. "You never know. It is definitely trial and error."

A primary goal for Coffee, Tea, and Thee—a goal shared by most fledgling e-businesses—is to get to the top of the search engines ladder. Mertes tried most of the recommended ploys, such as a long list of key words, but had little success in reaching the top 20. There were, however, occasional breakthroughs. "Our biggest success is GoTo, which we pay for," says Mertes. "But having to pay is eventually going to hurt small business." She suggests that, because each search engine page contains 30 to 40 names, it should be an acceptable goal for small businesses to be listed on page one.

In a pay-as-you-go search page like GoTo, says Mertes, key words are crucial. "You pay by the key word and you pay by the click," she says. "Avoid using big general key words and keep your costs down." Someone listing the key word *gifts* is paying $3 a click, even though attracted browsers may not be interested in coffee and tea at all. Rather, says Mertes, consider key words, like *coffee* and *tea*, that are highly targeted. Mertes admits that she needs more advertising revenues to get more e-visitors.

GET A LIFE

Coffee and tea distribution is a business that can benefit from online exposure while freeing the owners to have other lives. Mertes and Roberts enjoy not having traditional doors to open at 8 A.M.; they can keep their own hours. They needn't dress for the office nor wait for slow, seasonal buying habits to pass.

Also, they require only a small inventory in comparison with brick-and-mortar establishments. Reliable suppliers (who aren't always easy to find) can react quickly and reduce the need for on-site storage. Like a traditional business, however, Mertes keeps a merchant account at the bank and has purchased shopping cart software that runs on the company's secure server. "We use the credit card machine and process the charges in the office with the machine," says Mertes. "It's an expensive way to do it, however. We could probably do it cheaper."

The online Coffee, Tea and Thee is a business that rose to meet a social need in this country. Mertes and Roberts correctly reasoned that coffee and tea are symbolic in American culture—they represent tradition, celebration, and even romance. The next time you order an espresso *latté*, think about what you really expect from the steamy vapors of that cup.

Web address:
   www.he-and-she.com

Hot Foods

Start-up expenses: *Variable*
Special requirements: *Love of food*
Best advice: *"Quality is very important. Companies with their own food processing plants must repeatedly check on quality control. For those who use suppliers, it is good advice to review carefully all product lines, service records, and financial statements."*

This next Christmas season, don't forget lutefisk for Uncle Sven—and that limburger cheese from Sweden, the one that smells . . . Well, anyway, you love Uncle Sven, and he loves food from the Old Country. But where can you buy painfully stinky cheese and lye-soaked fish? Certainly not at Safeway or Winn-Dixie. Probably not even at the exotic-food kiosks in the mall. In fact, your best bet is the Net, where specialty food companies are prospering.

What do you want to buy? Truffles from Transylvania? Bonbons from Brussels? Without doubt, some click-and-mortar business is ready to take your order and send the package overnight. Click once for sausage from Sausalito. Click again for fruitcakes commemorating the Lives of the Saints. Keep surfing, and you'll find matzo balls, comice pears, smoked turkeys, rock candy, Greek olives, pepper steak, and sourdough starter. The Net provides the biggest and most bountiful menu in the world. The virtual market for specialty foods is hot.

Hot is also the theme of a rapidly growing company dedicated to spicy foods, sauces, salsas, and peppers. Hothothot.com operates online as part of Golden Holdings, a corporation that also owns other food processing and distribution outlets. In 1993, Hothothot began as the brainchild of Monica and Perry Lopez, who took their company online in August 1994. Subsequently, the e-business was purchased by Golden Holdings, which has its own manufacturing plant for hot foods and gourmet items. Hothothot sells its fiery lines to supermarkets, farmers' markets, and leading chains.

The company has been written up in *The Wall Street Journal* and *The New York Times* as an example of a successful e-business. The Hothothot.com story even appears in some college textbooks devoted to business methods on the Net.

BEING FIRST HAS ITS ADVANTAGES

Ben Arora, spokesman for Hothothot.com, says that when the e-company first ventured on to the Net, it was the only one of its kind. That advantage gave Hothothot a flying start and huge edge. Indeed, Arora confirms what so many people have said about e-commerce: being first in a niche is very important. Nonetheless, says Arora, the competition is in hot pursuit (no pun intended). "Every single day we scope out the competition," says Arora. "To remain market leaders is quite a task. We try to be more creative than the others. In fact, we have one employee whose sole job is to scan the different food sites to see what they are doing." The same is true for the technical department, where Hothothot technicians constantly review the customer base for feedback about what customers like and don't like at Hothothot.

Listening to feedback is one of Hothothot's best strategies. "We capture information from our customers," says Arora, meaning that the company has a survey program with forms asking about ways to improve service. Customers receive a bonus for filling out the forms. They receive free hot sauce in the mail after completing survey materials. "Listening to feedback is *very* important," says Arora. The competition in specialty foods is growing, and the e-company now has about 350 competitors. "That is tough," admits Arora, but he says that research and feedback have allowed Hothothot.com to remain foremost in its niche.

Keeping a bond with existing customers is also an important e-tool. For existing customers, Hothothot.com provides newsletters and *Newsflash*, a pop-up newsletter that appears when you log on to the site. In addition to menu changes and special promotions, *Newsflash* offers helpful information, such as the international military mail dates for overseas packages. Customer service is a high priority at Hothothot.com. "We do what we can to keep them coming back to our site," says Arora. Having a billion hits is not what is important in this specialty. "It's the dollars," says Arora, who notes that, unlike so many fledgling businesses on the Net, "Hothothot is actually making money."

KEY WORD: SUCCESS

Perhaps the financial success of Hothothot.com ties directly to its Web site, a light-hearted and effective series of pages that is consistently in the Top Ten with both Yahoo! and Hotbot, two of the biggest and best search engines. No fewer than twelve employees work full-time on the Web site. Even with the current successes, Hothothot is now redesigning its site; the current one has been online in one form or another since 1995. Arora himself is the content director for the Web site, and he uses his communications position to take a daily pulse of the buyers. "If someone offers a good comment, I make note of it," he says, "and keep it for later use. Feedback really helps me out."

The major difference between the real world and the virtual world, at least for e-companies like Hothothot.com, is the anonymity of the Web site. Arora can't see the buyers, and they can't see him. "There is no discrimination," says Arora. That's one obvious plus. But also Arora and other employees do not keep rigid hours. "I can work from home," says the Web director. "If I want to work at home, I can assign my duties to other people. The Internet adds flexibility. And things are so much smoother on the Net. I don't have to deal with difficult people and with the bureaucracy."

Like many e-businesses, Hothothot.com also has a presence in the real world. The company regularly appears at trade shows like the Fiery Food Show and the Fancy Food Show in San Francisco. "I love doing trade shows," says Arora with a twisted smile. "It is always fun when people come to our booth. It is fun to watch people with tears running down their faces. Yeah, it's the only time you can watch people cry and break down laughing at the same time."

Being first in its niche definitely helped this young but healthy e-company. Staying on top is always hard work, though, as shown by the persistent dedication to research and feedback at Hothothot.com. After all, there are plenty of other gourmet food distributors out there looking for a red-hot piece of the whole enchilada. By the way, do you think Uncle Sven would like some Five Alarm Garlic and Pepper Sauce for his pickled herring?

Web address:
   www.Hothothot.com

Organic Groceries

Start-up expenses: $2,000

Special requirements: *Reliable source for certified organic fruits, vegetables, and groceries*

Best advice: *"Be prepared for growth. You have only one shot at making a good impression. If you get caught off guard, it is hard to change, switch, and maneuver on the fly."*

If you think no one has noticed what you've been eating, you're wrong. You've been seen hanging around the corner deli, pretzel shop, and the donut joint. Is that chocolate icing on your lip? You could use a better diet, and here's a resource just for you: a home delivery service for organic produce and groceries. You can reach them on the Net at Urbanorganic.com. Start with the broccoli. It's good for you. For dessert, you can try some lemon yogurt or apricots. Mmmmm. This site is delicious—and very healthy.

ORGANIC PRODUCE RIGHT AT YOUR DOORSTEP

The Brooklyn-based company doesn't charge for local deliveries in Brooklyn or Manhattan. Elsewhere in the New York/Connecticut/New Jersey area, there's a small delivery fee. If you want your organic carrots in Sydney or the Yukon Territory, expect to pay more for shipping. All the produce comes from certified organic farmers and is guaranteed by independent testing organizations, "whose stringent standards ensure that no chemicals have been used in the production process," according to the site.

Urbanorganic.com is a membership service. After paying a $25 lifetime membership fee, customers receive weekly shipments of fresh organic fruits and veggies, with other food choices available. The standard Value Box has 16 to 20 different fruits and vegetables, varying according to season and availability. The shipments come in several sizes (Little Box, Value Box, Extra-Value Box, Super-Value Box, and Juicing Box). Locals can expect the shipments between 3 P.M. and 10:30 P.M. (after hours, shipments are left on the doorstep). Outside the company's delivery area, UPS handles the deliveries.

IT ALL STARTED WITH A HAND TRUCK

Charles Pigott is the owner of Urbanorganic.com but not the founder. The company was founded by two Australian emigrants who wanted to feed their children organic foods but found chemical-free fruits and vegetables too expensive in the markets. They put ads in the paper looking for buyers to join a cooperative. "There was a lot of interest," says Pigott, "so the husband thought it might be a viable business." It was, but not for the Australians.

Pigott bought the enterprise, which started modestly with a hand truck and some fliers, and in time, established an online presence. He also takes phone orders, but there is no storefront. Today, after seven years of operation, Urbanorganic.com makes 2,500 deliveries a week. After establishing a Web address in 1997, Pigott's company saw demand go through the cyberroof. Today the business doubles every two weeks.

With 28 employees and a 10,000-square-foot warehouse, Pigott's company shows no signs of wilting. They occasionally receive free publicity from New York area newspapers and magazines, as well as benefiting from a modest radio campaign. Their complete advertising budget for a year is about $50,000, a small amount considering its volume of business. Many new customers come from the search engines. As Pigott explains, they are not following an advertising carrot but seem to be people launching an online search for organic foods. "We have no ads on the Net at all," says Pigott, "yet people find us every day because we come up in the top ten on most search engines." On Yahoo! Urbanorganic.com surfaces as number one. "We are always in the first five on every search engine," adds the owner.

MORE THAN JUST MANGOS

In addition to vegetables and fruits, Urbanorganic.com sells organic groceries, soy products, breads, dairy products, herbs and spices, and specialty desserts. Each delivery box comes with a newsletter filled with useful information concerning health, cuisine, and food processing. Customers with special dietary requirements indicate their preferences, and Urbanorganic.com creates custom orders for a small additional charge. The company accepts cash payments and Visa, MasterCard, and American Express. Pigott prefers voice-mail transactions for cancellations and changes, reasoning that such interchanges create the best customer relations.

Occasionally, bad weather delays shipments, especially where organic vegetables and fruits are involved. As a result, Urbanorganic.com guarantees satisfaction, promising to "make it up to you on your next box." With referrals, customers can expect a complimentary thank-you box of groceries.

Although special orders are just fine, Urbanorganic.com usually prepacks boxes of produce for bulk sales. Says Pigott, "I buy in bulk, and if I can know ahead of time how much broccoli I'm going to need, I get a better value that day." To avoid the high cost of underordering, Pigott books his purchases eight days in advance. He says, "If broccoli is available and it's a good price, that's what's going into the boxes."

Pigott deals directly with local farmers and coops, also navigating through the necessary middlemen. Small orders are possible with a day's notice because Pigott has that flexibility with the distributors. The markup remains small on grocery items, and Pigott says he's not very competitive with such orders, asking what the chain stores charge.

SHIP IT NOW?

The biggest challenge for Urbanorganic.com is the perishable nature of the foods. Nobody wants wilted lettuce or moldy bread. Another concern is the fickle consumer. Sometimes the same box gets a "terrific" from one customer and a "just OK" from the next. As Pigott says, "There are varying degrees of expectations." Putting together a prepackaged box of groceries is difficult. Some buyers are thrilled; others, disappointed. Even though it takes Pigott half a day to plan and organize a weekly shipment, he's aware that at least someone won't be thrilled to receive kale, winter squash, or tangerines.

Another concern is the local climate and conditions. Unforeseen crises such as a water main break in downtown Manhattan have derailed some large shipments. "We deliver regardless of the weather," says Pigott. "Back in 1996, the post office didn't deliver due to bad weather, but my local trucks did." Pigott says that families in the New York area depend on his services. "In fact," he argues, "we are most in demand when the weather is bad."

The competition so far is negligible. Says Pigott, "I'm the largest supplier in the nation." While others may have 200 customers, they're concentrated in a given region. Urbanorganic.com offers nationwide delivery. Outside the area, of course, there are more problems. UPS does a fine job most of the time, but long-distance shipments tax the system, especially with highly perishable goods. "We tell the customer to send it back if they don't get a package within two days of ordering," says Pigott. "We just send them a new box." With such a careful system, there have been few complaints, says the owner, even with cross-country deliveries.

So put the Twinkies back in the box and forget about the Ding Dongs. Urbanorganic.com is just a few keystrokes away, and for tomorrow you can have a nice dinner of whole foods with no chemical additives. Enjoy!

Web address:
www.Urbanorganic.com

Personal Chef

Start-up expenses: $70 *(for domain name registration)*
Special requirements: *Cooking pots and utensils and cooking ability*
Best advice: *"Just be patient. Really build your business. It takes a while, even with an Internet site. You get a lot of inquiries and a lot of hits, but you might not get many people right away signing up for service. Let the business grow, and don't expect it to be a cash cow overnight."*

It's six o'clock, and you've had a hard day at work. Go to the fridge. Open the door. Uh-oh. Looks like another night of adventures with leftovers. What can you do? Well, if you live in a city like Omaha, where online chefs await your orders, you can solve this dilemma. By this time tomorrow night, you might be eating barbecued salmon with vinaigrette sauce and rice.

It's the new wave. People are busy. They don't have time to cook. If the hungry folks of America don't want to get freezer burn every night or risk injury from sharp can lids, they need an alternative—one that doesn't involve two hours of basting, baking, and broiling. In Omaha, the address you're looking for is www.easyelegance.com, the URL of personal chef Carroll Olson.

COST FACTOR

For a reasonable price, Olson comes to your home, cooks a series of gourmet meals, pops them into the freezer, cleans the kitchen, and pets the cat on the way out the door. Just leave a key or the security code, and your meals appear like magic, with instructions on how and when to defrost the marvelous packages. Olson specializes in entrées like halibut with pineapple and couscous or Mexican stroganoff and spicy corn stir fry. She tailors special menus to suit your needs, including dietary necessities and personal favorites. It's too easy.

At a cost of $220, Olson provides 20 meals—that's two work weeks of dinners for a couple. Singles get the same deal in individual servings. For an extra $60 per visit, Olson provides an added portion for a child, live-in grandmother, or Great Uncle Ed. The costs include the groceries, the cooking, and the packaging. Olson guarantees generous portions. Two children, for example, can share an adult serving happily.

A BACKGROUND IN MARKETING

Olson began with experience in marketing (no, not the shopping-cart-through-the-aisles kind of marketing but the corporate world variety). And she's always loved to cook. In 1995, Olson decided to start a business. Because her husband serves in the military—they move every three to five years—a shop or commercial kitchen made little sense. Olson decided she wanted to become a personal chef. She designed brochures on her computer and spread the word. The reception was positive. By 1998, she took her gourmet kitchen into cyberspace.

Olson's husband, who has a degree in information technology management, built her Web site. After an initial investment of only $70 for the domain name, the business was viable. There have been technical glitches. Olson uses *Frontpage* extensions, and some hosts won't accept those extensions. She says, "Some Internet providers won't pay for the Microsoft licensing, so they won't enable certain pages like the order form (if it's written in *Frontpage*). That could be a problem." She adds, "Fortunately, my host pays those fees, but not all will."

THE WONDERFUL AROMA

Her method is simple. She attracts visitors to her site and offers them a gourmet experience. When someone signs up, Olson devotes the better part of a day to buying and cooking the twenty meals. She does the grocery purchasing before arriving at the customer's home. It takes three or four hours altogether to shop, cook the meals—the entire two-week menu—and get it ready for freezing. Olson packages and labels everything carefully, then cleans up. She brings her own equipment and usually doesn't have to dance around the homeowners. Naturally, most of Olson's customers work outside the home during the day.

MARKETING MENU

Olson promotes her site through trade shows such as the Health Fair and the Home Show, where she hands out litera-

ture. After people arrive home, they can click on to her Web
site to get answers about cooking or to view the Easy Elegance
menus. "People like to get answers without having to worry
about being approached by a salesman," says Olson. "It has
worked out really well. The biggest advantage is that the shows
introduce me to hundreds of people." Olson uses the introduc-
tions to add to her mailing list and database.

Another ploy is a quarterly newsletter called *Hot Off the Grill*.
This sizzling periodical includes new menu ideas for the season.
People can visit the Web site without charge, especially apt for
those seeking quick meal ideas. Olson also e-mails offers and
ideas to people on her list, rather than having to pay heavy
postage fees for a more frequent edition of the newsletter.

Her marketing background also helps. Olson understands
the value of networking. She belongs to Internet groups such as
Homebased Working Moms. An ad at that site has drawn lots
of visitors. Olson says, "I don't register with a lot of search engines because I am not a national site. I'm only in Omaha." But
Olson does help her local cause by writing a column for the
Omaha newspaper, and she supports a standing ad in a local
magazine. "Whenever those publications hit the streets," she
says, "my hits go way up."

A GRADUAL EXPANSION
OF SERVICES

After five years in the business, Olson decided to print a training
manual—one that answers the sorts of questions people e-mail
from all over the country. With this venture, Olson is now consulting, sharing her method for filing her recipes and her instruction sheets for customers, as well as copies of her brochures, business cards, and marketing materials. In addition, Olson offers

teleconferencing and in-person training. Those who want to follow her lead can buy a packet of materials or personal instruction. She says, "A lot of people want to enter this business but don't have any idea how to start." Problem solved.

Olson believes she has succeeded because she knows the traditional world of commerce and marketing. In a small business, she says, you spend thousands of dollars for advertising without much response. For those who want to buy her prepackaged ideas, Olson thinks the how-to kit helps people avoid unnecessary mistakes and predictable pitfalls. She charges $1,500 for the full package of instructions and $1,000 for the manual alone.

Other chefs are training with Olson. She has instructed two others, not as employees but as independent contractors. "I am happy that I have people working with me," she says. "I have young children, so I can only do one family a day by myself." With added help, she can funnel business to colleagues, assuring that business will not be lost to overscheduling. "This is definitely a full-time job," admits Olson. "You could cook for two families in a day, but it would be tight for someone like me."

This site is delicious, and it's growing more typical of what's available on the Net. Time is valuable. You don't all have the leisure to cook tasty, wholesome meals. What would you like for dinner tomorrow? How about trout almondine with braised carrots and garlic mashed potatoes?

Web address:
   www.easyelegance.com

Restaurant Ordering Service

Start-up expenses: $20,000 +

Special requirements: *None*

Best advice: *"Operate in an e-venue where restaurant owners are willing to pay commissions to get more orders and where customers are likely to be wired. It's hard sometimes to get restaurants to go for something that isn't already built and working, so you have to look for people who are visionaries or early adopters. Get them going first."*

What sounds appetizing right now? A pepperoni pizza with olives and onions? Teriyaki pork with snow peas and rice? A bucket of the Colonel's original recipe chicken? Perhaps you'd like something more exotic. How about a Caesar salad from the Olive Garden or hot tamales from Chili's Tex-Mex? Or ethnic favorites like Pad Thai with shrimp, guacamole dip and chips, or a Reuben sandwich with garlic pickles? If you're not hungry now, plan ahead. Order the

Anchovy Lovers' Special (for one, please) for delivery during late-night TV. It's all available on the Net at no extra charge. And it's delicious.

Meal delivery service has outgrown picking up the telephone and placing an order. It was inevitable. Today people want halibut cheeks and havarti, apple chutney and chicken wings, cannelloni and Camembert. Diners appreciate special orders and unusual foods—delivered promptly or hot and ready at the restaurant door. They want variety, value, and convenience. In today's value-oriented world, folks want great food and prompt service. And they don't want to pay a surcharge. All these factors call for the same solution: order those enchiladas on the Internet cybermenu.

"HOLD THE ONIONS, PLEASE"

In 1995 Craig Cohen and Michael Adelberg founded Waiter.com, an online food delivery service. On their Web site, they describe the moment when the concept was born. One day, Cohen—then an employee of Sun Microsystems—wanted a vegetarian sandwich. He called the Silicon Valley number of Togo's sandwich shop to see if they would accept a faxed order. Nope. Togo's had a fax, they said, but it was reserved for corporate communications.

Subsequently, Cohen called his friend Michael Adelberg, a school chum from Massachusetts Institute of Technology and Stanford Business School. He proposed an online system for uniting hungry people and restaurant owners. Soon Togo's Eatery had agreed to their proposal, and Waiter.com was up and running. In short order, the owners quit their regular jobs and started cooking up software solutions for food distribution.

Other restaurants joined the revolution. Adelberg and

Cohen went online with 60 restaurants, each showing its menu on their Web site. By plan, the customers received their service free, with the eateries paying the Waiter.com tab. Now, when you want a pastrami on rye or a garbage grinder, you can log in, click on an order, and wait for the delivery van. In the meantime, the restaurant receives a detailed fax, including special requests like "no onions, extra mayo." Buyers can also have the food waiting at the restaurant for a sit-down meal or take-out. Waiter.com also has a low-tech solution to the munchies: 1-800-Waiter-9.

The numbers are impressive. Waiter.com caters to businesses such as Pizza Hut, KFC, Subway, Wolfgang Puck Cafes, Olive Garden, Domino's, and others, including small local outlets. The partners solicit orders for more than 1,300 restaurants nationwide, offering new cuisines and old favorites from a menu that spans the country. Cohen and Adelberg stress fast, trouble-free service and varied cuisine. Out of necessity, all participating restaurants are searchable by both location and cuisine. After all, the delivery time can be brutal on a giant double-cheese from the California Pizza Kitchen—for a customer from Cleveland.

Lots of Options Spell Convenience

Online ordering makes sense. There are no telephone conversations, meaning no tangled orders. The paperless menus allow for better communication and quicker turnaround. Also, the Waiter.com service has a memory. Buyers can save their favorite orders on the site or specify wild and weird new combinations (ham, olives, and peanut butter?). Like so many Web-based businesses, Waiter.com reduces the hassles of buying. Users simply click their way to culinary satisfaction, stipulating when they want the food prepared and where it will be eaten.

The Waiter.com site is filled with information. You can click to find a restaurant's business hours or get a map with directions to the front door. The site also hosts exclusive restaurant discounts and Waiter Points, a frequent-diner program that offers a series of prizes. This service even supports a personalized My Waiter start page, so that customers can "have it their way" as soon as they log on.

What advantages does Waiter.com have over conventional ways of dining? First, there are no drawers full of menus, no clogged phone lines, no delays while your waiter goes out back for a smoke. Second, browsers easily navigate an enormous potpourri of dining choices, which are endless. Third, special requests are easy—and recorded accurately.

DON'T TRY THIS IN PLEASANTVILLE

In the first minutes of the film *Pleasantville*, the locals are so conservative and parochial that they live in a world without color. Such a town would not support an online restaurant business. As Cohen says, "Silicon Valley was an ideal start-up location because people were not tied to traditional means of doing business. Online food ordering works where the clientele are willing to change their behaviors, willing to buy over the Net. But the atmosphere must also encourage restaurant owners to take a chance on paying commissions in exchange for higher business volume. That is the right business model. In this plan, perceived value is the key. There has to be something that works for both the restaurant owners and the customers."

"When we started in 1995," says Cohen, "there was not enough off-the-shelf software. You could get a Web server but not a shopping cart. We had to build our own." Luckily, the partners teamed with a technical wizard, Shakil Chunawala, who produced much of the essential software. They loaded the site with Netscape 4.0, and Waiter.com came alive with filled orders.

Cohen and partners also began to work with the restaurants to do comarketing. The Waiter.com domain address appears on hard-copy menus, helping to add a word-of-mouth advertising pitch. "We get a lot of viral publicity," says Cohen, meaning that the personal recommendations spread quickly. The two-times-two-times-two formula (you tell two people, they each tell two people, and so on) adds up to big business exposure in a short period of time. In this regard, Waiter.com is like many e-commerce ventures where carefully planned online strategies promote even more effective sales in the real world.

WHY SHOULD I COME TO YOUR SITE?

Having a Web address is not enough. Virtual businesses need visitors, and there are millions and millions of sites. What distinguishes one address from another? Cohen and his colleagues answer that concern by focusing on innovation. For instance, the first time you register at their site, it may take slightly longer than a phone order. However, when your registration information has been customized—and programmed with your favorite restaurants—you'll save time on every subsequent visit. "Then," says Cohen, "there's instant replay. Once you have saved an order, you can recall it with two mouse clicks and a twenty-second wait." With Instant Replay, customers can order a favorite sandwich or a special pizza, including all the unusual flourishes and garnishes.

"It's crazy that restaurants throw away this information every day," says Cohen. Such knowledge is valuable. "We have one gentleman who has ordered the same thing 320 times," he declares. "He orders it three times a week." With a simple click of the mouse, this diner—unadventurous as he may be—taps into his own ordering history almost instantly. It's convenient for everyone.

The Internet allows small companies to become big ones. It allows local companies to become regional, national, or even global. The main advantage of the Internet is a simple one: it commands a larger audience. The Net is an open forum for everyone. As Cohen says of his own experiences online, "This is a virtual business. It doesn't matter where I am." A company like Waiter.com can operate from Silicon Valley or from any location with an Internet connection and electricity. A good hot treat is only a double-click away.

Web address:
   www.Waiter.com

Specialty Wine

Start-up expenses: $60

Special requirements: *Background knowledge in wine*

Best advice: *"The Net is such a visual, educational way to tell your story and sell your product. Americans love information. The Net gives you direct access to your customer, so you can really have communication."*

Despite the testosterone factor in computing and cyberspace, women are gradually exerting dominance in the e-commerce world. An IBM statistic says by the year 2005, fully 60 percent of the sites on the Net will be owned by women. That's astounding. In many ways, the Net makes e-business easy and affordable. It is no longer necessary to seek venture capital or to have personal wealth to launch a serious enterprise. In large measure, women have been the beneficiaries of this leveling process.

Rosemary Zraly is one of thousands—perhaps hundreds of

thousands—of new business owners who have taken advantage of the Internet. Zraly worked for years as a marketing executive for champagne houses like Taittinger and Veuve Clicquot. She is a consultant, lecturer, and author on the subject of champagne. And she loves the Net. "Anybody can afford to get into business this way," she says. "It's cheaper than my cable TV bill."

When Zraly decided to open her own shop in January 1999, she went with what she knew: champagne. On her Web site, quaintly named Champagnelady.com, Zraly markets champagne and accessories, as well as her own books, *Uncorked!* and *Champagne Menus!* Zraly promotes her expertise in champagne with other publicity ploys, including lectures and television and radio programs across the United States and has come to be known in wine circles as the Champagne Lady.

BEEF RIBS, BLACKEYED PEAS, AND BUBBLY!

Zraly grew up in Texas, surrounded by the sound of corks popping. Gaining an early appreciation for the bubbly wine, she went on to study champagnes and gained membership in the prestigious l'Ordre des Coteaux de Champagne. After lecturing and writing about champagne for years, she started her own company, Champagne Communications.

Zraly's Web site is hosted by IBM and costs only $60 a month, encouraging her to describe the online business as "remarkably inexpensive." For that fee, Zraly not only gets hosting, but IBM provides Home Page Creator, a service for small businesses that makes it practically pain free to start an Internet venture. Absolutely no technical knowledge or skills are necessary to put up a Web site this way. IBM also provides (as part of the package) most of the back-office services, such as processing the online transactions and credit card verifications. Zraly can also check the traffic on her site and easily update or edit it at any time.

The site includes champagne recipes. In one section, the Gift Shop, browsers can find champagne products such as crystal flutes, sterling silver coolers, and jewelry made from champagne caps. The online profits come from Gift Shop sales, as well as from the commissions that accrue when her customers buy champagne from retailers linked to her site. However, the Champagne Lady does not sell champagne herself on the site; it's illegal. You must go through a licensed distributor to sell alcohol; and it's complicated to get a liquor license for international sales.

IBM MADE IT EASY

Zraly knew instinctively that her book *Uncorked!* was the right image for her home page. Says Vraly, "I was very intimidated, but I knew the book would dictate the look of my site. I started with just the book cover and the domain name. IBM helped me put in the extra visual touches like the champagne bubbles and the millennium countdown. And they didn't charge for that help. They were very supportive."

Today, with Big Blue guidance, Zraly doesn't worry about the security of online ordering. The IBM system handles security matters. "I don't even see the customers' credit card numbers," she says. "I get an e-mail to fill their order, and that's all I'm concerned with." IBM handles the approvals. Zraly needn't worry about crashes either. She says, "All I have to worry about is developing a product line and driving people to the site." With her growing customer base, however, comes more Web site concerns. Zraly admits that in the future she needs to hire another person to spend time online organizing the links program. Links maintenance, a necessary part of the business, is remarkably time-consuming. Zraly estimates that a new employee could easily spend eight hours a day at that task.

Driving people to the Champagnelady.com site remains the most important job for Zraly. She advertises with IBM and works the search engines. But her experience with search engines has been frustrating. "They are so disorganized," she says. "You have to keep plugging away, they're not like the Yellow Pages. I hope that will change in the future." Zraly prefers radio advertising to other forms. Radio spots have been profitable, especially a popular IBM-generated ad. "Everywhere I go, people know me from that commercial," says Zraly.

Furthermore, Zraly composed a video press release that was picked up in several major TV markets. As a result, she also received excellent exposure in newspapers. "Basically, you have to create a buzz, no matter what your market is," suggests Zraly. "But with champagne, it's easy. Champagne is such a magical word." As the Champagne Lady insists, when people hear the word itself, they stop to listen. That's the moment Zraly likes. She loves to tell stories about the history of champagne and its colorful traditions. At her champagne tastings, Zraly sells the fermented wine not only by flavor but also by spinning stories and anecdotes about the bubbly.

"I WOULDN'T OPEN A STORE IN THIS TOWN"

Zraly, who lives in New York, recognizes that the Net allowed her access to a huge market. Real estate is prohibitive in New York, and the Net overhead is minimal, almost infinitesimal. As an added benefit, the Net process promotes customer loyalty, something that is less common in malls and storefronts.

There are a number of champagne sites, but primarily ones supported by producers like Taittinger and Tott's. The Champagnelady site focuses on a variety of champagnes, not just one, and the Gift Shop increases buyer interest.

Zraly expects the market to increase for champagne and specialty wines. Why? The champagne market is still based on special occasions, not lifestyles, so it is still small but seeing definite growth. People are beginning to try new champagnes and become educated. "In the past, you always had to drink a champagne with a brand name you recognized," say Zraly. "But people are now getting sophisticated. After the millennium, they [are] even more sophisticated."

As the Champagne Lady emphasizes, very few people know a lot about champagne. The history, the traditions, and the stories about champagne are as much fun as the wine itself. Part of Zraly's mission is to educate her customers. And in that mission, she takes great pleasure. She's not the only one.

Web address:
www.Champagnelady.com

Wine Shop

Start-up expenses: $15,000

Special requirements: *State licensing to sell wine*

Best advice: *"Educate yourself. Know where your customers might be. You have to think where an average customer would go to buy wine online. Put yourself into the minds of the customers. People seem to think the Web has always been there, but it's remarkably new. I try to stay on top of things, to educate myself constantly. It's always a challenge."*

Good wine is expensive. No, not wine you buy on special at the local liquor store, but the good stuff, the quality wines that appear on the menus of fine restaurants. An exceptional wine costs $25 or more, even in a grocery store or discount shop. Don't even ask what the wine steward wants for an aged bottle of Valley View cabernet sauvignon at Chez Armando.

Does wine have to be expensive? Not really. The people at

Wine Country in Winter Park, Florida, have some remarkable buys for you. Each of the bottles is rated "very good" or "better" by *Wine Spectator* magazine, but not a single bottle is priced higher than $19.95. For a very reasonable cost, Winecountryonline.com supplies wines with ratings of 85 or greater. That's "very good" wine.

Since the 1998 holiday season, Winecountryonline.com has been selling wines with good noses and fruity bouquets to people all over the world, except in certain American states where it's prohibited. Adam Chilvers, owner of Wine Country, says, "The laws are a ridiculous mess. In some states, it's a crime. In some, it's just prohibited, even though there are no laws against online distribution. In others, you need to be licensed, perhaps meaning you have to establish a physical presence in the state."

Enologists and wine connoisseurs alike are clicking paths to this fascinating Web site. The company receives as many as 10,000 hits a day, with 10 percent of them turning to sales. That's a lot of wine. If you have a spare acre out back, you might consider planting grapes.

A CLICK-AND-MORTAR STORY

Adam Chilvers tells an interesting click-and-mortar tale. The Winter Park brick-and-mortar store cost in excess of six figures, he says. "In contrast, launching and maintaining a Web site brings in 100 times the number of people—on an international level—for a fraction of the cost." Interesting.

In fact, after only two years of operation, online sales accounted for 35 percent of total revenues, with Chilvers estimating a future rise beyond 50 percent. E-commerce seems to pay.

The retail outlet store opened its doors in Winter Park in November 1998, with plans for several more on the drawing table. In the meantime, Chilvers had a friend at an IBM affiliate who encouraged him to try the Net. He took the advice. Three months later, the Web site was launched, even though an online presence was not part of the original plan. Suddenly, with the incredible success of the Web site, the brick-and-mortar stores made little sense. Plans for more retail outlets were dropped in favor of an expanded Web presence.

Says Chilvers, "I'm 25, and I'm not a computer geek. At first, I didn't know anything about e-commerce." His friend at IBM, he concludes, was right about the Net's impact on his wine business. Putting his wines in front of millions of people is a phenomenal advantage, a remarkable shortcut to profits. "I sell to people I've never met," he says, "and to people who've never walked into the store. That's just amazing." With an initial investment of $15,000 for the Web site and all the refinements, compared with $125,000 for the store, Chilvers believes he has found the right business plan. The Web site, which he admits was "rather primitive" at first, has now evolved into a pleasant, easy-to-use address, with eye-catching visuals. And it's creating an ever-greater share of the total business profits.

BUILDING THE SITE

Chilvers chose PSR Software, an IBM affiliate, to build his site. Today they continue to provide the site maintenance. Says Chilvers, "They have taken good care of me. I just told them what I wanted, and it was done. I didn't have to worry about anything. I like that." You would, too.

The Webmasters at PSR also took care of the search engine placement. Chilvers handles the other marketing chores. "Most customers find out about our site through ads in publications such as *Wine Spectator* and *Gourmet* magazine," he says, "and there's some word-of-mouth publicity now as well." How does Chilvers know? He follows the "pockets" of orders from a region or an interest group. "For example," he says, "you get one guy ordering from Pensacola, then later you see a few more people from the area buying wines, and you can tell what's happening."

FINDING A SUPPLIER

Early on, the question of inventory was tough. When Chilvers was on the Web, he didn't know how much variety he would need of each wine. As he says, "What if someone calls and wants fifty cases of Fetzer chardonnay? We are not a multimillion-dollar company that could afford a lot of inventory. You don't want to run out and turn down a customer." The problem was to have enough of a particular wine in stock—but never too much. It sounds hauntingly like high school math.

The solution to inventory problems came from suppliers. Distributors, says Chilvers, have a twenty-four hour delivery cycle, so customers never know if Winecountryonline.com is out of stock or not. According to Chilvers, "I am selling inventory that I don't even own yet—a phenomenal situation."

CAUTION: 500-POUND GORILLA AHEAD

Yes, there's competition. Chilvers says, "It's a joke to say that wine.com is my competition. They are huge." The chore for Winecountryonline.com is to set itself apart from the major players in the field. The key? Simplicity. "Everything is $19.95 or less," says Chilvers, "and has a rating of 85 or more." The dominant wine site, he says, may be overloaded with information. While getting a lot of content, visitors to wine.com may also get lost. "When you sit down to buy something on that site," says Chilvers, "it can take a couple of hours."

At the Winecountryonline.com site, there is only one thing to do: buy. "You choose what you want," says the owner, "merlot, chardonnay, zinfandel—and you get a rating, price, and description. That's it." Boom.

Chilvers has some other advice for people interested in an online wine site. "Go to the Wine Institute site at wineinstitute.org," he says. "There you'll see the list of the states' laws. It's a total mishmash. After the repeal of Prohibition, laws were left up to the states. At that time, there was little interstate commerce, so it was no big deal. People would shop for wines in their local shops. That system is so outdated now that it's nuts. But we keep a list of the states that we can sell to. We'll work on the rest as we go along." Is your state on the can't-sell list? Check it out.

Web address:

www.Winecountryonline.com

Gardening

Exotic Plants

Start-up expenses: *As little as $2,000*

Special requirements: *Apparatus for shipping quickly and in volume*

Best advice: *"We put the Web address on everything we send out, like literature and a lot of how-to stuff. People pick them up and send them to friends. . . . We also try to get links with anyone who is worth having."*

Gardening is the number one hobby in America. Flowers, shrubs, and trees are available at the local nursery, of course, and even at brick-and-mortar outlets like Wal-Mart, Buy-Rite, and Fred's Feed and Seed. There's immense competition for the "green" dollars. But the garden supply trade also has lots of room for niche businesses, including ones that sell specialty garden tools, seeds, exotic plants, and other accoutrements. This burgeoning interest in plants and flowers is part of a Green Revolution that at first glance seems the antithesis of America's fascination with the Net. But an increasing number of American businesses are making use of the ties between cyberspace and green space.

In today's e-climate, both professional and weekend gardeners have come to rely on the Internet for supplies and stock. Throughout America, people with loam under their nails are downloading information from garden supply sites such as Blue Pagoda Orchids, a garden supply business located on a tiny peninsula 30 miles south of Sarasota, Florida. Blue Pagoda, like so many other nursery operations, is relatively new to the e-business fold. For 48 years, Marylou and Larry Evans raised orchids in their own greenhouses and began selling them commercially in 1969. Indeed, until two years ago, Blue Pagoda Orchids was an ordinary garden business, a flower shop with attached greenhouses. Often customers would wander into the shop, notice a prominent sign, and ask to see the orchid stocks.

The Evanses also belonged to the American Orchid Society, the publisher of an almanac for growers. "That's basically how we got business before the Web site," says Marylou Evans. But since adding the site, Blue Pagoda has done "very well." Now the American Orchid Society and its almanac are important in another way: as an e-resource, a valuable Internet link to their site.

The Evanses did not enter the e-business world by design. Their daughter, a Web designer, talked them into it. Since hitting cyberspace, they have noticed enormous differences between the traditional sales and the e-sales approach. One major advantage of doing business on the Web, says Marylou, is the easy interchange of information. Their Web site is packed with details, but often people have specific questions about care or selection of the orchids. The e-mail links allow the Evanses to respond rapidly while the customer is focused. "Sometimes we get two or three e-mails a day from people who order or ask for info. We try to answer them quickly so they keep their interest."

HELPING TO TAP THE GLOBAL MARKET

Instantaneous response is clearly important. So is tapping into the global market. Blue Pagoda is now receiving orders from overseas, including such far-off places as Zimbabwe, Uruguay, England, and South Africa. Recently, a man came into the shop who was originally from South Africa but had moved to Zimbabwe, where he had entered the spice business. He was able to locate Blue Pagoda because of its Web site. And, after an interesting tour of the grounds, the man left with several flasks of orchids. Clearly this is one connection that would never have flourished in the pre-Net era.

"With the Web site you get orders directly," says Marylou, "although it involves shipping, which is actually something we had never done before." Evans already had a computer when her e-business began, so her only investment—besides the nominal fee for hosting—was the cost of a secure site for credit card ordering. That innovation made a big difference for sales, says Evans. "Now if you read the list of orchid flasks and say, 'This sounds good,' you can type out the order form and it's done." Before Blue Pagoda had credit card ordering and a secure site, they had to e-mail or call prospective clients. Lots of people did not follow through on the initial impulse. Now that interest and orders are virtually simultaneous, business is, well, flowering!

To get customers to log on to their Web site, the Evanses put the address on everything they print, mail, and circulate. They distribute pieces of literature to friends and pursue worthwhile links whenever the possibility arises.

Keep It Simple

People looking for garden supplies are not necessarily interested in artsy Web sites. They want begonias, hollyhocks, and orchids, not elaborate screen designs with animation and award-winning graphics. "I spend a lot of time on the Internet," says Marylou. "I don't like clutter and waiting for all kinds of cutsie things and graphics to come up. If you are interested in orchids, that's what you're there for. We do have pictures [on our site], but you don't have to look at them if you don't want to." Rather than spending time and money on elaborate sites, says Marylou Evans, efforts are best spent on establishing valuable links with associated sites, such as Hauserman, the largest commercial grower in the country. That link has provided much of the new commercial business for Blue Pagoda Orchids.

Know Your Clientele

Despite their increasing success with professional orchid growers, the Evanses note that most online gardeners are casual growers pursuing a new or recurring interest in orchids, not a commercial one. Although the customer base is varied, most buyers want 15 to 20 orchid seedlings at a time, sold in special flasks. Almost every country and region has an orchid society, so the hobbyists pass information along, often by e-mail, and business at Blue

Pagoda expands as satisfied customers talk (frequently online) about their purchases. Recently, Larry Evans wrote an article for the *American Orchid Society* magazine. "We got excellent results from both that article and a local newspaper's write-up."

In addition to promoting word-of-mouth patronage, it pays to keep the business name in the news. Larry Evans also writes a monthly feature on the Blue Pagoda Web page, an editorial offering advice on planting and raising flowers and sometimes illustrated by "amusing stories culled from over 40 years of experience." A special benefit for site visitors is insider information on what can help or hurt the delicate and fragile orchid seedlings at various stages of growth.

COMPETITION CAN BE HEALTHY

Unlike some businesses, where the customer dollars are finite and limited, garden supplies offers multiple opportunities for companies to thrive. In a sense, the competition can actually drive up orders, creating the need for specialty items such as seeds, fertilizers, tools, and—in the case of Blue Pagoda—neem oil, a staple for orchid growers. As Marylou says, "The competition is out there, but we don't really bump into them. No problems."

To expand the business, the Evanses also added a recommended booklist on their site, one tied to the publishing supersite Amazon.com. The books on their list are favorites of the Evanses, not just a packaged list of Amazon.com titles. In fact, says Marylou, "We picked out the ones from their inventory that we found to be good books." The Amazon link allows customers to go directly from the Blue Pagoda Web page to Amazon.com, where each purchase returns a small profit to Marylou and Larry's business. The Amazon link is not only another profit center but

also a useful two-way path for customers—just part of the sophisticated e-world that drives the corporate business world while
nurturing small ventures like Blue Pagoda Orchids.

Web address:
   www.bporchids.com

Resource:
   www.orchidweb.org (American Orchid Society)

Landscaping

Start-up expenses: $3,400

Special requirements: *A knowledge of landscape design*

Best advice: *"There are a lot of people out there making unrealistic promises about how easy it is to build a Web site and make money. It takes a great deal of work and time to build a business, even an e-business. A good Web site is not difficult to put up, but building the traffic and running a retail business—then taking care of your customers—presents the same problems as found in an offline business."*

On his Web site, Tim Fahndrich, president of Landscape-USA.com, lists four of his favorite activities. Number one is "Mowing the lawn." Strange? Curious? Unbelievable? Apparently not. Number two is "Pulling weeds."

Tim and Daniel, father and son, are the owners and operators of this Web-based landscaping business. They appreciate plants and trees and the people who plant them, agreeing that "people who find enjoyment in working the dirt with their hands are also some of the friendliest people around." At the LandscapeUSA site, you can find valuable advice about planting and insights about different types of soils.

The Fahndriches, who boast 30 years of combined experience, come to the business with impressive credentials. Tim is a past president of the Oregon Landscape Contractors Association of Salem, and he has three years of experience as a representative for the Landscape Contractors state board. Daniel is a certified Master Gardener, licensed by Oregon State University, and past chair of the Landscape Contractors Board of Oregon, a position appointed by the governor. In short, the Fahndriches know the landscaping business. In addition to their online enterprise, they have a brick-and-mortar landscape design and installation company. Many of the ideas that they promote on the Net are ones they encounter in their daily projects around the Salem region.

The Fahndriches employ licensed landscape contractors, irrigation specialists, garden designers, master gardeners, and landscape designers. These employees are available to answer questions posted at the online store. In addition, the LandscapeUSA site features online tutorial courses, technical help, weekly tips, and other advantages, including landscaping products and personalized shopping.

AN ONLINE STORE
BRINGS IN THE GREEN

As their onsite literature explains, the Fahndriches were first online with a full selection of professional-quality irrigation supplies and landscape lighting, complete with photos, diagrams, and descriptions. Of particular interest is the vast line of products not usually available in garden stores and Grange greenhouses. Among other things, the online store sells arbors, greenhouses, bird feeders, low-voltage lighting, irrigation materials, deer repellents, bulbs, and seeds.

In the Tips and Features section, browsers find lawn and garden tips to help you battle sprinkler systems, lawn seeding, evergreen plantings, and so on. The company even posts case studies so that prospective buyers can study completed projects for ideas and inspiration. If you don't know whether deodora cedar will grow in your garden zone, LandscapeUSA.com tells you.

If you wonder about planting magnolias in Yukon Territory, the Fahndriches have an answer. No.

Furthermore, the site offers book reviews, where interested gardeners can use a link to Amazon.com and buy books. For others, there are chat rooms and an online forum for landscapers and gardeners. Want a list of upcoming Green events in your area? Log on to LandscapeUSA.com and get a calendar of gardening events. There's even a Find a Contractor search page, where companies and professionals are cross-referenced by city and state.

TARGET AUDIENCE: THE AVID GARDENER

It's not the occasional gardeners whom the Fahndriches want to attract but the dedicated ones. Says Tim, "They are people who are not afraid to pay a little more for high-quality products." To reach these customers, the company teamed with LinkShare, a leading affiliates network. Now the firm has more than 9,000 affiliates, the largest in the gardening industry. "Word of mouth is also important to our business," says the elder Fahndrich, "and, of course, we are listed in the search engines. That's a given."

The affiliate system had been a strong marketing tool, helping to promote the LandscapeUSA site. Affiliate locations include national ISPs, landscaping and garden sites, financial sites, building industry sites, online shopping malls, search engines, and so on. Says Tim Fahndrich, "Our affiliate program a win–win deal!"

DEALING WITH PROBLEMS

As for problems, Tim recalls that launching the site was more demanding than he expected. The site has excellent content, with a combination of tutorials penned by the owners and others contributed by suppliers. The National Gardener Association provides the tips that appear online. Because the elder Fahndrich had some technical expertise, he initiated the site himself but, in retrospect, wishes he'd brought even more technical experience to the project. Today, with the increased demands for Web maintenance, the company outsources more and more of its Web work.

COMPETITION IS LURKING

The competition is not dormant. The gardening industry is well established in America. Some of the seed and plant companies have been operating mail order businesses for a hundred years or more. Also, other gardeners are getting into the online mainstream at an even keel. In a crowded and growing field, a company like LandscapeUSA needs an edge. As Tim Fahndrich says, "We compete with quality." Some sites, he argues, have more products, but they don't cater specifically to avid gardeners. Another edge is the heavy concentration on content. The tutorials and online advice give buyers both information and confidence. What comes next? A shopping cart full of fertilizers, seeds, plants, tools, and booklets.

When the dark days of winter begin to lengthen, serious gardeners everywhere begin to survey their vegetable plots, sharpen their hedge trimmers, and prune their roses. But a fair number of them are preparing for spring in yet another way. They're logging on to LandscapeUSA.com for advice, for inspiration, or for a chat about begonias. Are you curious about Tim's number three and four favorite activities? Composting? Aphid eradication? Taming the ivy? There's only one way to see if your guesses are correct. The address is LandscapeUSA.com.

Web address:
  www.LandscapeUSA.com

Seed Supplier

Start-up expenses: $400
Special requirements: *Gardening expertise*
Best advice: *"Do a lot of reading. Research and learn as much as you can about whatever business interests you. The Web is a fabulous resource. Take it slow. Jump in now—absolutely—but go into your venture with your eyes wide open. I test new ideas one at a time. It's just a matter of common sense."*

The largest growing segment of the American population is the over-50 crowd. The kids are grown and living on their own, and life's pace has slowed. With so much time on their hands, many of the baby boomers enjoy simple, at-home chores, such as planting tomatoes, fertilizing the roses, or drying flower bulbs.

The interest in gardening is natural. The aging population of baby boomers has a penchant for working the soil. Older folks like to garden and have an enthusiasm for seeds and plants.

Parents get their kids involved, as well as their extended families and even their neighbors. Community gardens are popping up all over the land.

In the doldrums of winter, people throughout the country eagerly await the first signs of spring, dreaming about planting vegetables patches, tending herb gardens, and weeding flower pots. Well, friends, dreaming won't create a garden. You'll need bulbs, fertilizer, and seeds. Luckily, you don't have to plow out the driveway and head to the feed store. Just pull your chair up to the computer and start thinking about lettuce, zucchini, and chives. The next part is easy. You can order everything online.

Virtual Seeds Company is one outlet. Based in the mountains of Southern Oregon, the company communicates with the world through the Web, offering seeds from a variety of dealers and growers. Their virtual catalog lists more than 3,500 seed varieties. Virtual Seeds specializes in hard-to-find herb and vegetable seeds, mostly for the individual gardener. But they also ship in bulk to commercial growers.

Joyce Moore began her online business with a small initial investment and an interest in growing plants. One day, while taking a break from her own garden, she surfed the Net and found that a major seed supplier in the South was looking for distributors. Moore liked the commission rate and said to herself, "That sounds like fun." It was. Once she got a taste of the future with an online business, she began to think about a Web site.

Having retired as a paramedic, Moore created her own site in 1996. It took about a week to build the virtualseeds.com site. After making (and correcting) her share of design errors, the project went online. Moore's site is clear and easy to navigate, more informative than flashy—not unlike the simple design of her seed packages. Although the project began as a part-time endeavor, one that would bring in a few extra dollars and offer some challenges, Moore's business immediately bloomed. "It's a full-time business now," says Moore, "and I love it."

Yes, the huge seed companies like Burpee are online. But they deal in volume, meaning that the corporate distributors cannot afford to dabble in exotic plants or unusual edibles. Burpee and their major competitors market popular, well-known seed varieties. Moore's company, on the other hand, takes a different approach. "When you call to talk to Virtual Seeds," says Moore, "I'm the only one here."

IS THAT A CARROT I SEE GROWING?

Normally, browsers find virtualseeds.com through search engines, although word-of-mouth advertising is also taking effect. At first, Moore posted with the search companies herself, but the task became burdensome. Now she subscribes to a service that charges $10 for 100 engines and resubmits everything each month. This is where timing is key. Because it takes four to six weeks for the search engines to process an application into their databases and files, Moore recommends getting the information to search engines in October, so the search engines can have final postings available in January, when people start to think about spring orders.

To entice customers, Moore offers free information on her Web pages. She displays a gardening newsletter and various catalogs of information about seed growth and selection. She is available to answer questions about soils, growing zones, and plant varieties. With her secured shopping cart feature, customers can move around the site and shop for zinnia or carrot seeds in one location and move to another spot to buy.

A recent addition is Heirloom Edibles, a personal passion for Moore. An heirloom seed comes from a nonhybrid vegetable, one that is open pollinated. Heirloom vegetables are ones that have been in existence for at least 50 to 100 years. They are traditional breeds such as Brandywine tomatoes, popular in America since the 1800s.

TOMATOES AND MORE TOMATOES

Moore distributes tomatoes in a rainbow of colors, including white, green, and red. She also has exotic roses and rare potatoes. "It's a challenge," she says, suggesting that part of her job is to convince people to try new vegetable strains that might surprise the taste buds.

Tomatoes, for example, needn't be big, round, and red. Moore, who has tried exotic varieties in her own gardens, recommends several new and old tomato breeds, including Evergreen tomatoes, a favorite. "People love them once they try new kinds," she says. After a while, word of mouth takes over, and she starts new orders for choices such as the Evergreen. In this sense, Moore sees her company involved in educating people about vegetables, seeds, plants, and hybrids—especially about the older varieties of edible plants. For example, one man called asking about a white tomato grown by his grandmother in Kansas. After some research, Moore found the strain in her database. Now she recommends the white tomato to others who want to try an unusual (but delicious) veggie.

NOT ECONOMICAL, BUT TRUSTWORTHY

At virtualseeds.com Moore finds that quality control pays off. She sells seeds only from certified collectors or growers and carefully follows all federal and state laws involving seeds and plants. To guarantee safe delivery, she also packages the products in airtight, waterproof, reclosable plastic Zip-loc pouches. "This plan is not economical," she admits, "but it ensures an extremely high rate of success." The satisfaction expressed by customers makes the extra packaging expense seem like a bargain to Moore.

Like the Web site, Moore's mailings aren't fancy. The labels are matter-of-fact, and they feature no pictures. As Moore says, "We figure they'll be seeing the real thing soon enough!" Instead, each label displays the plant's common and botanical name, the proper planting depth, the right soil types, the height of the mature plant, the amount of water needed, the amount of sunlight required, the designation of annual or perennial, the average germination period, whether the plant can be raised indoors, and other special requirements.

Moore loves what she does. When the weather is nice, she's outside with her hands in the soil. In stormy weather or when Mother Nature spreads her icy hand across the ground, she has orders to fill from her Web site. Like so many enterprising e-commerce owners, Moore turned a hobby into a business. And, like the sprouts that are budding up everywhere in the yard, business is blooming.

Web address:
  www.virtualseeds.com

Gifts

Cakes for College Students

Start-up expenses: $1,500

Special requirements: *Working relationship with a local bakery*

Best advice: *"Plan everything. Think everything through from the beginning. You are going to overlook a lot of things from beginning to end. It is one big process loop, and you can't leave anything out. So lay out the plan and do a significant amount of research. Then execute it the best way you can—so that it fits your schedule. For me, it was looking for a business that I could run with a somewhat limited time schedule. Already I'm finding the business is demanding a lot more time as it grows."*

It's finals week. Your overachieving daughter has been studying hard for college tests in calculus, world history, French, and Renaissance poetry. How would you like to lift her spirits along with her glucose levels? Log on to CampusCakes.com, and order a wonderful German chocolate triple-layer creation to be delivered the night before finals commence. Now that's convenience!

The idea for Campus Cakes started back in the spring of 1993, when Tom McGinley was a junior at Loyola University in Baltimore. In his business management class, the professor asked everyone to create a fictitious company and build a business plan. At the time, McGinley was a fund-raiser for his crew team, so he wanted to put together a service for the college community that would also benefit the rowing squads.

STARTING A TREND

The plan for his cake business was to market birthday cakes and occasional presents to the parents of students. Until his senior year, McGinley's plan existed only on paper. Then he realized he needed more money; a trip to the Jersey shore during summer break had put a serious dent in his finances. "Unfortunately," he says, "I didn't save a lot of money for the fall term."

"I decided to make my business plan a reality," he says, "and I spent $600 for a mass mailing to all the parents of Loyola freshmen, a letter offering Halloween packages and birthday cakes. I was doing it by mail order with an 800 number. I got a good response rate from that first mailing." The crew team delivered the cakes and helped assemble the packages, so McGinley's efforts were cost-effective. After that experience, he decided to launch a business.

After distributing some of the profits with the crew teams, McGinley expanded to Johns Hopkins University and other Baltimore-area colleges and universities. He made an arrangement with a local family bakery to provide cakes. At first, the family members were skeptical, doubting that McGinley could really generate more business. "But as the orders picked up," he

says, "they began to love me." McGinley proved a valuable customer. In retrospect, McGinley says, "It was a win–win situation
for school, the team, the bakery, the parents, and for me."

NEW YORK, HERE I COME

Despite the money, McGinley closed shop until October 1999,
when he moved to New York for graduate school.

At Fordham University, McGinley considered reviving his
business as an e-commerce venture. He was working as an insti-
tutional banker during the day to pay expenses. Although he
doubted he had the time for a business, the small demands of
e-commerce allowed McGinley to launch a site where he could
sell his cakes. Finding a new supplier, a woman in New York
who had special skills in cake baking, McGinley turned to
the construction of a Web site, using Microsoft *Frontpage*.
"Fortunately," he says, "the business has been well received."

A DELICIOUS YAHOO! STORY

Like so many, McGinley counts on Yahoo! for customers. "I was
lucky enough to get a good listing in Yahoo!" he says. "If you
look under a couple of key words that are birthday related, my
site is second or third." Even though McGinley has eschewed
banner ads and mailing lists, his Yahoo! placement continues to
bring customers and profits.

Although the company is called CampusCakes.com,
browsers beyond the university system are clicking on to
McGinley's site. In addition to parents and students, elderly relatives, people in senior care centers, and folks in the military
are frequent buyers. Even overseas buyers are entering the site,

ordering cakes primarily for American relatives, not necessarily students. Fulfillment has been fun. It's the icing on the cake.

WITHOUT A BAKER, THERE'S NO BUSINESS

The local baker likes to bury her hands in flour and sugar, but she has no interest in marketing. She just doesn't want to deal with it, says McGinley. "That's what a Web site does," he offers. The baker has a busy retail store and is quite content with business. She has been asked by previous customers to send cakes to friends and relatives. But she says no. McGinley has filled the void, providing a private mailing label for customers. He says, "I pay wholesale prices and give her so many orders a week." Everyone is happy.

SHIPPING EVERYWHERE

The company has a reliable system for shipping through United Parcel Service. The cakes are packaged in an insulated box with Styrofoam that is molded for the cakes. McGinley knows the packaging works because he often sends himself a cake when he's traveling. No problemo! "I've gone to customers to make sure the cakes arrive in good shape," he adds. "That was one of my original concerns."

Previously McGinley had packaged the cakes himself, not always successfully. With the UPS Web site, McGinley tracks his cakes. After they're shipped, McGinley gathers the tracking number so that he can go to the site and find the dessert's exact location.

A PART-TIME PROPOSITION

Still in school—and working as well—McGinley truly has only part of each day for the demands of CampusCakes.com. He's aware that the business needs more dedication. "It is one thing to learn about e-commerce at school," he says, "but it's another to dive in and actually do it." His school training in information technology and marketing has helped. For one thing, the university classes stress the importance of customer service. As a result, McGinley has planned the business so that customers can reach him readily through e-mail queries. He checks his e-mail several times a day, promising to respond promptly.

McGinley even takes e-mail messages at work, forwarded from his site, so he fields urgent notices quickly. "But most e-mails are not urgent," he says, "and a lot of my business can happen in the evenings when I don't have classes."

Orders arrive online. The shopping cart software makes the orders completely automated. "And that is critical," says McGinley. "I have a database, and every night I fax a list of orders to the bakery. They process those orders." After they send the cakes (on a daily basis), they fax the tracking numbers to McGinley. It's easy. "It took a little while getting set up," he admits, "but once it was in place, the system ran smoothly."

HIS SHOPPING CART NEEDED ALIGNMENT

The biggest problem for McGinley's cake company has been the shopping cart software. "For some reason, I thought it would be a lot easier to incorporate a shopping cart into my site with *Frontpage*," says the owner. McGinley went online looking for shopping cart software that could work with *Frontpage*, and he found *CardIt*. It had a *Frontpage* add-on, so it seemed the perfect program, especially since *CardIt* cost only a few hundred dollars, with technical support included. Says McGinley ruefully, "I thought it would be easy to set up, but the system actually took a lot of HTML programming."

After many nights on the phone—more than a week's worth—trying to get help setting up the customized orders and credit card priorities, McGinley finally got his shopping cart problems worked out. He wrestled with a number of complicated variables, such as the kind of cake, the time of delivery, the message on the card, the message on the greeting card, and so forth.

Finally, the shopping cart settled down to run on all four wheels, and McGinley says that the tech support at *CardIt* was indeed helpful.

Web address:

  www.CampusCakes.com

Creative Gift Baskets

Start-up expenses: $700
Special requirements: *Photo scanner*
Best advice: *"You have to find what the market will bear in your niche area. So I try to keep my baskets affordable, and I offer a wide selection. I do a lot of custom work, and I don't charge exorbitant fees for it because I'm always out shopping anyway."*

Sometimes a business comes looking for you, and you have no choice but to comply. That happened to Yonnie Moncrief, owner of Yonnie's Signature Baskets. For years, Moncrief had been making gift baskets for friends and family. One day, Moncrief took a sample to work and placed it on her desk. By the end of the day, she had 60 orders in her pocket. As she says modestly, "Yonnie's Signature Baskets was born."

ALL IN THE FAMILY

Yonnie's Gift Baskets is a family business. As she says on her Web site at basketsbyyonnie.bigstep.com, "Chris has a flair for color and arrangements, Will runs the office, and Joseph handles local deliveries and shipping." But it's Yonnie who adds the personal touch, hand picking the gourmet treats and clever items that she knows customers enjoy again and again. The Moncrief family has made a lot of gift baskets—and a lot of friends.

FANNING A CREATIVE EMBER

"I always wanted to do something after retirement," says Moncrief, a long-time employee of the U.S. Post Office. In planning for her retirement, Moncrief devoted time to finding a business she could do on the side until she was able to retire. When the fateful day finally appeared, she reasoned, it wouldn't do to sit around or—even worse—toil for someone else. "I wanted to do something relaxing and creative," she says. After a long stint at the post office, Moncrief certainly deserved a retirement project that was refreshing, engaging, and fascinating.

After reading about this cottage industry in a magazine called *Extra Income*, Moncrief decided to market gift baskets. "I liked that you really didn't need much money to get started," she says. "So I decided to give it a try. I didn't know how creative I could be." After a career with the post office and a lifetime of raising children, Moncrief felt any creativity had fled long ago. "But," she says, "I was artsy when I was young. You get away from your hobbies when you have a family. So I took a craft class to see if I would enjoy such projects again." Moncrief found a creative ember burning low and fanned it into full flame. In no time at all, she was stocking sample gift baskets for the holidays. They were well received by friends and family. This feedback was enough to tempt her into business, where BigStep.com was waiting to help.

A "BIG STEP" FOR A SMALL BUSINESS

Since she wanted a home-based business, Moncrief thought about the Net. She came across BigStep.com in a "Tech Life" column in the *Philadelphia Inquirer*. It's paid off. "I had been looking on the Net at different ISPs and designers," says Moncrief, "but I never dreamed I could design it myself. I didn't have a clue." But with easy-to-follow instructions, Moncrief downloaded the BigStep programs and built her own site. Because BigStep.com is geared toward small businesses and not encumbered with massive site-building projects, they helped Moncrief launch her site much more quickly than she imagined.

Even though Moncrief someday hopes to own a shop, she recognizes that her best prospects lie on the Web. Since she's still employed at the post office, her Web site work begins after normal working hours. Nonetheless, the site is taking an increasing chunk of her time—for bookkeeping, inventory control, purchasing, and other tasks. Luckily, the Web site's technology does much of the heavy lifting.

PICTURES PAINT A PICTURE

Photographs lie at the heart of Moncrief's business. As the different holidays approach, she prepares baskets for the camera. She shoots and scans 35-mm photos and places them on the site. It hasn't been easy, she admits. "The biggest problem with the photos is learning to go with a lighter background." She also says that she's struggling with adjusting the image resolution so that the files remain small, allowing people to load the images quickly. "I have managed to reduce the sizes a bit," she says with resignation, "but I'm not an expert yet."

COST FACTORS

The Web presence has allowed Moncrief to reduce expenses in unexpected ways. For instance, when she first began her business, she bought supplies at retail prices, mainly because her purchases were so limited. On the Net, Moncrief can locate wholesale suppliers with dramatically lower prices. "The Web *really* helped me to locate suppliers for my baskets," she says. No longer saddled with shopping locally for gift items and decorating supplies, Moncrief expanded and improved her basket lines while significantly cutting costs.

In addition to hosting her Web site, BigStep helps Moncrief tackle the search engines. She submits her site through BigStep.com, and much of her business arrives through the keyword searches. Moncrief also prints business cards with her URL, and her basket labels also sport the Web address. With the addition of flyers and ads in the "Online" section of the local paper, Moncrief enjoys broad exposure. Even though most of her customers live within driving distance, out-of-state customers increasingly pop up online. Most are women buying for family members. Festivals and holidays are also productive, and celebrations like Secretary's Day and Mother's Day keep the Moncrief family especially busy.

PAID TO SHOP

Yes, there's competition on the horizon. Even entering the gift basket business, Moncrief knew there was standing room only. Competition comes from local florist shops and even food stores. Moncrief uses every shopping trip as research. She keeps an eye open for creative basket ideas and new trends. In her wanderings, she looks into shops to see what people are buying. Usually when an inspiration strikes, it takes only a day or two to find the requisite gift items and crafts pieces. The baskets are always changing, and the possibilities are endless. Recently, says Moncrief, she made a Valentine's basket for a man whose wife craved Snickers. Using a heart-shaped wire frame, Moncrief built a collage of candy bars, helping her customer win his wife's heart on Cupid's special day.

Web address:
   www.basketsbyyonnie.bigstep.com

Flowers

Start-up expenses: *$3,500*
Special requirements: *None*
Best advice: *"You can expect eighty-hour weeks, working from daybreak to moonrise, and there's always more to do. If you miss a day or two each week, it's like missing a month offline. Entering the world of e-commerce is like entering a time warp."*

Admit it. You have no idea what flowers were in that $65 floral arrangement that you sent to Aunt Alice on her 80th birthday—or if the blossoms were fresh, wilted, or ready for the compost pile. Let's just hope that the arrangement arrived in better shape than the Mother's Day tulips you received from your son in San Diego.

For years, FTD florists and similar businesses flourished, especially at holiday time, as Americans sought a last-minute all-purpose can't-miss gift for Grandma, Sweet Sue, or Little Nell. Today, the passion for flora has shifted to the Net, where flowers are among the top five products purchased online. Even as you read this, hundreds—perhaps thousands—of people are clicking on to Web sites in search of roses, Stargazer lilies, daffodils, orchids, forget-me-nots, and carnations.

The problem with places like 1-800-Flowers or BudsRUs.com is quality control. Will your purchase be beautiful, fresh, and fragrant when it arrives? Will the selection feature high-quality buds and greens from healthy stock, freshly cut and gorgeously arranged? Will you receive value for your dollar? Unless the package is going only across the street or across town, you can't be sure.

THE SYSTEM MALFUNCTIONED

One man who was disappointed with the quality and service of floral delivery companies is Jared Shutz, chairman and co-founder of ProFlowers.com. Shutz launched his online company in February 1998 after recognizing an unfilled niche. Shutz recalls, "I've been an occasional user of flowers, and it always startled me how much it cost, usually $70 or $80 to send a dozen roses to another city. At the supermarket they didn't cost that much, so that didn't seem fair. And the product delivered was never really good. You never knew what arrangement was going to show up. I saw that the system was broken. And I saw the Internet as an opportunity to cut out the middlemen and give the consumer a better price and a fresher product." And so he seized the opportunity.

With no experience in either flowers or technology, Shutz began his research. He met with growers and retailers, learning a lot about the industry in the space of a few weeks. Shutz decided to forego the usual business plan for flower delivery companies. Instead of using a network of local florists in various cities and towns to deliver arrangements in Denver, Topeka, or Mobile, Shutz organized his company on a different principle: centralized distribution. The folks at ProFlowers.com send the flowers from their home base, getting the packages onto delivery trucks within 24 hours of picking.

The biggest problem in the industry is the delicate and perishable nature of flowers. Bad things happen when shipments are delayed, jostled, warehoused, or frozen. Intense weather conditions create the greatest number of problems, but there are scores of other ways to ruin an orchid arrangement. Shutz decided that, rather than entrust these responsibilities to people he did not know—to people he had never met—he would fully participate in selection, packaging, shipping, and tracking. In centralizing the process, ProFlowers.com became a direct distributor, shortcutting the middlemen and lowering the total costs in the process.

Federal Express picks up the floral packages from the growers. To ensure quick and accurate processing, the automated ProFlowers.com software system provides direct links to both the growers and Federal Express. For added security, ProFlowers provides specially constructed shipping boxes, ones that make it difficult for handlers to crush the products. Nevertheless, ProFlowers.com expects a certain number of glitches, something to be expected with a delicate product. Consequently, the company guarantees all shipments. The ProFlowers guarantee is "a 100 percent no-questions-asked replacement policy," according to Shutz, smart thinking especially in the event of snow, sleet, wind, hail, tornadoes, floods, locusts, or any other kind of human error or disaster that can spoil a flower shipment.

A BLOSSOMING AFFILIATE
PROGRAM

Each week, Shutz's customer services staff surveys their customers to see if they are happy with their bouquets. Most are, probably because the ProFlowers.com selections are always fresh, lasting from five to ten days longer than normal floral arrangements. Also, they cost less. Shutz estimates that customers save from 30 to 40 percent on the average bouquet—an advantage wrought from eliminating middlemen. All told, satisfaction is high for customers of ProFlowers.com. Bizrate.com, the independent agency that tracks competition in each e-commerce industry, rates ProFlowers.com as the top floral site for customer service.

An integral aspect of the site's customer service is its 24-hour phone support on weekdays, and 9 A.M. to 5 P.M. PST operation on weekends. The company also offers full-time support through e-mail and a customer chat room weekdays from 7:30 A.M. to 3 P.M. PST.

But perhaps the greatest business advantage comes from ProFlowers.com's affiliate program, with close to 100,000 member sites linked. Shutz pays a commission to each affiliate whenever a customer places an order from a linked site. "That's where the bulk of our customers come from," says Shutz. "But we also advertise and buy banner ads on many sites." Shutz purchases lots of banner ads, unlike many in e-business, but measures their success carefully, calculating the exact cost per order based on the different banner sites. "We carefully watch them," he says, "and we scale up the effective ones while discontinuing the rest."

AN ORDER OF DAISIES
FOR MR. SPOCK

Everything on the Net happens at several times the speed of the rest of the economy. Shutz warns that Internet commerce is not easier than brick-and-mortar ventures, only different. He says you can expect 80-hour weeks, working from daybreak to moonrise, and there's always more to do. "If you miss a day or two each week, it's like missing a month offline," he explains. "Entering the world of e-commerce is like entering a time warp."

Without a doubt, the Internet has created a number of new businesses and business opportunities. A venture like ProFlowers.com is one such example. The Net presents a new and innovative way to buy flowers, one that couldn't exist previous to the advent of commercial cyberspace. Before the new computer age, the average customer could deal with only established flower distributors; calling a grower wasn't even an option. Today, with all the rules aside, people like Jared Shutz at ProFlowers.com can bring additional value to consumers, using a business model that is as new as the Net.

Web address:
   www.ProFlowers.com

Guy Stuff

Start-up expenses: $100
Special requirements: *None*
Best advice: *"The Net is the great equalizer. Just take a really good idea that you are passionate about, something you love to do (this business is a natural extension of my hobbies). Then take that excitement and build a business around it."*

Oh, yeah. Way beyond cool. This is the place. You can have your book clubs, symphony tickets, and museum tours. Forget about cutesy Web pages, self-help domains, and antique-gift sites. This Net address is for guys who like overstuffed chairs, potato chips, and long-neck brews. As John Riley says, "My niche market is the TV-watching, sports-viewing, beer-drinking guys (and the women who love them)."

It had to happen. Somebody built a Web site for the beer-drinking generation. John Riley is the guilty party, but he's loving it. And why not? He found a vacant untapped market and turned it into a high-income second job. "That's the beautiful thing about e-commerce," he raves. "It's there in your in-box waiting. When you get home from work, there are orders waiting to be filled!"

The idea for UltimateGuy.com came from Riley's wish for a few extra bucks. He calls it "beer money." Riley's site has exceeded all his expectations.

THE FULL MONTY

Here's the scoop. Riley was surfing the Net looking for creative ideas for a second income. On one site he saw a display of television remotes, ones that imitated *Star Wars* light sabers, football fields, and other "guy" themes. Riley thought, "Wouldn't it be great to pick a niche like that and dominate it? I believe dominating a niche is the correct e-business strategy. You pick something narrow and become the King of it." He did.

Riley started collecting remotes and, from that idea, began adding other products that qualified as guy stuff. "It seemed like the trendy thing to do," he says. Apparently, however, no one else had noticed the trend. Riley was shocked to find the domain name available. But he sent in his money ($70) and started working on a site. The first stop was Yahoo! Shopping Mall, where the technicians provided "some very nice and easy utilities for Web site building and tutorials on e-commerce." In short order, the Yahoo!Store package gave Riley the tools and information to create a successful commercial address.

From that point, Riley engineered a Web site, drawing on advice from his buddies. "It was such a great concept to talk about," he recalls. "We were all ultimate guys—shooting pool, drinking beer, going fishing. So it was easy to communicate the concept to the others." With this ease of information sharing,

Riley and group walked away from generic products—things that everybody sells—thinking instead of guy stuff that was "totally fun."

Riley's first goals were to learn e-commerce and earn extra money. But he also thought about quitting his day job to spend time at home with his three-year-old daughter. While such an arrangement is not yet possible for Riley, work-at-home schedules loom on the horizon.

A QUICK ENTRY, FAST RESULTS

In November 1999, Riley started his online efforts. In an amazingly short period of time, the site has evolved rapidly. "The hardest thing to do," recalls Riley, "is to take that first step and then, when you start walking toward a goal, things start rolling."

In the beginning, Riley sent press releases that received coverage in local papers. A local TV journalist soon picked up the story and featured UltimateGuy.com on a news spot. From there, potential vendors started calling, suggesting new ideas for the site. As Riley says, "Most are companies I would have never found on my own." From these roots came the current Ultimate Guy site, where Riley now carries such products as Aloha shirts, barbecue grills, and other outrageous toys for men. "Anything for the ultimate guy," says Riley.

Promoting his site caused Riley some sleepless nights. The media was cooperative and helpful, including a recent article in the *Milwaukee Journal-Sentinel*, the local paper for a town that Riley calls Ultimate Guy USA. Quickly he received lots of responses. But keeping the publicity levels active is the problem. As he says, "The article is great, but a day later it's gone, and I need to look for a sustained type of promotional activity."

THE VENDOR SEARCH

One great advantage for Riley is drop-shipping. Because his vendors have been wholesalers—people who are comfortable with the drop-ship concept—Riley depends on his distributors and avoids keeping inventory. "It dramatically minimizes my downside risk," he says. But he laments the loss of control at the same time, including contacts with buyers and customers. "My objective is to have good customer service," he says, "and I keep good contact with them so they know their orders didn't go into a black hole." Riley tries to keep customers informed "every step of the way," but that's possible only if he receives feedback from the vendors.

If the vendors don't respond, Riley finds himself unable to perform customer service. "That happened a few times during the holiday season because the vendors themselves were so overwhelmed," he says. "It wasn't a big problem, but there were a couple of situations where the vendors weren't as good as needed." Riley is glad to say that distribution glitches have been the exception rather than the rule and that, for the most part, his vendors have been responsible about feedback.

A SURPRISE IN THE DEMOGRAPHICS

Not all the customers at UltimateGuy.com are ultimate guys. Despite his assumptions that men in their twenties and thirties would be the main clientele, a full two-thirds of buyers are women buying gifts for men. "I never thought about women buyers," says Riley, "but in retrospect, it is obvious. A lot of female friends came over and said that the site is great, especially if you've only been in the dating game for six weeks or so. In that situation, you don't want to get him a serious gift. You want it to be fun." Well, the UltimateGuy.com site is the place to go for fun.

Beware, kids and women! Riley has you well targeted. He now owns UltimateKid.com and UltimateChick.com domain names, hoping to find products for these other special niches and repeat the successes of UltimateGuy.com. Says Riley, "I hope to build these sites with the same ideas, keeping a similar attitude." Admittedly, Riley is out in his own world. There are few competing sites, none with the same attitude and product lines. In fact, there are other gender-based sites, but the only one with any similarity, says Riley, is chickclick.com.

Riley believes his site is successful because he offers unusual products for guys who are truly focused. If life for the ultimate guy is really just a litany of beer, sports, and parties, then there's a place on the Net called Home.

Web address:
www.UltimateGuy.com

Refrigerator Magnets

Start-up expenses: $20,000

Special requirements: *None*

Best advice: *"Go narrow. Narrowly focused audiences typically aren't being served yet. Look for a market without a market leader, yet where you have something to add. You need to have your own interest in that market to come up with something appealing. Some people analyze business opportunities to death. At some point, you've just got to do it! That's the only way to find out if your idea is going to work."*

J*ust do it!* The long-standing Nike slogan has found its way into the thinking of many e-commerce adventurers. Chris Gwynn certainly agrees. He took one of the least likely business opportunities in the world—refrigerator magnets—and turned the idea into an online success. If he stopped to ask venture capitalists or Fortune 500 CEOs about the chances for success with refrigerator magnets, they would have undoubtedly said, "It just won't stick." Gwynn's profit sheets, however, tell another story.

Gwynn sells a wild and wacky variety of those do-dads that decorate appliances all over the world. We're talking about magnets featuring Monty Python, the Beverly Hillbillies, Elvis, the Beatles, and . . . well, you'll just have to take a look. So click on to fridgedoor.com and check out the zany possibilities. You can delight, educate, or shock family and friends, not to mention the occasional nosy kitchen guest.

SMALL MARKET, BIG PROFITS

When Gwynn says that he was looking for a narrow market, he's not kidding. The magnet business runs about $150 million a year. On the Net, Gwynn finds only a few other sites that sell magnets, and these companies feature no more than 200 items. Nevertheless, people seem to want these oddball decorations, and fridgedoor.com has them. As Gwynn suggests, it's best not to think too long about a strange idea like refrigerator decorations. Logic isn't going to help.

"I came from a background on the Internet," says Gwynn, who began in 1994 at a time when the notion of Web sites was still emerging. Although he worked in marketing, Gwynn had endured five layoffs, not a surprise in the high-tech world where change is the only constant. Even with the turbulent times, Gwynn gained valuable experience, and he knew there must be an idea out there with his name on it. Well, not exactly. The names on the idea were the Brady Bunch, Bon Jovi, and Snoopy. But at least Gwynn found a niche that was wide open and waiting.

Initially, Gwynn was looking for a side income to supplement his job as an industry analyst covering e-commerce for the

Andrews Group and to cushion those inevitable layoff periods. In short, he was looking to survive. But soon the magnet business became much bigger, a real opportunity. Eventually, Gwynn quit his day job and went permanently online.

WHAT TO MARKET

The first decision was what to sell. He realized that books and CDs, although perfect choices, represented a hugely over-crowded market, one that was long since closed to new players. Instead, he started thinking about an unknown market, one that nobody had really investigated. "I chose magnets as my product because they could be easily displayed," he recalls. "Customers can look at pictures of magnets and make their decisions."

Needless to say, refrigerator magnets are a low-tech item. Nobody really has to touch a magnet before buying or examine the quality of the workmanship. Magnets cost little to produce, and they're easy to ship. Furthermore, it's not easy to find refrigerator magnets at the mall or down the street. They're not standard fare at big-name department or grocery stores, at least not in the variety most buyers want. After all, a refrigerator magnet is more than a tool for securing a grocery list. It's a statement.

The usual outlets for magnets are specialty shops. Yet it's difficult to find magnets that appeal to people's widely diverse sensibilities, self-images, and senses of humor. That one magnet says "Bubba's Pizza" just doesn't do the job for everyone out there. For Gwynn the idea came to him one day when he was (what else?) staring at his refrigerator, contemplating a sandwich. He realized that his fridge was covered with magnets. Now there, he thought, is a niche business. After spending a summer investigating magnet designs, Gwynn launched his site for fall distribution, displaying 800 items, soon to become 1,500, far more than the closest competitor.

Gwynn finds that his buyers are between the ages of 25 and 54. In this category are two distinct groups. First are those who want to buy gifts. They are people looking for "interesting, fun gifts for lesser occasions." Some choose magnets to celebrate new jobs or as stocking stuffers at Christmas. The second group includes collectors, people who know the brands and producers. The collectors want both new products and established classics.

Before assessing the demographics, Gwynn assumed most of his customers would be women looking for gifts. In reality, half his clientele are men. He also believes that his lines must continue to feature depth (for the collectors) and innovation (for the gift givers). All things considered, refrigerator magnets looks like a growth industry.

EVERYBODY YAHOO!

To get online, Gwynn selected the Yahoo!Store program for Web design. "It's pretty easy to build with that software," he says. "I am not a technical person, but I learned what I needed along the way." Admittedly, fridgedoor.com is not a sophisticated site, but Gwynn thinks that his design is appropriate. "Finding what you want is as easy as possible," he offers. "There are not many graphics. They wouldn't add much." Sometimes not being technical has its advantages, suggests Gwynn.

His next step, marketing, represented an interesting challenge. Gwynn works with the search engines, but most customers come through the affiliates program. Gwynn's company pays 10 percent to affiliated Web companies that send customers, with Yahoo! providing a traffic and revenue report to the linked businesses. As Gwynn explains, "We try to get sites like the 'I Love Lucy' pages." Interested browsers can click from the Lucy site to fridgedoor.com and buy a variety of "I Love Lucy" magnets. Such an arrangement works exceptionally well for Gwynn because he pays only for sales, rather than spending money up front for advertising, which may or may not work.

Banner ads have not been productive. "I started out spending a lot of money on the ads," says Gwynn, "but our product is too hard to target. In this business, banner ads don't pay. We find our own affiliates, approaching them individually, rather than using a service to locate them."

FULFILLMENT—A CHALLENGE

OK, so you've got a great product. Now what? It's time to get those magnets out the virtual doors and onto those refrigerators. As Gwynn admits, he immediately recognized the complexity and significance of fulfillment. "There are so many parts," he says. "You have to maintain an inventory and stay on top of it. Then you need the right shipping boxes, and you must be sure that the right pieces end up in the right boxes." After those steps, it's recording weights and negotiating with UPS for delivery. There's also the matter of e-mail notices with tracking numbers. "It's a highly detailed process," sighs Gwynn, who hopes that others eyeing e-commerce take into account the challenges of the fulfillment process.

Those who don't win the fulfillment game can expect to lose customers—a simple fact. Gwynn says, "If you screw up the fulfillment process, you lose business. Even if you manage to put the right items in the box, the job isn't done. If you don't con-

firm the tracking number with an e-mail, customers get upset."
All the money and time spent attracting people to a site is
wasted if clients have hassles with shipping and receiving."

WHO PUT *THIS* SOAP
IN THE BATHTUB?

To grow his business, Gwynn is looking for new products and
sites. He plans to leave fridgedoor.com on Yahoo!, but he also
plans a more sophisticated magnet store elsewhere, one that
sells other items such as bath soaps. Gwynn envisions, for instance, a soap line with cute or catchy product names, cool
graphics, and a style similar to his own line of magnets. Gwynn
reasons that people looking at retro deco for gifts might also be
amused by unusual soaps.

In retrospect, Chris Gwynn is glad that he launched his business without worrying about an extensive business plan. *Just do
it!* is probably good advice for people willing to launch into cyberspace and move slowly into a growth position. And, if you
have trouble remembering this sage advice, click on to fridge-
door.com and order a magnet—the one that says, "Just do it!"

Web address:
   www.fridgedoor.com

Regional Products

Start-up expenses: $7,500
Special requirements: *Understanding of the retail industry*
Best advice: *"Prepare a business plan and stick to it. Revise the plan and update it while continuing to use it."*

Once you cross the Connecticut River heading north, you're in New England, the portion of the country that comes closest to Old World flavor. Not every town resembles the backdrop for *White Christmas* or *It's a Wonderful Life*, but places such as Stockbridge, Exeter, and Kennebunkport have that undeniable New England appeal and charm. And finally someone has gone online to prove that New England represents a nostalgic theme for Americans, whether they call it home or are just passing through. That someone is Elaine Y. Land, proprietor of NewEnglander.com.

Had America ever become Balkanized, like Europe, its regions would be recognizable countries such as the Bayous, Appalachia,

Great Lakes Territory, and the Pacific Northwest. But the free-flowing patterns of American life have had just the opposite effect. People from the Dakotas, Missouri, Pennsylvania, and Georgia wander and resettle, taking with them notions of life on the old farm or days in the homeland, even while adopting new lifestyles in California, Florida, and Kansas. Nevertheless, certain regions in America have a certain cachet, a style that represents the historical roots of the country, the beginnings. The most prominent region in this category is New England.

IT'S ALL IN NEW ENGLAND

In e-commerce, there's a growing awareness of regionalization. In the Northwest, businesses tout the outdoor life and its settings. In the Southwest or Florida, it's the sun. In the Mississippi Delta, it's the food. Businesses building on New England's appeal—call it the Ethan Allen effect—take advantage of the region's reputation for high-quality furniture, home furnishings and decorating materials.

As you'd expect, NewEnglander.com features specialty giftware and unusual products representing the six New England states. Don't look for Cajun rice cookers, raccoon caps, or fuzzy dice. The products are reminiscent of Colonial America, although not everything is Puritan black-and-white.

Land's company sells kitchen accessories, decorative pieces, home and personal products, outdoor toys, and gadgets. For example, you can buy pewter snowflake arrangements and pins from Connecticut, stoneware ornaments from Maine, silk chiffon kerchiefs and scarves from Massachusetts, and lobster whirligigs from New Hampshire. Log on to NewEnglander.com to find out.

Elaine Land recognized and capitalized on America's fascination with its Colonial roots. As she says, "New England gifts have tremendous appeal to native New Englanders, transplanted New Englanders, and wannabe New Englanders." In addition, travelers who have visited the New England countryside also like to purchase New England products as gifts. Look around your house— you're probably harboring a pen-and-ink drawing of the Old North Church or an Old Maine Maple Syrup can somewhere amidst the collectibles. Land has also found that transplanted New Englanders are great resources for product ideas. Out in the business world, she's constantly hearing anecdotes and stories that attest to people's ongoing loyalty to the Colonial heartland.

CHOOSING THE RIGHT PATH

As Land explains, New Englander.com faced serious hurdles as a mail order catalog and direct-mail business. She wanted assurance of an inexpensive entry into e-business and help with immediate turnaround time on products on the Internet. With a background in retail giftware—she was a marketing manager and product development specialist for a Manhattan firm—Land brought both market savvy and computer expertise into the venture.

The challenge, of course, was to launch a fully operational site with secure transactions for a small down payment. The Internet requires you to be flexible, because it changes so quickly, and Land wanted the option to revise the pages and her approach on short notice. The site had to be expandable and capable of being incorporated into a larger format once plans were in place because, for one thing, she wanted NewEnglander.com to include brick-and-mortar stores and a catalog department sometime in the future. Whew! A big order.

NewEnglander.com is available through traditional search engine routes, with listings updated frequently. Land has established links with several associated Web sites and built a print and online publicity campaign as well. "We are hosted by IBM," says Land, "and feel we benefit from our customers knowing that fact." The IBM logo is helpful, she suggests, implying a high level of service and leadership in e-business endeavors. Needless to say, the NewEnglander.com site is hosted on a secure server, and transactions occur in real time, 24 hours a day.

IT'S A DIFFERENT WORLD

Land likes the e-commerce approach. "Without a storefront on Main Street in Anytown, U.S.A., NewEnglander.com is not limited to local traffic and 'normal business hours,'" she says. For Land, the competition has yet to trample her territory. At least for now, Paul Revere can have another cup of tea, because he won't be needed to broadcast the e-business alarm. Although there are lots of mail order catalog companies and brick-and-mortar retailers in the "New England" field, no other e-business handles "All Things New England." Land's early entry into this niche market has her positioned well, and in the future the domain name will make it easier to maintain broad recognition when the market becomes crowded.

"The Internet is the wave of the future," says Land. She grumbles a bit about computer glitches and back-room business problems, but, as she says, "these difficulties are not unique to the Net." In the meantime, Land's regional approach continues to thrive. Other regionally oriented e-businesses may do just as well as NewEnglander.com. Anyone for Southwest pottery or watercolors of the pounding California surf?

Web address:
  www.NewEnglander.com

Sports-Related Gifts

Start-up expenses: *$9,400*
Special requirements: *None*
Best advice: *"Don't expect immediate results. It took three months for all the different search engines to find us. The first month I only took a couple of orders, and it slowly built from there. You can't set up and expect business the first day. There is too much that takes a long time. I recommend using a big server like Yahoo! because there are plenty of people who use Yahoo! for shopping."*

Where can you purchase a $6,000 chair shaped like a baseball glove? A golf bag barbecue set, a 14-carat gold football charm, a basketball wall clock, a soccer ball lamp, or a snowboarder's official guardian angel? Give up? Try Sports-Buff.com, a site launched by Amy Wagner and her husband.

Sports is an important theme in America, and it represents

big business on the Net. The Wagners sell the most unusual sports gifts they can find, often to coaches, sometimes to parents, occasionally to entire teams.

AN IDEA IS BORN

"The idea came to me on the beach in Florida," says Amy Wagner. "I have five daughters, and they all play sports. In the past I've had to find coaches' gifts and mementos for end-of-season banquets. I discovered that it's hard to find sports-related gifts beyond equipment." Wagner began to collect "I Love Hockey" paraphernalia, as well as "I Love [fill in the sport]" insignias from many sources. After determining that there were enough product lines to fill store shelves, Wagner signed up for trade shows and began to recruit suppliers. In 1997, she opened Sports Buff in Avon, Connecticut.

CYBERSPACE LAUNCH

In 1999, the Wagners added a Web site, and Sports-Buff.com was born. "It has done really well," says Amy. "I started the site just to enhance the business. This is a relatively small town, and we thought, if the idea was acceptable for here—if the people in Avon thought it was a good plan—then people around the world would like it, too." The Wagners constructed the site themselves, although Amy admits that her husband was the primary architect. He took advanced computer courses and gained enough knowledge to get the site up and running.

PRODUCT LINE

The business is a 50:50 partnership in the Wagner family. He handles the Web site, and she scouts the products. Since their first successful holiday season in 1999 the Wagners have added new product lines. Now that they have a better feel for their e-business and their retail store, they feel more confident with increased sales. Customers can buy some unusual products at their Web address, including a basketball T-shirt with an open court on the back. The shirt is accompanied with a pen so that players can "sign" their positions on the court. A great gift for a coach. The Wagners specialize in gifts for coaches. "When it gets to the end of the season of any particular sport," says Amy, "coaches' gifts sell the best."

The Wagners market about 500 items. The most popular sport is baseball, and the most popular items are ties. "But," says Amy, "anything associated with baseball is good, even furniture and jewelry." Hockey is growing in popularity, as well as soccer, partly as a result of the U.S. women's team and their successes.

The Wagners carry other exotic products as well. As Wagner explains, "You can find a thousand golf sites, but type in 'lacrosse' and you won't find much." Filling such niches is an important part of the business plan at Sports-Buff.com. The Wagners agree that having products for a wide variety of sports is their primary advantage.

ROADBLOCKS

A third of the orders are generated not online but by phone. Amy Wagner says, "Some people see the site, and they are afraid to give their credit card numbers online. In the beginning, we weren't set up for that situation. Now, when they are concerned, we're ready for their calls." During the 1999 Christmas season, the Wagners needed help answering the phones. But since then a full-time customer representative has been on duty. Amy Wagner says that customer fulfillment can be a problem, and she's glad that they've solved their difficulties over phone orders.

Another concern is the possibility of running out of products. It's a daily chore to remove items from the sales lists so that the Web is constantly up to date. According to Wagner, "It's very time-consuming. We need to write 'Temporarily out of stock' on the Web site and the date when the product will be available again." The Wagners are also fielding lots of international orders. For those, shipping can be worrisome. With the more complicated journeys came more complicated bookwork, but the owners solved their concerns with United Parcel Service. "We like the tracking feature that UPS provides," says Wagner. "That's important. As soon as people order, we e-mail them the tracking number, so they can follow the package themselves." For small items and local mailings, the Wagners still use the post office.

BUSINESS BOOM AT THE RETAIL STORE

Wagner was surprised to find that the site, in addition to creating its own business, drives more customers into the brick-and-mortar building. Located in the middle of Connecticut, the Sports Buff outlet is not widely recognized by the general public. But now, when people around the state and in neighboring states find the Web site, they often get into the car and drive to Avon, thinking, "Wow! They're only an hour away!" An increase in onsite traffic seems directly related to the Web presence. In fact, says Wagner, after contributing a 25 percent increase in business profits during the first year, the Web site also drove up brick-and-mortar business by 25 percent.

CLICK-AND-MORTAR COORDINATION

A click-and-mortar operation requires adjustments, but the two sales outlets work together nicely under the right circumstances. Wagner, in fact, thinks the Web site is relatively effortless. "We don't have to talk to customers, and we don't usually provide boxes or gift wrap unless they ask for it. The process doesn't take much time. Customers have already made their decisions by the time they order." She adds, "I love it."

However, Wagner doesn't believe the Web site alone is the answer. She thinks the business would be less effective with only the Net presence. She explains, "We have a lot more stuff in the store than on the site. We reduce the price at the store and sell things that won't move on the site. Yes, you can have close-out sales on the Web, but I like being able to offer a bigger variety to the people who walk into the store." Wagner argues that she doesn't like to put heavily discounted items on the Web site. The discounts fit better in the brick-and-mortar operation.

"Our lowest price on the Web is $8," she says, "but in the store we have several items ranging from $2 to $8. We also have greeting cards in the store, and we don't market those on the site either." When items don't move well in cyberspace, Wagner has the option of pulling them on to the shelves of her store, and vice versa. Also, space is a consideration. "For example," she says, "the baseball chair [$6,000] on the site is huge, and the store is teeny. The chair is available on the site but, for obvious reasons, not in the store."

The Sports-Buff.com site, however, really reduces the need for inventory—not possible in the Avon building. Manufacturers drop-ship lots of the sports items for Wagner, and that makes business operations so much easier. "I don't have to inventory so many things, especially $5,000 items that I can't afford to keep in stock."

Easy Does It

Taking a measured approach makes sense to the Wagners. The search engines won't find you immediately, they argue, so you might as well plan on a slow start. Besides, there are thousands of little details that need tending before the customers start breaking down the cyberdoors. Wagner is happy to have joined with Yahoo! "I pay a little more, but it's worth it," she says. "If a customer goes to Yahoo! and types 'basketball necktie,' this site will come up quickly." Wagner believes that Yahoo!—with its huge shoppers' base—attracts the most potential clients. Let's hope a few of them are looking for overstuffed chairs in the shape of baseball gloves.

Web address:
www.Sports-buff.com

Theme Gift Baskets

Start-up expenses: $2,000
Special requirements: *None*
Best advice: *"Come up with something new. Tap a market that is not out there. Don't try to copy from big successful companies because you think they are making the big bucks. Learn from them, but don't be like them. Set yourself apart and create something that is you. Find something for which you are the only solution."*

Here's a compelling reason to consider developing a gift-centered Web site: *Entrepreneur* magazine places gift lines in the top 10 for new business ventures. Want another reason? In e-commerce, after *computers*, the key word *gifts* grabs the biggest share of online sales. There are millions and millions of gift buyers out there clicking away at Web sites—not just at Christmas, but all year long. The dollar figures are staggering.

There's money to be made for those who come up with a

new approach and grab a niche position in this enormous market. But first, consider the buying audience. Gift giving is done largely by women, as it has probably been since the first "you shouldn't have" was uttered. And, although men were first to exploit the Net as a marketplace, women are rapidly establishing their financial presence. Today in America, women control 75 percent of the family finances, and about 46 percent of all women are shopping online. Those numbers will only increase.

Now that you're ready to launch your own site, stop to take a reality check. Unlike an e-business in designer dog biscuits or Transylvanian travel, this field is packed with competitors. Enticing and holding customers is an immense problem. Getting exposure on the Web is rarely easy, and in a venture like gift distribution, it's like trying to attract attention in the world's biggest convention center. What to do? Find a niche.

FINDING A SECRET TREASURE

One who found a niche in gifts is Angela Grieco, owner of Sundara.com. In July 1998, Grieco started her company after she researched the e-industry world looking for her own entry point into the gifts business. Grieco wanted to do something different, something exciting and new. "I wanted to be on the leading edge of the gift basket market," she says. "I wanted to build gift occasions—to turn gift giving into a series of surprises. I wanted to present gifts in a completely new way." She did.

The years she spent as the creative director at a mail order catalog company helped Grieco formulate her special plan. "I decided I wanted to do something independently, to pursue my own goal and dream," she says. "I realized my biggest pleasure in life was getting gifts for other people. I never liked buying something ordinary, and I felt guilty going to the mall at the last minute because that required no effort. My goal was to make people to feel good about giving." With a sense of purpose, Grieco tapped into the magical vision of a little girl opening a secret treasure chest.

Grieco started by remembering how exciting it was to open a special gift, a secret treasure. She seized on the idea of packing gift collections in decorated treasure chests. She worked with the idea and put together some prototypes. On each chest Grieco attached a scroll with a place for a secret message, one that suggested what's inside. She reasoned that the scroll would allow buyers to personalize their gifts.

Before Sundara went online, Grieco researched vendors on the Web and picked up some useful information. She began by typing in search terms like "sensual products" and "gourmet foods." In this way, she did an empirical Web study, developing her product lines according to trends and consumer interest. It took about four months to decide on her product line, to get samples, pick vendors, and establish gift categories. The product development phase finished in January 1999, and the Web site design, which had started in November 1998, consumed another five months. In March 1999, the Sundara site went live.

DO YOU REMEMBER WHAT YOU GOT LAST CHRISTMAS?

Well, what *did* you get for Christmas last year? That's OK, we can't remember either. On a recent "Oprah Winfrey" show, the host surveyed people on the street, asking them what gifts they received from their best friend last year. Almost no one could remember. The only passersby who could recall even one Christmas present described something intimate and personal—like a gift-filled treasure chest with a personalized scroll.

With Sundara, Grieco proposes a creative departure from the traditional gift solution. For most of us, gift giving is a problem, and running out to the mall at the last minute is the solution. "I wanted to provide a different, more personal alternative, something more thoughtful and intimate. I hope people can be remembered not for how much they spent but for the extra effort that makes someone feel special, for the thought and care that went into a present."

Grieco's signature idea is to have the gift create the occasion instead of the occasion requiring a gift. At Sundara.com, customers are encouraged to see any day as a special opportunity to celebrate those they love. "Those gifts," she says, "are the ones that will be remembered because they were not expected." Grieco believes that a good reason for giving a gift may seem banal on the surface: here's a little gift to "thank you for devoting a precious hour to listening to my whining on the phone." She argues that remembering and honoring friendship is at least as important as a traditional holiday.

BUILDING A DIVERSE LINE OF PRODUCTS

In the current line of treasures, Sundara.com has five separate categories of gift baskets. One is Sensual Moments, a classification that includes two different choices of baskets: Midnight at the Oasis and Sensual Secrets. Both are designed as surprises for lovers or spouses. The Sensual Secrets basket includes products like the *Kama Sutra*, sensual oils, pleasure balms, chocolate candies, scented candles, and Darjeeling teas. "It's an intimate experience," says Grieco, in what must be considered a classic understatement. Midnight at the Oasis is a smaller basket with oils, candles, and chocolates.

Another category is Gourmet Adventures, featuring four distinct food collections. Here, Grieco says, she wanted to do something "totally different" in the food line. "There are tons of gift baskets that are usually just a mishmash of foods thrown together. I want to take people to wonderful destinations when they experience foods from around the world." On Sundara's culinary journey to Italy, for example, you can expect fine Italian foods, a kitchen towel, a CD with Italian arias, and an Italian recipe booklet. Sundara.com offers a similar package for France, the Caribbean, and the American Southwest. "It's a whole little cooking adventure," says Grieco. "It creates an atmosphere that's special."

Each basket arrives in its own keepsake treasure chest—there are four different types. The baskets are priced from $35 to $145, and, because the quality is high, they are reusable.

A CROWDED FIELD OF COMPETITORS

Even with a creative and attractive gift line, Sundara.com struggled to find its place in the e-commerce world, primarily because the industry is overcrowded. Grieco began slowly, registering with search engines. But she got her biggest bang from links with other sites, including stress-relief sites and sensual products sites. "When I find one that looks like a good match, I e-mail them and buddy up," says Grieco. "The Web is a community-oriented place." Grieco likes to hang out on the Net, meeting surfers who eventually turn to buyers.

In all her business dealings, Grieco has learned the value of networking and patience. For her, the buyers are often people who have surfed past her site and remembered it. Later, when the need for a special gift arises, they return to her site with their credit card in hand. Grieco also notices that people are not just focusing on birthdays and holidays when making orders. There are lots of times when people buy a gift for no special reason. When Grieco sees the messages they want to send, she is reminded of the power of love and affection: "It gives me such faith in the human race. It gives me hope."

The Web is, for Grieco, "a private, intimate community." She sees people making personal connections through the Net. "It's just a vehicle for people to make friends," she says. But happily for Sundara, friendship is the basis for gift giving.

Fully 85 percent of Sundara's buyers are women—busy women. "They don't have time to go to the mall or to shuffle mail order catalogs," says Grieco. The customers appreciate the personalized Treasure Chest lines, and they tell their friends. The whole process makes Grieco very happy. "Whatever you do," says Grieco, "it has to be a passion." Her advice to others is simple. Find an online business that you love, one that fulfills your own dreams.

Web address:
www.Sundara.com

Health &
Fitness

Bodybuilding

Start-up expenses: $2,500
Special requirements: *None*
Best advice: *"Take a measured approach to expansion."*

Want a better body? There are two roads to fitness. One path is for those bodybuilders who use performance-enhancing drugs; the other is for health-conscious people who want an honest approach to muscle tone and weight control. According to Mark Mills, owner of the Better Body Company, the glamour end of the industry is geared to the egos and pocketbooks of eighteen-year-olds, who often want to look like Arnold Schwarzenegger but don't weigh the consequences of using unnatural supplements or drugs. Those who put health before performance, however, take bodybuilding seriously and see fitness as part of a healthy pattern of lifestyle choices. For these health-conscious consumers, there are online services such as Mills's better-body.com.

Even though the bodybuilders have a wide variety of magazines, catalogs, and product lines available to them, there is plenty of market space left for those who buy and sell natural health products. "We just want customers with an honest, realistic approach," says Mark Mills. "I've gotten offers to advertise for [performance-enhancing drugs and supplements], but I don't want to advertise what they are selling." Nevertheless, betterbody.com competes well in a niche market, one that Mills entered with a small purse. His business venture began with investments of $500 for software, $1,000 for *Shopping Cart*, and $1,000 for a computer, later upgraded to a top-of-the-line Dell model with desktop video editing capabilities.

FIRST A HOBBY, THEN A BUSINESS

Mills graduated in 1994 from Dartmouth College in New Hampshire, majoring in mathematics and premed. After receiving his degree, he decided to start his own fitness business rather than enter medical school. By 1996 the enterprise had become the Better Body Company. Oddly, Mills did not enter the market with an eye to making money. Instead, he says, "I started my own Web site because of my interest in fitness. I had been putting a lot of time and effort into creating manuals and videos. One day I heard about a thing called e-commerce and decided to give it a try." When people started placing orders on his site, Mills was both pleased and surprised. "That was when it became a business instead of a hobby."

Prior to launching his site, Mills had no business background. In fact, he knew nothing about the Net. He built his site by reading books and browsing other sites, particularly those with an emphasis on health. "That was my introduction," says Mills, adding that the process was made easier by some handy tools he encountered in cyberspace, including software.

Unlike many ventures in this field, betterbody.com stresses the practical approach to health and fitness. Says Mills, "A lot of magazines are making big money from advertising, which means that everything is geared to selling products." As a result, both newsstand magazines and e-zines in this field aren't entirely honest and useful to readers. Mills cites the predominance of "outlandish claims" in most health and fitness journals that feature advertisements for performance-enhancing drugs and supplements. On the contrary, says Mills, "we are real-world people. We don't advocate drugs, and that's really our advantage. It's one reason why we have lots of customers." The Better Body Company sells its own videos, magazine subscriptions, training manuals, and log books. The manuals and log books are hard copy; only the magazine is available in electronic form, appearing in PDF format.

The e-magazine has been an unexpected source of help for the staff at Better Body. Mills, who spends much of his business day on the e-zine, discovered that online customers who share his interests are sometimes willing to contribute. In fact, says Mills, "most of the stuff needed to finish the Web site came from customers I met on the site." For example, one customer bought Mills's e-magazine and later wrote, "By the way, I'm a software engineer." He offered to help because he appreciated what Mills was doing with his magazine and business. Later, a customer who works as a graphic designer agreed to create the betterbody.com logo. These contacts were obviously important. "You have to network with people you meet online," says Mills. "That keeps costs down, limits your time investment, and helps you get more done."

Does This Shopping Cart Come with Wheels?

Mills and his staff have learned to be versatile. "We do all our projects from start to finish onsite," says Mills, "including video editing, writing, shipping, and fulfillment—everything." Mills accepts payments by check, cash, money order, and credit card, with the cards processed in real time. Better-body.com has its own merchant account, but it's handled by a third party, Total Merchant Manager.

Mills spent more than a year researching merchant accounts before selecting Total Merchant Manager, and it's been a suitable companion for better-body.com. The software package cost about $1,000, and Mills found that it worked exactly as advertised. "*Total Merchant Manager* is the easiest software system to set up and use," suggests Mills, who became frustrated with the claims of other services. "Most companies want to sell you shopping cart software, but they won't admit that you need your own programmer to do CGI scripts and back-end programming. Without the programming, the software won't actually send the information to a credit card processor." In many cases, the merchant account companies charge $1,500 and claim that the software can be processing credit orders in 15 minutes. "But," says Mills, "it actually costs *another* $1,500 for a programmer—not to mention the lost time." Mills advises a thorough study of merchant account services for people starting an online business. "Be sure to ask what you need to do before taking the first order."

A Healthy Customer Base

Needless to say, any business needs a plan for attracting customers. At better-body.com, Mills decided to register with the top search engines, but he admits that he has not actively pursued high listings. "Honestly, I've read a lot about getting to the top of the search engines—how to do it, and that listings are important. But I just haven't taken the time." He does study the daily statistics about who's hitting his site and the demographics involved. "Lately," he says, "I've noticed more and more traffic is coming from Yahoo! and WebCrawler." In the past, Mills did numerous link exchanges but abandoned the practice. "I really think that link exchange causes your site to lose some value," he suggests, arguing that his company is ultimately responsible when customers link from his site to another. "What if it's an adults-only site, for example? I don't want that association. It's bad for my credibility and reputation." In fact, better-body.com has built a reputation primarily through word of mouth.

Besides the search engines, Mills concentrates on traditional mailing lists. He says, "You need to manage a mailing list and learn how to use it correctly." Most people, of course, consider unsolicited materials junk mail. But Mills argues that it's only junk if people are not interested. Therefore, it's important to target the customers through a service such as ListBot. He says, "They don't waste someone's time with something they don't want. ListBot allows my customers to decide whether they want to be included or excluded from my list." At present, Mills has an active mailing list of about 5,000 people. It has been helpful to work with a managed list, says Mills. "Before I let ListBot handle it, people drove me crazy with their constant changes—

addresses, for example." Today Mills pays only $100 a year for ListBot, noting that the service allows as many separate lists as he wants, so betterbody.com can target customers in a number of different marketing patterns, such as individuals between the ages of 30 and 40. ListBot also provides a weekly demographic report and general analysis of sales trends. "Because of that report," says Mills, "I now have a completely new idea of who is coming to the site, and it's much different from what I had originally thought."

WATCH OUT FOR COPYCATS

The competition has taken note of betterbody.com. In fact, several sites have registered with minor variations on the Better Body name, changing the URL by only a letter or a dash. Others sell similar products for the same price. But Mills says that reputation is important in the health business. "The difference—what makes us stand out—is that we run an honest business. A lot of people come to us after having problems elsewhere. I take the time to make sure they get what they need." The Better Body niche is not mainstream, but customers are loyal.

Mills explains that health sites are often littered with "lots of fluff and tons of pictures—mostly of people using performance-enhancing drugs." He argues that people get weary of both the pictures and the claims. He says, "The sites may get a lot of hits because people come to look at the pictures, but I guarantee they are not selling the products we are." In his opinion the standard business school formula does not hold for e-commerce, at least in the health and fitness business. "I'd rather have 10 people a day who are genuinely interested, instead of 3,000 gawkers looking at pictures." Apparently, those 10 people are pleased with the betterbody.com service, because Mills claims that his clientele have become more than customers. In many cases, he has gotten to know the buyers personally, often as a result of his policy on calling or e-mailing to see that people are satisfied with the Better Body products.

Although Mills could probably expand the online business immediately by adding new product lines ("the best way to grow this business"), he is taking a measured approach to expansion. Recently, he finished a graduate degree in biomedical science and is a full-time employee at a major pharmaceutical company. "So, for now at least, it is going to be a sideline," he says. "But I could see going full-time in the future. I really enjoy this business." Mills has fielded some buyout offers but does not want to sell. He enjoys helping people find their way to good health and enjoys the contacts made through the Better Body business.

Web address:
www.better-body.com

High-Tech Cosmetics

Start-up expenses: $3,500

Special requirements: *Ph.D. in biology or partner/employee with same*

Best advice: *"Do it yourself. Don't hire some group to set up your Web site, or they will bleed you out of money. You have to learn how to interact with your ISP. Use a small local ISP with a good reputation—one that is especially cognizant of security issues. Then get to know the people on a personal basis. Learn to put the site and the business together yourself."*

A re wrinkles inevitable? No, according to Dr. Loren Pickart, founder and owner of skinbiology.com, a Web site devoted to skin and hair regeneration products. In fact, he thinks it's possible in the future for people to live 400 years in relatively good health! In the meantime, why not look and feel good? Dr. Pickart, a scientist with a doctoral degree in biology, holds more than 150 patents on products that promote skin healing, hair growth stimulation, and wound healing.

What do you get when you cross a generation of baby boomers moving into their fifties with a multibillion-dollar cosmetic industry? An incredible opportunity for anyone with a product designed to erase years and produce a more youthful appearance. Major players like L'Oreal and Estee Lauder may rule in the department stores, but on the Web, it's anyone's game.

COSMETICS ON THE CUTTING EDGE

While conducting research on aging, Dr. Pickart discovered Iamin, the human regenerative factor, leading him to a series of products for clinical and cosmetic use, including wound healing products sold by Bard Medical, Merck, and Tanox Biosystems. The Web site promotes a special line of cutting-edge products, led by Protect & Restore, a copper peptide face cream. According to Dr. Pickart, copper peptides have been proven the most effective tool for increasing collagen and elastin in the skin—more effective than Vitamin C or fruit acids. Because copper peptides directly repair skin cells, the chemicals also reduce or remove scars. While Protect & Restore serves mostly to restore a healthy glow to the face, restoring skin texture in the process, it also removes lines or simply serves as a moisturizer under makeup.

Protect & Restore and other products in the line are not advertised elsewhere. The $18.95 price tag for a two-ounce bottle is modest, especially considering the competition's costs of $60 or more. Browsers to the site find an unusual display of medical reports and product displays. The site is content intensive—

each Web page reads like a condensed version of a book on aging, with a separate product featured in each section. Each display includes a full medical treatise on the science behind the product, as well as test results and product comparisons. The commercial realm lies in the background of each page. It's not necessarily a showy site, but it is compelling, thanks to strong, informative content.

THE SCIENCE BEHIND THE BEAUTY

Dr. Pickart's product lines began with a scientific interest in aging. For six years, while studying gerontology, Pickart reviewed patterns of aging. Then he began to seek ways to reverse or delay the aging process. For his Ph.D. thesis at the University of California at San Francisco, Dr. Pickart studied 20-year-old and 70-year-old men, investigating the effects of blood serum on cultured cells. It had always been known that younger blood was more effective at supporting cell growth and viability. But why?

Dr. Pickart looked at the differences between the age groups and found great disparities in levels of copper peptide, a compound produced during the breakdown of tissues. Copper peptides serve as an activator of subsequent tissue regenerations. In short, when old skin or organic material dies, copper peptides facilitate the growth of new tissue.

STARTING FROM HOME

In 1985, Dr. Pickart began his first home-based company, Procyte. He developed the ideas for clinical wound care, generating 25 products that are now sold around the world by different medical and pharmaceutical companies. With the patents in hand, Dr. Pickart had a secure commercial basis.

In 1991, following a bout of ill health, Pickart closed Procyte but within three years had launched a new firm, Skin Biology, with the goal of improving skin care in hospitals and nursing homes. The research scientist found a new, better technology for the application of copper peptides, one that "seems particularly appropriate for skin rejuvenation and improving the health and growth of hair—as well as for removing scars and repairing sun-damaged skin."

WEB PROBLEMS? JUST ASK A TEENAGER

Believe it or not, his middle-school daughter launched his Web site. Here's the story. Francois Dominique was working with her schoolmates to put up a home page as part of a class project. She got the idea for her father to build a Web site and offered to share her middle-school expertise. It worked! "She told me what to do," he says, "and then my daughter and I wrote the content."

Well, the price was right. Dr. Pickart had been receiving bids of $15,000 up front, with $200 a month in maintenance charges, for similar services. After brief consideration, he went with his daughter's suggestions. She worked in her father's office one summer, and by the time the school bell was ringing again, the two partners were selling products online.

"We are so happy with the Net," says Dr. Pickart. "Before, nobody wanted to sell our products. The big companies just wanted to sell expensive bandages. We decided to focus on the Net at a time when the company was going nowhere. But now, due to sales produced on the Web, the company has a good financial balance." Dr. Pickart especially likes the Web-based interactions with customers. Due to rapid feedback from customers, he constantly uncovers good ideas for new products and for improvements on the old ones.

HEALTH, AGING, AND LIES

Pickart admits that his industry has not been kind to consumers—a problem he wants to correct. He says, "We hear from women all the time who reach a certain age, about 35, feeling that cosmetic companies have lied to them for years." These women have a sense of being deceived in so many ways. To ensure effectiveness, Dr. Pickart's basic product for skin care, Protect & Restore, has been studied extensively by independent scientists and researchers. According to Pickart, Dr. Howard Mailbach, one of the world's most preeminent dermatologists—and the author of 80 books on the subject—has led four controlled studies of Protect & Restore.

Pickart feels it's his moral duty to promote good health and fitness. He also feels it's a high duty for people to remain healthy and to improve themselves. "Personally, I think women get better as they get older," he says, "but the media tries to make them feel bad about aging, urging them to turn back the clock." Putting the hype aside, Dr. Pickart wants to sell products that work on scientific principles, not because they're backed by multimillion-dollar ad campaigns.

PRODUCT ENHANCEMENTS

Another product that has been popular at skinbiology.com is Tri Reduction, a salve for scar and sunspot reduction. After hearing from women that Protect & Restore was reducing acne scars and age spots—even removing the most dramatic stretch marks—Dr. Pickart began to ask why. He increased by a factor of three the copper peptide levels from Protect & Restore, then added a 14 percent solution of glycoloic acid cream. The product worked very effectively, and Dr. Pickart began to produce Tri Reduction. According to Pickart, "One of the reasons this development is exciting is because there are no scar reduction methods on the market that don't produce pain or irritation."

Dr. Pickart's company also markets a folligen cream originally made for nursing home use. The product reached the hands of a younger woman, a 41-year-old executive whose blond hair was falling out. She had lost most of her hair and blamed it on stress. Nothing had worked to cure the hair loss, but after two and a half months of experimenting with the folligen cream, her hair returned to its former fullness.

Others then reported success at regrowing hair with the folligen cream. That news spawned several new products for hair regrowth. "We are going to keep experimenting and see what we can develop," says Dr. Pickart. "The goal of the company is basically to continue work on reversing the aging process—not merely to stop aging but to reverse many of the effects. There is no good reason why we can't have a good life for 400 years." That prospect sounds just fine to us.

Web address:
www.skinbiology.com

Medical Advice

Start-up expenses: *None*
Special requirements: *Medical degree*
Best advice: *"Have fun with your online business. I can't imagine—even though I know people who do have early success—that an e-business will be your primary source of income within the first year. Regardless of income, however, it's a lot of fun."*

In a recent interview with Susan Stamberg on National Public Radio, technology guru Esther Dyson talked about the "attention generation," the growing cadre of people who have all they need in life except personal attention. Dyson says the Internet represents a way to fill this great void. She says that consumers—who often have more "things" than they can reasonably use—increasingly key into cyberspace for something other than just great products. They want someone to treat them as individuals.

One niche takes the idea of personal attention a quantum leap farther—special services like financial planning, personal counseling, and medical advice. At these sites, customers deal one-on-one with specialists who, in addition to offering expertise, address the needs of the attention generation.

THE ONLINE DOCTOR IS IN

Forget the waiting room—sit on a cold chair in front of your monitor and type this Web address: Ask YourFamilyDoc.com.

There, that wasn't so bad, was it? The doctor on the other end is Michele C. Moore, M.D., FAAFP, who will answer your medical questions for a modest fee. Dr. Moore has practiced medicine for 23 years, first in family practice and, for the past 15 years, as a specialist in preventive and complementary medicine. If you want to know how to treat nail fungus, gout, or chicken pox, Dr. Moore renders a medical opinion and charges you $25. If the question requires extra research or a complicated answer—anything more than 15 minutes—the doctor will give you an estimate on the fee.

Dr. Moore does not prescribe medicine nor diagnose illnesses over the Net. Like a resourceful medical dictionary, she has answers about health. Unlike a dictionary, however, she can zero in on specific concerns and unusual circumstances with her e-mail responses. Furthermore, the doctor provides a monthly newsletter focusing on recently posed questions from cyberpatients. The doctor's newsletter archives are available without charge to patients and browsers. Happily, the AskYourFamilyDoc.com site is uncluttered, straightforward, and easy to use. It's also completely confidential. And there are no 50-minute layovers in the waiting room.

Like you would expect from a physician, Dr. Moore respects your privacy and has taken steps to assure that all online conversations remain secure. The information going both ways online is fully encrypted, using industry-standard protection SSL.

As Dr. Moore says, "Patient confidentiality will be in effect at all times."

Unlike many physicians, Dr. Moore uses many approaches to healing, not just the conventional medical school solutions. She solicits an open exchange of information with the online patient and wants medical choices to be made "jointly by the patient and the caregiver."

TOM HANKS STARTED IT ALL

Sometimes the chronicle of an e-business begins with an odd story. This one does. During Christmas 1998, Dr. Moore wanted to take her mother to see one of her favorite actors, Tom Hanks, in a movie called *You've Got Mail*. While watching the dramatic comedy unfold, Moore's mind was wandering, and "AskYourFamilyDoc.com" popped into her head. At that point, Moore did not own a computer and had never used the Internet. Needless to say, she was not ready to launch an online business.

Nevertheless, by tax day 1999, Dr. Moore was ready to hang out her cybershingle. She had started from scratch, first checking with patients, who said they liked the idea. Then the offers from parents started to roll in. "My son can build a Web page!" Sure enough, Moore chose one of the kids as her Webmaster. She told the young man what she wanted on her site and gave him a project goal of March. The month's delay was not a Web design problem but Moore's own slow progress at learning computer skills and Internet philosophy.

In an effort to learn about online practices, Dr. Moore discovered *The Internet in 24 Hours* on a bookseller's shelf and found it marvelously helpful. The book is recommended reading for people considering a similar journey from point zero.

Today Dr. Moore spends most of her time consulting with

online patients. She leaves the search engine duties to her Webmaster and does not have a marketing budget. Her recent book, however, mentions the Web site and has spurred some increased traffic. Apparently the word is getting out somehow. AskYourFamilyDoc.com takes about 5,000 hits a week without advertising.

SOME INTERESTING HITS

Moore's first online question was about allergic reactions to insect bites. The next broached the subject of preventive care tests, a favorite topic for Moore. Other visitors wanted prescriptions, something she does not provide over the Net. When people ask for prescriptions for illnesses such as migraine headaches, Moore only offers therapeutic advice. Says Moore, "I am sympathetic, but I can't." She explains, "There's always a small percentage of the population who are seeking controlled substances. A lot of them are legitimate. They have a problem with pain and haven't found a sympathetic ear in medicine." But others are clearly not legitimate.

But the drug seekers and con men are few in comparison to legitimate visitors seeking personal answers to their health questions. Dr. Moore has received queries from people in faraway places such as China and India—and from American travelers all over the world who don't feel comfortable taking their minor ailments to overseas health centers. When a stomach flu hits in Beijing or a rash in Kuala Lumpur, the typical visitor to Moore's site doesn't want to venture into the unfamiliar world of Far East medicine. She only wants to know "what to do next."

Perhaps a measure of Dr. Moore's success is the number of questions she receives from other doctors. Some physicians simply click on to ask how the cyberpractice is going. Others have serious medical questions. "Essentially, they want me to consult," she laughs. Moore finds such queries rather odd, but she also takes them with good humor. Also interesting are the e-mails from .edu addresses. When she checks her weekly hit lists, Moore discovers more and more questions from technical schools, universities, and medical schools. In a way, the interest of the educational community suggests that sites like AskYourFamilyDoc.com are filling an important role in American medicine.

ENJOY YOUR WEB SITE

Again and again the message from successful e-commerce entrepreneurs is the same: do it because you enjoy it. Dr. Moore admits she has not taken a terribly businesslike approach and could probably command a higher income with some marketing and advertising. Nevertheless, she likes the online routine. First and foremost, she says, AskYourFamilyDoc.com is fun.

The difficult part of the business comes in telling people that she can't offer diagnoses from a distance. She gives pointers and advice, often after picking up on some subtle hints in the patient's questions and responses. "On more than one occasion," she says, "people have been surprised by my answers because I've picked up on something they didn't realize they'd revealed. It's not as impersonal as it might seem." Indeed, the online doctor is not impersonal at all. Compared with the attitudes of HMOs, corporate clinics, and Fortune 500 hospitals, Dr. Moore's Internet-based health service must seem like a house call.

Web address:
   www.AskYourFamilyDoc.com

Nutritional
Supplements

Start-up expenses: $27,000
Special requirements: *None*
Best advice: *"The one problem we have found with the Web is the Now Generation. When they call at 3 A.M. to place an order—and decide to use the phone instead of the Net—they expect you to be there. We cover 14 hours a day onsite, and the rest of the time, we have an answering machine hooked up. We always call back or e-mail. If somebody e-mails, you must respond in less than 24 hours!"*

I f you've just chosen the value pack at Kielbasa.com, or if you're contemplating a big order from Stogies.com, you might pause a moment to think about your health. Several Web sites offer health products—everything from nutritional supplements to cholesterol-testing kits. At VesPro.com, the specialty is antiaging products, aesthetics, and fitness. When you log on to the site, you can scan pages of offerings that promote optimal health and wellness—items designed to "enhance immune function, monitor free radical damage, promote tissue regeneration and healing, build muscle, and metabolize fat."

FEELING BETTER

Wouldn't you like to increase your energy, look better, and feel younger? Of course you would. VesPro.com says it's possible. According to their experts, you can improve your health immensely with a variety of phytonutrients and phytopharmaceuticals, popular among baby boomers because they resulted from research in preventive medicine and antiaging.

A GROWTH HORMONE STARTED IT ALL

In April 1997, when the company started operations, VesPro's initial offering was a natural growth hormone releaser, a product endorsed in 12 nationally published articles. The supplement, called VesPro GHS, has become a staple in the antiaging industry. The product is designed to awaken the body's natural regenerative powers. Other products include antioxidant formulas, vitamin C serum (for boosting the collagen production in the skin), and cutting-edge sports performance products. For instance, Somatoplex is designed to promote athletic excellence. As VesPro.com says, the high-visibility clients who use the all-natural performance additive include many professional athletes, including several of last year's Super Bowl champions and the four-time Mr. Natural Universe.

There's more. At VesPro.com, you can also buy test kits to determine, for example, free radical activity in the body and oxidative stress. Others identify hormone levels. According to Chuck Heldstab of VesPro, "The tests are great because you can do a before-and-after approach and see in black and white that the products are working. I know of no other company site where such proof is available."

GOOD PRODUCTS, GOOD LINKS

Online operations and publicity patterns are sophisticated. VesPro.com has close ties to other health sites, including several that focus on alternative medicine and health supplements. VesPro.com also posts news articles from major medical publications like the *Journal of the American Medical Association*.

They also depend on opt-in mail, one of the greatest marketing tools available, according to Heldstab. "From our end," he says, "it is relatively inexpensive. You still have to pay someone to write the piece, but you don't have to pay postage. You already have the server and equipment ready to use." With three available servers, the chances of a crash are small. VesPro.com offers several opt-in services from its site, including a bimonthly newsletter called *Longevity Quest*, a magazine that presents brief but targeted articles on current scientific trends. Other opt-in services let you know when it's time to reorder products. An added option is a weekly notice of sales.

The Web has been an essential tool because the products at VesPro.com appeal to different customer groups. Flexibility is a great advantage. Heldstab says, "We've noticed that people in different parts of the country—as well as different age groups, want different products."

CHANGING DIRECTION

Ironically, the business began on a sour note because the Net was attracting too many Gen-X customers. When VesPro went online, the Web was crowded with youngsters. The site was reaching the wrong audience with its antiaging lines. "That is why we got into sports performance and prevention in the aesthetics products," says the marketing director. But now the demographics have shifted. "We're getting the baby boomers now," says Heldstab. Recently, he has seen a huge increase in over-60 traffic.

"The industry is incredibly fast-paced," remarks Heldstab. "We are determined to stay right up there." In a traditional mail order approach, rapid development and change is difficult, if not impossible. For instance, VesPro.com changes its site three times during an eight-month period. Why so often? "If you turned on TV and saw the same program all the time, you'd turn it off eventually," says Heldstab. "That's why stations change commercials every couple of months. People get bored. Even if your technology is flawless and cutting edge, the approach can get stale."

With about 200 active competitors in the market, VesPro.com remains cautious, watching the trends and times. The competitors will make some inroads, says Heldstab, but competition is not really a negative. "You wouldn't want it any other way," he says. Competition keeps every company on its toes.

THEY TAKE THE PRODUCTS, TOO

In addition to online orders, VesPro.com has a phone service. With 12 full-time employees, someone is always on hand to answer a call. Callers connect with one of several qualified people: two trainers, several specialists in medicine, and three information technology experts. Four of the VesPro.com staff have no medical experience, but one is an herbalist, and the rest have experience or training in medical disciplines. "Everyone has a good knowledge of the products," says Heldstab.

"If one person doesn't know the answer to a question," says

Heldstab, "someone else can help." If a question requires a consultant or reference check, the VesPro.com staff call the customer back.

In the staff room, VesPro.com products are highly visible. "Everybody here takes our products," says Heldstab. "And they're not free! We pay for them." VesPro.com staffers have confidence in the products because they see the research reports and know the results. The company consults various formulators around the world. After establishing an idea for a new product, the company sends the specs to an associated pharmaceutical firm. When trials are complete, successful products go into production. At any one time, VesPro.com may have 15 new nutritional supplements under research. Heldstab reports that VesPro associates with 12 international manufacturers.

HIGH VOLUME, LOW PRESSURE

In a crowded online market, Heldstab recognizes that VesPro.com must seek its own advantages. Anyone can establish a site and sell nutritional products, he says. So VesPro.com sets itself apart in several ways. First, they were the initial online company in this industry, so they already have a strong customer base. To keep that base intact—people always wander away and try new lines—VesPro.com markets on the Web through e-mail, using opt-in. "We are not high-pressure marketers," says the marketing manager. "We have a lot of doctors who use and prescribe our products. Most other companies have a single doctor on the team, someone who says whatever the company wants." VesPro, says Heldstab, has a list of 3,000 doctors who buy and use their products, sometimes acting as distributors.

The VesPro.com Web site appears in an elevated position on most search engines. Although Heldstab says the company doesn't resubmit excessively to the engines, his company has fruitful links to other sites, so when the search engines check the links, the VesPro.com site gains status. "Just having been out there so long really helps," he says. "If you go to any of our old sites, they still bring you to the newest site." VesPro.com has 150 domain names—all leading to the same updated location. These are not fully independent sites but gathering points for redirection to the clustered site.

It's like a spider web, says Heldstab, speaking of the site arrangements. There are sites linked into sites. Once caught in the "web," the customer moves toward the center. For example, if you click on the "Nitro Plex" logo, you find a twelve-page site for that one product, not including the order form. If you then click on "Other Products," you transfer to the main site, a sixty-page display area. Then you can go to any other product or to "More Information," which will take you to the specific site for that new line. With ease, you can also return to the home page.

How does the Web tangle work? "Each product and each page is under its own separate domain," says Heldstab. "They are separate sites, just linked together. High search engine placement is the point of this design." Heldstab also likes the spider-web intricacy for other reasons. For example, if he wants to add more products, he can put up a new site and link it without having to rebuild the whole framework. It eliminates the heavy work of refining and rebuilding a whole Web site just to accommodate new material.

Admit it. You could use a boost in energy level, some spring in your feet. Maybe it's time to look into supplements and nutritional boosters. Firms like VesPro.com have a cornucopia of health enhancers.

Web address:
www.VesPro.com

Weight Loss

Start-up expenses: *Variable*
Special requirements: *None*
Best advice: *"When you start out, do so with very good equipment and very good services—like a top-notch Web-hosting company and dial-up networks, as well as your hardware and software. Pay the extra money, get the high-end equipment. When you start to grow, it is going to be much harder to upgrade if you don't. You'll lose too much business while you're switching over."*

As a country, America is an extra large. Some experts consider obesity an epidemic, as waistlines are burgeoning from Manhattan Beach to Manhattan Island and Americans are fighting the battle of the bulge in every town in between. As a result, the weight-loss industry has become an economic Whopper. Jenny Craig and Weight Watchers are major corporations, while Slim-Fast products find their way each month to millions of homes.

It was only natural then that weight-loss programs would follow the trails to the Web. Online regimens usually include health advice, food selection tips, and workout plans—or some combination. A select number of the online companies offer an interactive health screening, while others offer the cyberactive version of Deal-A-Meal. It's all in cyberspace, virtual scales and all.

Well, as you can imagine, there's room in this industry for lots of ideas and lots of players, both in the major markets and in selected niches. Americans are not really enthusiastic about maintaining healthy lifestyles, but they're absolutely gaga for the next red-hot diet plan. Today it might be the newest wrinkle on the Thighmaster; tomorrow, a recycled imitation of the Pritikin Diet. It's hard to tell which lose-it-now trends will resurface first. But one thing is sure: America will continue to talk about—indeed, obsess about—weight loss. Perhaps e-commerce has some better answers.

A Guaranteed Health Program

Most weight programs are not personalized, but that is the advantage Randy Benton offers clients at Body4u.com. Benton's basic premise is that individualized exercise and food schedules, established by trained professionals, are good enough to earn his company's guarantee of success. As a member of the National Physique Committee, Benton has the knowledge and contacts to keep his company up to date in exercise physiology, diet, nutrition, and general health. Putting such information into play through the interactive features of Body4u.com has helped to make Benton's company a success.

Body4u.com began in 1990 with a program of research. Since then, Benton and his colleagues have tailored diet and exercise regimens for all kinds of people with different needs. The Web makes that service infinitely easier. In January 1999, Benton set up the Web site and turned his firm into an exclusive e-business immediately. There were two good reasons for Benton and his wife to take their business online. First, they had been engaged in health and fitness for a decade and loved it. Second, they both worked for Internet companies. They were fascinated by the possibilities of the Net and saw a promising, wide-open market for diet and fitness companies in cyberspace.

The Bentons liked both industries and put them together. Feeling that the fitness industry was slow to adapt to new technologies and concepts, Randy Benton reasoned that he would have to break new ground. Not many virtual companies were seeing the possibilities for a comprehensive approach to health, diet, and fitness.

The field, however, was not without competition. "A lot of competitors do diets. Some do exercises. Some do physical training," says Benton. "We count all these as our competitors." A site called ediet.com is probably one of the largest virtual competitors, and, as the name suggests, its focus is food issues and diet choices. Others include the American Heart Association and the American Health Association, which have sites that create personalized programs. Benton tried to be different with Body4u.com. "We differ from these others in that we give a more rounded and more in-depth package," says Benton. "Yet it is simple."

Benton's diet and exercise programs are easy to read, easy to use. "You don't have to know a lot about exercises and diets to do well with us," he emphasizes. The programs are computer generated, designed by Benton and his associates to perform comprehensive fitness analyses and diet schedules. The computerized program takes everything into account, including vitamin and mineral requirements based on the food-pyramid model. Benton's staff custom designs programs for clients with special needs, and they constantly work to fine-tune the online services.

Exercise is also specialized. People with bad backs or trick knees can get help at Body4u.com. Programs are keyed to help such people gain not only fitness but stronger backs and knees. Says Benton, "We definitely wanted to get away from being a generic program like the others out there."

Big Sky, Low Overhead

Although Body4u.com began in California, the Bentons eventually moved their operation to White Fish, Montana, to lower their overhead. Basic costs such as labor and office space dropped. The Bentons had originally lived in Big Sky Country before California and relished the thought of moving back. Happily, the Internet gave them the freedom to work wherever they wanted. It turned out to be White Fish, a place that Randy Benton describes as "a lot nicer" than Sunnyvale and one that allows a start-up company to invest more in the Web site, advertising, and basic services.

Benton's company did engage in advertising after testing several types—from e-zines to opt-in mailers, from banner ads to tile and button ads. But most of the time and money goes to service. As Benton explains, a small company must specialize in service because customers are precious and must be kept at all costs. "Once we get a customer," says Benton, "we want to help that customer as much as we can." Admittedly, there are not enough hours in the day, however. Benton says the backbone work is endless—updating the site, posting new articles, generating interesting recipes, and coordinating all the services.

Patience is a virtue in e-businesses. And Randy Benton

echoes that advice for other small-business owners. As for profits and success, he says, "It's not going to happen overnight. It will take a lot of time and consume much of your life. The funny thing is this: I probably work twice as many hours now as ever before. But we enjoy it. We love the freedom, and we find the challenge enjoyable." Many e-business owners feel the same. The whole process of planning, implementing, and adapting an online enterprise is part of the ultimate reward.

At Body4u, Randy Benton sells health advice, food plans, and exercise programs. But his real product is self-confidence. People who succeed at weight loss and fitness live better lives. In this regard, Benton realizes that his e-company has both a role and a mission. It is a pleasant and common footnote to not only the business operations at Body4u.com but to many comparable e-businesses as well. So, if holiday pounds have gained a permanent home around your waistline, consider an online weight loss program like Body4u.com.

Web address:
www.Body4u.com

Hobbies & Collectibles

Antiques

Start-up expenses: $800
Special requirements: *Digital camera*
Best advice: *"Advertising is a waste of money. Everything is word of mouth in this business. People find me exclusively that way. I hand out mailers and business cards with my Web site address on them. Even if I e-mail someone, I put my address at the end of the e-mail. For every item I sell to one customer, I hope ten friends will ask where it came from."*

Now here's an e-commerce story that warrants retelling. Gary Epstein was working one day in his brick-and-mortar antique shop in Cambridge, Massachusetts, a location surrounded by world-class colleges such as Harvard University and Massachusetts Institute of Technology. One day, a kid walked in and started talking, finally convincing Epstein to let the young man design a Web site for the antique business. Because Cambridge has a tremendous reputation for computers, Epstein gave it serious thought, then said OK. "This kid was a computer geek, a little eccentric, but very talented at what he does," recalls Epstein. The results were clearly worth the risk.

CHANCE MEETING

"What he did for me was fabulous," says Epstein, who specializes in rare old watches and jewelry. "I couldn't go out and pay $40 an hour to have a Web site built, but we bartered my merchandise for his services." The symbiotic arrangement paid off. Epstein got a great site, boston-antiques.com, and the computer whiz got experience and antique jewelry as well. "Hey," says Epstein, "You gotta do what you gotta do to get off the ground. And he used me as a guinea pig, too."

A PICTURE IS WORTH A THOUSAND WORDS

After moving the business to Brockton, on Boston's South Shore, Epstein changed his approach, utilizing the new technology of the Web. One of the first innovations was the use of a digital camera to replace old photos and photocopies of inventoried items. As Epstein says, "Now when I bring new inventory into the store, I catalog it, take a picture, and download it to the site." With a daily schedule of photo sessions, Epstein keeps his site up to date. He also takes that time to remove the photos and descriptions of sold items. Many people, he complains, don't bother to upgrade the inventory on a daily basis, leading to unhappy surprises for buyers.

Share the Wealth

The antique world is a strange one, admits Epstein. "It is controlled by people who have been in business for 30 or 40 years. Many are burnt out, and other old-timers just aren't interested in the Net." For Epstein, however, the site is inspirational, a great way to get people to look at an antique pocket watch or broach. He also deals extensively with eBay. Several customers from the auction site buy on eBay, then follow the links to boston-antiques.com, a simple matter that involves clicking a button at the bottom of the page. "I put the button there for people who want to deal with me directly," says Epstein. "It's a good way of advertising."

Generally speaking, the East Coast is a hot market for antiques. People travel to Boston and New England, says Epstein, because quality artifacts may not exist in many other parts of the country. As a result, prices are a little higher in the East. Epstein's particular niche is high-end decorative pieces and art deco. He also keeps a large number of vintage watches in stock—about a hundred at one time.

In addition to sales, Epstein's partner, Rob Cohen (whom Epstein calls "the best in the country"), accepts watch repair and reconstruction jobs from customers all over North America. The added watch repair business has necessitated a second site. Says Epstein, "People can send their watches from anywhere. Rob Cohen is the last line of defense when it comes to watches. When nobody else can fix it, he will do it."

Communication Is the Key

After working in the family business for a while, Epstein had second thoughts. Entering his late thirties, he decided it was time to take a risk and go into something he loved, such as antiques and fine art. "I think I have an eye for items." Admittedly, opening the brick-and-mortar site was difficult for Epstein because, as he explains, "even though the economy is good, people in Boston tend to be tight with their money."

About a year after opening the real doors, Epstein opened the virtual doors. Boston-antiques.com immediately made a tremendous impact. "It's nice," he says, "when people call up and ask what I have. I can simply say, 'Go to my Web site and look at the picture.'" The sales technique could not be better.

As with so much that works in e-business, Epstein's site emphasizes communication. The Web presence gives his products more exposure, even while Bostonians are sitting on their wallets. Even though it's tough to do business in Boston, people in other parts of the country or overseas may scramble to buy a tea cozy or a pewter cup at retail prices even if the item is cracked or damaged. "It's a great way to unload merchandise and keep money moving," says Epstein. "The Net stimulates the business." With the Web advantage, Epstein has sold antique pieces in ten countries and throughout the United States. With a current mailing list of 700, he has a strong customer base, but new buyers primarily come from the Web. Even Epstein's mailings and flyers include the Web address.

DAILY UPDATES

Why have a site? "For the most part," says Epstein, "my Web site shows that I have a real store and a location. That lends legitimacy." Epstein also believes that most everyone who deals with him at the site is happy with purchases. He offers a year's warranty on everything mechanical, including vintage watches, a huge part of his business. Those guarantees, displayed on the Web site, give customers a sense of security.

When Epstein first went online, he was already behind. Just bringing the inventory photos up to date took four months. Today he has the leisure of snapping new pictures everyday as watches and other antiques come through the door. Epstein stresses the importance of remaining on top of Web site updates. Why, he asks, would someone want to go to a site that hasn't been updated for over a month? "On mine," he says, "you'll see it's updated daily. I listen to what people tell me and if they give me a criticism or suggestion, I take advantage."

IF YOU WANT IT, I WILL SHIP IT

Although you can't normally buy furniture at boston-antiques.com, Epstein is flexible. "If somebody wants to pay, I will ship anything," he ruminates. "A lot of antique dealers don't want to go through the hassle of shipping large items. But if I buy a kitchen set for $100 and a customer wants to pay $800, I will ship it." Epstein admits that furniture is usually a problem to ship. "But if business owners say they don't want to ship, it means they are lazy business owners," he adds. For most items, Epstein employs Priority Mail. He likes the post office's new dedication to service. These days, Epstein says he can go into the U.S. Postal Service site to get free shipping materials such as boxes, tape, and "all sorts of stuff to make it easy for you."

Web address:
  www.boston-antiques.com

Antique Quilts

Start-up expenses: *$3,200*
Special requirements: *None*
Best advice: *"You really must have patience. Plan to put a lot of time into the business. I am very happy we entered at the beginning of the e-commerce era. I wanted to have an outstanding site, so rather than do it myself, I hired someone. I think it was good to contact someone who knew what he was doing."*

In the Academy Award–winning movie *Witness*, Harrison Ford plays John Book, a Philadelphia cop who seeks protection in a Pennsylvania Amish community while he flees from police corruption at home. In one scene, Book labors at a barn-raising, perched high in the rafters with hammer and nails, while in the shadows below, the Amish women spread out their sewing on long tables. The women are making quilts—beautiful quilts of traditional design and color. In this single scene, the director captures the historic essence of the German Amish community. While the men labor at the barn, the women—three and four to a table—create a communal quilt that records the gathering for posterity.

Quilts are more than just fine sewing projects. They are artifacts, representations of ethnic values and traditional ways in American history. And western Pennsylvania, the home of the Amish community, is the cultural center of quilt making in America. When Alicelee Graf launched her Web site, Antiquequiltsource.com, the traditional communities of the West Country were in her first thoughts. In the Amish, German, and Mennonite enclaves she found antique quilts from the last half of the nineteenth century. These treasures became the specialty of her business.

WEB SITE GIVES THE ADVANTAGE

But there are other quilts as well. Gray's company gathers textiles in excellent condition, with outstanding workmanship, graphics, and colors. Then, as she has been doing for 20 years, Graf sells the quilts and garments worldwide. She operates a personal, home-based mail order business from western Pennsylvania, but she is the only antique quilt mail order company with a Web site. Eschewing a brick-and-mortar shop and the trade shows, Gray has established a new business model for this cottage industry. "We are more focused," she says, establishing her distance from the competition. Instead of scrambling to demonstrate wares at trade shows, Graf is happily ensconced in her office surrounded by fine embroidery and batting.

AN INDIRECT ROUTE
TO THE QUILT BUSINESS

Graf did not always live in the horse-and-buggy ambience of Pennsylvania Dutch Country. She graduated from the University of Massachusetts with a degree in textiles and design, then started as an interior decorator in Boston. Next she earned an M.A. in reading instruction from Boston University and became a remedial reading teacher in several locations throughout the United States and overseas, frequently moving because of her husband's military career. At one point, Graf even opened her own reading center.

Even with such a busy schedule, Graf always sewed her own clothes, being fascinated with textiles and garment making. While the military was packing her family to the next destination, Graf also began to collect antique quilts. She says, "When I bought my first quilt, I just feel in love with it." She bought two more, and suddenly, she knew exactly what she wanted to do—and it wasn't teaching reading. Her interest in general antiques faded to the background, and Graf started to sell older quilts from her home. For nine years, she advertised locally, and people came to the house to browse.

The next step was a mail order business. For eleven more years, Graf gathered quilts and sent them from the post office, hoping to offer these antiques to the whole population, not just the few thousands who lived in her region. She says, "I tried doing trade shows on weekends, but that proved too time-consuming and hard on my family." When she placed traditional print ads, Graf got good responses. She followed up with direct mail. "My first ad was a one-inch blurb in a popular national magazine," she says, "a country-type magazine. It took a while, but the ad worked. We did well enough to continue."

THE NET CALLS

"I wanted to be in on the innovation called the Net," says Graf proudly. "We had a computer, and we felt this direction was the best way to go." Graf launched one of the first quilt businesses on the Web after hiring a designer. "We wanted to do it right," says Graf. In late 1997, the Antique Quilt Source became an e-business. "We weren't sure it was going to work," admits Graf, "but we felt we had to try, even if the project failed." It didn't. After a bumpy start, Antiquequiltsource.com pulled all the stitches tight.

The Grafs maintain their own site with the help of "a couple of whiz kids." The Web allows them to constantly change the selection of quilts, updating the photos of the available spreads. Because antique quilts are one of a kind, the Grafs spend considerable time replacing one photo with another at the site.

ALL OVER THE GLOBE

Several international customers have come on board, and Antiquequiltsource.com is acquiring a solid overseas following. Because her print ads appear in overseas magazines, Graf is finding a sharp increase in international orders. Sometimes phone conversations are tricky. "They call on the phone, and you have to make yourself understood to people who speak another language," says Graf. "That's a challenge."

CUSTOMERS AND MORE CUSTOMERS

The clientele at Antiquequiltsource.com don't fit one particular mold. Graf says that some buyers and homeowners want a colorful addition with style and character. Others work in drab office buildings and want something traditional to upgrade the ambience. Still others own commercial buildings and hotel suites. Maybe they're looking for a focal point for a lobby or boardroom. A great many customers, she says, are collectors and homeowners who simply love quilts and want to add to their collections.

SEARCH ENGINES LEAD THE WAY

The search engines have brought plenty of business to Antiquequiltsource.com. People who haven't encountered Graf's print ads find her company through Yahoo! Just typing in "antique quilts," says Graf, regularly brings up her site. "Yahoo! is best," she declares. But Amazon.com has also been productive. Amazon discovered the quilt site and asked Graf to join their auction page and z-shops. Although Graf has to pay a small fee for the privilege, she thinks the association with Amazon is fruitful. Graf admits, "Amazon hasn't perfected its site for merchandise other than books." She believes that book buyers have yet to find their way to products like garments and quilts. But Graf remains guardedly optimistic about the online shops and auction sources.

STAYING CURRENT

Keeping the Web site updated has been the biggest problem for Graf. "Even with our people adjusting constantly," she says, "there are unexpected problems." With great regularity, her staff needs to update the picture displays and add or drop new lines. "A major problem," she suggests, "is people whose computers don't have enough power to pull up the photos rapidly." These visitors think the site is flawed, even though the fault lies with an old computer. People who can't raise the photos properly then complain about the Web page.

On the other hand, those buyers who "know what they're doing with their computers" have nothing but compliments for the Antiquequiltsource.com site. They like the close-up photo views and the ease of navigation through the pages. Graf has been pleased with the technical quality of her site and its design features. She believes that the money she invested in a professional Web design was well spent.

In a well-known American drama called *How to Make an American Quilt*, a group of women sit in a small circle, working on their embroidery projects while they ponder values, traditions, and relationships. In many ways such a scene embodies the rich ethnic heritage of Colonial America. But even more, quilting suggests the ways we're part of a living history. It's no wonder that Antiquequiltsource.com has a devoted following.

Web address:

www.Antiquequiltsource.com

Collectible Horses

Start-up expenses: $20,000
Special requirements: *In-depth knowledge of the product line*
Best advice: *"You need to know about and stay on top of the search engines."*

We are a society of collectors. Out there somewhere, people are searching for Barbie dolls and GI Joes, matchbook covers and fire extinguishers, first editions, and closing-night programs. They want bubble glass and isinglass, Olympic pins and bowling pins, guitar picks and swizzle sticks. Collecting is big business today, and the market is virtually unlimited.

Look in the attic. Stroll through the basement. Rummage in the garage. Those old toys, games, and tools are probably on someone's wish list. Grandma's movie posters and that sugar bowl marked "Nippon" might be worth some serious money.

And if you happen to find an old Ty Cobb baseball card, start looking for a good tax dodge. But it isn't just the rare and unique items that command interest. In fact, it's virtually impossible to avoid having some collectibles around the house, even if they're just Mickey Mouse ears or 3-D glasses. We are all potential buyers and sellers in a market that is a close cousin to the garage sale phenomenon. And in this Internet-inspired era, the collectors of the world are beating new paths to your door to find out exactly what treasures you're hoarding.

DOUBLING THE BUSINESS
EACH MONTH

Sue and Tom Schutz inaugurated the Horse Collector in August 1997, beginning as a traditional consignment business, even though their goal was to go online as soon as possible. Initially, Sue Schutz left model horses at a local crafts shop. As a child, Sue had collected the miniatures, finally giving them to her daughter. When the daughter was grown, the two of them began buying others, gathering a good-sized inventory for resale. Soon, says Sue, "I realized this was an upcoming hobby. Recently I watched the local toy stores and saw the local inventory turn over. It clicked that this hobby had red-hot potential."

That potential turned to cash flow when the Horse Collector found its way to the Internet. Originally the Schutzes had placed their hand-painted Breyer horses with Country Sampler, a chain of stores accepting only handcrafted work. Despite relative successes, her husband, Tom, an experienced Web designer, argued for launching the business onto the Net. At first, Sue was against the Net move, believing their best strategy was to continue consignment selling of miniature horses, a market without much competition. But the move to the cybermarket was indeed successful. "It was a gold mine!" says Sue, noting that today 95 percent of sales come from the Net.

Success was not immediate, however. The Horse Collector had been launched in August to take advantage of Christmas sales. But the online portion of the business was not realized until November. By then, it was too late for an effective holiday campaign. "Because search engines take a while to get registered," says Tom, "we didn't do much that first year. But in the second year, after I did a lot of work with the search engines, our numbers doubled every month. We still double our business every month after three years."

Marketing for the Horse Collector has concentrated on the search engines—a strategy that the Schutzes recommend for similar online endeavors. Like many small businesses, horse-collector.com has benefited from a simple approach to Web page sales. "The main emphasis is to be user-friendly and search-friendly," says Tom, who subscribes to a number of search engine services that keep the partners updated. "That way," Tom says, "I can adjust the page or adjust the strategy." Banner ads have not been productive for businesses like the Horse Collector. After preliminary research, the partners concluded that banner ads are not worth the investment. Links have also been a concern. The owners are "very finicky" about links, not wanting to give exchanges to competitors unless they're "somewhat exclusive." As Tom Schutz says, "I want to keep my own customers."

Some of the larger pay-for-service engines have been troublesome thus far, leading the Schutzes toward a heavier reliance on free search engines. "The engine GoTo concerns me, and I don't know at this point if they are going to work out. GoTo hasn't had any impact on us. I've never heard anyone say they use GoTo. But I have the most difficulty with AltaVista. Because one supplier can have six or seven pages, they keep repeating the same information. So today I don't target AltaVista, but I do register with them." Schutz insists, however, that Yahoo! is indispensable, even though it's "a fight" to get a listing. Schutz says Yahoo! has some serious hoops to jump, including having to submit two listings before making inquiry about status. "Until you register twice," says Tom, "they don't pay any attention." Then it remains a battle to get Yahoo! to respond to questions.

Tom Schutz notes that Yahoo! now has services where you pay for a higher search listing. "It seems like a conflict of interest," complains Tom, who also says that, with Yahoo!'s paid services, it's even harder to receive feedback and talk to a Yahoo! representative. Nevertheless, "Ya gotta have Yahoo!" says Tom. "It can take six months or more, but once you're listed, you will see your numbers climb instantly."

A DIFFERENT APPROACH TO SALES

Unlike a standard storefront business, the Horse Collector went online without much overhead. The Schutzes needed a $2,000 PC, a scanner worth about $4,000, and inventory totaling $14,000. Instead of taking profits, however, the partners built up computers and inventory for almost three years, then began pulling profits from the receipts—a relatively quick turn compared with most brick-and-mortar enterprises. They admit that their Internet enterprise has been all-consuming. "In general, people think it's easy to start an electronic business. It's not. Even after two years, I still spend 12 hours a day. Finally I learned to take Sundays off and maybe a half day on Saturday. It's definitely full-time. It takes work, and it takes devotion."

Luckily, the cyberworld offers a well-lit path to success for businesses like horsecollector.com. "The future is the Internet," says Tom, who says that e-business today is in its Wright Brothers stage.

Also he notes that, until two years ago, e-business was for men, who bought more computers, more hardware, and more software than women. Today, at least at horsecollector.com, most customers are female. "It's a girly product." Because some people, primarily the older generation, remain shy of computers, the Horse Collector ads include not only the company's URL but also the firm's 800 number. "If they don't have computers, they can ask for catalogs," says Tom Schutz, "but mostly they come to our business through the Web site." Interestingly enough, despite its high-tech evolution, the Horse Collector remains a standard mail order business. While the Net has added an entire new look and scope to the marketing, the Schutzes still spend most of their long workdays taking orders and mailing shipments.

The competition has not been asleep. The horsecollector.com site is one of several challenging the same market. "The competition ranges from people who are doing it for a few bucks over cost to wholesalers and full-price retailers," says Sue Schutz. "We have about eight other sites directly competing with us. Five of these sites deal predominately in model horses; others, like toy stores, have the horses as part of a larger inventory." In this marketplace, the main concern is the big-money players, large companies like Toys "R" Us, corporations that have delayed making the Net connection but now see that it's "go online or don't play." And the field may become more crowded. "I expect even more competition," says Sue Schutz, although she also notices a number of small players who maintain a Web site for a few months and then disappear. As in the real world of storefronts and neon signs, attrition will take its toll.

Tom does video conferencing as an assistant engineer for an established company. For him, doing Web pages has been a hobby and a source of extra income. Since beginning horsecollector.com, he has had numerous inquiries about Web page consulting but has resisted the temptations. "I just don't have the time," he says. "My emphasis is to get home-office people on the Internet and not to get involved in large projects." Because he has always worked with the public either face-to-face or through the video conference medium, Tom Schutz recognizes that Internet business "is not personal." He laments the loss of human contact and envisions the day when e-businesses will also use video conferencing. In that situation, an agent will come on the line through the browser, adding to the human touch but also raising the cost of business.

MORE THAN JUST A WEB PAGE AND SOME STAMPS

Dealing with customers online is not entirely trouble free. The biggest problem is understanding and registering with search engines in a timely fashion. Paying for search services is not always the answer. Rather, diligence in dealing with search companies seems the best advice. Many people lose patience with the process and lose business in the interim. A comparable problem is finding someone who knows how to promote the site and create the Web page. When business owners put together Web sites, they want fancy effects and sophisticated designs. But most customers have low-tech browsers. In a word, they are *slow*. The complicated designs look good on high-powered equipment but load and display poorly on lower-end PCs. "You have to keep the browser dumb," says Tom Schutz, "to reach the broader audience with this product." And the page has to be fast as well. "I started using Java stuff, and people said they couldn't see my text or designs," says Tom. The catchphrase here is the same for most new online businesses: keep it simple.

Another complication comes from outstripping the inventory. In an online mail order business with serious up-side potential, there is a real danger of not having items to ship when the orders pour in.

The Horse Collector owners needed a business records program that was affordable and useful. "A bookkeeping program like *QuickBooks* is not set up for mail order," says Sue Schutz, "and you don't want to go into the high-end programs that cost thousands."

The partners also had trouble with establishing a merchant account. Finally, after lots of Internet research, they found a local company, Eagle Merchant Services, that met their bookkeeping needs. In this set-up, customers order over the phone. There is a form on the Web site, but the Schutzes have not yet put up a shopping cart. Says Sue, "I want to grow the business and get more products there first." The Schutzes do like the 800 number service. "It makes business more personal," says Sue, "and they can ask questions, so we know for sure what people want. It is a warm and fuzzy relationship. I have developed some loyal followers."

While first searching for those followers, the Schutzes started an AOL account, where members get a free site so they don't have to pay $50 or more a month to host their sites. "It worked well," says Tom Schutz. "And then, when we surpassed what AOL could do for us, we got another server." The Horse Collector went into the marketplace cautiously, staying with AOL for a year before upgrading to another server. "It was a good way to test the waters," suggests Tom.

The market for collectibles is huge and growing—a cybermarketplace that plays on our natural human tendency toward nostalgia. And the business seems weatherproof to economic storms. When the economy is good, collecting is good. When the economy is bad, people want to spend $30 on a treat for themselves. In the meantime, it is never more than 364 days to Christmas, that magic season when an old-time Lionel caboose or an "I Like Ike" button is the only thing that will do for Jimmy's stocking.

Web address:
www.horsecollector.com

Collectible Sports Cards

Start-up expenses: *$175*
Special requirements: *None*
Best advice: *"Depends. If people have experience, I think they can do a fairly decent job of building and promoting a site. Any novice should find a reputable Web site builder, though, and pay the price to get started. In the long run, that plan would save a beginner a lot of problems."*

Pssst! Check the attic. Root through the garage. What's in that box marked "My Stuff: Don't Touch!" Let's hope it's sports cards. Yesterday's playthings are today's collectibles. Do you have a rookie card for Alex Rodriguez, Walt Michaels, Michael Jordan, Bobby Hull, Jackie Robinson, Frank Gifford, Red Schoendienst, Bart Starr, Walt Hazzard, Don Havlicek, Gale Sayers, Wilt the Stilt, or Tiger Woods? If so, your retirement years will be a little easier.

In the past few years, the mania for baseball cards has spread.

Today collectors are hoarding football, hockey, and basketball sets as well. Even golf, gymnastics, and soccer cards are starting to surface. Furthermore, the collectors aren't just kids anymore. Middle-aged men and even businesswomen are in the game. As you might expect, there are also online card shops. One of the best is the Strictly Mint Card Company, founded and owned by Mike DeLuca at wwcd.com/smcc.

ROOKIE GOES TO BAT

DeLuca was a rookie in 1996 when he opened his shop in Forest Hills, New York, with an investment of $175. In those years, sports memorabilia was interesting to collectors, but few were using the bubble-gum-scented cards as investments. DeLuca began with individual cards—rookie offerings and insert cards, as well as the complete sets. Later came the interest in other major sports and, of course, the collectible cards for the National Football League, National Hockey League, and National Basketball Association.

DeLuca began with no special experience or expertise. He just loved cards. "There is no way to get experience in this field," he says. "You learn as you go. I did get a degree in accounting, and that background has helped some." But the real advantage was sound business practices. After more than a decade in the card business, DeLuca was stressing the fundamentals—good selection, competitive prices, and strong customer service. "These are essential," he says. "Without each, you won't succeed."

A GLIMPSE OF THE FUTURE

DeLuca had another advantage. He saw the wave of the future, the Internet. Today, says DeLuca, "very few people we knew from the beginning are still around." Those without a strong business sense could not compete, and those who did survive had to be ready for the new business paradigm of the Net. Not surprisingly, the Internet drove many unprepared dealers into early retirement.

These days, working from his online site at wwcd.com/smcc, DeLuca sells "mint condition" cards in New Mint and Mint + + grades. All his factory products are sealed in the original wrappings, and the rookie and insert cards are guaranteed "to be clean, well centered, and have that fresh-from-the-pack look." Sorry, no gum.

AN ONLINE HOME RUN

How did the Web site start? In 1996, DeLuca wanted to get a jump on the Internet market. After checking with several possible hosts, he chose WWCD, one with a long list of dealers in collectibles.

Competition is strong, and eBay dealers flood the field, as well as other dealers who have built clever Web sites. DeLuca believes his success comes not only from an emphasis on business fundamentals but also from three additional factors. First, the Strictly Mint Card Company handles complete card sets with great variety and selection. Second, DeLuca accepts credit cards, even Discover and Amex, something rare in the online card businesses. Third, DeLuca's company sells to a strong international market—again an unusual ploy. All told, DeLuca is well positioned for a profitable market share, even though the lineup of online players is getting rather long.

As for problems, DeLuca laments having to deal with faceless people in cyberspace. Many are less than professional, failing to handle transactions in a timely and efficient manner. With every "Tom, Dick, and Harry" trading cards on the side, DeLuca finds his online business more problematic than the face-to-face transactions of the storefront card shop.

ADVERTISING LEADS THE WAY

Nonetheless, DeLuca is pleased with the results of his online forays. He uses newsgroup posts to attract customers. Also there are references to the site in his print ads, the ones that run in sports and collectibles magazines like *Tuff Stuff*, *Beckett's*, and *Sports Cards*. His average customer, the 20- to 50-year-old male, is still collecting, buying, and looking for a Ty Cobb rookie card. In the meantime, DeLuca is happy to meet the demand for this year's collectible sets. After all, maybe the rookie card for the next Ken Griffey, Jr., is included, neatly wrapped in plastic, a future treasure for some lucky card collector.

Web address:
   www.wwcd.com/smcc

Dollhouses and Miniatures

Start-up expenses: $400

Special requirements: *A love of dollhouses*

Best advice: *"It doesn't matter where you're located. Location becomes irrelevant in the virtual world. But you have to provide more information on your site than if you had a store. At a store, people can see, touch, and feel the products in person. On a Web site, you need to be able to describe things at a level where people can thoroughly understand the product. That is a challenge."*

Dollhouses are not just for little girls anymore. They're part of the collectibles craze. In fact, men and women of all ages, including a growing number of retirees, are visiting sites like Suzisdollhouses.com. From Suzi Otis's Web pages, you can order a hand-carved rocking chair or a gilded art-deco dresser, cleverly created to fit your dollhouse. In fact, says Otis, "Anything you can buy life-size we can find for you in one-inch scale."

EVERYONE WANTS A MINIATURE

Golf clubs? Bread machine? Boom box? Wow, Barbie never had it so good. What's going on here? Well, after some well-planned research, Otis discovered that all kinds of people are interested in dollhouses. Some people have been collecting miniatures for years. Others are new parents buying for a baby, thinking ahead to when the child is old enough to play with the toys and small-scale furniture. Still others are artisans who like to paint intricate designs on small furniture or want to try their hand at creating dollhouse artifacts in miniature scale.

The craftspeople are perhaps most interesting. They see the dollhouse furnishings as a challenge, a piece of delicate sculpture or design. In some cases, the best artisans produce pieces that look like the real thing, only soaked in hot water and shrunk to size. For the arts devotees and hobbyists, Suzisdollhouses.com is a place to get new ideas, shop for materials, and buy pieces as models for their own work.

IT'S ALL AVAILABLE AT SUZI'S

The range of products sold by Otis is enormous. She carries a full line of dollhouses and miniatures from major suppliers. "Everything is discounted," Otis adds. "We have kits, assembled dollhouses, furniture, wallpaper, carpet, building materials, one-inch-scale dolls, decorating accessories, electrical and lighting, even landscaping." For serious collectors, Otis features furniture that is not only scaled perfectly but made perfectly. If you're serious about quality, consider the $300 hand-carved dinette set or the designer table lamp. This site isn't just a furniture warehouse for toddlers.

HOBBY TURNS A PROFIT

Otis has been online since September 1999, filing with the major search engines a month later. Her mother is her partner, and both women have been building dollhouses "for years and years." Like so many others, Otis entered the e-commerce world not only to turn a profit but to pursue a personal interest.

When they were involved with dollhouses only as a hobby, Otis and her mom could not find miniatures at a discount. That problem made them frustrated and curious. They saw a need and built a business to fill it. At first, they sold "room boxes" (a room from a house in miniature) at doll shows. Soon after, they decided it was prudent to go online, primarily because they found themselves turning to the Net for their own shopping needs. Says Otis, "We saw a few good sites in this market, but none met the need that we saw. In the end, we figured we could do it. And we have."

RESEARCH IS THE FIRST STEP

In contemplating the business, Otis drew on her background in information systems and technology. Her technical background helped, even though she wasn't a programmer. "I looked into software," she says, "so we could build our own store with a shopping cart. We looked at hosting and decided Yahoo! was the way to go." At Yahoo!Store, Otis found everything she needed: technical assistance, a secure site (very important!), search engine listing, and other benefits. Otis also liked Yahoo! because, in her opinion, as the largest search engine it offered the promise of bringing the most customers online.

After deciding that dolls and dollhouse products appealed to a large number of people, Otis launched her site, eventually drawing customers not only from Yahoo! but from other search engines as well. But it wasn't easy. "That is the biggest challenge," says Otis, "getting ranked high in the search engines." She recognizes that each engine has different requirements, different strategies, so what works at Yahoo! may not be as effective elsewhere. "And to be honest," admits the owner, "you can't play games with the search engines. People have tried. It doesn't work. They're smart."

In addition to the search engine route, Otis has parlayed links with other sites to her advantage. She also appreciates the convenience of an 800 number, where customers working on their own designs and construction projects can phone in with queries. "They'll ask all kinds of interesting questions," Otis says. "Sometimes they want specific advice with building problems or just general recommendations on design." That's where the fun begins. "Just sitting here and taking orders is a big part of the business," she offers, "but it is certainly not the most fun. Getting involved with the customers is the best part."

HIGH SPEED, NO BUMPS

Otis says that the Internet's speed is the greatest surprise—not only the speed of transactions but the speed at which interest has grown in Suzisdollhouses.com. "We weren't quite prepared for that!" says Otis. "It grew so fast!" Because she began business on the cusp of the Christmas season, Otis opened her cyberdoors to a world full of eager customers with long gift lists.

Normally a business begins with the usual bumps, false starts, red herrings, and retrenchments. Not so on the Net. "We didn't have the normal period to work out all that stuff!" exclaims Otis with both pleasure and frustration. "We could have used more time to put things in place and get used to the software." Yes, an adjustment period is helpful in any business, but—and we can't stress the notion enough—there is no speed limit in cyberspace.

For others contemplating the e-commerce highway, Otis has a couple thoughts. First, have a sound business plan. Second, forget about the advantages and disadvantages of brick-and-mortar shops. Although buyers cannot touch the merchandise on the Web, they need to get a "feel" for the products. Therefore, it's necessary to display and describe miniatures (or any products) accurately, carefully, and thoroughly. "That," says Otis, "is a challenge."

Web address:

www.Suzisdollhouses.com

Science Fiction Collectibles

Start-up expenses: $500
Special requirements: *Tricorder and communicator*
Best advice: *"Make sure that you help the customer have the best experience possible. Ultimately it is not about whether they are ordering on-or offline but how they are being treated. Even the most technologically savvy buyer is not going to remain at the Web site unless it is structured to satisfy the customer."*

If you are prepared to "boldly go where no one has gone before," people are already ahead of you in line. *Star Trek* aficionados and fans of the paranormal long ago paved the way to the unvisited galaxies of cyberspace. Take a number.

Science fiction and the Net—could there be a better match? For sci-fi fans, the "Truth Is Out There. In the midst of the search, the faithful are making daily online contacts with sci-fi characters like Data, Dr. Who, Agent Scully, Rod Serling, Flash Gordon, Roswell aliens, and the arrogant "Q." It's almost too marvelous. With a click of the mouse, *Star Wars* fans, Trekkies, "Twilight Zone" viewers, and *Dune* patrons can visit their own M-class planets in the virtual world. Simply log on to www.800trekker.com and "Engage!"

SCI-FI FANS

David Blaise is the founder and CEO of Brainstorms Internet Marketing, an online company that has a large piece of the sci-fi pie. In 1994, Blaise founded the Friends of Dr. Who organization, which now reaches more than 10,000 members. "Friends" features a newsletter, but in recent years Blaise added a centerfold merchandise spread as well.

After a short time, the merchandise inventory expanded to include *Star Trek, Star Wars*, and other sci-fi paraphernalia, creating a larger fan base. "Going with *Star Trek* products," says Blaise, "was the obvious way to expand. "I wanted to have a vanity 800 phone number, something that would be impossible to forget. The word *trekkie* would just annoy people, so I tried *trekker*. I had to jump through a lot of hoops, but I got the 1-800-trekker phone number in February 1994, and I incorporated the company a month later."

In March 1994, when Blaise launched his catalog company for science fiction fans, he was humoring his own fascination with film and literary brave new worlds. In starting the catalog business, he was primarily following his own interests. Originally, the catalog business offered merchandise, including items like the Tardis key, a feature of the *Dr. Who* series. When Fox made a *Dr. Who* movie, Blaise's company provided the Tardis key. On the evening of the movie's opening, Blaise's employees held a party to watch their keys "star" in the film.

"As soon as I added that merchandise spread," says Blaise, "it became clear that a lot of people who were receiving the newsletter were interested in merchandise, so the natural step was to put together a *Dr. Who* catalog." Blaise's first print run, a black-and-white booklet, went only to fan club members. According to Blaise, the response was "incredible."

Today the offices of Brainstorms Internet Marketing have a Tardis key on display, a proud memento of their cinema cameo. But the company is no longer simply a catalog operation. In 1998, Blaise took the operation online, adopting the address of www.800trekker.com, a domain name that speaks to several generations of Kirk and Picard fans. The catalog is still available but is used as a direct marketing piece to promote the Web site. In addition, people can still use fax, mail, and phone services to order. But, says Blaise "We are encouraging people as much as possible to order online."

"Science fiction fans are technologically savvy," says Blaise, "so the transition has gone well." Trekkers and other space travelers are generally well educated and left-brained. They understand computers and Web sites. As a result, the switch toward Internet operations has been fairly smooth for Brainstorms.

CYBERSPACE IS CROWDED

Science fiction sites are rampant on the Net. Blaise has analyzed his own company's success in a crowded market and points to three significant factors. First, the browsers at 800trekker.com are experienced. They know the lore and the technical side equally well. Second, Blaise offers a fully integrated e-commerce site. Competitors sell science fiction merchandise, but few integrate it without a glitch in service. Third, Blaise's company offers ordering entry 24 hours a day, seven days a week, either online or by phone. Customer service desks are manned eight hours a day, with any overflow handled by an inbound telemarketing company. "We're always covered," says Blaise. "Whenever the phones ring, someone capable answers."

Besides top-notch customer service, Blaise's organization boasts a reliable credit card system. Once the card number is received, the order processes automatically, with a copy immediately going to the shipping department. If an order arrives by 11 A.M. it ships the same afternoon. "That kind of smooth process happens on mainstream sites," says Blaise, "but seldom on sci-fi sites. Traditionally, there has been a problem with fulfillment in the industry." By insisting on careful and accurate processing, Blaise hopes to derail some of the skepticism about sci-fi sites. It's a clear advantage, he says, that fans would rather order from other fans than from corporations.

Another important feature is Blaise's guarantee. His company offers a 90-day, no-questions-asked guarantee on all products. Also in place is a 90-day "best price" policy. If customers find a better deal within three months of purchase, Brainstorms Internet Marketing provides a 110 percent rebate or a merchandise credit, again with no questions asked and no hassles. A good deal, yes?

A Good Affiliate System Is Crucial

Blaise's company takes special advantage of the affiliate system of the Net; most of his customers arrive from other sites. His site is tied to 4,500 other Web addresses such as the *Star Wars* and the *Buffy the Vampire Slayer* sites. Originally, Blaise made contact by sending out e-mails, letting them know they could earn money by sending customers his way.

Today a visitor to the *Buffy* home page, for example, can click on a banner that goes not only to the 800trekker.com site but directly to the *Buffy* store at Blaise's Web site. This direct link, without a lot of clicking and searching, is one reason for success, says the 800trekker owner. This online targeting increases Blaise's chances for sales and reduces the number of visitors going to a different site to buy merchandise.

Blaise uses affiliate programs that run through LinkShare.com and BeFree.com, third-party facilitators. Here's how it works: the third-party companies track the number of click-throughs, the number of impressions (how many people saw the banner on an affiliate site), and the number of sales. Says Blaise, "Third-party verification like this is important. The affiliates don't have to take my word for anything. They can check on progress and get a report at any time."

With a strong affiliate system and a bevy of popular products, www.800trekker.com is poised for a profitable voyage through cyberspace. Blaise wants to have not only the best sci-fi site on the Net but "the best catalog Web company in any industry." That goal is an ambitious one. But with 1,000 hot products—including action figures, apparel, autographed books, comics, DVDs, and other paraphernalia—prospects seem bright.

Web address:
   www.800trekker.com

Stencils for Home Decorating

Start-up expenses: $20,000
Special requirements: *Laser stencil cutters*
Best advice: *"We were the first in our industry to have a Web site, and that certainly moved us along. Today, unlike when we entered, you need all the bells and whistles to compete. All our competitors are copying our site, and you have to be constantly aware of what the other guys are doing. Try to keep above the fray."*

Making a homey place to live doesn't have to be expensive. Sometimes the secret is refinished furniture. Sometimes the key is window treatment or well-chosen knickknacks. Whatever you need to add warmth, it's on the Net. One inexpensive decorating solution is laser-cut stencils. Jan Dressler, founder and owner of the Dressler Stencil Company, has 300 designs for you. Just navigate your way to Dresslerstencils.com, and the fun begins. You won't believe the possibilities.

A CLICK OF THE MOUSE

Dressler's full-color catalog offers stencil designs organized by themes: animals, florals, cave drawings—even accessories for any theme. If you think a stencil project or creative mural sounds like a good idea, tap into Dressler's site and choose a category. From there, you'll reach a thumbnail overview of the selection for that category. For further information and details, click on the thumbnail. It's that easy.

A detailed reference guide helps you find everything, and it includes all the necessary information about how to use stencils, build murals, or create scenery. The site also offers stencil brushes, acrylic paints, natural sea sponges, and instructional videos. It's all there. An interesting addition to Dresslerstencils.com is the Resource Guide. In these pages, browsers view several interesting stencil projects, complete with instructions and samples of the finished murals.

FIRST VISIBILITY, THEN A WEB SITE

The Dressler Stencil Company began as a mail order operation. Dressler produced print catalogs and advertising—the traditional method of marketing. One of her strategies was to join a professional organization, a move that helped make her contacts and finally led to editorial coverage in magazines. These early publicity efforts gave Dressler some visibility in the business and kept advertising costs down. Nonetheless, the mail order business had a high overhead.

When Dressler moved toward print ads, the business grew. She says simply, "The more ads we placed, the more business we got." But the huge, constant advertising bills were unwelcome.

"You have to spend more to make money," she laments, remembering the invoices. Once the company made a name for itself, however, Dressler found it easier to get free exposure. Television producers called, and she began doing weekly spots (and more) on cable shows like "Christopher Lowell," "Decorating with Style," and others. With numerous reruns, Dressler finds that her stencil line gets plenty of media exposure.

But everything changed with the Web site. In 1996, Dressler's husband fired up the computer and began building a presence. Dressler says, "Once the site went up, things really started sparking." Even though the site was small—and although not many people were Web shopping back then—profits surged. In 1998, the Dresslers revamped their site. Since then, the Web has been by far their biggest moneymaker.

Dressler enjoys marvelous exposure with no advertising costs. She loves it! Even though it eventually cost tens of thousands of dollars to launch a Web presence and maintain it, she argues that the cyberstrategy has been "amazing in terms of sales figures." The site has outsold Dressler's print ads by a remarkable percentage, and she even sells the catalogs online. Some people still want a print copy, even though the entire text is published online.

The Dresslers host their own site with their own server, hoping to maintain control over the technical side of operations. They also employ a consulting group to intercede if the server crashes—a company called Northwest Computer Support, which provides 24-hour monitoring.

A BUSINESS IDEA
HATCHED AT THE MALL

"It was a fluky thing," says Dressler, remembering the first time she encountered the notion of selling stencils. She visited a country mall where they sold stencils, and her friend said, "Let's go look!" When Dressler peeked, she had no idea what she was viewing. "What are those?" she asked. Even though she didn't like the designs, Dressler liked the concept. She thought, "Why can't I draw something and paint it on plastic—then cut it out?" Well, she could, and she did. Today, the stencils are laser cut, and Dressler's company is busy. They operate six days a week with 20 employees. It's an effort, she admits, just to get all the orders out the door. Dressler remains the primary designer, but she has begun to feature the artwork of new designers.

CUSTOMER BASE

The customers in this business are women between the ages of 35 and 60—usually women who either have small children or don't work outside the home. "They are people who have left the workforce for the most part," says Dressler. "They are searching for a creative outlet." Designing with stencils seems to fill that need.

Dressler's advice for those thinking about e-business is simple. "Don't be afraid. Go for it!" She suggests that early entry into a niche is certainly the best plan, but even if you're entering a crowded market, this is the time. The virtual business world will only become more crowded, and the opportunities will never be better. In short, move now. Write your name in virtual ink and stencil it onto the Web.

Web address:
www.Dresslerstencils.com

Turkish Plates

Start-up expenses: $5,000
Special requirements: *Import connections for Turkish goods*
Best advice: *"Try a free service for Web site building first before constructing a huge Web site and investing a lot of money. There are a number of places you can go where you can build your site for free. That way, you can experiment and do what you need without investing a lot of money. Why spend thousands of dollars on a Web design when it may not work?"*

The Net has a curious spin-off effect, not unlike the process that creates new TV shows from old ones, such as "Rhoda," "Benson," and "The Jeffersons." Here's an example. Laura Kazan visited Turkey, the homeland of her husband, and brought back some plates. She began to sell them on eBay, following the lead of her little sister, who had been selling books on the auction site. After a while, some of her eBay customers asked about ordering directly, and an e-business was born!

After starting with a few Iznik plates from Turkey—just a handful—Kazan also gathered some Turkish tiles and copper plates. She decided she needed a way to display her merchandise, and a Web site seemed perfect. Now a plethora of the auction buyers have followed her to Kazan.bigstep.com, and she's adding new buyers as well. Kazan still uses eBay and other auction sites to sell Turkish plates, but she utilizes eBay primarily as a means of advertising, a method of introducing the lines and attracting buyers to her own site.

MARKETING STRATEGY

After frequent visits to the old country, Laura Kazan typed in "Turkish" on a search engine. Not much came up. She was intrigued. Later, on one of her trips to Turkey, she considered the sales possibilities for Turkish goods, thinking that there is a good market in that country, not only for Turkish emigrants but for others with interests in the history and culture of the region. Bringing back a few Iznik plates, Kazan found she was right. People wanted to buy. Today she's marketing a broad range of ceramic plates and tiles—a good selection of mostly handmade wares from Kutahya.

Iznik plates is an art form traditional to Turkey. The ceramic plates (and tiles), all imported through a buyer in Istanbul, feature designs from the Ottoman Empire. They're considered souvenir items. Iznik plates from Kutahya sell well in this country, especially the ones with Arabic writing. Since most plates are individually crafted, the designs are all different. Collectors are especially fond of the Iznik ceramics.

Sorting Through Search Engines

In the beginning, Kazan attached information about her own site to her eBay auction postings. "I linked it in from there, and eBay is where most of my sales generate from. I wandered through the Net looking for Turkish directories and art directories and got myself listed. That connection brings some customers, too." After attempting a listing on iMall, Kazan decided she was wasting her money. She says, "iMall didn't work at all because you are not going to get people there who are looking for these kinds of items."

Kazan's foray into Yahoo! was more productive, and she ranked number one for a period of time. She also ranked well with AltaVista. But in the end, she found it impossible to maintain a prominent rank with Yahoo! and the other search engines, so she decided instead to seek listings in appropriate directories. That plan worked.

But eBay is still the source of most customer traffic. According to Kazan, most of the people on the auction site are ready to buy when they enter. Usually the browsers begin by typing "Turkish," and that key word leads them directly to Kazan's Turkish Treasures, aka Kazan.bigstep.com. Because her customers are well defined, Kazan likes the advantages of eBay. She can expect browsers to be interested in Turkey and highly motivated to buy her products. Using eBay as an advertising base seems particularly astute. Kazan lists items on the auction site that have drawing power toward her own Web pages. "I think of it as an advertising cost," says Kazan, "so it doesn't matter if I don't get the full price." In fact, Kazan's eBay link offers a 10 percent discount to the winning bidders for each item. That ploy attracts new customers to Kazan's Turkish Treasures, and it often results in double sales.

Bringing a Piece of Culture into Your Life

Kazan spends no time trying to inform the public about Iznik plates or Turkish ceramics. She believes that people without previous knowledge will not seek her site. But those who already know something about Turkish art and culture are prepared to buy.

Indeed, the average customer at Kazan.bigstep.com has visited Turkey. For example, says Kazan, one summer she heard from a number of people who had recently been to Istanbul and wanted mementos. "They knew about the items and wanted more," she says. Besides travelers, she also sells extensively to people with Turkish heritage. Several of her buyers are married to Turks and want to decorate their homes with plates or tiles from the homeland—or to give them as presents to relatives and friends.

Some Concerns: Price and Shipping

In the beginning, pricing her merchandise presented a problem for Kazan. Primarily, she wasn't asking enough. Curiously, it's not always a price cut but a price hike that brings in customers. Originally she priced a select group of copper plates at $9.99, thinking they wouldn't sell well. After raising the prices to $50 and $60, she sold stacks. Although she's not entirely sure why the copper plates became so popular, Kazan theorizes that the Arabic calligraphy on the rims is a major attraction.

Most ceramic plates on Kazan's Web site sell for between $45 and $55, and her tile collections range from $40 to $90, depending on the sets. She says that the best-selling collections are in the lower price range, each set having four tiles. Also available is a tile trivet for $12.50, a product that has sold especially well.

Shipping was, of course, a serious concern. On the first shipment from Turkey, some pieces were broken. Another time, the entire shipment was damaged due to packaging problems. Says Kazan, "We will be going to Turkey soon to train people how to pack the merchandise more carefully. We also had to learn to do that ourselves in order to get our own shipments to customers intact."

With a shipping routine now in place, Kazan employees are breaking fewer plates. They've secured the correct style of bubble-wrap material and the right-size boxes for their in-house packaging chores.

A PART-TIME VENTURE

Laura Kazan runs her e-business from her house, partly to stay home with her family. After initial successes, her husband wanted to get involved, too. He also works at a local restaurant and goes to school, so his contributions are not as great. Luckily, their association with Bigstep.com reduces some of the Web site maintenance pressure, so business has been smooth since its inception in August 1999.

Competition hasn't been a problem. Laura researched other sites, finding only three—all in Turkey and all with "ridiculous" prices. Kazan's products come exclusively from Kutahya, a city famous for ceramic design. Everything is made in artisans' studios there, where local competition keeps the prices constant. Kazan feels her price lists are more than fair. "What I sell for $55," she says, "the other sites in Turkey sell for between $150 and $350."

With a large inventory, including such items as silk-screen tiles, hand-painted tiles, plates, and clocks, the Kazans have Turkish art products that have a large appeal in the United States. Using eBay strategically for advertising, the e-tailers have created a business plan that promises steady profits and strong growth. Besides, the Kazans get to travel regularly to the Turkish homeland, where there are always exciting new product lines to consider.

Web address:
www.Kazan.bigstep.com

Personal
Services &
Lifestyles

Childcare and Eldercare

Start-up expenses: $40,000
Special requirements: *None*
Best advice: *"The Net has changed dramatically. The days are over where you can start a viable business like this with $35 or $40 in your pocket. To pull it off now, you need a clear vision, and you need the funding. If you have a good idea, there is always a 500-pound gorilla lurking out there, so you absolutely must have the resources to stake your claim."*

The start-up stories for e-businesses—the tales and anecdotes of the first month of operations—make fascinating reading. Consider, for example, Oliver Mittermaier and Michael J. Goldberg, partners in CareGuide.com, a resource site for child-and eldercare. The two men began their venture at the local library, hauling stacks of telephone books. At night and on weekends, Mittermaier and Goldberg labored to photocopy the Yellow Pages listings for childcare in Topeka,

Hartford, Mobile, Bedford Falls, and Tacoma. When they had finally run out of nickels, the men had amassed an enormous database, one that was entirely original and unique.

In the beginning, CareGuide.com was intended to be only a childcare site, but soon the partners realized the obvious applications of their approach to the elderly as well. As they began to expand their business plan, the two men almost pushed themselves too far, working their regular jobs and spending nights at Mittermaier's studio apartment shuffling piles of photocopies and resource books. In the end, the "ridiculous hours" of night work resulted in a Web site that combines useful services for both the youngest and oldest members of the American population.

Today, the CareGuide.com site has two distinct components: childcare and eldercare. For each, browsers can consult, without charge, a database that lists caregivers in their local area. The business also lists extensive articles on topics such as how to choose health care providers, stages and options in Alzheimer's disease, answers for specific questions and recommendations, and problem solving with caregivers. Finally, there's a Tool Box with information written by both men where visitors find the Child Care Center Checklist, the Nanny-Au Pair Phone Screening Form, the Nanny Interview Form, and the Nursing Home Checklist. In short, the Care Guide site offers people all the necessary resources to care for children or the elderly.

LOTS OF HITS IN THE FIRST MONTH

All those ink stains and paper cuts paid off. As Mittermaier recounts, "Without any advertising whatsoever, we got 15,000 hits in the first month. We thought, *Gosh, this is huge!* The site immediately fielded e-mails from all over the country asking for listings in new areas. For another nine months, the partners worked part-time expanding their database and seeking new caregivers using the Yellow Pages again. But the company couldn't remain a part-time endeavor for long. Mittermaier and Goldberg quit their day jobs. CareGuide.com has become the largest online resource for information and services for child- and eldercare. Their e-catalog has lists for more than 10,000 American cities, with in-depth information on more than 90,000 childcare providers and 75,000 eldercare providers.

INSIGHT OR INSANITY?

In retrospect, Mittermaier sees that his vision for the company was not entirely tenable. The double-pronged approach of child-and eldercare now "seems insane," he admits, especially because eldercare services are quite complicated. Nonetheless, the company found its footing and grew rapidly, partly because the competition was still thinking it over. "The saving grace," says Mittermaier, "is that we got in early." Amen.

Today CareGuide.com is big, really big. Mittermaier and Goldberg have more than 50 employees, and they expect to double that number soon. They spend a majority of their time contacting and screening caregivers, especially concentrating on keeping the database current. Although the employees at CareGuide.com don't rate the caregivers, they check on licensing and registrations, making every attempt to assure the public that the recommended caregivers are capable and reliable.

"We promote our Web site online," says Mittermaier, "but there's mostly word-of-mouth advertising." The partners also work with human resource managers, who take

CareGuide.com's Web content and put it on another company's extranet or intranet pages, thus creating a kind of "private label" caregiver information page for employees. Mittermaier says that he has similar arrangements with women's health sites on Yahoo! and Excite. "For instance," he recalls, "if you go into Women.com to search for childcare, the content looks like theirs. Actually, it's ours." This method has been an integral way for consumers to get tapped into CareGuide.com content.

How Does an Information Database Make Money?

Mittermaier says that a key driver in their business vision is to provide information without charge to consumers unless there's a transaction where an online visitor purchases a hard good or service. "In essence," he says, "we think of ourselves as a classic infomediary. We capture the interest of consumers, cater to their needs, give them solutions. And on the back side, we go to the vendors that market to those consumers." Both the child-care industry and the eldercare business have enormous potential, says Mittermaier. He finds it easy to locate companies that want to market to these groups, so providing free advice and referrals is not a drain on resources but a solid business arrangement with a huge profit potential.

Mittermaier contacts companies with products such as diapers, syringes, and toys. Then he explains how his business caters to individuals caring for children and the elderly: "If a consumer asks for information, we forward that request to our associated companies, and they pay us on a per-lead basis." Such a strategy makes CareGuide.com a good alternative to direct marketing. As he says, "We protect consumers from getting unwanted things while delivering highly motivated buyers to the companies we partner with."

Problems so far have been minimal, but Mittermaier admits that it's difficult to maintain focus with a site that has such a wide audience. Even though CareGuide.com has the resources and flexibility to follow several different courses, Mittermaier wants to avoid competition with general interest sites such as Women.com. He doesn't want to go broad but wants to remain focused on caregiving only. "Our focus is caregiving," he says. "The challenge is not to get sucked into the appeal of starting to do things for the easy money—like straight advertising or meaningless sponsorships. Such activities dilute the value of what we want to do."

In the end, CareGuide.com distinguishes itself from its competitors, especially the larger ones, by avoiding an emphasis on daycare centers and nursing homes, since that's only a fraction of their caregiving spectrum. They deal primarily in information, and Mittermaier feels that the information must be broad-based and comprehensive. "Nobody else," he offers, "is providing information or services or solutions for the entire spectrum of family caregiving needs." Mittermaier sees his business emblem as an umbrella, one that covers any caregiving situation. For example, people with fibromyalgia or Krohn's disease or diabetes can search for help with specific questions. Others who care for the elderly or the very young can seek out strategies, health products, or caregiving services at a single site.

Web address:
www.CareGuide.com

Delivery of Web Purchases

Start-up expenses: $1,000,000 (*significant marketing expenses*)
Special requirements: *None*
Best advice: *"Personally, I like to do stuff through the computer. I thought, if I could buy everything through the Web, I'd be much happier."*

When you consider the impact of Internet shopping, especially during the holiday season, you should also remember that all those Pokémon dolls, Sinatra CDs, and snowblowers need to be delivered. United Parcel Service and Federal Express trucks are already jamming the freeways and clogging the arterials. But every year, from now until the Net self-destructs during one incredible overload period, the number of deliveries will multiply exponentially. You may be wondering: Who's going to bring all these extra packages? Who's going to deliver the goods waiting on the loading docks?

ENTREPRENEUR STEPS UP
TO THE PLATE

Ari Friedman asked himself the same question and decided that somebody needed to direct the Net-borne traffic. He said, "I will." Friedman owns HomeDelivery.com, the only online delivery service that doesn't actually make deliveries. HomeDelivery.com is best described as a clearinghouse, a facilitator for merchants who deliver purchases. Friedman felt that people needed delivery services for normal, everyday online purchases from local grocers, pet food distributors, wine and liquor stores, dry cleaners, pharmacies, and pizza parlors. "It's nice for the store owners," says Friedman, "because it gives them an affordable way to get online, to open this channel, and service customers." Friedman even believes that Internet ordering through one central Web site is easier than picking up the phone. In addition, participating businesses benefit from Friedman's ad campaigns and the traffic that is driven by others to the site. But the big advantage—and one that others seem to have overlooked—is that HomeDelivery.com doesn't have to deal with storage costs, shipping hassles, and fulfillment nightmares.

COMPETITOR HAS TOO MUCH
OVERHEAD

From a business point of view, this model makes more sense than the method employed by major competitors like Kozmos.com. To handle fulfillment, Kozmos keeps all its products in storage and distribution centers. They must maintain a huge inventory of books, videos, snacks, and other products. When customers order a product, they deal directly with

Kozmos.com, and the company loads its own trucks at the Kozmos warehouse. The company does an incredible job of getting your latest whim to you in minutes, but at what cost? Obviously, the incredible inventory demand, as well as the need for a huge fleet of trucks and enormous warehouses, represents a significant financial burden. Overhead, overhead, overhead.

SPREADING AROUND THE COUNTRY

If you live in Boston, Chicago, New York, or San Francisco and have favorite shops you frequent, they're probably part of HomeDelivery.com. If you live in Bismarck, Tidewater, or Sioux City, it may be a while. While you're waiting, however, consider Friedman's business plan. Consumers want to deal with brick-and-mortar shops that they trust and know. It's natural for them to want to do business with Gino's Bakery or Pellegrini's Dry Cleaners. Now the local shops can list their goods and prices (including delivery fees) on the HomeDelivery.com site, and everybody benefits.

THE LAUNCH

In 1999, Friedman launched his site. The first priority was getting merchants to enroll for the Web service. That argument was an easy one. Small-business owners, said Friedman, would not have to develop their own Web sites to participate in the e-commerce trend. They could get great exposure and advertising without investing in a separate Web presence. Finally, Friedman says, the big argument is the oldest one in commerce. What do you get from HomeDelivery.com? Location, location,

location. In one central and highly visible spot, buyers find everything they need and have it delivered right to their door. It's a great idea!

The actual concept was Friedman's own idea. When he imagined the future of the Net, he saw Home Delivery as a prime opportunity. "Personally," he says, "I like to do stuff through the computer. I thought, if I could buy everything through the Web, I'd be much happier." Now he can. Friedman claims he hasn't visited the grocery store or the pet store in more than a year, and he likes the freedom from crowded aisles and long lines. "It's a convenience thing," Friedman says. "We save customers' orders in memory, so they can regularly replenish orders for recurrent items like pet food. One click, and you're done!"

Customers start the process at HomeDelivery.com by entering their ZIP codes, then choosing a category such as shopping, pet supplies, toiletries, flowers, take-out, wine, or dry cleaning. After finding an appropriate merchant, the customers place their orders for toothpaste or flea collars. Then the merchant delivers the goods.

ONE MORE TIME: THEY'VE GOT NO TRUCKS

The notion of a delivery service that doesn't deliver takes time to grasp. Merchants, of course, must have their own delivery methods to join Friedman's troop. The absence of a warehouse or a fleet of trucks sets HomeDelivery.com apart from the competitors. And it makes Friedman wonder how companies like Kozmos.com draw a productive bottom line. "That would take a huge investment," says Friedman, who seems thankful not to be involved with shipping and storage. "It's a big debate in the industry," he adds. "How are those companies like Kozmos.com going to manage all those deliveries and still make a profit?"

Friedman likes his position. He knows he's helping local merchants, opening new channels for sales, and cementing business relationships with old customers. The entrepreneur says, "We brought in a grocer from Long Island. He's ecstatic. He used to have people on the phone trying to write everything down while people yelled their orders. Now the orders come in directly on the Net. He thinks it's great!"

In the future, HomeDelivery.com will continue a nationwide rollout, continuing to grow the merchant base and then increasing the customer base. Friedman predicts, "We will be incorporating new features and services—like being able to tie a number of errands to one delivery." In the future, he says, large numbers of the merchants in your neighborhood will belong to his system or one like it. Why? A lot of merchants don't want their own Web site. "It's too expensive," says Friedman, "and they can't manage the same kinds of promotions we have." That argument is compelling.

HomeDelivery.com required a large capital investment in the beginning for marketing, programming, operational costs, and so on. Friedman's faith in the system, however, is justified. The public is finding his business through online partners, through conventional advertising, or through participating merchants' promotions. And they're ready to buy.

Web address:
www.HomeDelivery.com

Matchmaking Service

Start-up expenses: $10,000
Special requirements: *Publicity resources*
Best advice: *"Don't believe that you have to do things the same as everyone else. Don't waste your time going through the proper channels if you don't have to. Remember, timing in cyberspace is critical."*

The "Personals" section has gone online. The current singles scene is hectic, complex, and wired. But human emotions remain deceptively simple. Unattached people, from Ally McBeal to John Q. Public, want to make connections, to find the ideal match. In the modern information age, people seeking love and companionship can skip the bar scene and travel directly, through cyberdating services, to Cupid's home page, learning with speed and accuracy precisely where the winged god is pointing his arrows.

"We're talking about breaking the ice, not about breaking

your wallet," says one of the headlines at eCrush, a computer-based dating service launched by Karen DeMars and Clark Benson. The eCrush service features a free registration form, where you give the names (in total confidence) of those you adore. Then the company sends e-mail to the intended one(s), saying in essence, "Someone has a crush on you." According to the blurb, "This is usually intriguing enough to get them to come to the site and register their own eCrushes, which could include you!" Once the matches are registered in the company computers, eCrush informs the potential lovers—for a fee.

UNLIMITED POSSIBILITIES

Even though DeMars and Benson did no market research, simply following an idea they thought would be fun, the two are tapping into an interest base that is virtually unlimited. The idea for eCrush came from Benson, 31, an entrepreneur with three music-related businesses. Benson shared his idea with Northwestern University fund-raiser Karen DeMars, 29, one day when the couple were walking the Hollywood hills. Benson had chosen the name SecretCrush.com and had the capital to begin. DeMars wasn't feeling challenged at her position at Northwestern and was ready to quit the development office. "I kept trying to get a promotion," she says, "and people kept saying, 'You need to spend more time around Northwestern,' but I thought, 'Well, I could keep sitting here, but I wouldn't learn anything.' "

There was plenty to learn once DeMars committed to the dating service. First order of business—the name. She didn't like SecretCrush.com and said so one night over dinner. So she and Benson brainstormed names until eCrush came to mind. They both loved it and found the name wasn't registered as a Web site.

The name, taking full advantage of the "e" connotation, probably was an important factor in the company's early success.

From there, the partners wanted to do market research but found it would cost $5,000. "We decided to do this no matter what," says DeMars. "People [we talked to] either loved or hated the idea. They said, 'Don't quit your job' or 'This is the best thing you could do.' " Together the owners adopted the motto "Build it first and see what happens." Shortly after, DeMars quit her job and started working on the site in December 1998. With few resources, she spent four hectic weeks designing and preparing the Web pages. "We decided to launch for Valentine's Day," says DeMars, "because I had no marketing money, and I was absolutely determined to get that public relations angle for launch." Indeed, eCrush met the February 14 deadline, taking full advantage of the built-in publicity surrounding Valentine's Day. In the first eight months of operation, the dating service made more than 12,000 matches. As DeMars says, eCrush is an electronic icebreaker. Often, someone who's been surreptitiously eyeing someone else at the water cooler for months signs up as a lark, only to find that the feelings of attraction are mutual. "It's like a high-tech approach to junior-high note passing," she adds.

BEING FIRST IS IMPORTANT IN E-BIZ

Companies like Amazon.com and eBay have made it clear that the first company to launch a revolutionary idea becomes the bully on the block. Taking that lesson to heart, DeMars and Benson launched eCrush with incredible speed, noting that "in e-business, there is no time to come up with a better solution. There is always going to be a better way to do things, but if it takes two months, it's too late. We might have had something more polished, but we wouldn't have been the first. And *being first* is important in e-business." The rapid launch of eCrush squeezed potential competitors. "There are a couple of similar sites," says DeMars, but none with a similar database. And, of course, the name eCrush has now become synonymous with the dating service industry.

DeMars and Benson quickly grasped one of the big differences between the virtual business world and the real world. In the real world, there are roadblocks—"processes and procedures" that slow the business traffic. The information superhighway has no stop signs. "It's an attitude," says DeMars. "In the virtual world people are less formal. Business is based more on relationships. *There are no rules*, so whatever works goes." DeMars says that eCrush has concluded deals with firms such as Capitol Records on the basis of a lunch appointment, with "no courting, no formal proposals—whatever works." Like many e-businesses, the dating services are populated by young entrepreneurs. And yes, while the average owner is a thirtysomething or even twentysomething, DeMars agrees that the key to success is not counted in years but in outlook. It takes a youthful approach to succeed in e-businesses.

Having a youthful approach breaks many of the conventions taught at business schools. For instance, one of eCrush's most important employees is a 24-year-old programmer who never previously held a job. "That's completely unheard of in the real world," says DeMars. The programmer, who became the chief technical officer for the company, would never have gotten past the first interview at a brick-and-mortar establishment. "People would laugh you out of the boardroom in the real world if you tried to hire him," says DeMars. But the e-world has room for employees who drive skateboards to work. DeMars emphasizes that the virtual world is not linear like the real world. "It's like funny money," says DeMars.

TIMES ARE CHANGING

The Internet does not entirely make sense to older generations of entrepreneurs because they think the "kids" are playing with "funny money" and ignoring the bottom line. Benson disagrees, saying that Internet companies have different goals. "In the real world, a business will have an actual value while it is running, but in e-business, the goal is to build up a valuation and be acquired by a bigger fish like Yahoo! or something." On the Internet, the goal is *market share*, where owners are hoping to build up traffic to a certain level. It is less important (perhaps even irrelevant) to make a profit. "That is the reality," says Benson. "Only a few are actually bringing in profits. In the short term they are trying to grow as fast as possible." At eCrush, the partners are spending "less than most" and constantly looking for ways to cut costs. Not everyone in the e-world is trying to keep costs under control.

Even the "big guys" rarely turn a profit today. "The Internet is in gestation," says Benson, "for at least a couple of years anyway." The financial numbers of companies such as eCrush are difficult to gauge but coming closer to reality every quarter. Right now, says Benson, even companies like Amazon.com are a year away from turning a profit, so it's important to remember that Internet businesses are growth-based propositions rather than profit engines, as in the real world. "When the company is growth-based," says Benson, "you need a lot of financing to get to a certain level, and the good thing is that the investment community understands, so they are willing to finance companies that are not turning profits but are growing. It takes a change in thinking. It's a whole different mentality."

As Benson notes, considering both his own business and others on the Net, growth (like profit) is a valid way of evaluating ventures in the new business climate. Some people are scratching their heads and saying, "This is crazy," but it's not the first time in history that companies with positive growth and negative income have been viewed as successful. "It's like the early days of the auto industry," says Benson, "when the public was so enamored by the car. Long before it made money, they invested in it."

THE LAUNCH

DeMars notes that there are several ways to launch an Internet company. Some people go to a firm for design and service. Here the up-front costs can run between $250,000 and $500,000. However, if you're "smart about it," says DeMars, you can get freelancers who can save you about $80,000 on total costs. Another option is to work with someone who "wants to be with you on the ride" and might work for less. At eCrush, quotes from firms ranged from $25,000 to "a few million." The partners finally selected a friend who was willing to put the pieces together for $10,000, taking on eCrush as a personal project, even though he had never designed a Web site. "We took a chance on each other," says DeMars. "That's the way to keep costs down." Normally a firm would begin with a business plan and some venture capital, which is a safe, traditional approach. "But if you take the back-door approach," says DeMars, "you're in the same position as someone who got $500,000 in financing."

In the early stages of growth at an Internet company, creativity is the cornerstone—lovingly set with the mortar of thinking outside the box. "That's the difference," says DeMars, speaking about the creative approach to problem solving. "If you went to your boss at a traditional company and said, 'This is the only way we can do this job—to get a guy who moonlights to develop this big part of our business, and we're going to have to depend on him to pull it off,' your boss would think you were completely baked. But in the e-business world this solution may be the only rational choice."

DOES HE OR SHE HAVE A CRUSH ON ME?

Benson and DeMars were pretty creative about the company they chose to launch. At eCrush, the software "lets you find out if somebody you have a crush on has one on you, too—with absolutely no risk of rejection." Most people have reveries about those they work with or want to date at school, but they're afraid of approaching that person for fear of rejection or concern for jeopardizing a relationship. If Suzy Creamcheese has a love interest in Joe the Cable Guy, she logs onto eCrush.com, fills out a short profile, and lists Joe's name. Then eCrush sends Joe an anonymous e-mail saying, "Somebody has a crush on you." Without revealing Suzy's name or personal details, eCrush then invites Joe to register and list any people who entice him. "If there's a match," says DeMars, "we get them together." Bingo. Electronic love.

By necessity and design, eCrush is completely confidential and risk-free. If you put Jody Foster or Ben Affleck on your crush list, no one will ever know unless the Hollywood stars list you as well. Of course, Ben and Jody have to be registered with eCrush for any possibility of a match, But the odds of connecting with someone significant are not unreasonable. So if the Hollywood stars aren't enamored with you, perhaps the cute new employee with the Porsche will have you listed.

GUERRILLA MARKETING (IT'S A JUNGLE OUT THERE)

Costs are important for any fledgling company, even in the Internet era. At eCrush, the owners save money through guerrilla marketing. "Marketing without spending a dime is the challenge," says DeMars. "That means swapping links, cobranding, partnerships. Sometimes it means things as stupid as putting matchbooks in bars." The dating service takes full advantage of spiraling, a word-of-mouth publicity ploy that exponentially increases the exposure. People who log on to the Net service tell two friends, who in turn tell two more friends. "What we're doing is working," says DeMars, "so we're doing more of it." Apparently the creative approach has a punk-rock quality to it, making the site "cool and accessible as a dating site." DeMars suggests that personal ads and traditional dating services are "cheesy," while computer link-ups resonate with the under-30 crowd.

In the midst of a successful guerrilla marketing campaign, DeMars and Benson are adding a marketing budget to pay for, among other things, some new features on the Web site: surveys, games, and chat rooms, for instance. In creating new publicity opportunities, DeMars made good use of her personnel skills, probably well practiced at Northwestern. She says, "You have to be an outgoing person and a good spokesperson for your site." For example, using the site, DeMars made contacts with *Seventeen* magazine and became their guest spokesperson for a month. That column not only increased business for eCrush but expanded their contacts as well.

IT'S LIKE ROCK 'N' ROLL

The owners at eCrush warn that e-business is not all creativity and dropping matchboxes in bars. At some point the company brushes sleeves with the real world. "When you start getting to a point where you have investors coming to you with offers, then you need to know your basic business," says DeMars. Especially important is having a grip on the technological aspects of the service, a glaring weakness in DeMars's background. "It's hard to know whom to trust technically," she offers. "You can't necessarily trust a big firm, and the cybergeek may not know anything really; he may just be a good talker." Everyone has an opinion about technological innovations and strategies, not only for eCrush but for most new businesses. DeMars says technology is the key, and only a "young mindset" enables businesspeople to take full advantage. "It's a willingness to accept the technology," she emphasizes, "and not just think it's a passing fad. Not unlike rock 'n' roll."

"Don't necessarily think that you have to do the same as everyone else," says DeMars. Avoid proper channels when possible. They'll only slow you down. And always remember that timing is critical. In the Internet world, being first with a new service, design, or technology is crucial. Finally, says DeMars, have fun. It's important to remember that, in e-business as in brick-and-mortar shops, you're dealing with people. Computers may make eCrush and other Internet business endeavors possible, but people spend the money. If they're enjoying themselves and having fun at a site, the growth (and even profits) will follow.

Web address:
   www.eCrush.com

Personal Shopper

Start-up expenses: *None*
Special requirements: *A flair for style and fashion*
Best advice: *"Take your time and really think out your site. Find avenues and ways of making your site special, whether it's the coloration of the music or pages that flip a certain way. The site has to fit your business. Music works for a personal shopper site, but it wouldn't for a truck dealership. Give the browser a positive feel for your business."*

Does your wardrobe need a little work? Would discount store fashions be a step up? Well, shopping takes time and a good sense of fashion. And few of us have both. But don't give up hope. And *don't* go back to the closet for those disco pants or that Hawaiian shirt. Instead, log on to www.-wardrobestudio.com, the Web address of Cherys Jenkins, personal shopper.

Initial Charge

For $150 an hour, Jenkins will wander the mall, check out Nordstrom's, browse the aisles at Ross Dress for Less, and haunt the boutiques. When she returns with your new outfits, you're set for any occasion, from a rodeo to a grand opening. Jenkins charges you only for chasing down clothes you keep, not for tasks such as paperwork on computer files, including what she bought, where she bought it, and how much she spent. In addition, she adds other useful information, such as the receipt number, so that when the statement arrives, you'll recognize the purchase.

Some may think that $150 an hour is too much to spend for someone to do your shopping for you, but Jenkins believes that a resourceful personal shopper actually saves you money. Recently she shopped for a woman who needed to make an appearance at a film festival. In the end, the personal shopper found a perfect gown retailing for $2,000. But Jenkins also knew where to find it for less, and the customer paid only $299, plus the shopping fee. Jenkins is unapologetic about the per-hour rate. In fact, she says, "If you're good at what you do, then that's what you charge for."

Jenkins doesn't work alone, but she's the only one in her company who shops. Other employees handle the Web site and crunch the numbers. She understands that not everyone needs a personal shopper. Her clients pay for her sense of style and critical eye. Jenkins admits she has some limitations. For example, she doesn't advise clients on what colors look best on them or shop only for a particular designer label. So, while she may find the perfect outfit at a discount barn or a chic dress shop, the idea is the same: the right outfit at a good price.

AN OLDER TRADITION

Most of us don't know much about the tradition of sending representatives to shop for clothes. As Jenkins says, "I am 45, and my generation had never heard of a personal shopper. But my mother's generation knew. It's something that goes in cycles."

Jenkins encountered the personal shopper idea several years ago while studying at the University of California at Davis. To pay tuition bills, Jenkins interviewed for a position with the high-end department store Nordstrom's. The manager offered her a job, and her first task was to "take a paper and pen out to this wealthy woman in La Jolla. Listen to what she wants." In a few hours, Jenkins was learning firsthand about shopping for others.

After a few years, Jenkins became frustrated that Nordstrom's didn't handle all the lines that her clients wanted. In response, she quit to start her own company in 1984 in San Mateo. "The concept came from really wanting to take care of my clients," she says. "My attitude is simple: if your time is extremely valuable, then let me do what I do best while you're using your time to do what you do best." In a short period, Jenkins had her own list of clients, both men and women—busy people who wanted quality clothing but didn't relish shopping or felt incompetent to do a first-rate job.

IT'S A LONG PROCESS

Don't expect Jenkins or any other personal shopper to speak with you briefly, then rush out and purchase the dream wardrobe. Jenkins warns that personal shopping is a process, one that begins with a lengthy interview. At wardrobestudio.com, you first fill out an image profile. "People say my information is a long read on the Web site," says Jenkins. "Perhaps it is. But we have things to work out. If you want my services, I need to know your lifestyle, why you want a personal shopper, and other information." Jenkins requires a profile from all applicants, and she says firmly, "I do not move without first having an image profile."

The profile is similar to a character sketch, followed by a meeting where the customer gets to know Jenkins and establish rapport. Why is rapport necessary? Because the next step is for Jenkins to solicit a credit card or a check. A certain level of trust is absolutely necessary.

From there, Jenkins begins the wardrobe planning. She visits the existing closet and works from the client's current wardrobe. "I don't have to gut your wardrobe," she says. "That is devastating for most people." Jenkins can update a piece, take in a skirt, remove the cuffs from pants. She takes each customer's needs into account and tries to begin by working with the functional pieces already occupying a hanger. Certain vendors appeal to Jenkins because they excel in fit, style, or design. But no single approach works for everyone. Each shopping spree must be personal and unique.

Next, Jenkins begins her shopping treks, sometimes to places that the customers never consider. In addition to Saks and Nieman Marcus, Jenkins also searches Ross Dress for Less and the Bon Marché. "I shop according to what's on the shelves," she says, adding, "I am frugal." Jenkins says she can visit a discount store or the Ross outlet and pay $3.99 for Donna Karan hosiery, whereas the same item costs $17 in most department stores. Such savings, she insists, more than pay for her services.

"You're going to pay for my time," she says, "so I might as well save you money." Jenkins reports that over a three-month period, she bought a $36,000 wardrobe for one client. But the bill came to only $18,000. "She's a happy camper," says the personal shopper. "That woman was not an average client," she adds, "but the shopping was typical." In fact, most shopping assignments are considerably more modest, but varied in type. For example, some people want Jenkins to buy clothes for special events; some want purchases at the beginning of each month; and others seek her services seasonally or biannually.

PERSONAL SHOPPER, VIRTUAL WORLD

Most of Jenkins's customers don't arrive in a rush. She receives many referrals, and her client base grows slowly but steadily. It was only recently that Jenkins added her Web site, but it has already attracted considerable interest. Lots of people log on simply to ask questions. One man wrote, "I have a yellow shirt. Can I wear it with a French blue tie?" Feeling that her business is at least partly informational, Jenkins answered promptly, as she does with every query. She explains, "The Web site is a good way of letting people know that the business is available."

In 1999, when Jenkins launched her site, the Wardrobe Studio started to attract a global audience. "It's a good vehicle for knowledge and marketing," says Jenkins. Because she wanted a certain classy image for the site, she moved slowly toward a Web presence, using the time to create pages with the right colors, music, and message. "I want my Web site to be an experience," she says, "and I want people to enjoy the Wardrobe Studio. That was my whole idea behind building the Web site."

Her friends and colleagues urged Jenkins to put wardrobe-studio.com into cyberspace more rapidly, but the owner balked, recognizing that her image was her business. She didn't want to give any potential customers the idea that the Wardrobe Studio was an impromptu notion or a pedestrian business. She says, "Anything worthwhile takes time. A good site doesn't happen overnight."

The effects of the Web presence have been positive. Even though several of Jenkins's clients have moved from the region—even out of the country—they keep in touch through the Net. Some have helped with Internet referrals to friends and colleagues. In those cases, Jenkins conducts an image profile over the phone, asking finally for a photo and some direction on handling the shopping expenses. She sends purchases through Federal Express and walks clients through the process before she sends the packages, making it clear that the pale green sash goes with the evergreen skirt and the vermilion coat goes with the suede shoes.

There have been some light moments for Cherys Jenkins at the Wardrobe Studio. One man received a Christmas gift certificate from his wife. When he initially contacted her, Jenkins discovered that he thought her service was "ridiculous." But, says the personal shopper, after a few purchases, the man became "like a kid in a candy store." Now, after six years, he tells his wife, "Don't buy anything for me. Just call Cherys!"

Web address:
www.wardrobestudio.com

Religious Specialties

Start-up expenses: $10,000
Special requirements: *None*
Best advice: *"Don't expect overnight success. It'll take longer than you think, just like any other business. There's been a lot of hype saying, 'Just hang out your Web shingle, and you're gonna get rich.' But instant success is the exception."*

Where do you go to get incense or a ceramic Buddha for your home altar? How do you find holy water or a St. Christopher medallion? What store features *The Lives of the Saints* or selections from *The Book of Mormon*? Can you find a prayer shawl or a *yarmulke* in the local mall?

Shopping for religious specialties has just gotten easier. With the Internet, people can shop for a remarkable variety of religious icons, devotional books, home altars, specialty books, and other accoutrements. In cyberspace, the click-on option is significantly easier than a conventional search for religious specialties. In the past, devotees could find catalog or brick-and-mortar outlets featuring Catholic and Buddhist materials, for example, but seldom a clearinghouse for an eclectic supply. Today, with the advent of e-businesses like DivineImages.com, it's possible to order a Sikh incense burner, a Seder candleholder, and a graven image of Martin Luther all in the same Web visit.

INFORMATION: STRAIGHT FROM THE WEB

Michelle Ritan entered the Web world in September 1998 with very little business experience. Her only contact with the commercial world came from working as a dessert caterer for a coffee shop for two years. But the Internet fascinated her. She talked to several experienced people and began reading about the rapidly changing world of e-commerce. She met a husband and wife who had launched a successful site in a similar venture, and they shared their success story. Ritan knew she did not want a storefront, with rents and overhead. To her, an online business seemed ideal. But what business should she choose?

Ritan decided to stick with what she knew best. "When it came time to decide what kind of business I would start online, I took a good look at my longtime interests and habits. I've always had an interest in spirituality and world religions. So I decided to choose a business involving religion." Still, there was the problem of how to launch such an enterprise. She began with the obvious. "A lot of information I got straight from the Web." First she looked online for materials on Internet marketing and e-commerce. "Of course," she laughs, "even if the advice had a 1998 copyright, it was already out of date." But the online reading offered a good crash course in business terminology, and Ritan learned a fair amount about promoting products through search engines. Despite the dated advice, Ritan appreciates the rich resources of the Web for new business owners.

Ritan also went to the library and the bookstore, finding hard-copy texts on e-commerce. Furthermore, she read *The New York Times* business section daily and was surprised that the stodgy old *Times* editors were devoting most of their print space to articles on Net commerce. She then subscribed to the Internet-inspired magazines *Wired* and *Red Herring*. The overall effect was informative but also confusing. "The e-commerce world is changing so quickly from even a year ago," she laments. "It makes my head spin."

Divine Images began with an investment of about $10,000, including expenditures for a new computer system and professional Web design. The investment also covered the costs of merchant services, inventory, advertising, bank services, telephone lines, 800 numbers, and office supplies. As Ritan says, however, "It could have been a lot more expensive. If this were a storefront, I'd also have rent, utilities, taxes, and countless other onsite costs."

A CONTRADICTORY PROPOSITION

Ritan studied religion formally, so she had a broad background in theology. Early on, she ran a key word search in her areas of interest and scanned the offerings of her competitors. Eventually she decided that sacred-space creation was her niche. Ritan began to focus on personal altars and the objects people use to supply those sacred spaces. Sacred space may exist in the home or the office, says Ritan. It's simply a special place for devotion. She says, "I saw what was on the Net, and there weren't many appropriate sites."

Her own interest in Zen Buddhism led Ritan to search for products for her own home altar. The search was unproductive. "I couldn't find anything locally and not much on the Internet either. Some competing sites feature products like statues and incense, but not many personal altar products. I knew other people who were interested too, so I decided to invent the product line myself." Ritan designed three types of altars and made sketches. She took the sketches to a fine woodworking company in her home town. The carvers worked from Ritan's sketches and produced handsome versions of the home altars. Then Ritan thought about what customers would need to furnish the sacred spaces. She developed a line of devotional statues, candleholders, wall art, and plaques with devotional themes—all items appropriate to creating a home or office sacred space.

In the course of developing the product line for Divine-Images.com, Ritan wrestled with a paradox. She reasoned that the home altar is part of a very old tradition, particularly in the Far East, but not common in North America, although more and more people are showing interest because "it helps people get spiritually connected in their personal lives." Ritan wanted to create a Web site that not only sells products but also provides a spiritual atmosphere for visitors and customers. She says, "I wanted an e-commerce site with elements of inner peace in a hurried world. I wanted to provide educational materials, information on how to create the personal space, books and manuals—things that would be helpful for a spiritual quest." Nonetheless, she recognizes the inherent contradiction: the Internet is the ultimate metaphor for today's fast-paced "click-through" society. As with many online businesses today,

DivineImages.com operates in a gray area, where the business concept—in this case sacred space—seems incompatible with the business engine, the Internet. Nevertheless, the odd pairing works.

SLOW, STEADY PROGRESS RATHER THAN A SPRINT

Unlike some Web businesses, DivineImages.com advertises outside the Net. "You *need* print advertising as well as the Internet," says Ritan. "I advertise in three or four selected publications. I tried to promote with search engines, worked hard to get mine into top twenty results, but it takes a lot of surveillance." Ritan does use *Web Position Gold*, search engine positioning software, and reports that it saves her time and frustration. "*Web Position Gold* goes out and polls the big search engines. Nobody would have time to keep up with it by hand." Ritan also uses local advertising in a New Age newspaper, and she has placed some brochures with businesses in Atlanta, taking advantage of districts with a strong predilection toward spirituality. However, banner exchanges have not been part of the business plan. "It wasn't appropriate for my content," says Ritan. Link pages were appropriate, however, and Ritan says she will do exchanges "if it's truly appropriate."

Ritan, like many small e-commerce entrepreneurs, warns against inflated expectations. "Don't expect overnight success," she says. "It'll take longer than you think, just like any other business." Regular merchandising on the Net is not the way to instant wealth for most people. In fact, like any traditional business, there's a series of small decisions and steps that precede a leap onto the Fortune 500 list. One of those decisions involved shipping procedures. Ritan was asked by a large business to do a drop-ship to increase volume. But she says, "Volume has not been a problem." Ritan has a close relationship with UPS and a shopping cart that is secure and actually calculates shipping weight and cost. "It's really slick," she beams. Ritan does some handling herself, but she sends all large shipments to Mail Boxes Etc.

Another important decision involved Web site design. Although Ritan had done network consulting for seven or eight years, she decided to hire a professional, Jennifer Youree at 3cats1dog.com (see "Web Site Designer"). She says, "When I evaluated what it took to learn HTML coding, I decided I had too much on my plate already. I just wanted to go ahead and launch quickly. It was a worthwhile investment to hire someone who was up to speed." Ritan thinks she made a wise decision, leaving her time free for what she really enjoys and understands: research, design concept, and seeking vendors. "That's my fun," she says, adding that she really likes dealing with new vendors and finding new products for her site.

One key to Ritan's success is her universal approach to sacred space. "My site is eclectic," she says, meaning that people of all religions (or no religious persuasion) could use her site comfortably. DivineImages.com is not dedicated to any one religion or sect. In fact, Ritan is proud that people can find Buddhist statues and Catholic vestments side-by-side on her site, as well as icons and books from many other religions. She is pleased with the quality of customers to her Web site, noting that, unlike traditional business fronts, people on the Web do little browsing. "They know what they want," she says. Divine Images customers have to be more educated about sacred space products than brick-and-mortar customers. It is decidedly a challenge to buy on the Net. Not being in the same room with the products requires some preliminary research from prospective clients. Ritan also appreciates the e-mail dialogues that come to her through the Web page. She feels she has benefited from the e-contacts and found new ways to enrich the experience of her own sacred space.

Web address:
   www.DivineImages.com

Pets

Animal Gifts

Start-up expenses: *$1,200*
Special requirements: *None*
Best advice: *"Research your idea and don't be afraid to try it. Once you've researched, don't sit on the sideline and think about it. Jump in and always be concerned about where your traffic will come from, as well as how you're going to tell folks about what you're doing."*

I f Rover or Felix could work a mouse, UPS couldn't carry all the orders for dog treats and cat toys. As it is, pet owners are doing a pretty good job of keeping the big brown trucks rolling. In the process, these motivated buyers are assuring profits for the owners of creative pet sites such as AnimalDen.com, a husband-and-wife venture initiated by Chris and Johnnie Oberst.

ANIMAL HEAVEN

Near the end of 1998, the Obersts launched their site, primarily in response to Johnnie's lifelong interest in animals. Living in rural Oregon, the Obersts recognized that the Net provided a global clientele, one they could never reach from a brick-and-mortar storefront in the countryside.

The Obersts also realized that a real-world pet store would fall into the middle of a tough market. Says Chris, "We wanted a site that had something to do with animals and decided to move forward in the gift area, rather than open a store, which is a fairly competitive market." Both owners had business backgrounds. For ten years, Chris owned an exporting company and Johnnie ran a mailing business. In 1997, they went online after following some discussion groups on the Net and realizing that pet products presented a doggone good market. Immediately they realized they weren't barking up the wrong tree.

The resulting online store features gift items for animal lovers. "These are items that are hard to find in a lot of areas," says Chris, "so we felt just having a national or worldwide reach would be a remarkable advantage." The Obersts' pet market differs from the normal pet supply companies. Instead of selling cat collars, fish tanks, and dog chews, the Obersts concentrate on products for the owners themselves. Typical items include coffee mugs, sweatshirts, coasters, and jewelry—usually embossed with a picture of Rex or Spot or Polly. Other interesting doodads include a wolf suncatcher, a longhorn oil lamp, a reining horse umbrella, and a gecko thermometer. A portion of each sale goes to support organizations that help animals and wildlife.

THE ONLINE ADVANTAGE

Pet lovers are everywhere. In fact, the Obersts have fielded orders from places like Turkey, Australia, Japan, Morocco, and Germany. Needless to say, it's possible to make such deals from a country store in the West. "The buyers are pretty spread out," says Chris. "If we were to open a store in a retail location with only a local market, it wouldn't work." The specialty gifts don't appeal to everyone, at least not in the way that suppliers might sell bird feeders, cat chow, and flea collars. Not everyone is interested in a Koko the Gorilla sweatshirt.

More than anything else, the Obersts are surprised at the worldwide market. They enjoy receiving orders from distant corners of the globe, and, even though they never expected an international response, it's still fun.

A remarkable advantage of their online presence is the cost factor. Instead of a traditional mail order business—the other possibility—the Obersts reach a huge audience while avoiding large capital investments in catalogs, mailing lists, postage, and other kinds of overhead. With such burdens, most mail order companies find it difficult to turn a profit, especially early in the game. "The Internet," says Chris, "is *so* cheap in terms of operating costs. You can change your information and adjust products constantly on the Net." In comparison with the slow, expensive plodding of mail order operations, the Web approach is a breeze.

GETTING THE WORD OUT

In their advertising plan, the Obersts use both online and offline methods. Offline, they advertise in dog and cat magazines. Online, they trade advertising with other Web sites. The Obersts also sponsor affiliates, who earn commissions each time they bring a customer to AnimalDen.com. The owners also receive some traffic from Yahoo!Store and through word-of-mouth recommendations. Although such viral advertising is slow, the Obersts believe it's particularly effective. "It snowballs as you go along," says Chris.

BUILDING A CLIENTELE

Customer service is a big emphasis. In fact, at AnimalDen.com, you can read more than 100 letters from satisfied customers. "We stopped posting more," says Chris, even though the letters on their Web page represent only a small portion of those received. "We've been fortunate that people seem to be happy," he adds. "We get lots of feedback."

Nonetheless, there are always customers who are dissatisfied, no matter what you do, suggests Chris. But the Obersts follow a policy that helps brighten the mood of even the gloomiest buyer. "We are like everybody else," he says. "The customer is always right." The Obersts take returns and exchanges without hesitation. "That is important online," Chris says, where reputation is hard won and easily forfeited. This policy keeps problems to a minimum.

To keep browsers interested, AnimalDen.com has an uncluttered, easy-to-use home page, which mentions the added pages of free offers, samples, and services that are accessed by clicking on the Special Friends icon. There the customer encounters free animal-oriented greeting cards, books for kids, and endangered species slide show, animal jokes, crosswords, and word games. Visitors can even listen to bird calls, whale songs, and other animal sounds.

All things considered, AnimalDen.com seems a wonderful place to visit, even if you don't have a pet.

Web address:
www.AnimalDen.com

Aromatherapy for Pets

Start-up expenses: $3,000

Special requirements: *Aromatherapy products and knowledge of how to prepare them*

Best advice: *"Trademark problems can grind up precious dollars and time. A lot of times, when you start a new business, you don't think about these things," she says. "Nobody is holding your hand, so a lot of concerns get overlooked."*

How has old Rover been feeling lately? Is he lethargic? Prone to bouts of depression? Does his coat look mottled? Do you suspect a flea condo lurking somewhere, waiting to attack? Perhaps Rover needs a New Age approach to health and good grooming. It's time to try aromatherapy. Yes, that's right. You can now get a sweet-smelling potion for your dog or cat, an herbal concoction to drive away the blues, to strengthen the immune system, or even to discourage those nasty fleas. Dogs, cats, and other animals are prime targets in e-commerce, and sites devoted to pets are ubiquitous. Kristen Leigh Bell is the owner of one such site, Aromaleigh.com.

THE NAME GAME

The company was formerly called Divine Dog Company, with a line of products called Aroma Dog. Bell had researched names and felt her choices were appropriate and available. After six months, however, she heard from a trademark attorney, who claimed that another business held the rights to Aroma Pet. "I got all upset," says Bell, "thinking my business was over."

Her own attorney told Bell that she could win her trademark case but that the fees and problems would be overwhelming. So Bell started looking for a new moniker. After two months and eight different trademark searches, she settled on a combination of *aroma* and *Leigh*, her middle name. After all her hassles, Bell suggests that e-commerce venturers really do their legal groundwork before launching a new site.

STARTING OVER

With a new name and outlet, Bell began again. She invested her own time and resources in the Web site, creating pages that she feels would cost about $20,000 to build with hired experts. Her own costs centered mainly on raw materials like bottles and labels. Bell doesn't purchase a lot of prepackaged scents, nor does she engage in mass manufacturing. Many of her herbal packages and nostrums are ones she has researched and produced herself. In a few cases, however, the basics, like unscented shampoos and conditioners, arrive from a manufacturer who makes them by the gallon. "Then I just add the essential oils," says Bell.

RELAXATION IS THE ANSWER

The idea for an aromatherapy site came from Bell's own circumstances. She says, "I have severe allergies, so I started using natural products and getting into aromatherapy. I would make potions for myself, other people, my pets, and other people's pets. It became a hobby." She started with shampoos and deodorizing sprays, ear-cleaning products, flea and insect balms, and products to calm a dog's anxieties. From there, the aromatherapy lines grew naturally. When friends and colleagues heard she was promoting aromatherapy for pets, they had the same reaction. According to Bell, "People thought I was crazy!"

Bell was working 70 to 80 hours a week for someone else and wanted to put efforts into a project of her own. She considered the aromatherapy lines and decided to launch a Web site. Using her own recipes, she envisioned a target market of people who don't like synthetic chemicals and have special concerns about health. Using herbs and homeopathic medicines, Bell produced a series of all-natural products, mostly for animals but some for the owners as well. She says, "After the owners try some of these preparations for their pets, they get addicted and buy a few things for themselves."

YAHOO! STORE TO THE RESCUE

With a background in advertising and graphic design, Bell knew she could do her own site work. She started an association with Verio, an ISP, and maintained her own site. But it soon became difficult to track the e-commerce tendrils because she featured more than 200 products. Prices, sales figures, and other accounting matters began to overwhelm her system. With so much programming work involved, Bell switched to Yahoo!Store—a drastic change, as she describes it.

Yahoo! has its own store software that automatically handles some of the largest accounting chores. Says Bell, "It makes it really easy to change prices across the board on every single product you have. You can feature products at the click of a button. They had written the software specifically for e-commerce and virtual stores. It definitely works. Yahoo! is a lot simpler." Since the change from an ISP, Bell's business has doubled, and the hits have tripled. "I have lots of new customers," she says. "I always had repeat customers and referral customers before," she adds. Those people would e-mail her and talk about the products before buying. The new customers brought from Yahoo! are different, she says. "They don't want to talk. They just order my products!"

RESEARCH IS IMPORTANT

Bell uses Yahoo! to see what products her competitors are offering and what special offers are generating new business. She says, "It allows me to gather a lot of information on my customers, meaning how they perceive the sites and how they navigate."

It was definitely an advantage for Bell to have worked in advertising. Otherwise, she could have spent thousands and thousands of dollars for her logo and catalog identity. Doing the work herself kept costs low. The Web site has evolved rapidly, having been completely revamped five times in the first eighteen months of operation. Formerly the site was flashy, with lots of animation and Java rollovers. After realizing that people were getting lost or sidetracked, Bell revised her pages, making the format easier to use and more comfortable for browsers.

Bell constantly surveys her customers, offering free samples for feedback. This feedback has helped her discover potential problems with site navigation and move quickly to stave off trouble. Research is a way of life for Bell. She regularly visits competing sites to see how they present products. Because people remain wary about ordering on the Net, citing security problems, Bell constantly looks for ways to make buyers feel safe and comfortable. "People want as much information as possible," she says. Bell provides lots of background on her products—as well as blurbs about her company and her history.

ADS AND E-MAIL

At Aromaleigh.com, Bell started her marketing campaign with small ad space in dog magazines and several banner ads on pet-related sites. "I was just trying to get links and listings wherever I could," she says. Now Bell has a different approach, seeking more editorial references and trying to get specific products featured in different magazines. The Yahoo! connection, however, is most productive. It means daily growth. According to Bell, "If I go into Yahoo! and type in 'skin care,' a lot of my stuff comes up first. I'm getting really good placement at Yahoo!"

Since business is growing, Bell now needs help. She hires temps when things get really hectic. There are lots of e-mail questions, some of which are technical and specific, so she can't farm out too much work. She says, "My customers like the fact that they are talking to a real person who knows about what they're buying. That's why they keep coming back." This advantage is important. The Net is faceless, and buyers who can gain some confidence from a phone conversation are much more likely to place orders.

Aromatherapy for dogs and cats is certainly an unknown business. It's one of those e-commerce ventures that appeared improbable five years ago, before the virtual world came into full flower. Today it seems almost mainstream.

Web address:

www.Aromaleigh.com

Dog Daycare

Start-up expenses: $300
Special requirements: *A passion for animals*
Best advice: *"Every time I come across a name of someone who might be interested in Dogma-Daycare, I capture the lead and manually drag it into my database in Outlook. Then the person's name becomes part of my regular mailings of updates, specials, and news."*

Arf! Bow wow! Ruff! Ruff! Imagine a warehouse in downtown Washington with thirty (yep, thirty) dogs in daycare. When you called, Benji was having a birthday party, and simply everyone had a cold nose (the dogs were eating ice cream cake!). But it's a business for Rebecca Bisgyer, and you can reach it on the Net. Bring references. Not every Rex, Fifi, and Ginger gets into dog-ma.com.

If you live in Dogpatch or Pawtucket, forget it. You'll have to pay Billy down the street to walk your dog while you're at work or traveling. Dog-ma.com operates only within a stick's throw of the White House. In fact, Rebecca Bisgyer uses the Net not to promote a nationwide business but to regulate her Washington bookings, removing some of the seasonal fluctuations for her local dog-care venture. What better way than through the Net?

THE CORPORATE WORLD LEFT A VOID

In a business where you always have to watch where you step, Bisgyer made some pretty strategic moves, many by necessity. She began in the corporate world as an expert in currency trading and marketing, heading up sales in the client services division of her company. She always worked in small corporations, seeking a level of comfort that never came. Recently, she and her husband felt huge frustration with "Business as Usual, USA." They felt unfulfilled, empty, and shallow. Bisgyer's husband started his own company, and while business began at a slow pace, Rebecca secured a new position with a large financial trade association.

When Bisgyer went to her first board meeting, the president, who had just completed the negotiations for her hiring, was fired. Bad timing. "It wasn't going to be the same job," she says, "so I left." With no income and little security, the couple decided it was time for a radical step. Rebecca asked herself what kind of business she could launch, and the answer came up "dog sitting." Yep, dog sitting—something that thoroughly involved one of her passions, a love of animals. As she explains, "Sometimes it takes real motivation to make a big change in life." We think this one qualifies.

START WITH A CONCEPT

Bisgyer says, "I had conceptualized the idea of doggy daycare for two years. I had two dogs of my own, one with terrible separation anxiety. Essentially, the dog was my child." After daily morning scenes at the back door, Bisgyer thought, "There has to be a better way." Already she was paying $15 a day to have her dogs walked. Now she was facing bills for doggy psychiatry unless she could find a solution. "The dogs brought a lot of joy into our lives," she explains. "They deserved good care."

After seeing a story about the San Francisco ASPCA, a group that offers a "sitting" service for animals, Bisgyer took note. The ASPCA used the incomes from the service to pay bills at the shelter. Since the San Franciscans were a nonprofit organization, Bisgyer reasoned, they could help people with some useful information. With that idea in hand, she started visiting shelters and dog-care facilities.

MARKETING STARTS EARLY

Bisgyer started promoting her company six months before opening doors. She interviewed potential clients at home, admitting, "They had to be pretty interested in my service if they were talking to me before there was any real business." Although she was right about the level of interest, Bisgyer was wrong about the demographics. She expected groups of people who lavished considerable expenses on their pets, including buying such things as dog walkers. It wasn't true. Normal folks who loved their pets and wanted them looked after during the day were her clients.

Early on, Bisgyer placed inexpensive ads in newspapers to

test her idea. She found a downtrodden building on the wrong side of the freeway at a dead-end street. "But," she says, "it has excellent access to the Washington freeways." Finding herself only a few blocks from the Capitol rotunda, Bisgyer knew the place had possibilities. She began to fix the building on a shoe-string budget and to look for ways to become visible. Without any money to invest, Bisgyer could not advertise convention-ally, so she chose local neighborhood papers, adding a number of flyers targeted to dog parks, veterinarians, dog trainers, and so forth.

Slowly the spiral advertising caught on. Bisgyer noticed that her first customers loved the service. "Until they used it," she says, "they didn't understand. They soon learned there was a better way to live than to let the dog chew up the house or live in a crate all day." Now when Washingtonians pick up their dogs, they don't come home to monsters with twelve hours of frustration to spend but calm, docile, obedient animals who've been "working out" during the interim.

Public relations on a budget was a challenge, of course. Bisgyer implemented a modest campaign, providing monthly press releases. She kept an updated press list and—because she's a good writer—wrote articles of interest on dogs and pets, fo-cusing especially on trends in the pet industry. For instance, Bisgyer completed a survey of Washington hotels, showing which ones allow dogs in the rooms. The story attracted re-gional and national interest as well, and some useful exposure.

BARK IF YOU LOVE OUR WEB SITE?

After seven months in the business, Bisgyer started a Web site, even though she had no money. Luckily, a friend with a Web site business wanted to pad his portfolio. He offered to put up a small site for Bisgyer. She says, "I knew little about the Net, and I wasn't sure it would benefit me that much, considering the local scope of my business." But Bisgyer wrote the content, and her friend created the site. Soon Bisgyer began to receive lots of useful feedback online. The Net idea was a good one.

Next came the ever-present problem of registering with the search engines. Bisgyer thought it might be easy. She wasn't exactly competing with Friskies or Petsmart. "There weren't eight million businesses like mine," she says. Nevertheless, Bisgyer couldn't crack the top ten on the engines, even though she was hosted by an ISP, a major player, and even though she had finally purchased their most expensive service. "It was completely ineffective," she admits.

"What I finally figured out was that you shouldn't care about the 400 search engines that submission services boast about," she says. "You should only care about the top ten search engines." Now she resubmits to the large services every few months, using *Web Position Gold*, software that constantly checks her site and makes suggestions for resubmission. After laboring for nine months to get well placed on Yahoo!, Bisgyer now ranks number three.

A Glimpse Ahead

Future goals include finding ways to expand her business. "There's tremendous growth in the pet industry," she says with calculated understatement. "People feel differently now about their pets than even five years ago." The high-end markets for cat and dog care are burgeoning, and Bisgyer sees nearly unlimited possibilities for the right Web business.

In the meantime, dog-ma.com is still throwing birthday parties. Those in the Capitol area who want to see what happens in the warehouse can click on and get information about the company, see pictures of the pets, view published articles on animal care, and link to galleries of pictures (doggies doing their daily routine at Dogma Daycare). Interested folks can e-mail for more information, set up appointments, or even apply for admission online. However, prospective clients must interview for open positions. Get out the dog brush. The competition is keen.

Web address:

www.dog-ma.com

Exotic Pets

Start-up expenses: $8,200

Special requirements: *A game breeder's license, scanner and digital camera, inventory of animals*

Best advice: *"Offer a very clear presentation of your information on the Web site. Update frequently, and respond to inquiries quickly. There is so much out there now. Try a unique slant. You have to find something new that is appealing."*

Web sites like Petopia.com have multimillion-dollar budgets, and they sell everything from aardvark food to zebra shampoo. But you don't have to have millions. The world's immense interest in pets and pet supplies has also created a healthy business environment for niche industries. Today on the Internet you can purchase gerbil cages, snake food, turtle vitamins, and falcon hoods; you can also buy rodents, marsupials, crustaceans, and arachnids. If it flies, crawls, swoops, or slithers, you can probably buy it on the Net. Just open the package carefully.

Kathi and Gary Martin have been in the pet business since 1998, when they began advertising from their 20-acre farm in rural Iowa. At Cuddly Critters, the Martins feature a line of exotic animals, including Chow Chow and St. Bernard puppies and Bengal kittens. The Bengals are a cross between domestic cats and wild cats, resulting in a fascinating feline with distinctive markings that, like the Bengal tiger, enjoys frolicking in the water. As Kathi Martin says, "There is no market for exotic animals in the Midwest. We advertised in the Omaha paper but got no response. But if you can hit the Coast, they're heavily sought after." And that's just what the Martins' Web site did. It offered them exposure not only to the trendy West and East Coast clientele but also to opportunities across the globe.

ARE LEISURE SUITS STILL POPULAR IN DES MOINES?

Those who log on to cuddlycritters.com will find a number of in-vogue animals like the Bengal kittens. As Martin explains, "Trends like this start on both coasts and move inward. A lot of people on the coasts want the latest thing to enhance their images. It happens to be exotic cats right now." Before their recent marriage, Gary Martin owned an exotic animal business in an ideal high-exposure area, but the move to the Midwest reduced the business visibility considerably. In Iowa the Martins knew they could not expect much of a customer base. Kathi predicted that fewer than ten people a day would wander into a brick-and-mortar site devoted to exotic pets. So they decided to operate Cuddly Critters entirely in cyberspace, a decision that has given the new business a fast start.

Shipping is perhaps the largest concern for the Martins. Crating and shipping of animals can cost between $100 and $175, making the costs prohibitive. Birds, on the other hand, are cost effective to ship. They can be air expressed in crates. And because birds are light, the fees are less. Furthermore, birds need less care and attention in travel than raccoons and cats and koala bears. Shipping for birds usually runs about $25, including transportation to the customer's doorstep, a service provided by the airlines. "That's pretty good service for $25," says Kathi Martin, "and the price doesn't seem to vary whether we send them to Ohio or to California." Consequently, the birds, priced in the $15 to $100 range, are the most successful products in the Cuddly Critters line.

"WE'RE NOT FANCY, BUT WE LOAD FAST"

Despite the infancy of their online business, the Martins have devised a careful and effective sales plan. First, they offer wide variety in their catalogue of exotic pets. "The wider appeal you have, the better the response," says Kathi with conviction. Also, the Martins have made the most of their Internet ties. Originally, Kathi submitted to every search engine she could find, frequently using (and paying) Internet launch companies for the service. Soon, she says, "I found out it was better to do it myself, because it was hard to tell what they did for me. Now, every time I hear of a search engine, I go there and look for the 'list it' button."

Kathi Martin says she has learned a great deal about meta tags and key words from her own cybersearches. She has purchased software that checks the feedback from her lists, and she uses free classified ads on the Net whenever they're available. Finally, Cuddly Critters is affiliated with the Dove Association and other professional organizations appropriate to their animal-sales business. "Usually," says Kathi, "organizations like that will provide some free space, or at least they'll include our URL and e-mail address."

Other keys to success include fast response and customer service. The Martins answer every inquiry promptly because, as Kathi says "people love that." Most people call with questions or are seeking advice. But "you never know," says the Cuddly Critters owner.

Communication is very important, as is a good Web page. The Martins built their site themselves, using *Frontpage* software. Their site is simple and direct, not cluttered with animations and eye-catching features that, despite a certain appeal, slow the loading. As Martin says, "We're not fancy, but we load fast. I think that's important." Also, Cuddly Critters is in a highly targeted marketplace. People who enter the site are not usually casual browsers but potential customers looking for special animals or, at the least, advice on pet care.

Cuddly Critters handles a large variety of pets, setting them aside from most pet-sales sites. There are many breeders and businesses that handle just one type of animal, like Shar-Pei puppies or boa constrictors. Variety is their slant, according to Kathi Martin—their appeal in a complex and crowded e-market. Thus, the Martins have a large inventory of several exotic species. One of the complications brought by such diversity was the necessity for special licenses and permits. Gary Martin needed to have a game breeder's license, for example. Also, there are restrictions and rules for taking exotic animals from the wild and for shipping them into foreign countries. "The rules are very stringent," says Kathi. "We get global hits from Venezuela, for instance, and from overseas. You have to become very knowledgeable about regulations. If it's someplace foreign, I send the application back to the customer. They have better access to information, so I ask them to get the information on regulations. The state regulations [for America] I post on the site."

NOT JUST KITTY LITTER AND A BAG OF FRISKIES

The launching of a pet supply business like Cuddly Critters takes some careful planning and funding. The Martins had to make an investment in a scanner and a digital camera, for instance, costing some $3,000. They also needed an initial inventory of animals—another $5,000 investment. Luckily, the Martins own 20 acres of rural land, a huge advantage in breeding and raising the exotic animal stock. You can't raise raccoons and foxes in a Manhattan brownstone.

The Martins emphasize that it's important to have realistic expectations. Their site is not Petopia.com, and their customer base is narrow. Nonetheless, there are uncomplicated and easy ways to make the most of opportunities. Kathi stresses always saying "Thanks" in an e-mail to online customers and always including a hyperlink back to cuddlycritters.com. Whenever possible, she also encourages people to return to her site by asking people to bookmark it. On average, the Martins receive about 10 actual inquiries each day from their normal volume of 100 hits. They have not quit their day jobs (Kathi is a professor, and Gary is a carpenter), realizing that Cuddly Critters will provide a business for their retirement years (about five years hence) and, in the meantime, "enough money to have fun."

Web address:
   www.cuddlycritters.com

Pet Locator Service

Start-up expenses: $25,000 *Canadian*
Special requirements: *Searchable database*
Best advice: *"It's much harder to start a small business than I thought it was. You need to study everything you can get your hands on and surf the Web for ideas."*

Lost a pet? If Rover has roved or Petey the Parrot has flown the coop, what can you do? Every week, desperate pet owners tack scores of flyers on telephone poles and begin to speed-dial the animal shelters, but the results are usually disappointing. One promising solution is the online search engine for pets.

In North America, pets have special status, often becoming members of the family. "They give us joy, companionship, and love and ask little in return," according to a prominent pet retrieval service. Nonetheless, about 25 million cats and dogs are reported missing in the United States and Canada each year.

While some of those animals find their way home, most will not. That problem led Phil Belanger and his partner, Craig Kachor, to found Creatures Global Pet Registry, an online service based in British Columbia.

"I actually lost a cat," says Belanger, "and we started off thinking about all the problems of finding a lost pet." For one thing, there's little organization to the current systems for locating a lost Puff and Spot. "If you want to find a pet, you have to go to all the shelters, and you have to go every day. After a couple of days, people give up because it's time-consuming." Belanger and Kachor realized that there are efficient ways to track lost people. Why not use the same processes to find pets?

OKAY, FIDO, SAY, "CHEESE"

In imagining creaturesglobal.com, Phil Belanger thought a photographic identification system was essential. "There are photographic systems for people," he says, "but not for pets. Why not?" He realized that governments use photographic records to find missing persons—for good reason. He also wanted to take the process online and create a search engine. "Other sites have pictures of pets but are not searchable," he says. "This way, owners can look at specific criteria and not have to look through thousands of pictures. For example, you can look for 'gray cats lost in mid-May in Vancouver.' "

Creatures Global offers some clear advantages to pounding the streets calling, "Here kitty, kitty, kitty." Belanger wants people to register their animals with his online service before they wander away. "If people register beforehand," he says, "it will work better than tattoos and even better than microchips." Although the implants are an excellent idea, lots of places don't have scanners. Also, the chips tend to migrate, making it harder for a scan to locate the chip. Photographic records, on the other hand, are reliable. Belanger says, "I've never seen two animals that look exactly alike. Even with 50 black cats on our site no two look alike." Creatures Global also offers identification tags as a back-up system. But the photo display onsite is the key. "If an ID tag falls off or you can't get close to the animal you're covered anyway," says Belanger.

"I DIDN'T KNOW HOW TO WRITE CODE . . ."

"We got the idea two years ago," says Belanger, and spent one and a half years researching the idea. Belanger went to his friend Craig Kachor and proposed a partnership. Belanger decided to buy a computer and write the database program, even though initially he didn't even know how to turn the machine on. Belanger designed the structure of the database in text format, then decided he had reached his limit. The partners hired a designer and told him what they wanted. "It was too complicated to do without help," admits Belanger, arguing that he could write neither code nor CGI scripts. "I found a small independent guy who did it for a good price," he recalls. "It was actually his last project. We made sure the contract says he can't do this for anyone else."

Belanger worked with the designer and helped take the site through several revamping stages. "It's still not perfect," he admits, and the site needs an upgrade so that animal shelters can begin a search restricted to the immediate region. There's no reason for the North Vancouver Society for the Prevention of Cruelty to Animals (SPCA) to be publicizing a lost Doberman in Topeka and Pompano Beach. "We'll be adding search fields as we go," says Belanger. "Right now some are shut off until the database has more animals in it." Then, with upgrades, owners will be able to search for their pets by tag number, by microchip number, and by registration number. As it stands, the company features free searching, but it costs $15 Canadian for the information on how to make contacts. People who want to make inquiries, to search for their lost pets, or to ask about adopting pets must have the $15 membership.

THE NET OFFERS OPPORTUNITIES FOR EXPANSION

Creatures Global is not yet global. In fact, the company will only gradually add animals outside the British Columbia area. For now, there are site bases for Kentucky, New York, and Hawaii but no pet pictures for the sites. Belanger says "We have some features turned off temporarily. We don't want people to find 'NO MATCHES FOUND.'" While they upgrade the system to include all states and provinces, Belanger and his partner want to be sure that people do not engage in fruitless searches for Benji in Birmingham or Otto in Ottawa. "Right now there are hundreds of pets," says Belanger, "but soon there will be thousands or millions."

Going online was clearly a huge undertaking for the partners at Creatures Global. Belanger is a nurse, and Kachor is a teacher. Neither had prior Web design knowledge, and both learned their Web skills from surfing other sites, asking "How did they do that?" Then they would take the design apart and look at the pieces. "But we don't copy anything," says Kachor. "It's all original. Even the content is ours."

Belanger is the first to admit he had no idea how difficult and frustrating a small business could be. First, Belanger's partner came to the rescue by being "a logical and technical problem-solving person." Kachor read numerous books and viewed sites on and off for more than a year. Then the partners sank $25,000 in Canadian currency into their venture—only to lose $10,000 of that amount to computer thieves, who also bagged the scanner, printer, and other hardware just as the database was about to come online.

Regardless of trials, creaturesglobal.com leapt into cyberspace on schedule. The partners ran some local newspaper ads and registered with search engines. Almost all the Vancouver-area animal shelters (other than the SPCA) are using the system. The pet retrieval service is free to the shelters, which are enthusiastic about Creatures Global because normal advertising outlets are inconvenient or expensive. Typically, the shelters' only options are the free 3 A.M. slots on public television or black-and-white newspaper ads, which are prohibitively costly. Creatures Global is available 24 hours a day, seven days a week.

SPEED AND FLEXIBILITY ARE CRITICAL

For best business advantage, the photographic search is speedy. "The way our database works," says Belanger, "is that you can do a search and look at a page with six thumbnail photos. Then you click on one picture for a bigger one." The site is organized so that clients can move through the thumbnails rapidly. The photos are small; downloading time is minimal. "We looked at other sites where photos were large," says Belanger. "These were places where anyone with a slow modem would wait forever. Most weren't searchable anyway. We made ours very fast. You can click through hundreds in a short period of time." Clicking onto one small photo brings up a picture about half the screen size, with text offering details about the pet's coloring, breed, special markings, and so forth. Beneath the picture is a button marked "Click paw to give this pet a home." Here, clients can send or receive e-mail about a pet on-screen or about a lost pet. Creatures Global also helps people adopt unclaimed pets or to make contact with animal shelters. The $15 fee is never for the initial communication and photo display—only for the details.

As with many fledgling businesses, the owners of Creatures Global admit, "We don't know anything about marketing." They remain somewhat dependent on the Society for the Prevention of Cruelty to Animals. A business association with the SPCA can offer both name recognition and credibility. Belanger is confident that such an association is forthcoming. The partners are planning a pet show—an expensive proposition—in hopes that a number of animal shelters will take part. The reasoning seems valid. According to Belanger, "The SPCA doesn't want to house any more pets than they have to. This is for their benefit. If it fails, they're stuck. Online there will be more people looking at pets. It will increase the number of pets going out the door."

Web address:

www.creaturesglobal.com

Unique Pet Supplies

Start-up expenses: $20,000
Special requirements: *None*
Best advice: *"Have realistic objectives. A lot of hobbyists are looking for supplemental income. For them, it's impractical to compete
on a serious level. For those looking to enter at a commerce level, the
best advice is to remain pragmatic. Be fiscally conservative. Allow
your creativity and energy to drive your project. Don't constantly
bring in experts and pay for things you don't need."*

Talk about great business names. How about Cool Pet
Stuff? Pet Vogue? Imagine cats in wraparound shades and
dogs in designer collars. Wroof! Cool Pet Stuff and Pet
Vogue are businesses begun by Steven Kirsch. As advertised, the
stuff is trendy and in vogue. Cats and dogs, of course, are not particularly fashion conscious unless they live in Brentwood, but
their owners often qualify. People who shop for their own toys at
upscale retail stores are the target buyers. Whether it's a laser

pointer to entertain Spot or a hand-painted "Welcome" sign announcing Fuzzy's breed lines, CoolPetStuff.com and PetVogue.com deliver.

FILLING A NEED

Steven Kirsch started CoolPetStuff.com as a family business in 1997. While looking for a dog collar, he and his wife became frustrated with the prices and the lack of variety. Even the catalog businesses, although less spendy, offered surprisingly little selection. They decided they could do better, and the Kirsches launched their online site.

According to Steven, the business plan of Nieman-Marcus was the standard they wanted to emulate, at least in terms of service. "We can get it for you" became their motto, and the Kirsches took pride in meeting the challenge with their initial business. Finding creative people with unusual products helped CoolPetStuff.com grab its share of the huge pet supplies market. In all dealings, the Kirsches stressed quality and customer satisfaction.

SERVICE, SELECTION, SECURITY

In short order, CoolPetStuff.com became the Sharper Image of cats and dogs with a Nieman-Marcus emphasis on service. The concept flourished, to the extent that Steven Kirsch's business recently grew 1,000 percent in one year! How did it happen? Well, here's the story.

"We got involved with the concept of starting a small business a few years ago," says Kirsch. "We were looking for something we could really use to express our personal interest in quality. We were thinking either kids or pets." Obviously, Kirsch and his wife chose pets.

The business partners looked for unusual pet products, rejecting the general product lines of places such as Petco and Petsmart. First, they considered a catalog business, but the lure of the Net prevailed. "We basically invested in the future of technology," says Kirsch. "We believed a Web store would surpass more traditional commercial vehicles."

The Kirsches built their own site but also constructed a Yahoo!Store thumbnail site, thinking of the smaller project as a "sampler." In this respect, they followed Sharper Image, which did the same thing. "We had to use guerrilla marketing," says Kirsch, "because we had no budget, maybe $20,000 total for operations." That penny-pinching meant the Kirsches would engage in networking to a large extent. "We made a lot of friends on the Internet," says Kirsch, "and did anything we could without paying a fee or charge."

Mass mailings through e-mail helped, and Steven Kirsch spent a great deal of time talking to reporters, gaining as much free publicity as possible. The partners also explored the search engines. "Together," says Kirsch, "it all worked. With a huge run-up in business, the Kirsches saw profits soar. He says, "We attribute our success to being in the right place at the right time—in the correct sector and on the Internet." For Steven, "the right sector" means retail pet products. But the particular angle that ensured success is the niche market they carved.

"A lot of people feel as we did that pet supplies should be interesting," says Kirsch, who complains that new ideas are not popular at the major distributors. He estimates that an innovation or trendy new design takes up to eighteen months to appear on the shelves at Petsmart or Petco, if at all. "We found we could do it in a week," he declares. There's the niche. For a business plan, the Kirsches decided on a "three *S*" concept. They stressed exceptional *service* to the customer, a rich *selection* of products, and heightened online *security* for credit card purchasers. A wise combination.

UNUSUAL PRODUCTS

At CoolPetStuff.com, Kirsch debuted nifty new products like the Tidy Feed, a dog bowl with a little globe in the top cover. The feeding aperture is big enough for Rover's mouth but not those big floppy ears. People with cocker spaniels are thrilled. Washing doggy ears is no treat. The number one seller at CoolPetStuff.com is a cat drinking fountain. Another favorite is a wine barrel doghouse, suitable for svelte St. Bernards.

Customers love the CoolPetStuff.com site because unusual products and special orders are the norm. One customer called Kirsch and said she was getting married. She wanted her dog to be the ring bearer. "Could you get me a tuxedo for my dog?" Well, yes. Kirsch later received a photo of the ceremony, with the dog foremost, dressed in his trendy tux with a little pillow strapped to his back for the ring. Too cool.

A NEW BUSINESS ADDRESS

After just a few years of business, Kirsch and his wife recently sold CoolPetStuff.com to Pets.com, one of the top players in the pet products market. CoolPetStuff.com will be absorbed into the larger site. But the Kirsches remain in the pet supplies business, seeking a new clientele. PetVogue.com is a niche within a niche. It's an upscale boutique featuring the high end of products originally featured on the CoolPetStuff.com site.

Says Kirsch, "It's a very sophisticated site, simple and clean."

But very trendy. "We have things like dog beds for $400 or $500 and custom-built doghouses selling for as much as $6,000." At the new PetVogue.com site, you can pay $20,000 for a cat necklace or get a tiara for your poodle (even more expensive). There's also a line of fashionable clothing. Whoa. *Do you have anything from Paris in a size three for my Shar-Pei?*

The Kirsches remain confident that their new site serves a vibrant market. They have people from several top design firms creating new pet designs—clothing that sells for $200 to $300 apiece. And for the discriminating buyer, there are pet carriers in fine leathers and exotic pet collars (also in rich leathers) for both cats and dogs. Says Kirsch, "All of these products sell well because, with the shift of wealth in this country, there are increasing numbers of very rich people. The demographics are amazing now."

So, if your pet shelter mixed-breed cat is looking a little scruffy, or if that toothless old hound in the backyard needs a makeover, think about the Net. The Kirsches are glad to sell Blackie or Felix a stunning new outfit or the in-vogue accessories that will make the other pets on the block howl with envy.

Web addresses:
    www.PetVogue.com
    www.Pets.com

Real Estate & Home Improvement

Antique Reproduction Furniture

Start-up expenses: $2,900
Special requirements: *Digital camera*
Best advice: *"Try to use your Web site in a supportive way. Most of the people I know in my industry with sites use them as a tool to get the name out there and to dispense information. At this point, we're using the site as an advertising tool."*

David T. Smith is a furniture maker. He specializes in custom-built and stock renditions of eighteenth-and nineteenth-century American furniture. He uses traditional furniture-making techniques, including dovetailed drawers, mortise-and-tenon joinery, and hand-forged hardware. With a choice of colors and finishes, buyers can order authentic reproduction designs. Of course, the furniture is on display, but not just in a showroom. Clear digital pictures of pieces show up regularly on Smith's Web site: davidtsmith.com.

20 Years and Still Going

Twenty years ago, according to the literature on their Web site, the Smiths settled onto farmland in rural Ohio. Around them grew a community of artisans, some 40 strong. Today the craft center is known as the Workshops of David T. Smith. Here people view and buy "custom-crafted, museum-quality repro- duction furniture, pottery, and kitchens," all built onsite.

David began work with his father's table saw and a box of hand tools. One of his first projects was an antique table, bought for $11 and repaired by Smith. When a dealer offered $350, Smith knew he had talent. He kept the table.

With a lifetime devotion to fine craftsmanship, Smith and his 50 employees use old woodworking techniques, regularly pro- ducing new and repaired products that appeal to dealers, muse- ums, and high-end buyers. These creations appear often in magazines such as *Country Living* and *Early American Homes* and on television programs such as "Home and Garden TV."

Design, Rebuilding, and Reproduction

With a community of workers and an onsite designer, Smith is prepared for most antique furniture requests. His designer works privately to draw new creations for buyers, or customers can order from stock items. Most of the products appear on the Web site either in a photograph or basic design. Buyers can or- der a particular finish as well. As anyone familiar with antiques knows, the quality and look of the finish is critical.

Smith shares one story, recounted from the television show

"Antique Roadshow," of a man who owned a beautiful antique highboy. Because the piece was dirty and grungy, the owner commissioned an artisan to refinish it. On the show, an assessor told the owner that the piece was worth $3,500 but would command ten times that much with the original finish. As Smith explains, "Our specialty is doing aged finishes that look like old finishes." It's easy to see why.

In addition to Early American furniture, the artisans at the Workshops of David T. Smith throw pots, many of them replicated to look like old redware—some even with authentic-looking chips and mars. Also, the workers turn wooden chandeliers, all in Early American classic style. "Our products are high-end classics," says Smith. "We did a number of pieces for the Ralph Lauren Lighthouse Collection, and we sell wholesale to 50 or 60 dealers around the country." The Smith business is also brick and mortar, with stores in Ohio and Naples, Florida.

A DIFFERENT VIEW OF THE WEB

Unlike many online sellers, Smith and friends maintain a site primarily to show their merchandise. Most sales are direct. When customers ask what's in stock, Smith simply says, "Look at the site." There, digitally displayed, are the usual wares and inventory pieces. The virtual showroom stocks about $400,000 to $500,000 of inventory at one time. "Many," says Smith, "are one-of-a-kind pieces." These offerings have a special finish and are crafted from select woods. "It's hard to have a printed catalog for these kinds of presentations," says Smith.

Indeed, the Web site is a display showroom, updated every two or three weeks. Everything in the showroom is for sale, but people also like to propose new finishes or tops for tables and hutches. If so, the Smith workers take a digital photograph with the right combinations of colors, woods, and styles and pop it onto the Web site. Voila! Instant showroom!

Smith says, "I'm amazed, but my laptop probably has 5,000 or 6,000 images on it." He constantly stores new designs but can also dip into his archives on demand to resurrect old patterns.

BUYING OPTIONS

Although it happens, most sales don't occur at the Web site. Most of the Smith items are quite expensive. People want to see what's available, but they don't want to wait ten weeks for a print catalog. As Smith explains, "They might be out of the mood by then or on vacation when it comes. But on the Web you can browse when your interest is at its peak, and instantly see the creation." Because Smith accepts many custom requests, he has become accustomed to people who peek at the online catalog but want something changed—small or large. "That's our specialty," he says. "Instant gratification."

The main advantage, as Smith sees it, is speed. The Net resource allows people to have what they want now. "I like things that are quick, too," he admits, recalling that if he's driving his car through traffic, he's also likely to be downloading inventory on his laptop or scanning designs.

TECHNOLOGY DRIVES THE BUSINESS

Even though Smith's furniture is based on centuries long past, he has a new-millennium grasp of the technical end. "We try to stay on top of technology," he says. "I've got a guy who's computer literate. We go to someone's house and design a kitchen right there on the laptop, then e-mail the drawings back to the shop. If you need specs, you can go to the Web and get refrigerator sizes from Frigidaire, for instance." Wow! Because many sales are high-end custom orders, Smith expects lots of impulse sales. For that reason, quick response and rapid-flow information are essential.

Advertising is not a problem. People find the Smith company in many ways. As stated earlier, they've had write-ups in prominent national magazines, and they place print ads with the Web address wherever they draw the most business. With an early entry onto Yahoo!, Smith's antique company gained a foothold in the big search engines. He says, if you ask for reproduction furniture or Windsor chairs, davidtsmith.com shows up in the top ten. Who would have imagined such a thing in 1812?

Web address:
   www.davidtsmith.com

Asian Home Furnishings

Start-up expenses: $50,000

Special requirements: *Expertise in design, production, sales/marketing, and the import/export business*

Best advice: *"Make sure you have a solid organization that can support the e-business as it grows and expands. Pay careful attention to order responses, customer service, and follow-up."*

Would you like to help people create new design themes in their homes? Today, the Net can help. A growing number of sites are devoted to home furnishings and designer creations. If the credenza is an embarrassment and the dining room a disaster, perhaps it's time to go online. If you're intrigued by furnishings with the Old World charm of Vietnam and the trendy fashion sense of Paris, consider xamaison.com, the business address of designer Lan Vu.

Traveling the world looking for textiles—the best a country can offer—sounds like a vacation. For Vu, a former fashion forecaster and writer, it's her job. Recently in her search for one-of-a-kind prints and designs, she returned to her native Vietnam, where she was captivated by both the land and the fashion. When Vu returned to her home base in Paris, she sought to capture the essence of the Asian countryside in her new collection of home furnishings. At first, she wanted to market her unique designs in limited quantities throughout the United States but soon realized that an e-commerce Web site provided a better business opportunity. Her company, Xa Maison (*xa* "distant," and *maison*, "home", is a pure expression of her vision.

Finding a Home in Cyberspace

With her product line completed and in production, Vu needed a vehicle—her Web site. After only a few weeks of work with *Dreamweaver* Web page software, she constructed a site that reflected her company vision. Having an online store, she suggests, allowed her to reach a worldwide audience and presented an inexpensive alternative to funding brick-and-mortar shops in major cities. The Web enabled Vu to start business operations immediately "with a minimum investment."

Today, Xa Maison attracts visitors primarily through press releases sent to magazines, as well as through Web links to associated fashion and furnishing sites. "Running an e-business has taught me to think more abstractly," she says, "and on different levels." Because orders are received online and the products are made in Southeast Asia, Vu spends enormous efforts to coordinate data, track monies, and traffic merchandise.

As the Web site explains (amid glorious photos), xamaison.com offers originally designed table settings, silk cushions, and bedding, along with other home accessories—all hand-made by local Vietnamese artisans. Many of the textiles are traditional weaves, including several from ethnic hill tribes. Vu says, "Xa Maison is based on the idea of interactive journeys—selected artists traveling to different locations, capturing designs in a limited collection." At the Web site, buyers can read the entire chronicle of the artist's journey and "understand the full story" of the creators behind the products.

Using traditional craft techniques, Vu's artists produce only a set number of the same design before moving to another project. Although Xa Maison lines appear in select boutiques throughout the world, most sales are transacted online. One of the problems Xa Maison faces is the impression that Vietnamese crafts are low-end, poorly designed, and cheaply made. Vu has worked hard to create a new image. After she completes the designs in Paris, the products are made in Asia by well-known crafters and artisans that she "hand-picks," thus ensuring the quality of their work. "Our focus is high-quality goods," says Vu, "those made using traditional techniques." Though such methods cost more at the production level, the care and skill of the artisans makes for a superior product. She hopes to capture a niche market with her designs, leaving mass market distribution to companies that manufacture generic home furnishings.

Despite competition on the horizon, Vu recognizes that her best business position lies in the middle—neither competing with the major manufacturers nor maintaining a small custom-designs-only shop. Says Vu, "We offer the service and originality of the small home sites, but also the professionalism and fashion-forward ideas of corporate sites. We would compare our site to an online museum gift shop, which offers finer-quality products designed by selected artists." Unlike the museum shops, however, she wants to carry lines that continue to change, so that each artist crafts a different vision and journey—one that constantly transforms itself.

TIMING IS EVERYTHING

Online businesses offer certain pros and cons compared with traditional storefront operations. While Vu has a remarkable advantage by not having to fund and maintain shops all over the world, she also must live with the specter of abstraction that the Net creates. For instance, instead of walking down the hall to the production room, she has to deal with the fact that the sewing machines and looms are operating half a world away. Also, there are problems with the back-end services. Recently, xamaison.com stopped receiving orders. For days Vu wondered if she had processed her last order. She soon discovered a glitch in the credit server, one that derailed the entire process. "That problem," she says, "resulted in the loss of valuable business."

Another factor is timing. Every day Vu faces the challenge of coordinating "the artisans who create work at their own pace and the customers who are accustomed to the microsecond responses of the Internet world." In short, while the weavers and builders are taking their time, the buyers are banging on the cyberdoors. To face the challenges head-on, Vu has to pay careful attention to scheduling and accommodation. Sometimes, says Vu, she has to allow extra time for production and realistic sales projections—not estimates based on twenty-first-century expectations of efficiency.

In retrospect, Vu recognizes that Xa Maison is a return to traditions. She was so impressed with the rich quality of traditional textiles in Vietnam that she believed they should be available in the international market. Moreover, she wanted to start a business that would generate profits on the one hand but contribute to the community on the other. As a result, she found a school for the deaf and mute in Vietnam and contracted the students' services, hoping to help support the school's programs. In addition, by using local artists and craftspeople, Vu hopes to supplement incomes for the Vietnamese, as well as to showcase their skills in a high-end market. These dreams are materializing for Lan Vu, who has integrated distant home in a unique and charming way.

Web address:

www.xamaison.com

Hardware Store

Start-up expenses: $2,000
Special requirements: *None*
Best advice: *"If you own a brick-and-mortar store and are think-*
ing of going online, get involved with a portal like Yahoo! or
About. They're relatively inexpensive, so you can get your feet wet
without an outrageous outlay of money."

Since the first coin changed hands, the mantra in business has always been "location, location, location." What happens to Mom's Coffee Shop when Starbuck's opens across the street? That's right—Mom's out of business. The problem of invasion by competitors is a concern for all business owners and can be deadly. At least that's what Robert and Karen Ludgin, the owners of Coastal Tool, thought in 1995 when Home Depot opened its doors two miles down the road. Actually, Home Depot simply nudged Coastal Tool from its comfortable storefront location into the wild and wonderful world of cyber-space, where profits have been great.

Coastal Tool opened in 1981 in Hartford, Connecticut, and began selling power tools. At that time, Coastal Tool was probably the only place on the East Coast where the business model was to offer low prices everyday. The discounting concept is common now but wasn't in the 1980s. The Coastal Tool store was modeled on a similar store on the West Coast, one owned by friends of the Ludgins. At one point, Rob Ludgins decided to visit the West Coast operation for a few weeks to learn more. He came back with a truckload of products. Soon after, he ventured into a mail order business he operated from his storefront. Catalog sales flourished until 1988, when distribution of catalogs peaked at 750,000.

GOING VIRTUAL

In November 1995, the owners decided to put up a Web site. Todd Mogren, the current Web designer, was in on the decision. He says, "I had finished doing some computer work here and wanted to extend my stay," he admits, "so I had to come up with something." That something was an early-entry site that launched Coastal Tool into the big leagues of tool sales. The site was online in 1996 and soon added a shopping cart program. In the first full year of operations, sales jumped from $187,000 to $887,000. And because Home Depot and other megastores were muscling into the neighborhood, Mogren and the owners felt that an active Web site would broaden their market reach.

"Going in," says Mogren, "we thought we could do about $100,000 in sales, so we doubled our expectations when it came in at $187,000. From the beginning we intended to use the Internet to sell products, rather than just serving an informational site. We really wanted to list products and take orders online." Coastal

Tool did just that. By 1998, sales stood at $1.5 million, and 1999 sales were more than double that amount. That same year, Coastal Tool processed over 19,000 orders online.

One special feature of the Coastal Tool site is "The Tool Doctor." In this window, you can e-mail any question and have it answered the same day. "The Tool Doctor" also refers do-it-yourselfers to tool repair centers near their homes. By November 1999, the good doctor had received and answered 52,201 click-in questions about tools.

STILL IN TRANSITION

Despite the online successes, Coastal Tool has not gone entirely virtual. Customers can still request catalogs online. And catalogs are regularly included in equipment shipments. Nonetheless, the only way to get on the Coastal Tools mailing list is to request a catalog online. Coastal Tool no longer bothers with bulk mailings, but, says Mogren, "We still have a pretty catalog."

Like many businesses making the shift to cyberspace, Coastal Tool stands in a transitional period, one that's likely to remain for another two years (by their own estimates). Those people who have been comfortable with mail orders but have migrated online still want the security of a hard-copy catalog. "In many cases," says Mogren, "they haven't made the complete leap to online transactions."

Coastal Tool still gets 150 requests per day for catalogs. Mogren sees the catalogs as a business advantage, rather than a liability. "Having a catalog actually gives you credibility," he says. "In the eyes of a customer, the catalog legitimizes a company that has put up a Web site." During this transitional period for Net businesses, many companies are discovering—as with Coastal Tool—that virtual sales methods work best when

complemented by traditional ones such as catalogs, print advertising, and 800 phone numbers.

No Slow Movers in Cyberspace

Some aspects of sales are remarkably different in e-commerce
than in the real world. For instance, if at a local storefront you
advertise a price advantage, you get some added business. But a
price advantage online can bring huge sales. Consider the number of people on an average day shopping on the Net. Lots.
Even if you count only those looking for a Sandvik saw or a
Makita drill, the totals are substantial. "If you're the price
leader," says Mogren, "your sales will grow exponentially."

But that's not the real news. In cyberspace, there are no slow
movers. In a small market, which describes most operations in
the real world, companies may need to stock one special item
and (with reorders) might sell five or six. Once you go online—
keeping in mind that there are very few other resources available to find that particular saw or drill at a good price—you can
dramatically increase your sales.

But here's the real kicker. A business can actually feature
slow-moving or unusual items on the Web site, and these lines
will drastically increase sales for every item. That paradox de-
fies the business logic of the real world. "In a brick-and-mortar
shop," says Mogren, "you would normally take the price-sensi-
tive items and build on them. There are a lot of places that sell
tools, but they're not tool stores, so having the hard-to-find
items also legitimizes your operation. Then ship on time and let
people build up rapport. They will soon be comfortable with
your online business. At that point, they don't try to price shop
nearly so much if they believe you're reasonable and fair."
Online merchandisers can establish user loyalty even while

moving tools (or any products) that would probably gather dust at a brick-and-mortar shop.

Repeat Customers Spell Profits

Getting customers to the site at Coastal Tools was not difficult. In 1996, the company was perhaps the only exclusively tools site on the Net. The search engines had little trouble finding the firm's address and—believe it or not—back in 1996, the electronic paperwork for registering was simple. In March 1996, says Mogren, a customer could type in "Makita," the name of the best-known tool manufacturer, and find that 55 of the top 60 positions belonged to Coastal Tool. The other five would be sites surrounding personal names, like Stan Mikita Beef and Brew or Joe Mikita's Cleveland Browns Web Site. "So we pretty much had the market to ourselves," says Mogren.

Things changed, of course. Today the market is flooded with competitors. But Coastal Tool is hanging on to its customers. Because sales are strong, the company can now invest in a significant advertising campaign. However, very few advertising dollars go to print sources. Ninety-five percent of the ad dollars are spent online.

Coastal Tool has made wise decisions involving the Net. In 1997, they were one of the first to install a shopping cart. "It sounds so silly now," says Mogren, "but in 1997 so few businesses had carts!" As for advice to others, Mogren suggests getting involved early with prominent portals like Yahoo! or About. The cost is reasonable and, for those who aren't quite sure how to enter the virtual market, a big advantage. "You can get your feet wet," says Mogren, "without spending an outrageous amount of money." As the business grows, entrepreneurs

should not take large profits but reinvest the cash into upgrades, getting on your own server, and tying it onto your back
end.

"People are put off at the amount of money you can throw at
the whole process," admits Mogren. "You'll get quotes in the
hundreds of thousands for site design. But you can get past
those expenses by partnering with portals that offer built-in
traffic. They take care of the back-end complications." In short,
then, business owners entering the Web world for the first time,
especially those with some trepidation about the whole experience, might take special benefit from the services of Yahoo! and
other such portals.

LOOK WHO JUST MOVED INTO THE NEIGHBORHOOD?

When Coastal Tools started its operations in 1981, they were
housed in a small building with 1,500 square feet of retail space
and 6,000 square feet of warehousing spread over three floors.
There were only four parking spots, and cars whizzed by on a
busy street. It was not a good spot for business.

Recently the company moved to a 30,000-square-foot building—a direct result of success on the Internet. All those saws
and drills take up space! "We went into the Web business to
combat Home Depot and other chains," says Mogren. It clearly
worked. Now the retail site has 30 to 40 times as much walk-in
traffic as before.

Ironically, Coastal Tool has a new neighbor. There's a new
Home Depot directly across the street. It's been good for a
laugh. Says Mogren, "Lots of customers come through the
doors and think we're nuts for staying in this location. They get

up close and whisper, 'How're you doing?' We just whisper back, 'We don't know.' "

Of course, the folks at Coastal Tool know exactly how they're doing. Business is booming. And the means to hammer down big profits came from a predictable source: a well-conceived Web site on the Net.

Web address:

www.CoastalTool.com

Home Contractor
Referral Service

Start-up expenses: $5,000

Special requirements: *None, although handy skills include networking, sales, and organizational ability*

Best advice: *"You have to sell yourself, even if you have all the tools necessary. Investigate all your options carefully. Figure out what you're good at and what drives you. Most of all, though, you have to love the job in order to succeed."*

Leaky roof? Broken banister? Electrical outlets that shoot sparks? Welcome to home ownership. Now where do you call to get things fixed? There's always the classified ads, but that's a decided gamble, not unlike picking a wife or husband from the Lonely Hearts column. To be sure, everyone on the block has a story that, with variations, repeats the phrase "I just couldn't get them to fix it right."

Getting the roof sealed and the banister repaired are projects beyond the scope of the average homeowner, especially busy two-income households. For many Americans, work hours are long, and patience is short. When you get home from work, there's dinner to prepare and homework to supervise. But there's also a Girl Scout meeting, volleyball practice, the Rotary fund-raiser, Aunt Janet's birthday party to plan, and the Investment Club meeting (at your house this week, of course). Besides, home repair requires more expertise than most adults can muster, even though the brave and the foolish sometimes fake it, at least until there's water running in the hallways.

WHERE DOES IT HURT?

Enter Debra Cohen, who started Home Remedies in August 1996. The cleverly named company, a referral service operating from Hewlett, New York, brings carpenters, painters, landscapers, plumbers, and other skilled workers into contact with homeowners. The homeowners receive free referral service from Cohen, but the contractors pay a 15 percent commission on new business arranged by Home Remedies.

Cohen maintains a database of approximately 50 local professionals, each with steady references, good work histories, and, above all, pleasant manners. Cohen checks contractors' licenses, insurance, and bonding before adding new workers to her database, so that she can assure homeowners that work is done capably, at reasonable cost, and on schedule. To run her business, Cohen spends about 15 to 20 hours a week on the phone and at her computer.

Everyone needs help, argues Cohen, in finding the right resources for home repair. Most homeowners don't have time to check references and often end up choosing a name from the Yellow Pages. Plumbers and electricians make serious money, so choosing the right contractor is important. Cohen's Net-based referral service takes the fear and risk out of the process. She not only helps homeowners find skilled laborers, but Cohen also provides follow-up service, seeing that each job is completed to everyone's satisfaction.

When Cohen started thinking about the Home Remedies Company, she was a publishing executive in New York. For eight years she edited an aviation magazine with a large circulation base in South America. In addition to publishing, Cohen managed properties globally and traveled extensively. When she decided to start a family, Cohen imagined a Web service that would free her to be a stay-at-home mom. Strangely enough, her New York job was excellent preparation for Home Remedies. "Being vice-president of a magazine may seem totally unrelated to this business," she says, "but it gave me the basic skills I need, like networking and communication."

When she began seeking referrals, Cohen was untrained in Web business. "I knew how to type," she says. "That was it." But Cohen taught herself the basics of computer operations, then looked at the requirements for creating a Web site. She decided to hire professional designers, but, she says, "I monitor everything carefully." Today homeownersreferral.com uses an extensive Web marketing campaign. Cohen focuses on writing e-zine articles and reregistering with search engines as often as possible. As she explains, "I do a lot of publicity on the Web—making link exchanges and writing for women's and home-based business sites. I have an extensive publicity campaign in print, too. My business has even been featured on television and radio."

With so many publicity outlets, Home Remedies has an increasing customer base. She does monthly mailings to about 300 residences in South Nassau County, focusing on two-income families, her major market. Cohen checks contractors' references carefully, using a five-point evaluation system, and she insists on quality and reputation.

The biggest problem at Home Remedies is filling job orders. Home building is booming, and contractors are at a premium. Keeping up with the demand is a challenge. "I have 400 gutters waiting to be fixed," sighs Cohen.

A Prepackaged Business Opportunity

As so many entrepreneurs are discovering, the Net offers a remarkable difference from normal brick-and-mortar referral services. In her role as liaison between homeowner and laborer, Cohen has built a client list of hundreds of satisfied customers. Recently Cohen added a global emphasis to her business, one that allows her to market a prepackaged business opportunity. "When I'm on the Web site," says Cohen, "I'm dealing with people all over the world. It's easy to keep in touch, although you have to keep an eye on time zones. Nevertheless, my site is working 24 hours a day. Even in my sleep, my autoresponders are working, giving out necessary information." As Cohen explains, the Net saves her time and offers unlimited exposure. The world is her marketplace.

Cohen's prepackaged business opportunity is for others who want to enter the referral business. For an investment of $2,995, anyone can buy the Homeowner Referral Network Business Package. This business plan, which outlines the necessary steps for entry into the business arena, allows others to learn from Cohen's experience as Queen of the Electronic Rolodex.

Business can be simple if, like Cohen, you figure out what you're good at—and what you enjoy—then follow through on it. Cohen's home repair referral service, like so many nascent e-businesses, is demanding. "You must be disciplined," she warns. But it also helps to understand your strengths—in her case, organization and networking. By the way, with a little paint, some more electrical outlets, and a bank of new cabinets, that home office of yours could be perfect for an e-commerce venture. Now, have you thought about contracting for the necessary repairs? Well, we recommend the services of Home Remedies.

Web address:

www.homeownersreferral.com

Home Improvement Information

Start-up expenses: $5,000

Special requirements: *None*

Best advice: *"If you're posting a content site (which describes most sites), make sure you have searchable archives, so that people can find information quickly. Otherwise you need search engines. That's what frustrates most people; they can't find what they need."*

Web-based businesses like home improvement information services sometimes seem to operate in a surreal world, one that leaves traditionalists gasping for air. Consider, for instance, an e-commerce anecdote about AsktheBuilder.com from the pages of *Striking It Rich*: "Imagine this. You decide to launch an advertiser-supported content site. You make several cold calls to companies that manufacture products related to your enterprise, with the hope they will advertise. On the fourth call, you sell a banner ad for $12,000, get

paid instantly . . . and your site hasn't even been launched yet."
This isn't sales. It's Alice's tea party.

In the sometimes surreal world of Web-site sales, the kind of
events that were unimaginable five years ago are now becoming
trends. To women and men who pound the mean streets promoting products and services, this Mad Hatter's tale of instant
success must seem dizzying. For Tim Carter, who actually lived
this fantasy, it was an auspicious beginning, but hardly the
whole story. From its surprising start, Carter's Ask the Builder
Web site blossomed into a cyberadventure that earned more
than $600,000 in 1998 alone.

A TIM-OF-ALL-TRADES

Carter graduated from college in 1974 with a geology degree.
He put his diploma in a drawer and immediately entered the
home improvement field, first by performing handyman jobs.
Soon he was working on room additions, then custom homes.
"The next thing I knew," he says, "I was a licensed plumber, a
master roof cutter, and a master carpenter." In 1993, with a tool-
box full of talents, Carter found himself chosen as one of the
Top 50 Remodelers in America and traveled to Washington to
be formally recognized. "That was the changing point of my
career," says Carter.

Twenty years of physical labor was beginning to exact a toll
on Carter, who, like Tim the Toolman Taylor, has the stitches to
prove it—approximately 500. Add that to the considerable
stress of the contracting business, and Carter felt the need to
find another niche. He didn't know what to do, but his wife
said, "Why don't you take your home improvement ideas and
write a syndicated newspaper column?" So he did.

"I didn't realize I had writing talent until I tried," says Carter. "That started a whole new career." Carter syndicated his column by beating on doors and, in 1994, he added a local radio show. That show is now also syndicated. Then in December 1995, all the pieces fell together when Carter launched his Web site. It was one of the first home improvement sites on the Web. Carter knew instinctively that content was the key to success online. He began with a self-composed rich and varied archive of information and adds new information constantly. For instance, Carter supplies a brand-new column every week in addition to a regular feature, "Builder's Bulletin."

The Internet, says Carter, allows him equal footing with publishers such as McGraw-Hill and *The Chicago Tribune*. He has something to sell and an audience to listen. Normally, home improvement books and columns benefit the publishers greatly but don't offer much financial reward for the authors. On the Net, Carter became his own publisher. "Let's face it," says Carter, "publishers are the ones who make the profits. As a publisher, I can do anything. I can sell advertising *and* do e-commerce, *and* I get to keep the money." Isn't America great?

WHY DOES BOB VILA ALWAYS LOOK SO UNRUMPLED?

Recently Carter made the jump from self-syndication to Tribune Media Services (owner of *The Chicago Tribune*). That frees him to devote energy to his Web site. Carter also provides a ninety-second home improvement vignette on WCPO TV. In his spare time (what spare time?) he filmed a pilot for a national show called "Ask the Builder." "My show is going to be awesome," offers Carter. "The current TV shows are not realistic.

Bob Vila always shows up clean. His materials are ready, and the crew is prepped. The truck is spotless and shiny." Carter promises to tell the truth about home repair.

In real life, there's a problem every day on the job, he suggests. "I was always in damage control, constantly solving problems and making the best of it. That's the *real* world of home improvement." Carter says that TV hosts like Vila may look relaxed and organized while connecting water pipes under sinks, but the scenes are misleading. "I sweated, wore jeans, and my truck was always dented," says Carter. On his show, Carter says he will even tell viewers the ultimate truth about home repair: "Hey, this is a job you can't do. It will take weeks and look terrible. Call a professional." Carter talks about his site on the show and puts content from the show on the site.

WEEKLY ADVERTISING BUDGET: $8

Getting customers is the bottom line in Web sales, of course. Being early online gave Carter a real advantage. Also, his newspaper column includes his Web site address. Carter recognizes the value of this business plug. "Maybe 99.9 percent of Web sites do not get free advertising, but I did." As always, advertising had a domino effect, leading to word-of-mouth publicity. In Carter's words, "People visit [my site] and tell others about it. Then the media find out and spread the word. Even the BBC got the story."

Carter has never bought a banner ad (although he's sold several), and he sees no need for extensive advertising. "The only ad I pay for is one in my church bulletin," says Carter, "and that costs eight dollars a week." Actually, he admits, he also sprang for a banner in the school gym, but "people only see that for the three months of basketball season."

YOU CAN COMPETE
WITH THE BIG BOYS

There are direct competitors to AsktheBuilder.com. Even though he entered the cyberworld early, Carter was not the first. That distinction goes to Housenet.com, a service started by two East Coast syndicated columnists. But Housenet.com sold to a large publishing company. Then came Hometime.com, which also has great content, according to Carter. But the competitors do not match Carter's depth of content, nor can they offer advice and free service. AsktheBuilder.com makes most of its profits selling banner ads to home improvement supply companies; the rest come from product sales.

Sometime in 1996, Carter began selling an oxygen bleach product, one that he had written about in his column. Selling the bleach online was a good venture, says Carter. "Before I found this product, I thought bleach was bleach, but it's chlorine bleach that is so nasty. This oxygen bleach takes out stains and doesn't hurt fabrics, fade colors, or kill plants. I wrote about it originally, saying it was a great deck cleaner, but then the manufacturer told me all its other advantages. I sell a lot of it." But bleach is not Carter's only line. He also sells an intellectual property called a Bid Sheet. Carter compares the sheet to a "test" for home improvement companies, a questionnaire that should reveal the contractor's professionalism and experience.

"I used to sell the Bid Sheet the old-fashioned way," says Carter, "through mail orders." But, he adds, "It was horrible doing business that way. When I converted to the Net, it was completely different. Now I take the money when people order, and the product goes to them automatically in an attached file." Because product sales have been a low-effort, high-margin aspect of business, Carter is looking for more lines to distribute, including both intellectual properties and shippable products like oxygen bleach.

BUILD A FOUNDATION

Carter began his foray into Web site advertising and sales with no technical skills. He says, "Before I saw the Web for the first time, I was terrified of it. I hired professionals to put my site together. Why professionals? That's what I preach in my columns: Use professionals." From his on-the-job experience, Carter knew that homeowners often made matters worse with their own uninformed repairs. "So I knew intuitively that I shouldn't design a Web site myself," he adds. "Man, I'm glad. I got it done right!"

As for AsktheBuilder.com, Carter acknowledges that he has kept his site simple and easy to use. "Most other sites have all these links," he complains, "and you can't back out because you may be 15 levels deep. On my site, you're never more than three levels deep. That's by design." Ease of access is terribly important. "Don't go crazy with graphics," Carter adds. AsktheBuilder.com has no extraneous graphics, and, once the Web page is loaded, the remaining pages are instantly loaded as well. Content is more important than "fancy stuff" in such Web designs.

Carter spends most of his Web efforts on answering e-mail questions. He receives more than 100 queries daily—almost anything can go wrong with a house. Since Carter strives to have enormous amounts of home improvement advice and to organize it in such a way that people can find answers quickly and easily, he's adding a section to the site called "Tim's Tips." He'll post ten e-mail questions (and the answers) at one time. Carter says this service is unique. "Most other sites are not answering e-mail like I do. I've tested other sites, sending e-mail

questions. I never get a response or, if I do, it's just a generic signature response."

BRICK AND MORTAR FOR THIS BUILDER'S SITE

Like many e-commerce adventurers, Carter finds the virtual
world faster and more precise than the real world. For example,
formerly Carter had to depend on "he said" and "she said" phone
communications in his home improvement business. He had no
permanent record of these phone sessions with customers. Now,
with the Web site and e-mails, there's always a digital fingerprint.
Carter can say to a customer referring to a posted e-mail, "Look,
this is what you said and what you ordered." No longer are business arrangements dependent on memory and interpretation.
Credit hassles are reduced, too. "Now I get paid for everything in
advance," smiles Carter, "even for advertisements." The days of
billing once (or several times) and waiting for payment are over.
On the Net, payment is instantaneous, aided by the automated
credit card services available in cyberspace.

At the same time, cyberspace has its drawbacks. What was a fast-
paced world before has now become hyperkinetic. Furthermore,
expectations are high. "Everyone on the Net wants instant gratification," says Carter. "If you can't deliver, you've got problems."
Luckily, Carter has been able to deliver.

THE THREE Ds—DILIGENCE, DETERMINATION, AND DISCIPLINE

The world of e-business is not for talkers, says Carter, but for
doers. "I believe in the 3 Ds: diligence, determination, and dis-

cipline. You have to have all three. Nothing about Web business is easy. You hear all the success stories, but to get overnight success I had to put in 20 years—working out in the rain, in the cold, and getting 500 stitches. It's my accumulated knowledge that makes it work."

Despite the obvious rewards, Internet business is not for the meek. Carter didn't have the money to launch his site. He borrowed it. The decision was not easy. Says Carter, "My wife and I were hurting. It was a huge gamble. But I was determined to work. I decided I was going to *make* it work. Sometimes I'd wake up at two in the morning, pop out of bed, race to the office, and work on an idea for two or three hours."

Web address:
www.AsktheBuilder.com

Sports &
Recreation

Cycle Retailer

Start-up expenses: $700
Special requirements: *None*
Best advice: *"Find a usenet group like I did. Whatever you are really into, find a group of people who do that for a hobby, and you might have a built-in customer base. Don't come across as arrogant. Just ask questions, and they'll be eager to help. Also if you can find somebody to give you an endorsement, that's great. It would be hard for us to pay Michael Jordan, but most people involved with unicycles know John Foss. When he started recommending us, we saw a big boost in sales."*

There's something hilarious about a unicycle. Maybe it's the herky-jerky lurching of the wheel or the improbable flailing of the rider. For some, it's probably just the entire silly notion of making do with half the requisite number of wheels. Whatever the cause, people's faces usually light up when a unicycle weaves its way through the streets or down a grassy knoll—at least until the crash.

John Drummond woke up one morning with a desire to get into shape. Instead of rolling over like most of us, he followed through. When he thought about fitness, the image of bicycles came to mind. His father's 84-year-old friend biked 20 miles a day, usually leading the pack when riding with the kids. That image stuck with Drummond, as did the troubling notion that his brother-in-law, who ate "like a horse," remained thin and fit by pedaling 200 miles every weekend.

Drummond agreed that cycling was the right fitness plan, but when he went shopping, he came home one wheel short. At that time, Drummond was 42 and thoroughly ensconced at IBM. With 21 years of experience, he had gained some status and a modicum of respectability. Riding a unicycle was a decided risk to that reputation. Only clowns and acrobats rode unicycles, he thought. However, throwing caution aside, Drummond mounted his cycle and hit the road, immediately and continually drawing gawks, chuckles, and pointed fingers from passersby.

After a while, people began to ask about the unicycle. "Where did you get that thing?" they would say. Drummond soon saw a market. He called the man who'd sold his cycle and asked to become a local dealer. "At first," he says, "I thought maybe I could make enough to get a better one for myself." But in a short time Drummond realized the potential of this untapped business. Not everyone in the family was so enthused.

When he broached the subject with his wife, she said, "That's nice, honey," but didn't take him seriously. But in about two months Drummond launched a site and finally opened his virtual doors. Nothing happened. The cybersilence was deafening. "It was a real learning experience," suggests Drummond in what has to qualify as a classic understatement.

ONE WHEEL TURNS, SLOWLY

"What you really need to do is register with the search engines," says Drummond, "but I didn't know that then." Instead, he logged on to a usenet group for unicyclists with about 200 subscribers worldwide. "I was a lurker," he admits, "not saying anything, just reading the postings." But Drummond noticed that one man knew more than anyone else. The man turned out to be former world champion unicyclist John Foss, also president of Unicyclists of America and owner of his own Web site. "So I called him one day and asked for help," says Drummond, "something to get my site known." Foss built a link to his own Web page, and Drummond began to see some online responses.

At first Foss thought it would be nice to sell five or ten cycles from his site. But soon business exceeded his modest expectations. He began to think that 30 was a nice round number—maybe even contributing enough profit to replace his wife's car. Later he decided 60 or 70 unicycles was a lofty goal, but the demand did not stop there. Now Unicycle.com averages 100 sales a month, and Drummond recently sold 600 bicycles in a two-month period in the dead of winter. "I had no idea the business was going to pop like that," says Drummond. "We got into it for fun, and as it turns out, I left IBM in November [1999], and I haven't missed the income." Despite trying, Drummond found he could not do both jobs. He chose the fun one.

Signing up with Yahoo! helped immensely. Not much happened from the day Drummond submitted his site plan until Yahoo! sent a confirmation letter. In the meantime, Drummond found a company called WorldSubmit.com that "has the best price for registering with search engines." According to Drummond, WorldSubmit.com registered his site with 100 search engines each month and charged only $89 for six months of service.

"It's well worth it," says Drummond, "considering the fact that I don't have to worry about it anymore." He estimates that, without the service, Drummond would spend two or three days a month registering with search programs. "You don't have to give them key words," muses Drummond. "They go by the meta tags on your site." Because he built his site with *Home Page Creator* (which does not require the user to know anything about meta tags), Drummond simply follows the template, and the program does the rest.

FIRST A HOBBY, THEN A BUSINESS

Drummond entered the e-commerce world with a small bankroll, less than $700. The continuing costs total only about $150, mostly for Web hosting. He started slowly, in part because he saw the online site as a hobby. But once the orders started to flow, he asked himself, "Why hasn't anyone done this already?" Now he's having fun with his hobby and turning a hefty profit as well.

One distinct advantage was the limited competition. In fact, there was no competition. Only one other person in the United States was distributing unicycles, and his business was custom vehicles. Despite the absence of players, Drummond could not obtain his choice for domain name. He found that Unicycle.com was registered elsewhere. The owner didn't want to sell but leased the name for $250 a month. After three months, Drummond wanted to print labels and asked again for the rights to Unicycle.com. This time, the owner agreed to sell for $4,000. That in itself says something about the value of domain names, even to those in fields virtually void of competition.

Also successful was Drummond's convoluted attempt to get

the 1-800-Unicycle phone number. It originally was tied to another company. Despite his inquiries, Drummond kept running into an information barrier. After six phone calls, he finally convinced the phone company that he was serious. "Ironically," says Drummond, "it was available the whole time." The five-month wait was frustrating, he admits, but worth it. "The two things you want for your e-business are a great domain name and a clever 800 number," says Drummond. Well, he's got them.

"THESE GUYS ARE NUTS"

As his business grows, Drummond sees virtually unlimited possibilities. He wants to expand the business outside the United States—certainly possible through the Net—and he recognizes that IBM's *Home Page Creator* is a big help because the program allows users to publish in a foreign country's native language.

Drummond has also expanded into mountain unicycling. "These guys are nuts," he admits, "but there's a convention every year, and at the last one a bunch of us took the lift to the top of the mountain, then took the trail down. It was a blast!" There are other e-commerce opportunities in mountain unicycling besides selling the vehicles. "You need pads," says the businessman with a straight face. At any rate, the mountain adventurers need skill and cunning to navigate upland trails and switchbacks. Bandages also come to mind.

From its humble beginnings, Unicycle.com has grown to being a distributor of about 100 products from a variety of vendors. Just think how many doodads he'll sell if Barnum and Bailey gets news of this site!

Web address:
www.Unicycle.com

Destination Travel— Dude Ranch

Start-up expenses: $4,000
Special requirements: *Ranch and horses*
Best advice: *"The biggest challenge is trying to make your site concise yet diverse. There are so many great ideas, but you have to keep it short and sweet for most people. No long layouts with lots of verbiage—such clutter overwhelms the browsers. Mostly, people just want to see pictures. Even so, the site should be as interactive as possible."*

Okay, cowboy, saddle up and start movin' that herd." If John Wayne did it, so can you. Out in Big Sky Country, where the air is crisp and the view is forever, you can take a trip to any number of dude ranches. In Wyoming, Montana, and other Wild West states, some fascinating educational experiences involving geology, ornithology, history, zoology, and even cowboy poetry await you.

The concept of dude ranches is changing. Sure, there's

plenty of riding and even a little roping for the adventurous ones. But it's not all *City Slickers* and Norman the steer. At a location such as Breteche Creek Ranch in Cody, Wyoming, summer guests can expect plenty of diversions, including classes, lectures, and projects. Jim Franklin, director of the ranch, describes a rustic ranch experience where hands-on activities mix with rides, study sessions, bird-watching, and rock hunts. Breteche Creek Ranch isn't your run-of-the-mill dude ranch.

Breteche is an educational foundation, an organization dedicated to self-discovery and study. Established in 1991—and inspired by recent developments at the Center for Range Management—Breteche nestles into a valley of the Shoshone River's north fork. At the edge of the Shoshone National Forest, Breteche Creek Ranch and its neighbors, such as the Rim Rock Ranch, thrive in the heart of both Shoshone and Crow territories. Teaching is central to their mission. As Franklin says, "The ranch was designed to be a nonprofit center to teach people about the environment of this area and about issues that are important to the West." In fact, the Wyoming experience is a wonderful opportunity to see fox, coyote, bears, elk, deer, hawks, eagles—even moose—in their breathtaking settings. Situated just 35 miles east of Yellowstone Park, the ranch's 9,000 acres lie in natural migration paths for many animals. The area stands at the center of the largest wilderness system in the contigious 48 states.

COWBOY COFFEE AND POETRY

"How do you make cowboy coffee? Put in coffee grounds, water, and a horseshoe. Boil the coffee until the horseshoe dissolves." Now there's a recipe that old John Wayne would love.

Yes, guests at the ranch get to taste Old West flavors as well as ride and study. Usually, the ranch invites guest speakers such as Chuck Preston from Buffalo Bill's Historical Center and university professors to speak on birds, rocks, stars, and animals. Nature trails traverse the Breteche Creek site, and visitors learn about beaver ponds, wildflowers, and shale deposits from the visiting experts. In addition, for those who don't get enough exercise on the trails, there's a 22-foot climbing wall, raft tours, fishing trips, and rock climbs.

During a seven-day visit, guests from the ranch learn about the migrating birds. They stand on ridgetops and talk about escarpments and volcanic cones of the surrounding Absaroka Mountains, an old volcanic field with diverse terrain. At night the dudes gaze at the stars and hear lectures on astronomy. And around the campfire, there's occasionally a cowboy poet and songs. Yee-haw!

Saddle Up and Go Online, Pardner

Breteche Creek Ranch went online when manager Kerry Strike was looking for a way to bring guests back for subsequent visits. First, she initiated an online visitors survey, then established a database. From that information, she sent out newsletters to groups that might have interest in the ranch programs. Finally, Strike and other employees began to use e-mail as a way to communicate with previous guests and to gather demographic information.

The firm started its Web site through Bigstep.com, a cost-effective way to establish and manage a site. The ranch personnel quickly realized that the Net was a great way to reach lots of people without huge advertising expenses. They also discovered that updating and technological revisions were relatively easy through Big Step's software.

Once launched, the ranch's Web site became its primary marketing method. "The Web is where we probably reach 90 percent of our market now," says Franklin. "Another ranch down the road—Rim Rock Ranch—has gone strictly to Web-based marketing, and they're filling up now." By comparison, says Franklin, Breteche Creek Ranch did a traditional mass mailing in 1999 and received the usual 5 percent response. "But that's not good enough anymore," admits Franklin, who says that expanding the Web site is the only solution to reaching more potential guests in the e-commerce era.

The ranch's Web site initially contained only 20 to 30 pictures but now boasts about 150 images and includes some interactive applications. "The Web site made us realize what we could do," says Franklin. "It opened the doors, and we've just started seeing what's coming in marketing." Franklin says that a company can spend a lot of money in marketing through magazines or newspapers, but "you just don't hit the variety of people that come to the Web."

The results have been formidable in the dude ranch neighborhood. Rim Rock Ranch, usually dormant in December with two or three guests, is now operating at more than half full during the winter season, despite marketing limited to online approaches. At BretecheCreek.com, the lesson has taken hold. Franklin realizes that the competition from other dude ranches and destination resorts is growing. By touting the educational programs online—as well as the natural splendors of the ranch—Franklin and his colleagues have been able to build a loyal and growing clientele of "dudes," nature lovers, and escapees from the Concrete Jungle.

As a final bit of advice, Franklin suggests that a Net site needs special consideration. People seeking destination vacations do not want to read a lot of words. They want pictures—lots of pictures. "Keep it simple," says Franklin. Even though browsers react well to an interactive site, they also don't want to have to work for information. After all, this is supposed to be a vacation.

So hit the trail, you old Cayuse, and remember to wipe your boots before you go into the bunkhouse.

Web address:

www.BretecheCreek.com

Golf Pro Shop

Start-up expenses: $5,000

Special requirements: *None*

Best advice: *"An e-business is not even close to being like a traditional business. We try to make it as formal as possible, but the Net is a very informal medium."*

Golf is big. Really big. Not only in America but all over the globe. It's immensely popular in Pebble Beach and Torrey Pines but also in Tokyo, Paris, Madrid, and Munich. Wherever there are doglegs and sand traps, golfers are shopping for the latest oversized driver or sand wedge.

Golfers also have money to spend. They tend to form a relatively affluent crowd, often sprinkled with lawyers, doctors, business executives, and corporate types. Golfers like to invest in this sport, where a competitive edge is not unlike an insider stock tip. Many golfers are constantly on the lookout for a new club, a ball, or a book that will chop three strokes from their scorecard at the upcoming company tournament. Now they can shop—where else?—on the Net's virtual pro shops.

GOLF IN ANY LANGUAGE

How do you say "I have a bad slice" in French? Or "It's out of bounds" in German? David Schofman could probably tell you. He's the owner of the International Golf Outlet, a supplier of golf equipment for duffers and scratch players around the world. He keeps pace with the fanatical links fans through his Web site, www.igogolf.com, an address that draws customers from more than 100 countries. Schofman went online in October 1995 and within two years was making birdies and eagles in the golf supply business. The igogolf.com business is not only flourishing in English. Demand has led Schofman to make his site available in four other languages: German, Japanese, Spanish, and French.

Most success stories begin with a single good choice. Schofman's began with a bad one. When he chose a name for his online golf business, he went with igogolf.com, even though golf.com was still available. At the time, admits Schofman, he had no idea how important domain names would become. He thought golf.com was too general, too vague. Nevertheless, after two years of online operation, Schofman's International Golf Outlet was making more than $2 million a year. Apparently the domain name was Schofman's last questionable business move.

"THE GAME ITSELF IS HARD ENOUGH"

Schofman launched his electronic mail order business with discount prices on a line of golf equipment and accessories—items that suffer a severe markup in the pro shops. For several years previously he had sold links equipment in traditional fashion. His business goal is a worry-free experience for customers. As he reminds everyone, no one needs hassles in buying golf supplies. "The game itself," he says, "is hard enough." True, too true.

As for advice, Schofman suggests that online businesses can be more expensive to start than most people realize. Everything from technical operations to advertising to infrastructure has a price tag, one that many neglect to consider. "Most people underestimate the costs and think you can buy a $200 piece of software, throw up a site, and that's it. If all you want is three orders a year, that's OK. If you want a *real* business," says Schofman, "you'd better invest."

To attract customers to igogolf.com, Schofman depends considerably on CBS Sportsline, a parent company and the largest sports Web site in the world. Links to igogolf.com provide many potential buyers. Web advertising accounts for an additional 15 to 20 percent of the business customers, and 10 percent comes from partners and affiliates. Another source of income is print ads.

HELLO, VIRTUAL WORLDS

The virtual world is an unusual kind of selling atmosphere for many people, including the executives at igogolf.com. In the real world, an experienced sales representative can charm a customer into a huge purchase. But online, suave looks and comforting smiles have no impact. Also, people are more price conscious on the Web. "Customers are more willing to say things over the Net that they wouldn't say in person," says Schofman. Apparently, online customers have fewer reservations about asking for steep discounts or special deals.

There is already a handful of competitors in the online golf supplies business. Schofman, like so many others in similar circumstances, is thankful for making an early entry into the virtual world. In addition to the current legitimate contenders, Schofman can name more than a dozen other competitive sites that come and go. "Most will run out of money," he says, "because they don't know what they're doing. It's tough getting into the game this late." Schofman worries about the new names and faces on the Net but remarks, "I won't lose sleep over them." The formula for success at International Golf Outlet has worked for several years, and Schofman has no plans to change. Whatever he's doing, it's par for the course.

Web address:
    www.igogolf.com

Kites and Wind-Powered Equipment

Start-up expenses: $1,000
Special requirements: *None*
Best advice: *"Make sure you practice your HTML skills and try different strategies so you don't get burned out. Get feedback from customers, coworkers, and peers. Update as much as possible."*

Imagine a sky full of color, with kites streaming across the blue-gray horizon as delighted children, awestruck parents, and middle-aged folks who don't care how young they look navigate the kites. A wonderful scene, you say. Now all you need is that special kite, the one that flies through your dreams and floats in your reveries. Here's an address for where you can get the kite you want: Windpowersports.com, the outlet for the Wind Power Sports Store in Las Vegas. In a day or two, you'll be running barefoot in the grass, chasing a sleek, long-tailed sky-racer.

KITES TAKE FLIGHT

The Wind Power Sports Kite Store is a brick-and-mortar shop in Las Vegas that opened its doors in 1996. Larry Park, speaking for the management, says that the owner, Scott Dyer, collects kites as a hobby. When Dyer decided to launch a business, he followed his interest. Originally, the company was part of another venture, BFK Sports. But in 1999, Dyer and his colleagues caught a huge gust of entrepreneurial wind and went independent, adding later the other wind-powered products and the Web site.

Today the Wind Power Sports Kite Store, both from its brick-and-mortar shop and through the Net, sells kites and accessories of all kinds, including single-line stable flying kites, quad-line steerable sport kites, and elaborate competitive kites. The company features kite-building materials such as spars and fittings. It's all there. According to the Web site blurb, the Wind Power folks offer "art kites from around the world, as well as fighters, tumblers, lifters, and power kites." You can even find land-sailers and buggies—sounds like a wild ride!—and all the accoutrements to keep them flying.

Buyers are many and varied. Especially in the spring, when March winds hint at a change in the weather, people start thinking about taking to the air. The kite community is fairly large, says Park, with recurring festivals in Washington State, Indiana, and elsewhere. There are even championship competitions in Muncie, Indiana, where the wind always blows, and in other gusty spots around the world.

An Increasing Role for the Web Site

Today the Web presence handles about half the sales for the Vegas business. Park agrees that the Net carries a huge potential for international sales, even from places such as Hawaii and Alaska. "It's far more cost-effective than a print catalog," says Park. "We have always been a pretty good mail order business, but the Internet really increased that business tremendously."

The Wind Power firm still prints catalogs and mails flyers. They have a large database of traditional customers. But Park likes the Net for sales, especially because it takes little advanced preparation and no mailing. To stay current, Park updates the site weekly, adding new products and announcing new offers. The company no longer prints quarterly catalogs. Now, with Internet access handling so much business, the catalogs are sent through the mail once a year.

Park wants his customers to take advantage of the Net whenever possible. He likes to assist customers by referring them to local libraries and college computer centers, where they can access the Web site online. He says, "We encourage people to go to the Web site so that we don't have to keep sending flyers."

Getting the Business Off the Ground

The first goal for the management team at Windpowersports.com was to create a site with top-notch ordering capabilities. Without delay or complication, visitors to the site can select their favorites and start looking for the UPS truck. Park's company buys regular online advertisements through search engines like GoTo, Excite, and Yahoo! They post messages on rec.kites, a news net group, and Windpowersports.com has its own e-mail list. Interested? You can join from their home page.

For additional exposure, Park sponsors a monthly giveaway, urging participants to consider joining the e-mail list. He says, "Before we put anything out, like postings and ads for sales, we tell the people on the e-mail list first. Then a few days later, we'll post for everyone else to see." Park also works with affiliates. He uses *ClickTrade* to manage the affiliate programs.

MARKETING MADNESS

Another marketing method of value is the survey on the Web site, a poll asking questions like "What kite do you fly the most?" Customers may answer, "Maneuverable kites," "power kites," or "dual kites." These answers drive the future plans for Windpowersports.com, especially when Park decides which lines to purchase and which trends to back. If customers want an emphasis on power-kiting, Park loads his virtual shelves with more "buggies." He says with candor, "The survey is our market research vehicle."

Being part of a business community has been important for Park and his colleagues. Windpowersports.com belongs to the Kite Ring, a European consortium of sites devoted to kites and sails. Organized as a networking tool, the Kite Ring group serves as a promotional tool for participants—not unlike a banner exchange program.

Park says that the Web's primary difference from real-world sales involves speed. Doing business on the Net simply takes less time—lots less time. "When we receive an order," he says, "everything is written down. We don't have to spend time typing in credit card numbers or addresses."

Buyers who know what they want have an easy time ordering on the site. Park says, "We're getting customers from all over the world with our dual approach—the Web and the mail order side." As an added benefit, word-of-mouth advertising has also brought a brisk breeze of new customers.

LOTS OF CHOICES

Kites are either affordable or expensive, ranging from $20 to $1,000. In March and April, when business really catches the wind, dual-line kites are the most popular. People also like to order kite-carrying bags, wind meters, and videos for learning tricks. Of course, Park's company is not the only distributor. Park allows that there are many competitors in the market, but they deal primarily through catalog sales and brick-and-mortar stores. "We offer a bigger variety of products," he says. "That's how we compete." With only a small investment—about $1,000—Windpowersports.com gave Park and his company a large advantage in the niche market. "It pretty much paid for itself right away," he offers. Apparently the wind was just right that day in cyberspace.

Web address:
   www.Windpowersports.com

Mountaineering Gear

Start-up expenses: $50,000 +
Special requirements: *Mountaineering experience*
Best advice: *"Stress fast-loading pages and excitement. Don't have links that lead out of your site. Keep everything logical and working. Think negatively now and then: What's wrong with this picture? What does the customer see on the site?"*

Imagine climbing the Eiger with Clint Eastwood: ice, wind, frozen hands. Don't you wish you had shopped more carefully for mountaineering gear, especially clothing? Well, everything you need to scale K2 or Mt. McKinley or Old Baldy is now available online at Jagged-edge.com.

What do you need? How about great clothes for mountain ascents, including jackets, pants, hats, scarves, and clothes? The gear is virtually bomb-proof—well, at least abrasion-proof. You can slide down rock faces, climb over outcroppings, and belly up to razor-sharp fissure lines without tearing the gear. Jagged-edge.com also has Tibetan jackets tailored from a design brought from the Himalayas. Whatever you need for that special climb is waiting for you in cyberspace. Margaret and Paula Quenemoen, founders and owners of Jagged-edge.com, have pushed themselves up many a mountain in the past few decades. They know what it takes to get to the top in relative comfort and safety.

LUCKY NUMBER 13

The owners of Jagged-edge.com didn't seem likely candidates for high-flying business careers. But for Margaret Quenemoen, hard times soon became good times. Living in Colorado at Telluride, high in the mountains, Quenemoen had a big problem. She was broke. In desperation, she decided to sew a series of hand-made headbands to sell locally. A local restaurant displayed them, thirteen in all.

The thirteen headbands sold quickly. She knew then that her own trials had been instructive. As an extreme athlete with years of experience in harsh climates and conditions, Quenemoen learned to be resourceful and creative in difficult circumstances. She began to think about a business.

In due course, Margaret Quenemoen convinced her twin sister, Paula, to join the enterprise. Paula, also a mountaineer, had faced her own adversity in China, wandering through the Himalayas in frozen weather wearing a Yak hair sweater and skirt. The sisters joined forces for Jagged-edge.com, first a wholesale business and then, by 1993, a retail business. Today, they offer both a retail site and an online presence. For good measure, they also feature catalog sales.

The sisters sell high-end and fashionable outerwear for extreme athletes and the Eddie Bauer set. With the Web, a catalog, and on-site sales combined, the partners earn about $3 million a year. For Margaret, it's been a long journey from Telluride.

THE "MOUNTAIN LOOK"
SALES

At Jagged-edge.com, the Quenemoens remain active. They organize company hikes and climbs, all the while testing clothing and equipment. They climb, bike, ski, and hike together, physically pushing themselves and joining in a spiritual effort that they call "the path, the way, the journey." With philosophy at the forefront, the sisters operate Jagged-edge.com "like a well-run expedition, embracing innovation, initiative, and a commitment to succeed."

Much of the outdoor gear at Jagged-edge.com uses eco-fleece, made from recycled plastic bottles. Special lines include children's apparel, outdoor accessories, fleece vests, jackets, and pants. Following the business lead of L. L. Bean, the partners compete well in a tight clothing market, one that grew 33 percent in the years from 1991 to 1996.

Growth in the outdoor gear market is not a result of America's new-found fascination with exercise and fitness. Look around. In fact, the sales trends are driven by fashion. The "mountain look" is in. Jagged-edge.com stays at the vanguard in style by marketing clothes that capture the look. The Quenemoens even have their own Jagged Edge brand, complete with a Chinese-character logo that represents "the way of the path, the journey."

A POTPOURRI OF APPROACHES

The Web site of the business began in 1996. Back then, the sisters were true pioneers in e-commerce, even though they predated shopping carts. "There was zero effect on business from the Web back then," says Paula. "People were just warming to e-mail." Without any serious investment capital, the

Quenemoens built their e-business on sweat equity, calling their efforts "a labor of love." For years, they lived in their store and slept on the floor to save time and money while building a Web presence and walk-in clientele.

Competition has been heavy in the field. Paula Quenemoen says that Jagged-edge.com stays ahead of the wolves through hard work. "We just do our best to get whatever business we can," she says, "and by having the best site we can afford in terms of time, money, and manpower." She asserts that Jagged-edge.com is a moderately successful site. "Some sites are worse, some better," she says. The main concern for Paula is the site's download time. "No matter how good the site is," she says, "if the download time is slow, customers will leave."

Although Jagged-edge.com has a number of sales approaches, the partners are relying more on Net commerce. "The Web site is a better bet, business-wise," says Paula. "The catalog costs money and paper, but the Web is free and environmentally safe." Using traditional advertising, the sisters direct traffic toward their site and their catalog. The Web address is available on all their printed materials and paraphernalia, including Jagged-edge business cards, stationery, coffee cups, lip balm, magazine ads, and catalog copy.

Survival has been an important theme at Jagged-edge.com. From difficult beginnings to a successful present, Margaret and Paula Quenemoen react like well-trained athletes prepping for a climb. Their business is a natural outgrowth of their philosophy, one that encourages an environmentally safe world and a healthy, active lifestyle. They are following a path, one that just happens to lead up the side of a mountain.

Web address:
   www.Jagged-edge.com

Racquet Sports Supplies

Start-up expenses: $300
Special requirements: *None*
Best advice: *"Start small if you're not sure. If you want to be a major player, then get the money and set the foundation. It's a lot of work. I intend to keep my site as it is. I'm not trying to get bigger. It's profitable, and I don't have to do anything. The way I have things set up—well, it's easy money. Not a lot of money, but it's plenty, considering all I do is send e-mail attachments. For me, the work is done, and the potential is huge."*

OK, raise your hands if you've played racquetball. No, not tennis. Not squash. Not Ping-Pong. Racquetball. That's what I thought. It's a specialty sport, one that requires speed, dexterity, and athleticism—but not much money. Most YMCAs have racquetball courts, and so do most universities. The downtown athletic club and the local fitness center also have a few courts. To get started, all you need is a can of rac-quetballs ($3.95), a set of goggles ($6.95), and a racquet.

You can get a decent racquet for a few bucks at Goodwill, but if you want to beat your law partner or your sales colleague or even your girlfriend, you might consider a lightweight, flexible racquet with a name like Ektelon or Spalding. Because racquet-ball is a one-of-a-kind sport, one that doesn't pay the big com-mercial dividends like golf or soccer, you'll probably need to go online for that special implement. And a good place to start looking is Mitch Derr's Back Hand Sports.

RACQUETS AND ONLY RACQUETS

At backhandsports.com, Derr sells only racquets. You can't get Gore-Tex warmup suits, *The Beginners' Guide to Racquetball,* or Adidas cross-trainers. Derr likes it that way. He is a fourth-grade teacher with an after-school business, one that allows him to do virtually nothing while the checks roll in. Derr is dabbling in a sport he loves and seeing a profit as well. Furthermore, he has time to play racquetball every day after school—at least on those days when it's not necessary to haul the deposits to the bank.

Even with a modest advertising plan, Derr fields 100 hits a day on his Web site, up from an initial number of 10 per day. He likes the gradual approach even though he realizes that an aggressive marketing plan could accelerate the business. In the meantime, Derr is happy with a staff of five and a market that no one else seems anxious to enter. While the profit totals may not be a threat to Wilson or Nike, having an open playing field is one distinct advantage of untapped sports businesses. Derr has only five competitors, and none of them specializes in racquets. In the future, he plans to branch into tennis and squash racquets as well, but he's dedicated to only selling products with strings.

An Idea Born in the Trenches

Uncle Sam takes some credit for Derr's success. While he was with the army in Bosnia, Derr found a copy of *Flyer* magazine and read about e-commerce. Immediately he became interested in online business opportunities. When Derr left the military, he went back to college, graduating with a psychology degree. For a year, he worked in marketing for a major corporation but found the work unsatisfying. He quit the corporate world and began thinking about more appealing choices, including the idea of teaching children.

Soon, while teaching about long division and the Louisiana Purchase, Derr returned to the idea of a Web business. But which one? "At that point," he admits, "I had no idea what kind of business I would start." He read, studied, and asked around, but the inspiration finally came from his fiancée. She reminded Derr that he liked racquetball and suggested the sport as a business. "It was pretty obvious," says Derr, "so I decided to take her suggestion." With his own Web design program, Net Object Fusion, Derr created a racquetball site, simply by following the tutorials.

Derr's first step was to find suppliers. It wasn't easy. He contacted about 100 other racquet sellers by e-mail to ask about supply firms. When he sorted through the feedback, Derr discovered there were only five major manufacturers of racquets. But to deal directly with the companies, he needed a huge deposit for inventory. Not possible. So, with a little searching, Derr found a representative who buys from the manufacturers and then drop-ships for a fee. It was simple and easy. Without having to keep an inventory or pay in advance, Derr found himself in the racquet business.

HANDS-OFF SELLING

It sounds too good to be true, but Derr stumbled across a business plan that requires virtually no effort on his part. When an order comes into his site, Derr's software processes it and sends him an e-mail. He admits that he felt the need to do *something*. "I could have made this step completely automatic, so that I didn't even step into the process at that point, but I didn't." Instead, he developed a packing slip with Microsoft *Excel*, one with the customer's name, product description, and shipping address.

Derr then sends the *Excel* information through e-mail to his supplier, who prints the invoice, pops it into the mailer, and ships it with the racquet. "I don't touch the products or even see them," he says. "It works out very well for me." Derr's supplier gives him a good price and—when all is said and done—there's plenty of profit and almost no labor on Derr's part.

MARKETING STRATEGIES

After building the site, Derr faced the problem of marketing his products. He started with the basics, registering with search engines by hand. In short order, he tired of the process and paid a $30 fee for a service to do the registrations, choosing from among the scores of registration services available on the Net. Sadly, Derr found that the search engine route was not appropriate to his niche business.

The next step was establishing links. He typed in a search for "racquetball" and explored all the sites that popped up. Through e-mail, he tried to get links with sites like the U.S. Racquetball Association. "That site," he says, "is where most of my customers come from." Other links were not so productive. Some business owners made unreasonable demands, like free racquets or other concessions. But, in the end, Derr located enough connections to establish a useful network. He knows that he could expand his business exponentially with a strategic marketing campaign, but he has lesson plans to prepare and racquetball to play.

THE POWER OF THE NET

Backhandsports.com is still a young business. Derr went online in 1999 with a real-time online credit card processing system. Buyers can view the racquets they want to purchase at the Back Hand site, and the credit system allows for instant purchases and rapid shipping. Derr says that all orders are shipped within three days.

There have been few problems, but his five competitors clued him to one complication early on. At one point, Derr lowered his prices significantly, breaking an unwritten industry rule about pricing. Immediately he received tons of irate e-mail from a number of sources. He found he was upsetting everyone in the industry and had to back off. Derr still offers great deals, however, including holiday rebates and free shipping promotions, but he's aware that others are watching.

As for advice, Derr believes in some popular e-commerce axioms: start small and do what you love. He believes that online entrepreneurs should enter their markets cautiously unless they have serious financial backing. It's still possible to lose money in cyberspace. Derr also recognizes that he would not have prospered selling widgets or Swiss Army knives. Because he loves racquetball, his e-commerce business isn't work—it's fun. Besides, he gets to try out all the new racquet models, and who knows when that competitive edge will come in handy.

Web address:
   www.backhandsports.com

Sports League Scheduling

Start-up expenses: *None*
Special requirements: *Love of sports*
Best advice: *"First and foremost, establish where you're going to sell your goods. It's important to meet your audience before launching."*

Turn to the sports pages. Now check the small print. There you'll find rows and rows of statistics. Wins and losses, fielding percentages, field goals from both inside and outside the 40-yard line. Those small numbers and tight columns are there for a reason. Sports statistics are important to lots of people. For the average basketball fanatic, free-throw percentages and assist-to-turnover ratios actually make satisfactory reading.

But the obsession with statistics goes beyond professional sports. For all the guys and gals playing in the amateur leagues, their own personal on-base percentages, batting averages, and slugging percentages really do matter. For one thing, they determine who buys the drinks after the next doubleheader. The same enthusiasm characterizes the Little Leagues, where the kids (and their parents) are fascinated with the numbers that would appear in small print if they were available.

Well, those numbers are now available on the Net, thanks to sports league scheduling services. One of these online companies is LocalSportsOnline.com, a partnership dedicated to helping amateur and professional sports manage their teams and leagues.

AN AMAZON.COM AFFILIATE

Using LocalSportsOnline.com is a simple and easy way for teams and leagues to post and update their schedules, to list the team standings, and to identify player statistics. The founders invented powerful software that enables any sports team or league to keep track of lineups, scores, statistics, and so on. The programs work for baseball, football, basketball, soccer, lacrosse, roller hockey, softball, and volleyball. Other useful Web pages include links to the weather channels (helpful for checking field conditions before the big game) and links to pro sports team sites and pro sports sites. Fans can use the Message Board to argue about such timeless issues as whether Babe Ruth was better than Mickey Mantle. Visitors can also calculate baseball numbers (including their own) with the Stat Calculator.

Company president Robert Smith also devised the online Sports Store with selected sports team items like Mariners watches, Patriots key chains, and Pacers duffel bags. The company's online Sports Bookstore carries recommended sports-related titles. Both the Sports Store and Bookstore provide revenue for Local Sports Online, although local teams also pay a fee to register. Finally, Smith's organization is an Amazon.com affiliate, so clicking on a title takes browsers to an Amazon.com order page, where buying a book initiates a sales commission for Smith's Local Sports Online firm.

FIRST TO THE STARTING LINE

In 1996, Local Sports Online started operations as a Web design company. One of the founders was playing in a recreational sports league and was in charge of managing the standings and schedules for the league—a huge task that involved a significant commitment of time and energy. He and his partners decided to build a program to automate the process. They created software that could publish schedules and scores on the Net, if only to save time. As Smith muses, recasting the ancient axiom, "Necessity is the mother of all invention."

After that success, Smith and his colleagues looked hard and identified the need to produce sports number packages on a large scale. "Lots of other people wanted sports scores and numbers, too," says Smith. "So we set up one person to spend most of his time working on the software side of the program until we perfected it." Local Sports Online was the first to enter the market at a time when the Net was still a novelty. "At that time," says Smith, "our biggest obstacle was not the program or the concept. It was the Net. People weren't used to the Net. They just weren't online in big numbers, so it didn't occur to anyone that they could manipulate sports team information this way."

After people started to become comfortable with online services, a remarkable shift occurred. The cities and parks departments—exceptionally slow to embrace the new technology—

finally began to get it. Now, sports and recreation bureaus constitute the largest market segment for Local-SportsOnline.com. Even though the local sports associations were especially slow in adapting to the Web concept, business has boomed. Smith estimates a 300 percent increase in online traffic with the recreation crowd. As he says, "It was worth keeping after them."

IT'S ALL IN THE MARKETING

To expand business activity, Smith's company focuses on grass-roots marketing, as well as direct marketing to local Little Leagues, soccer leagues, and school leagues. They also provide services for city recreation programs, indoor arenas that promote soccer and roller hockey, industrial recreation and church leagues, and various educational programs that involve sports. The teams and leagues pay for Local Sports Online services, with fees charged for each sport. Smith's company charges $149 per year for hosting each sport for a single season. That includes the software for scheduling, the data, and customer support.

Even though Local Sports Online was first to the Net, others have taken the cue. "When we first started," says Smith, "there was no one else online. We were ahead of the curve. Now there are 15 or 20 companies involved."

Running a business online is not terribly different from traditional business practice, says Smith, who says that he must think more often in terms of automation, trying to get away from mundane day-to-day algorithms like compiling statistics by hand. "Whatever program you have in place," says Smith, "you're just a little more aware of the technology and open to new and different business ideas." If anything, the Net reminds small business owners like Smith that the computer has far greater applications than we have yet envisioned.

So if Little Susie is batting .408 for Barb's Hair Palace, you just might be able to read about it in the local paper next week. Companies like Local Sports Online are making such notions more and more reasonable. And if your bowling team is leading the league in the thirteenth week, perhaps the details can be plastered across the company bulletin boards, courtesy of such a sports service. Sports is an integral part of American culture, both at the professional and the local levels. Local Sports Online is taking advantage of that involvement and adding something else to the mix: fun and enjoyment for the players and their fans.

Web address:

www.Localsportsonline.com

Water Sports Outfitters

Start-up expenses: $2,800

Special requirements: *None*

Best advice: *"Good contact with suppliers is as important as customer relations. I try to make personal acquaintances with suppliers. If you don't, you can get lost in the shuffle. Whenever possible, talk to them about family and make a few jokes. It helps them remember you, especially when it comes time to make big orders or special purchases."*

So you want a We-no-nah open-water kayak for navigating fjords in Greenland? For those who are into water sports, online is the place to shop. On the Net, you can buy Sorel boots, Wigwam socks, Tyr swimsuits, Teva sandals, Woolrich jackets, and Columbia snowpants. The adventurous sort can find O'Brien water skis, Body Glove wetsuits, and Coleman heaters. And if you have a really big mailbox, you can even order skis, an outboard motor, or a canoe. Just log in and make your choice.

Traditionally, the outdoor outfitting business was a storefront operation that did many things well, but there were limitations. If you wanted mukluks in July or beach sandals in December, you were out of luck. Similarly, such stores couldn't afford a large inventory of unusual sizes or one-of-a-kind items. Catalog companies often filled those niches, but even L. L. Bean and Eddie Bauer don't have the space to stock whole warehouses with canoes, motors, and rafts.

With online shopping came the clearinghouse concept. Northlandmarine.com operates from the Great White North town of Three Lakes, Wisconsin, and draws their products from many companies, including Sorel, LaCrosse, Ryka, Gramicci, Hi-Tec, and Minn Kota. If you can use the product to stay warm or be cool, it's probably available at Northland Marine.

UP AND RUNNING FOR FREE

Northland Marine was a brick-and-mortar operation for many years, spanning three generations of family ownership. They opened their doors in 1976, growing at a steady but slow rate of 5 percent each year. In 1997, all that changed, thanks to owner Laura Boers's father, Roy, a retired printer. Roy Sobolik, who had no training in Web design, offered to learn the craft of Web site design and build a site for the business. Promising to keep the costs at zero, Sobolik bought books and tackled the Net.

Says Boers, "My dad learned everything on his own. He had absolutely no instructions. He just picked it up himself. He was retired, so he had the time. He's very artistic and had some useful knowledge from his years in the printing business. That experience really came in handy for him. He thought we could pick up business outside our local area, so that's why he suggested it." Well, it worked. Not only did the Boers family start receiving orders from faraway places like Greenland and South Africa, but the online approach shattered the growth charts. In the first year of Web operations, Northland Marine doubled its sales. In the next, they did $1 million in business.

Sobolik completed all the Web site designs and included catalog pages from the suppliers' workbooks. With clever positioning, Sobolik got Northlandmarine.com to the top of many search engines, largely by stressing brand names. As Boers says, "If I type in 'Sorel boots' (a top category for us), we come up number one." Boers and Sobolik are not sure how they got to that lofty position, but Boers thinks research may be the key. "My dad reads a lot of books," she muses.

Rising to the top of the engines is a bit of a mystery considering the number of large sporting goods firms hovering on the Net. "We even come up higher than some of the biggest," says Boers, "like fogdog.com." Whatever the reasons, Boers is proud that Northlandmarine.com stands in the top ten for every search engine whenever customers enter the product name as the key word. "Nobody looks for our company name," adds Boers.

"My dad tries to keep the site as simple as possible to navigate," says Boers. "Basically he doesn't want people to get lost." The family agrees that Web visitors should be able to move easily through the site without bells, whistles, or detours. With their success, Boers fully expects a larger company to attempt a takeover, but so far none has appeared on the frozen horizon. In the meantime, she smiles, "People just keep bookmarking us."

A HIGHLY MOTIVATED CUSTOMER BASE

Buyers of outdoor equipment and X-treme Sports gear are not casual Web browsers. When they go online, they're on a mission. Unlike shoppers in brick-and-mortar operations, the customers at Northlandmarine.com know what they want. "Most are sold [on what they want] before they call us," says Boers, "as opposed to those walking in the door of our shop in Three Lakes, where you really do have to sell them." The difference between the real store and the online store is startling. When it comes to the Internet, once people find a location like Northlandmarine.com, with products that they recognize, they want to complete a purchase. Most Web visitors don't continue to check with other vendors. "When they come to us, they're ready to buy," says Boers. "We have to make it easy on them so they don't have to go any further."

As for the most important online role, Boers says simply, "We answer their questions. The Internet shoppers know what they want. We're just finalizing what's in their mind. The biggest thing is making sure you give them what they need, not just what they *think* they need."

Satisfying customers' needs is not only good sales—it's good business. A major drain on profits comes when people return products. As Boers explains, if parents just want warm footwear for their kids to play in the snow, they don't need ice-fishing boots. Normally, return rates on the Internet can be as high as 35 percent. That figure seems way too high to Boers. To avoid high return rates, Northlandmarine.com purposely avoids online orders. Customers must pick up the phone and call. "That policy makes sure that people get what they want," says Boers. Often the phone call allows Northland people to talk customers out of making bad choices. The policy seems to work. "Our returns are only 7 percent," she says. Boers explains that Northland is not just supplying products—they're matching products to people.

BUSINESS REPS, PLEASE PARK
YOUR CAMPERS IN BACK

With competition ever on the horizon, Boers and her family keep a close eye on customer relations and suppliers. Their biggest product lines are boots and shoes, with Sorel the primary footwear line. During the winter, Northlandmarine.com receives surprising footwear orders from Hawaii, where people want sandals even though they're not available in retail stores. Similarly, in summer she gets orders from Alaska for waterproof boots.

"We're providing clothing and gear year-round," says Boers, "while retailers put products in storage during the off-seasons." Interestingly, that approach has also spilled over into the Three Lakes store, where Boers's employees now leave sandals out all year long. To her surprise, Boers regularly sees Wisconsin folk buying sandals and hauling them through the snowdrifts to their cars. "Maybe they're going on vacation," she smiles.

Hard-to-find sizes are also big business for Northland Marine. In the storefront, Boers carries size 16 boots. Online, the selection is even larger (no pun intended). Without the need for high-volume inventories, a Net-based business like Northlandmarine.com can even offer a fashionable footwear selection for someone the size of Sasquatch.

Contact with suppliers is as important as customer relations for Boers. She tries to make personal acquaintances with each supplier. If you don't, she says, "You can get lost in the shuffle." Whenever possible, she recalls, "I talk to them about family and make a few jokes. It helps them remember me, especially when it comes time to make big orders or special purchases." Although Boers never meets most of the company representatives, sometimes she has nice surprises. One time, the suppliers from

Columbia Sportswear, a woman and her husband, came through town, and they parked their camper in the backyard. As Boers says, it was a good business connection. "The Columbia representative really came through for me, helping me get things done when I needed it."

Whether it's talking about hunting or spinning tales about the big fish that got away, Laura Boers recognizes that personal ties are critical to business, even one that has millions of dollars in sales. "We're not just filling out forms here," she says. Boers receives a lot of letters asking her to visit both customers and representatives. "Mostly they want to invite us down and give us some fish," she chuckles.

Go with Quality Lines, Keep Up to Date

As Northlandmarine.com becomes a big business, Boers reminds herself of several business principles, ones that are worth sharing. First, she suggests, keep your site as accurate as possible, because people who call about a product that's no longer available will lose faith in the operation. Second, she says, "Don't give products away!" It's important to make a solid profit margin. Third, maintain the integrity of products you sell. Even though Northlandmarine.com experiments with new product lines and experiences some disappointments, it's necessary to try new ideas. Just be sure that you're always offering high-quality goods and apparel, warns Boers. Finally, keep things simple. As Dad showed with his Web design, ease of operation is more important than glitz and glitter.

Web address:

www.Northlandmarine.com

Travel

Bed and Breakfast
Reservations Service

Start-up expenses: $2,500
Special requirements: *None*
Best advice: *"You need to do a lot of legwork, as far as advertising is concerned. Advertise in print as well as on the Internet."*

ecently, Scott McKay's daughter was accepted for study at the University of Texas–Austin. While his daughter attended freshman orientation, Dad stayed in a cozy bed and breakfast near the campus. But how did Scott McKay survey the B&B choices in Austin from his home on Oahu? Simple. McKay logged into TNN, the National Network of Bed and Breakfast Services, a networking system with no actual staff, only a confederation of service owners who periodically take turns routing inquiries to members around the country. From there he located the Web page for Bed and Breakfast Texas Style, a reservation service based in the Lone Star State. In a matter of minutes, McKay found a charming Victorian with reasonable rates and a Texas-sized bed. When Scott McKay said "Aloha" to Austin, he was wearing a ten-gallon hat, a Longhorns sweatshirt, and a winning smile.

For an ever-increasing number of people, bed and breakfasts are the first choice in accommodations. Over the past 30 years, the industry has reshaped itself in America, taking its cue from Western Europe.

Bed and breakfast lodging is a growth industry. In 1980, there were only between 5,000 and 6,000 inns operating domestically, according to numbers from the U.S. Travel Data Center. In the early '80s, demand was high but options were few. Since then, enterprising people throughout America have been restoring brownstone walk-ups and Craftsman classics, creating a national treasure of fashionable and comfortable inns, many in historic homes. Today it's difficult to find a town of any size without several B&Bs. Unfortunately, not all are as clean and comfy as the one Scott McKay found. A reservation service like Ruth Wilson's Bed and Breakfast Texas Style takes the guesswork out of finding an elegant room and a yummy breakfast soufflé.

GET ONLINE AND TAKE OFF!

Ruth Wilson was a teacher who in her own words "burned out." One morning she picked up the *Dallas Morning News* and read about a B&B reservation service in Colorado. Wilson called the owner and before long was on a plane. She stayed a week in Colorado and learned everything she could about the business. Within a month, Ruth Wilson had collected her permits and papers, and since then (August 1992) she has been running both a bed and breakfast and the Texas-based reservation service. Wilson was first attracted to the personal connection associated with innkeeping ("You have to be a people person") but soon learned she no longer had time for both businesses. Bed and Breakfast Texas Style won out.

Three years later, Wilson's husband, "a computer nerd," talked Ruth into letting him build a Web site. She admits that she began with very few technical skills. From its unsophisticated beginnings, though, the reservation service, spurred by the Internet, grew to meet the demands. "I have about five desks, a fax machine, a credit card swiper machine, and a PC," says Wilson, in addition to the Web site. And she has a competent staff to help, especially with the software applications.

Nonetheless, competition is heavy. "Everyone is on the Web now," says Ruth, "and that has gotten to be a real challenge." Ruth Wilson goes head to head with the competition by personally inspecting each inn for cleanliness, ambiance, and special services. Consequently, "travelers trust us to find a nice clean place, particularly when it's in a city they've never been to." Part of the strategy is to be very picky. "Believe me," she adds, "we've turned down plenty."

A SMALL INVESTMENT PAYS BIG DIVIDENDS

Bed and Breakfast Texas Style is a great example of an e-business requiring little start-up expense. It is home-based, so it has virtually no overhead. Wilson began with minimal up-front expenses, just a computer. In addition, she secured her business name without any expense.

Wilson has found that lots of old-fashioned public relations legwork is involved in this Web business. She prints plenty of promotional material and finds that pamphlets are a valuable source for new business: "I leave my brochures *everywhere,* and that does help." She advertises in print as well as on the Internet and makes public appearances whenever possible. "I do speaking engagements like civic groups, and women's groups, where I inform them about the availability of reservations services and present a slide show of my B&Bs." Recently, for example, after dropping a pile of brochures at the local Chamber of Commerce, she received a phone call from a Chamber member who wanted to buy a gift certificate for her parents. Like so many small businesses, Bed and Breakfast Texas Style uses the Internet as an important resource but is not solely dependent on cyberspace for referrals and new customers.

Although a substantial portion of Wilson's business comes from word of mouth, the Internet has been a happy surprise. "I get a lot of customers off the Internet," says Wilson. "We have our reservation form on the Web so that people can fill it in, and it comes to us directly. People just surf to find it. Doing business on the Web is a lot more convenient and quick."

Bed and Breakfast Texas Style charges the individual B&B a standard 20 percent to 25 percent reservation, with no charge to the customer. Some services impose a small fee for customers who use credit cards. Wilson does not. She also belongs to the National Network of Bed and Breakfast Services (TNN).

YOU HAVE TO BE A "PEOPLE PERSON"

Innkeeping is demanding—of both time and energy. Running a B&B service shares many of the same demands. But Wilson especially enjoys hearing the stories of satisfied customers who find "just what they want" through her service. And she enjoys the guests saying, " *'The hosts are so wonderful.'* This is what we hear all the time. The guests just brighten up the hosts' lives. They love being treated like special people, with fresh flowers, candles, and so forth."

For those looking for a high-intensity business with low start-up costs and few complications, a B&B reservation service might be an option. As Ruth Wilson says, with obvious pleasure, "There have been *very* few problems."

Web address:
www.bnbTexasStyle.com

Resource:
The National Network of Bed and Breakfast Services
    (TNN): www.go-lodging.com

Business Travel
Accessories

Start-up expenses: *None*

Special requirements: *None*

Best advice: *"Remember that you're the master of your destiny in this matter. The more people you talk to, the better you'll do. It's that easy. It's a numbers game. The less you do, the less you do."*

I f there's an ongoing theme in e-business start-up stories, it's "have fun." Repeatedly, the people who love what they're doing seem to find a path to success. Take Stuart Brotman, for example. For many reasons, Brotman likes to bicycle to work. One day, having arrived at the office in a rumpled suit, slightly damp from an unexpected storm, he decided he needed a suit bag that he could fold into a backpack, something he could carry every day on his own commute. So he designed and built the foldable garment pack.

Today Brotman owns Travel Dynamics, an online retail store that sells garment bags, backpacks, travel satchels, and other accessories for both men and women. Now there are thousands of commuters out there biking and hiking in the rain, in the heat, in the humidity, who carry work clothes, shaving kits, shoe bags, and other paraphernalia in one of Brotman's creations. Every time he encounters one of his own carry-alls in the streets or on the trails, he gets a good laugh. Brotman, in addition to making money in a growing second business, is having fun.

IT'S A BIG STEP

In 1992, when Brotman first envisioned a foldable backpack, he was working at Nordstrom's and needed a clothes carrier and shaving kit so that he could "put himself together" in the back room before hitting the sales floor. One of his associates, a seamstress, helped him put together the prototype. Brotman was pleased with the result and even secured a patent, although he didn't sell the first models. But from that experience came a nifty shaving kit, one that other people really liked. He began making sales, and the idea caught fire.

First, Brotman went to small stores and chains, marketing his shaving kit by bicycle. Then Sharper Image took an interest. "That changed everything," says Brotman. "It really hit well there." Other stores heard the rumor and started calling. Although Brotman was then only taking wholesale orders, by 1998 he was also thinking about a way to reach the retail Web market.

"I didn't know anything about Net businesses," he admits. "I didn't even know where to start until I met a man who had knowledge about the Net. He introduced me to BigStep, and within 48 hours I had my site on the Web. I designed it myself."

BigStep is a do-it-yourself Web program that allows owners to side-step high-priced software and big-fee technicians. With

BigStep.com, Brotman established a sophisticated site that fed into the search engines, even though he began the process with virtually no Web design background. BigStep offers a step-by-step instruction program, one that even works for "technophobes," a term that Brotman uses to describe himself.

THE ASIAN CONNECTION

When Travel Dynamics went online, Brotman's business changed entirely to a retail outlet, eliminating the need for two-wheeled marketing. With increased demand, Brotman sought a larger manufacturing base. He found it in Asia. On the advice of a relative with business connections in Asia, Brotman went to Korea, where he met several people with expertise in making travel bags and totes. "I went to the factories in Korea, and it was all pretty amazing," says Brotman. "It opened up all sorts of fascinating possibilities."

With the Asian connection secured, including a Far East agent, Brotman began to receive high-quality nylon and leather bags on the West Coast. These he often fills with travel accessories—brushes, combs, lathers—from as many as seven vendors. Initially, Brotman went to the Yellow Pages to find his vendors, but he also asked for recommendations as he did his research. Eventually, he admits, it was "a lot of work" tracking down the right vendors with the appropriate products. A Travel Dynamics bag may carry as many as 21 different items, each designed to avoid leaks, spills, and breakage.

In the United States, Brotman outsources the bag "stuffing" and packaging to Commercial Support Services of Richmond, California, an organization providing work opportunities for the mentally challenged. They assemble the pieces, pack them, and ship the bags. "They're wonderful," says Brotman, who appreciates the group's dedication and industry.

BIG BROTHER WANTS YOU TO FILL OUT THESE FORMS

Brotman has taken a measured approach to his online business. He continues to ride his bike to his "day job" as a kids' counselor and fund-raiser. Nevertheless, Travel Dynamics threatens to "break out" and command much more of his time. His Web site has helped to get his business name into circulation. People locate Travel Dynamics through the search engines or through viral advertising.

Brotman actually finds the e-commerce approach less time-consuming than he expected. And, as for difficulties, there are few, with the exception of learning how to put images on the Web site. "Your success depends on your computer skills," says Brotman, "and mine were not so great." Nonetheless, Brotman managed to apply the BigStep programs successfully with a few trials. Now, he says, "I download the images to a file, and the BigStep software asks me where I want to put them. It's that simple. I use digital images that come from scanned photos." Voilà. Done. Complete. That's all, folks!

Brotman continually looks over his shoulder for the competition. Lucky for him, there isn't any yet. The bags and totes are made of washable leather, the kind found in children's shoes. "There are similar things available," says Brotman, but the quality is not there. Brotman attempts to keep his price point reasonable, and thus far the strategy has kept the business growing at a strong pace.

Despite the low costs of start-up, the smooth entry into the

Net world, and the lack of competition, there is a snake in Brotman's garden. Yes, that's right. It's Uncle Sam. On more than one occasion, says Brotman, he has sat on the linoleum in front of his post office box crying because the government regulations are unreasonable and complicated.

"When I started this business, I heard Hillary Clinton say in a speech that people should go out into the world and invent something—start a business. Well, I did. But then the biggest thorn in my side is the government." As Brotman suggests, government rules and regulations—the paperwork—are by far the greatest barrier to a successful young business, Web-based or otherwise.

IT'S IN THE BAG

Web businesses are catching the wind at the rate of hundreds per day. Entrepreneurs such as Brotman have discovered that the Internet makes it possible to start a venture with little or no capital. Not long ago, Brotman was backpacking with one of his own creations on his shoulders when he passed someone on the trail who said, "Hey, look, I've got one of those!" Those are the moments that make Brotman feel the best. He says, "It's just a kick—a fluke that turned into something really fun."

Making money while having a good time—what a concept. In the face of such a paradox, people used to say, "Only in America!" Today the phrase is changing. All over the world, people are exclaiming, "Only on the Internet!"

Web address:
   www.tdforme.BigStep.com

Specialty Tours

Start-up expenses: $10,000

Special requirements: *Travel experience*

Best advice: *"I hope that people starting an e-business don't start counting their money. Even today e-business is more about sharing information and letting people know about you. It's not really about the actual selling, although it will become that way in a few years."*

Sail around the Greek Isles while reading *The Odyssey*. Learn basic Japanese during an escorted tour of Kyoto and Tokyo. Bicycle from Paris along the Tour de France routes. Play golf at St. Andrews and Troon in Scotland. Solve the crime of the century on an Agatha Christie cruise of the Mediterranean. These are specialty tours, a growing market in the travel industry. Today, more and more people are choosing unusual travel packages—tours with a theme.

"IF IT'S TUESDAY, THIS MUST BE BELGIUM"

Specialty tours are a refreshing vacation from the huge generic packages offered by most travel companies. In every Sunday "Travel" section of big-city newspapers, people find packaged programs to Berlin or Rome or Antwerp, complete with hotel, air travel, food, tips, and buses. Such tours, despite their convenience, deny travelers the most interesting things about foreign travel—the true native taste of each destination. Eventually, such tours make travelers feel like part of the herd, and the experience is often less than memorable. Specialty tours, on the other hand, are endeavors of love—travel packages created by people who are passionate about Scotland's golf courses or veteran readers of Agatha Christie's novels, who love the French back roads and valleys, or who want to share the hidden mysteries and traditions of Japanese culture.

One of the most intriguing specialty tours is sponsored by Undiscovered Lands, a California-based company. Partners Otto Szilagyi and Horea Anderco offer a tour of ancient Transylvania, the homeland of vampires and the Undead, at the Internet address DraculaTour.com. They market guided tours of the Transylvanian mountain regions, which they call "lands forgotten by time, shrouded in mystery and mysticism." Their Web site offers opportunities to "meet vampires, witches, ghosts, and alchemists . . . seekers of eternal youth, mystics, clairvoyants, and fortunetellers." For the brave, there are séances. And for everyone else, there are dances, feasts, historic walks, and music fests. Shadowy Transylvania is the primary destination for Undiscovered Lands, but other out-of-the-way places in Eastern Europe are available as well.

THINGS THAT GO
BUMP IN THE NIGHT

Szilagyi and his partner envisioned their company while still living in their Eastern European homeland under the veil of communism. When the Berlin Wall fell and "the Evil Empire" faded, Szilagyi came to the United States, opening an accounting practice. Anderco remained in Transylvania, working as a successful engineer and local politician. But both men kept alive a dream of uniting American and Eastern European cultures in a business that would be part Old World, part New World. Today, Undiscovered Lands operates from the East Bay area in California, also with offices in Transylvania. They use the Web to offer a complete travel package, one that draws clients from all over the world. And while some business propositions have "legs," this one seems to have fangs.

Undiscovered Lands opened its real and virtual doors in 1999, with Szilagyi and Anderco adding another partner (one with Web site experience) and a CEO. They reasoned that the Internet was a distinct advantage, allowing the business to reach out globally for customers. Traditional marketing, they felt, would restrict their advertising efforts to the Bay Area, unless the partners were willing to embark on an international effort, a very expensive proposition. "The Web doesn't have boundaries," says Szilagyi, "so we don't stop at the border of California. We make ourselves available to anyone who can find our site."

Szilagyi stresses that Undiscovered Lands is more about education than travel. He wants his Web site to inform people about Transylvania and Eastern Europe, to interest them in traditional cultures, and to provide resources for those who want to explore new lands, either physically or intellectually. In that regard, Undiscovered Lands is like the old Star Trek show, says Szilagyi, with a mission to "seek out new worlds," wherever they may be.

CHOOSING A GUIDE

One of Szilagyi's biggest concerns is the quality of the guide service in Transylvania and beyond. The company has guides in the home country, he says, "but I go over there myself quite often to make sure everything goes well. We have trained the guides so that they will have the necessary level of knowledge and professionalism." Ideally, the DraculaTour.com guides make clients feel comfortable and want to return. "It is very important how they present themselves," says Szilagyi, stressing that he wants each guide to share the owner's knowledge of European history and geography. The tours average $1,750 per customer, covering all expenses: airfare, lodging, meals, entry fees, and guide service. Szilagyi suggests that a tour participant leaving home with $100 should still have the bill in his wallet when he returns home. OK, maybe $99, if you consider the dollar it costs for a necklace of garlic.

While Transylvania is the main draw, Undiscovered Lands also presents tours of Slovakia, Hungary, and portions of the former Yugoslavia. There are two firms in Southern California doing tours of similar regions, and one in the San Jose area. But Szilagyi discounts their chances of seizing a significant share of the market. "They don't organize the tours with the same level of thoroughness and professionalism," he says. "Some new travel companies will pop up as people realize the potential for forgotten lands, but right now we are not afraid of the competition." Szilagyi observes that the big tour companies (which are mainly interested in travel to Hungary) operate on an entirely different level. "They look at Eastern European countries as secondary places to take clients." For Undiscovered Lands, the unfamiliar cities of Eastern Europe are the main prize.

TWO LEVELS OF QUALITY CONTROL

Sending tours to Eastern Europe has some inherent complications, which Undiscovered Lands has anticipated. Szilagyi offers insurance to clients at no additional cost, noting that most travel companies charge $50 to $80 for the service. The partners also have business insurance and, most important, a trust account for clients' deposits. The money paid up front for services goes into this trust account until travel is complete, allowing an added level of security for prospective customers. The firm also carries general liability insurance with substantial limits. (You can never tell when a ghoul will strike.)

Undiscovered Lands operates a joint venture with a local travel bureau in Transylvania so that the onsite company stays on top of regional rules and regulations. The local travel company owns its own hotels and arranges restaurant service as well. Szilagyi appreciates the convenience of these connections and sees the Transylvanian tour company as a "second level of control." The California partners reimburse their Eastern European service providers through the local agency, eliminating a potentially harmful level of bureaucracy. "The bottom line," says Szilagyi, "is that we try to avoid any problems."

Szilagyi and his partners have rejected the big-business approach to international travel. They do not want to be the tour company that takes people to big hotels in big cities, where a Big Mac is just as available as *krautronza*. Rather, they have put together an idea, a plan of education and culture. Then they create a tour to take advantage of the idea. According to Szilagyi, Undiscovered Lands wants "to explore the cultures and reach people in their natural surroundings." He insists that "our clients can search out little villages that few in the outside world have seen—little hamlets where people live as they did one hundred years ago. We want our visitors to participate in the dances, spend an evening with the locals, listen to their music, and enjoy the spectacular natural scenery."

NOT AN OVERNIGHT SUCCESS

Like many nascent e-businesses, Undiscovered Lands is not a pot of gold. Szilagyi warns that e-businesses today are "more about sharing information and letting people get to know you." The money comes to those who build reputations and establish a niche in the e-community. But for now, says Szilagyi, "Most people who find your site and like your services will send an e-mail asking for brochures or asking questions." Maybe these browsers will buy services later, maybe not. But without the human touch, there is little likelihood of ongoing commerce. Unfortunately, says Szilagyi, many people believe that if they put a Web site together, people will log on to make purchases. But the Net is not like a Sears catalog. Some e-industries are turning a big profit early, but most aren't, including Undiscovered Lands. "The rest of us," says the owner, "must be patient and wait until e-commerce stands on its own." He agrees that the Internet is a "beautiful media" to sell services— and an even better place to make business contacts. Even though direct sales of services may not be booming, it is useful to remember that e-commerce is about making connections.

"Making contacts," says Szilagyi, "is more lucrative in the long run than making hundreds of direct sales on the Internet." Such is the power of the greatest tool in the history of commerce.

KNOW YOUR MARKET

Even though the Internet is the wizard's wand for Undiscovered Lands, Szilagyi and his partners focus much of their marketing outside the Web. They advertise in local papers and have produced promotional videos. The company also bought a CD burner. As a result, they can send audio and video samples to travel agencies. The response has been good, says the owner. "Most want to feature our tours or at least include them." But the Web continues to be the tool of the future for DraculaTour.com. As Szilagyi says, "We will do everything possible to keep our Web site popular and visited." The company has recently expanded its advertising to national magazines and is beginning to draw a larger portion of its clientele from foreign countries. As with many service businesses, it appears that the combination of traditional print advertising and Web messages has been profitable for Undiscovered Lands.

HIDDEN BENEFITS OF THE WEB

Undiscovered Lands is yet another e-business where profits are certainly welcome, but it's not the only reason to keep the Web page flickering. Szilagyi and his partners have learned to appreciate each other. "The close relationship that we have is wonderful," says Szilagyi, speaking not only of Horea Anderco but of his other two associates as well. They revel in teaching others about their myth-filled homeland. They enjoy the travel and the opportunity to meet people from all parts of the world. And, like many entrepreneurs in the specialty tour business, the partners at Undiscovered Lands feel that the Internet is a magic carpet that can make their dreams into real-world itineraries for people across the globe.

Web address:

www.DraculaTour.com

Travel Auctions

Start-up expenses: $4,000
Special requirements: *A background in outdoor sports and travel*
Best advice: *"Be aware that everything is going to take longer than you think—the programming, the testing, everything. Don't put up a site until you're sure it's fully functional. We had problems with scripting, and we ended up losing some customers because of it, so debug as much as possible. You have to sell the site first, then sell the product or service. It's a concept that differs from one for a traditional business."*

The e-commerce chronicles are full of Horatio Alger stories, but this one sounds like a Hollywood script. Kim Garrett was employed by one of the largest rafting companies in the United States. As part of her duties, she was working on a Web site for the company. After a grueling 18 months, she proved herself indispensable, especially on the technical side. So she quit. And with her former boss, Verle Duerden,

Garrett created a partnership in a high-adrenaline online business. Today adventurebid.com is the largest outback travel directory and auction on the Net. And Kim Garrett is the chief operating officer.

Adventurebid.com bills itself as "The Ultimate Resource for Travel and Adventure." It's an auction-style site with links to scores of professional outfitters, all prepared to give you special deals on outdoor vacations with pizzazz: biking, eco-travel, boating, hunting and fishing, off-road wheeling, paddle sports, wilderness tours, winter sports, hiking, and climbing. Wow!

The concept builds on the Priceline.com model. You simply bid on an adventure trip. If you're the high bidder when the auction closes, you get the tour, provided that you make arrangements for payment within 48 hours. If not, the next lucky bidder gets a whitewater boat trip down the Rogue River or a spelunking holiday near the Carlsbad Caves. By becoming a member at adventurebid.com, you can apply for deals, discounts, special tours, and even a monthly prize.

COMPUTERS AND WHITEWATER RAFTING

Once again, in a story that keeps replaying in e-commerce, Garrett's combined her two loves into one business. With her husband and daughter, she always enjoyed rafting, hiking, camping, and other outdoor adventures. When she was away from the mosquitoes, Garrett thoroughly loved computers and the digital world. She used her computer skills to organize an outfitters' directory (the people who organize and orchestrate the trips), one that currently boasts more than 1,700 members. Coordinated with the directory is an auction site, where customers bid on the outfitters' packages for rates that vary between 20 percent to 80 percent below retail.

The adventurebid.com business was a natural outgrowth of Duerden's whitewater trade. Duerden was always looking for ways to get people to the rafting company's Web site. So, with Garrett's help, the company began to auction empty spaces on raft trips. Not only did the idea sell empty seats in the boats, but the auction process dramatically increased hits at the site.

The following year, Duerden and Garrett talked to people in the tour industry who were interested in filling their empty spots as well. Within a short time, the soon-to-be partners were running an auction business. Because most outfitters operate at only 60 to 80 percent of capacity, there was plenty of demand for auction sales. "So we built an auction Web site around the concept of selling unclaimed trip space," says Garrett. "At that point, I stopped working for the rafting company and started building the auction site. We worked on the design for about 18 months, then put a beta site online in February of 1998." Although the site functioned only three months before being redesigned, Garrett knew they were on the right track. When adventurebid.com returned to the Net in August 1999, it surfaced with a much larger directory and new attractive features, such as links to other sites and "insider information."

Although Garrett didn't do the Web site programming, she was the liaison and designer of the site. She says, "I mapped it out. Then once we started growing a little, we added more people. We made sure that the directory integrated successfully with the auction concept." From there, it was smooth sailing on a bright green sea. At present, Garrett feels that the adventurebid.com site has real advantages over the competition because the designers speak the language of travel. Garrett and her colleagues are not travel agents; they are outfitters who know the hills and valleys of adventure travel. As a result, Garrett's company helps people feel secure about the outback trips and Xtreme Sports ventures.

REPUTATION IS KEY

Bidding on a vacation two time zones away is risky. People need assurance that they're not signing up with inexperienced guides. Therefore, Garrett's first rule of thumb is security. The company doesn't want to become booking agents. They prefer to put travelers in touch with outfitters. But they also see the value of experience. Garrett's group stresses communication with the outfitters and can vouch for the reputation of the guides. Because Garrett and her partner have worked in the rafting business, they are more than travel agents and can speak "outdoors" with both outfitters and travelers. In working with Garrett's company, customers know they're dealing with reputable guides, and outfitters know they're dealing with educated travelers.

Tours are almost always discounted. A typical auctioned trip is six days of salmon fishing in Idaho, which retails for $1,100 but sold recently for $599. Pricing policies are flexible. As Garrett explains, "We generally don't recommend an outfitter listing a trip unless there will be at least a 20 percent discount. They can go as low as 80 percent, but that's not the norm. Half off is more like it." Nonetheless, there are instances where the auction price actually exceeds the retail listing. For example, Grand Canyon trips book up to a year in advance. If there are only two spaces left at auction time, the bids could actually rise above retail. But such a circumstance is highly unusual.

With more than 1,700 outfitters, there's a trip leaving from somewhere almost daily. Generally about 20 percent of the outfitters in adventurebid.com's directory offer trips for auction at any one time, meaning that the customer can usually peruse descriptions online of about 250 different trips (except in midwinter). April and May, the glorious spring months—a time when people are seeing the last of snow, ice, and dark days—are the biggest travel months, with about 1,000 trips happening in any given week.

THE BUSINESS SIDE OF OUTDOOR TRAVEL

How does adventurebid.com make a profit? Garrett says, "We make our profit by taking a small commission from the outfitter. It's not unlike being an affiliate." For the most part, the money comes from promotions. For instance, the outfitter pays adventurebid.com for a banner ad, especially value-added banners, ones that are strategically placed on the site. A value-added banner promotes merchandise for a topic you're exploring. So if you're looking at bike trips, you see a banner ad for bike tires or bike seats.

In addition to link sales and banner ads, Garrett's firm has engaged in a broad and comprehensive marketing plan, one evenly divided among online targeted e-mails, search engine placement, and their own banner ads. The company also advertises in industry magazines such as *BackPacker*, *Men's Journal*, and sport and outdoor magazines. Garrett's group has even organized a few adventure travel shows. Of advertising, she says, "Anything we can think of, we're trying. It's all working. Our hits are increasing." Indeed. Adventurebid.com is taking 300,000 hits a month. And, according to their two tracking systems, between 50,000 and 75,000 new visitors log on each month.

Doing business online for Garrett is unlike doing business in the real world. "We talk to a lot more people," she says. "Before, they would have to buy a travel book or make a million calls to outfitters before figuring out where to go." Now a directory of several thousand trips is available at the touch of a mouse.

Web address:
www.Adventurebid.com

Travel Information

Start-up expenses: $3,000
Special requirements: *None*
Best advice: *"I wouldn't suggest people go into selling tickets because airlines have cut their commissions from 10 percent to 5 percent, and there is a cap, so you can't get more than $50 per ticket. It's better to work with specialty tours."*

T ravel sites are among the top three favorites on the Net. People want to see the world, and they want to do so at a discount. For several years now, travelers have taken the initiative in planning their own ventures as opposed to using brick-and-mortar travel agencies. And the competition in cyberspace is fierce. While companies such as Priceline.com may have the large-market advantage, there are plenty of niche markets available. Creative, innovative programs can succeed—if you have a bold new idea in travel, now is your platinum opportunity. The market is huge.

Someone who got in early is Rik Brown. In high school, Rik took an aptitude test, and the scores added up to "travel agent." He had no interest. However, in 1980, long before the birth of the Net, Brown found himself a world traveler, including a working stint in Japan, where he decided to get a degree in Japanese. One day in the local Japanese language paper Brown saw an ad for a travel company, which he decided represented an outstanding opportunity to remain in Japan. Soon after, Brown found himself employed by the Japanese office of Thompson's Vacations, a large British travel firm.

While still in Japan, Brown had begun to dabble in computer programming, well ahead of his time. In the mid-80s, Brown returned to America and by 1986 he changed his focus to on-line travel services. At that time, he was dealing only with CompuServe and other nascent programs such as Prodigy. By 1992, the Internet was surfacing, but only for messaging and other such primitive tasks. E-mail was still in its infant stages, and e-commerce was little more than a gleam in the eyes of computer nerds from Silicon Valley.

BEING FIRST COUNTS

In his early days, Brown was managing travel information, like dispersing the State Department's travel advisories. Then he moved into providing travelogues online. Various people published the travelogues, and Brown would use those publications to attract people to his Web site. "I just wanted to develop information services for travel," he recalls. "I just kept adding content. In those days, the Internet meant I could do newsgroups. And I used a satellite dish to downlink in '94, meaning that I could send everything by phone lines." During 1994, the Net expanded significantly, and browsers came into existence. That's when online magic began to happen.

Through inspiration, insight, or sheer luck, Brown had grabbed the name Travel.com in 1992, a choice that virtually assured him success in later years. "I was surprised, even in '92," he says, "that the name was available, but I got it." The URL itself is probably worth millions. Recent auctions, such as the record-setting bid for Business.com, demonstrate that a propitious domain name can almost assure monumental profits in e-business ventures. Obviously, the name Travel.com brings people to the site. As Brown explains, "The name itself is a powerful draw. In any one week, I can see from the logs that every country in the world has logged on. Even when there's fighting in the Balkans, people from Bosnia will log on. It's almost as if everybody in the world has taken one year of English. They all know the word *travel*. They type it in, without even using a search engine."

As Brown says, he gets "a lot of offers from the name and the business title." Even though it is tempting to take Travel.com into the public arena—and the offer sheets are staggering—Brown is happy with the firm's progress for the present. He will probably delay a stock offering until much later. For now, says Brown, the business is in good hands—his.

Travel.com is a testament to the Horatio Alger notions of the Web. The company is run by one man with a computer working from his home. There's no venture capital money here, and the site didn't sprout from the brow of a corporate executive. Brown began his business on computer bulletin boards even before the Net existed, and now that online commerce has blossomed, Brown is in position to write his own e-ticket.

IT'S ALL HERE!

As the name Travel.com implies, you can get just about *anything* related to travel at the site. You can shop for the best fares on 500 airlines, at 33,000 hotels, and with 50 rental car companies. Click on this site for every kind of travel and vacation package. It's all here! Profit is basically divided between banner sales and travel sales. "There are no particular problems in this business," says Brown, "because we're not really selling anything. The other companies are selling. I'm just helping them market the products." To protect himself, Brown places a disclaimer on every page of his Web site. He doesn't want to hear from irate travelers left by the roadside in Tonga.

The travel sales, says Brown, are actually marketed by other online companies that are accessed through his Web site, like Delta or Alaska Air. "It's like a huge shopping mall," he adds. Travel.com is the affiliate, so Brown makes a small commission on each sale negotiated through his site. But that plan will change. In the future, Travel.com will become the "grocery store," keeping all the brand name products but adding a few private label items as well.

THE NET IS STILL A BABY

In some cases, an Internet business is hands-on. Daily maintenance is the key to success. Not so with Travel.com. "I could die, and the system would just keep going for months," says Brown. "The system has an electronic life of its own." Indeed, Travel.com established its position so early—and with such a great name—that the business runs with robot-like efficiency.

Rik Brown advises e-commerce types to note the progress of

successful ventures. Why, he asks, do some firms get millions of hits while others don't? "It's hard to say" is his honest answer. Some businesses advertise on TV and spend millions promoting their e-products or services. Others seem to profit without any effort, even though the competition for e-business dominance is ferocious. Nevertheless, it's still early in the game, he says. Only about 2 percent of the world's population is linked globally. "It'll be five or ten years before this phenomenon reaches maturity," says Brown. In that time, the key is to pick a niche and do it better than anyone else.

For those who find a niche, the lifestyle is grand. "Anybody can do e-commerce part-time," says Brown. "I started full-time, but then a couple of years ago, I switched to part-time because I wanted to get more experience in the travel industry. I decided to work for TWA, and I was able to run my e-business evenings and weekends." A leisurely schedule is one of the perks for cyberbusiness owners, assuming the profits are forthcoming.

"You can try a part-time approach to see if you really like e-commerce," suggests Brown. "You can get a lot done on evenings and weekends." Punching a clock is not important— not even necessary. "Today I was wondering if I should play golf," muses Brown. "The weather's nice. Why not?" It sounds like the good life. Moreover, you don't even have to be a travel agent to start an e-travel business. Of course, it's not so simple as hanging out an e-shingle. The airline, hotel, and travel companies decide whether you can sell their packages. But there are plenty of positions in travel these days. Creativity and innovation are the keys.

Web address:
www.Travel.com

Wedding

Custom Wedding Accessories

Start-up expenses: *Under $1,000*

Special requirements: *Digital camera, adapter, and* Easy Photo *software*

Best advice: *"Plan on spending time, especially in the beginning. I spend about two hours each day just surfing the Web—seeing what's out there, looking at different sites, checking the search engines, and looking for people to exchange links with. Exchanging links is a wonderful tool for getting business."*

Cakes, flower baskets, ring pillows, figurines—they're all part of a business that until now has been the domain of bridal shops and catalog stores. But Annette Faulkner, who created A. Faulkner originals, has added a new twist to the search for the perfect wedding centerpiece or cake top. She has taken the process online. Faulkner can even color the hair of the figurines on top of the cake, making sure they match those of the bride and groom. Faulkner's wedding materials are handcrafted or, at the very least, personalized with details such as the couple's names and wedding dates. And such details are perfect for the interactive features of online selection. In short, wedding accessories and the Internet constitute a marriage made in cyberheaven.

"Don't expect that mad rush of customers—any more than you would in a real shop," says Faulkner. It just isn't going to happen that way. You hear a lot of hype about e-commerce, but it has taken four months to get going. Plan on taking a year to get known. It's really no different than any business in the real world."

Despite the track record for marriages in today's world, people still keep saying "I do." Some do it more than once. Considering the repeat customers, the sales of wedding accessories must certainly qualify as a growth industry, for better or for worse.

LOOKING FOR THE RIGHT COLOR?

Often, the intended bride or her mum is looking for something special, something unique. Unfortunately, customized wedding accessories are hard to find, especially for people in low-density markets. Imagine looking in Dubuque for parachute-style napkins for a pair of skydivers who are taking the plunge. We don't think so.

When Faulkner was helping her daughter plan her wedding, the two women had trouble even in Sacramento, a very large marketplace. "She looked everywhere," says Faulkner, "and couldn't even find her own wedding colors." Shop owners essentially said, "Choose from what's available." But Annette Faulkner bought fabrics and papers (in the right colors) and outfitted the wedding. Her daughter was thrilled, and Faulkner saw a need that she could fill. That moment marked the beginning of Faulkner's e-business.

Faulkner had been working in telecommunications and was laid off. Because she had time on her hands and lots of experience making wedding accessories for friends, she launched her wedding accessories business online. "I *only* do business online," says Faulkner, reasoning that even a large market like Sacramento is too small for a niche operation like hers. Faulkner took 20 digital pictures of cake tops and featured them on her Web site, as she says, "just so people can know my abilities."

E-Business Is a "Big Step"

Faulkner's online business focuses exclusively on personalized wedding accessories. She lets clients choose their own colors, decorations, and themes. Faulkner's role is to customize the products. For example, if people are marrying in a hot-air balloon, she offers a balloon-shaped cake top. If they're getting married under the water or in the forest, Faulkner will oblige these special whims. "One customer was getting married at Lake Tahoe," she says, "and I did the cake top in rustic style with trees and a little lake. I know that whenever the bride looks at it in the future, she'll remember the ceremony by the lake under the trees." Increasingly, she observes, people are looking for something unique, something they'll never see anywhere else. How else could you explain Las Vegas?

Going online was a wise decision for Faulkner, who first looked around Sacramento for a shop. She realized that a massive ad campaign, plus building costs, was her only recourse. It was a simple decision and a productive one. "Once I was out there on the Web and getting some recognition, I realized it was the place to be," says Faulkner.

Faulkner spent well under $1,000 to begin. Putting up the site cost practically nothing because she used BigStep.com, a Web site service. But Faulkner went through a frustrating time before connecting with BigStep. Initially, she spent about five weeks wrestling with some expensive software and building her own page. When at the last minute she decided to add two cherubs to the home page, the entire site crashed. She said, "Forget it."

Fortunately, Faulkner found an article about BigStep, a free service. She pays only for the allied credit card service called Card Service International. Says Faulkner, "I had checked into Visa for a merchant account. But I can take three major credit cards through the service that BigStep set up, and it only costs $14.95 a month, plus about $1.50 for the transaction fee." Faulkner had to qualify and fill out a single-page form, but otherwise the process was easy and painless. "I was thinking it was worse than the paperwork for buying a home," says Faulkner. It wasn't. When the packet came in the mail, she was astonished at its simplicity.

With BigStep, Faulkner found she could start taking credit card orders three days after filling out the application. Card Service International has great customer service, too, says Faulkner. "You can actually talk to someone there if you need to."

Faulkner has received orders from all over the country. She makes all her products from her home and keeps her own hours. "When I used to work for a corporation, I would put 100 percent of myself into my job," she says. "Now I'm donating that time to myself. I highly recommend it."

FEEDBACK IS THE TICKET TO SUCCESS

Faulkner submits to all the search engines. She agrees that it takes a lot of time to attract people to her site. BigStep will submit to three engines—Lycos, Excite, and AltaVista. But Faulkner personally continues to submit to other engines and services like BriefMe.com., which sends newsletters to people who have signed up and expressed interest in sites such as Faulkner Originals. Subscribers to BriefMe.com receive free newsletters in areas of their interest. For example, Faulkner regularly receives the Arts and Crafts newsletter regularly. As an added bonus, when BriefMe.com publishes her reviews, they include her name and Web address. It's good publicity.

On the days when the BriefMe.com reviews come out, Faulkner also receives a daily report telling how many people are visiting her site and where they're from. The report is produced by *Referrer* software. "I can get it daily, weekly, or monthly," says Faulkner. "It's great." With the software, Faulkner can tell whether the big numbers are coming from Yahoo! or BigStep. She also discovers if they typed in her Web address, meaning the visit came from a referral. If Faulkner doesn't see many hits from the search engines, she knows it's time to go back to work there. She likes the services of RankThis.com, another free service. RankThis.com tells Faulkner if she is in the top 200 on eight separate search engines. With ten key words, it takes time to check out each one individually.

The competition has not been sleeping. Faulkner was number one on Hotbot "for a long time" but has been recently replaced. "It's really motivating, though," she offers. "I actually like having to compete."

Some Good Advice

When building her business plan, Faulkner decided to purchase a digital camera. With the camera and an adapter, she provides pictures of her products, loading them onto the site with *Easy Photo* software. With *Easy Photo*, she can crop her pictures or change the darkness—even shrink them if necessary. Faulkner puts thumbnails (stamp-sized photos) onto her pages that customers can click on to get a bigger picture.

Faulkner advises prospective online sellers to spend the time investigating the e-commerce world. It takes about two hours a day to just surf the Web, seeing what's out there, she suggests. The time online is best served checking the search engines, looking for hot links, and surveying the crafts sites. Further, she says, business doesn't rain down on you immediately. A year of struggling for position and market share is about average, she believes.

Finally, says Faulkner, keep in mind that the Web can be fun. "It's almost like a family," she submits. "I e-mail someone and say, 'I'm with BigStep,' and they say, 'Oh, yeah? Me, too.' The next thing you know, we're chatting up a storm and doing business." Doesn't that sound like fun? Many people are saying that online selling, although not without its difficulties, is easier and more rewarding than brick-and-mortar sales. In fact, for Faulkner, it's a piece of cake.

Web address:
   www.afaulkneroriginal.bigstep.com

Honeymoon Travel Agency

Start-up expenses: $50,000 +
Special requirements: *Insurance and a travel agent license*
Best advice: *"The flexibility and adaptability of the chat room is a strategy that seems underemployed in the travel industry. Chat has been a really powerful tool for us. I have been surprised nobody else has embraced it."*

If you want to spend your honeymoon at Motel 6, that's fine. But you probably won't need the services of a specialty travel agency like Click Trips. Upscale package vacation companies like ClickTrips.com want you to *enjoy* your honeymoon or anniversary tour. Niagara Falls is out. Cancun is in. Click Trips builds custom vacations to a limited number of destinations. Such specialization allows the company to excel in pricing, product knowledge, and customer service.

In a nutshell, Click Trips creates honeymoon packages and wedding destinations, with a few specialty vacation packages thrown in the mix for variety. Jack Benoff, who has a publishing background in the travel industry, is the president and founder of the firm. Benoff spent 18 months consulting with travel companies interested in marketing on the Internet before he realized that very few people in the industry had the nerve to sail with the new paradigm. After doing his homework, Benoff felt no hesitation.

Fear and Trembling in Las Vegas

When travel agents spoke with Benoff about the Net, they didn't see opportunity; they saw danger. Traditional brick-and-mortar agencies were scared because they saw airlines and hotels offering the public direct Net access. They figured cyberticketing would leave them out of the loop. When Benoff tried to market online services to travel agencies, he told them they could benefit. But most didn't make enough profit to fund a healthy online presence. Says Benoff, "I spent a year and a half telling them what to do and they ignored me, mostly because they didn't have the $100,000 in the budget. I figured if nobody else was going to do it, I would." Agents felt that he would put them out of business, and instead of joining the wave, many simply entrenched themselves in traditional booking practices. They didn't get it. Benoff, however, saw the chance and sought a successful niche. What he discovered in his search was fascinating: the people who were getting married were the same people who were surfing the Net regularly.

Benoff realized there were many travel sites that enabled consumers to book their own airline tickets but few sites that allowed the users to build custom vacations. Wisely, Benoff chose not to compete with the big names in travel, such as Travelocity and Preview. He also decided not to market his firm as a travel agency. Not only was the competition too steep, but he wanted to avoid a business based almost exclusively on booking airline tickets, where airlines are offering fewer and fewer incentives in the click-and-book era.

Honeymoon travel became Benoff's niche, and he revels in the challenge of putting together fun-filled travel packages for newlyweds. His staff has an accumulated 20 years of experience in the travel industry. By focusing on a select few destinations, Click Trips quickly established a reputation for excellence. Benoff is especially proud of his e-mail guarantee—that someone will return a call or e-mail within 24 hours, no matter what time of day the query comes in.

THE UNEXPLORED ADVANTAGES OF CHAT ROOMS

Click Trips was never a brick-and-mortar agency, even when the company was only part of Benoff's imagination. "My goal from the first was to be an online agency," says Benoff, noting that his initial strategies focused on an innovative use of chat rooms. Today the chat room is an integral part of the business, even though they're unusual in the online travel world. "When we started using chat rooms," says Benoff, "we were the only ones."

The chat rooms are available during business hours from 9 A.M. to 8 P.M. Eastern Standard Time. On Saturdays, visitors can click into the chat rooms from 10 A.M. to 4 P.M. On any given day, ClickTrips.com has one to three agents in the office. People can enter the rooms, ask questions, and—when they're ready—book tours.

Benoff believes his chat room concept has facilitated better communication and stronger sales. "It's great that people who have never gotten a brochure from us—never even walked into our office—will book several thousand dollars worth of travel," says Benoff. The intimacy of the chat room serves to personalize service in ways formerly possible only at a travel agency desk. Once people click in to the main chat room, an agent guides them to a private room, where the customer gets more details. From the chat room, Click Trips books honeymoons and tours for people as far away as Pakistan, India, and Japan.

"Recently there was a customer from Tokyo," says Benoff, "who booked an $8,000 honeymoon. We never spoke to the man or e-mailed him. Our agent was able to answer his questions, and that was enough."

ELECTRONIC HAND HOLDING?

To get customers to the ClickTrips.com site, Benoff has developed links with sites such as TheKnot.com, a site exclusively for wedding services. Click Trips also works with other bridal and honeymoon sites, sponsoring contests or providing content. At the AskTheExpert site, Benoff's company is the "honeymoon expert."

Happily, the honeymoon experts have benefited from viral publicity. As Benoff says, "We have satisfied the demands of the customers, so they refer us to friends. Instead of calling an 800 number, they come into our chat room. If someone is in the office, an e-mail is answered within half an hour. People don't wait days to get responses." As with so many electronic businesses, the real product is customer service. The travel package is important, of course, but secondary.

Honeymoon planning is big business. As Benoff says, "This is not just booking a flight or a hotel." The average vacation plan costs $3,000. As such, the service can't be automated. It can't be a shopping cart system. No one is likely to click *Bermuda Hilton, king-sized bed, no smoking,* for $3,000. Customers still need "hand holding" for that decision. The chat room is part of an electronic hand holding system that personalizes the process at Click Trips. The results have been solid. Says Benoff, "In less than a year, we have gone from a nonexistent agency to number one among independents with Travel Expression (the travel division of American Express)." Benoff muses that, when he started his online business, people said, "It's a stupid idea." Today he has the last laugh.

HAPPY CUSTOMERS, GOOD BOTTOM LINE

While chuckling, Benoff surveys his progress. "There are agencies that have been around for 20 years. We have just blown by them in dollar volume," he notes. For those who are squeamish about entering the e-commerce world, afraid perhaps of the technology or the paradigm shift, he offers ClickTrips.com as an example of a business that not only survived the changing business climate but prospered.

In the midst of these successes, Benoff recalls that his business "is not based on price." He's convinced that customer service remains the most important key to growth. "We can tell you more about the resorts we sell than anyone else," says Benoff. "So when you go, you'll feel as if you have already been there before."

Indeed, Benoff says that he gets a constant string of e-mails from people who say, "When we walked into the lobby, we felt at home." ClickTrips.com has benefited from its online presence in an exceptional way. Instead of creating distance between the agent and the customer, the Web site, with its series of chat rooms, personalizes the experience for the traveler. And Benoff guarantees the quality of travel, something that chains and major agencies cannot do. "If you don't like the resort," he says, "you can call us, and we'll do something about it. We can work to get your money back for you, unlike hotels, who truly don't know what customer service is about."

Web address:
www.ClickTrips.com

Wedding Registry

Start-up expenses: $100,000 +
Special requirements: *None*
Best advice: *"We get a lot of traffic simply through word-of-mouth referrals. Ours is viral marketing at its best. I tell my people that every weekend is like a movie premiere for us. Soon after the ceremony, we'll be getting the buzz from people who attended the wedding and learned that the great centerpiece came from us."*

The next time you receive a wedding invitation in the mail, consider not only the happy couple but also the jubilant entrepreneurs who will profit—from the jeweler who provides the ring to the photographer who captures the special day on film. Yes indeed, that sound you hear in the background isn't wedding bells; it's the joyful *ka-ching* of cash registers. By any measure, including financial statistics, the wedding industry is huge. Here are some stats from industry leader TheKnot.com:

- $45 billion is spent on weddings per year.
- 2.4 million couples marry annually in the United States.
- $17 billion is spent on wedding gift registries per year.
- 26 is the average age of a bride; 28 for the groom.
- $51,591 is the average household income of married couples.

NOT A WEB SITE FOR MOM

David Liu, CEO of TheKnot.com, an online wedding service, says his company brings a "much needed alternative to the white-gloved, outdated advice of antiquated etiquette experts." In other words, it's a site for engaged couples, not their parents. On the site, Liu bills his services as wedding *advice*, but the company is really a high-end retailer with ties to scores of providers. TheKnot.com is not an intermediary but a comprehensive sales site with more than 10,000 products for sale. It's a good thing they're well stocked. TheKnot.com is visited by a million people a month.

The average American wedding has a budget of $19,000 plus, but the demographics for Liu's company are a little higher. Visitors to TheKnot.com spend about an average of $25,000 on their wedding. Despite the discouraging statistics on marriage as an institution, the wedding business itself is remarkably stable.

MORE THAN JUST CHINA

Remember when the wedding registry used to include only china, crystal, silver, and linens? Well, those items are still on the list, according to Liu, but a few things have been added as well—power tools, camping gear, PlayStations, and casual china pieces. The bridal registry is different today because 80

percent of people getting married already have the same address. That living arrangement changes the wedding scene dramatically. People are looking more for leisure activities and services, alternatives to what our parents wanted. As a virtual
retailer, TheKnot.com can provide all those innovative services
and products.

The company has prospered because the old way of planning a wedding was cumbersome and disappointing. In the
past, at brick-and-mortar shops, the registry process suffered
from timing problems. When the future bride went to Crate &
Barrel, for instance, to register, the clerk would recommend
registering for the store's basic line because inventory turns
over every two months. But etiquette dictates that the bridal
couple should register four to five months before the wedding,
while friends and relatives should make their purchases a mere
three or four days before the big event. By then, of course, what
the bride wanted is no longer available.

This paradox of supply and demand plays out as the primary
constraint for a lot of brick-and-mortar stores, even though
most people don't realize it. The timing issue has seriously
compromised the registry process. An online service can sur-
mount these roadblocks, according to Liu, who says, "Our inventory doesn't have to turn over like that, for seasonal reasons
or any other. The customer can count on us."

AN AMAZON.COM BUSINESS MODEL

The operation at TheKnot.com is instructive for potential online business owners. There are plenty of wedding registry sites,
but TheKnot has a different outlook. While others form business partnerships with retailers and act as intermediaries,
collecting commissions for whatever sales they refer, Liu's

representatives go directly to the manufacturers. The "knot" becomes the actual retailer, not unlike Amazon.com. Says Liu of his business plan, "It gives us a level of flexibility to provide the products and services brides really want, not just what a store wants to give them. If you go to Macy's, or any other store, you're subject to their seasonal offerings. They're general merchants, not specialists like we are. We ask what a couple wants these days and market to them specifically for their wedding needs."

Flexibility and innovation are important to businesses like TheKnot.com. The information exchange between people at weddings is very rapid. "We get a lot of traffic simply through word-of-mouth referrals," says Liu. "Ours is viral marketing at its best. I tell my people that every weekend is like a movie premiere for us. Soon after the ceremony, we'll be getting the buzz from people who attended the wedding and learned that the great centerpiece came from us."

Although David Liu's online operations appear to run smoothly, a million hits a month is a terrific traffic pattern. TheKnot.com needs to be prepared. As such, distribution is their primary concern. Being ready to deliver is paramount to success. The obstacles of distribution can multiply exponentially in any similar business if the products and services are not available in a timely fashion. The careful wedding of good products and professional distribution is one important key to success in modern e-trade.

Web address:
www.TheKnot.com

About the Authors

The Philip Lief Group is a Princeton-based book developer that produces a wide range of books for small businesses, including *The 101 Best Businesses to Start*, *220 Best Franchises to Buy*, and *Moonlighting*. The Philip Lief Group has been singled out by *The New York Times* for its "consistent bestsellers" and by *Time* magazine for being "bottom-line think tankers."

An award-winning writer with 16 years of experience, Lynie Arden has published 11 books and more than 50 articles on business, careers, employment, travel, and consumer awareness. Her books include *220 Best Franchises to Buy*, *The Work-at-Home Sourcebook* (which won the "Best of the Best" award from the American Library Association), and *Franchises You Can Run from Home*. Her work has appeared in dozens of newspapers and magazines, including *Success*, *Working Mother*, *Family Circle*, *Compute*, and *In Business*. In addition, she developed and taught the course "Starting Your Own Business" at Sacramento City College, University of the Pacific, and The Learning Annex.

Tom Nash is a professor and writer who has received study grants at Yale, Princeton, and the University of California at Berkeley. He is also the author of *Ten Days to a More Powerful Vocabulary* and co-author of *The Well-Traveled Casket*.